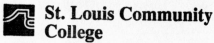

Licence to Thrill

LICENCE TO THRILL
A Cultural History of the James Bond Films

James Chapman

Columbia University Press

NEW YORK

Columbia University Press
Publishers since 1893
New York; Chichester, West Sussex

Copyright © 2000 James Chapman

First published in 2000 by I.B.Tauris & Co Ltd in the United
Kingdom

A full CIP record for this book is available from the Library of
Congress

∞

Printed in Great Britain by MPG Books Ltd

C 10 9 8 7 6 5 4 3 2 1

Contents

Illustrations

General Editor's Introduction

The James Bond films are a cinematic phenomenon. The series was launched in 1962 and is still running after nearly forty years and – if we exclude the spoof *Casino Royale* – five different actors in the leading role. The critics have frequently been vitriolic about Bond and his world, branding it variously as sexist, racist, snobbish, violent and juvenile. But this has not been reflected in the films' continuous box-office success worldwide. This disparity between critical perceptions and audience appreciation is one of the many subjects tackled by James Chapman in this wide-ranging analysis of the cultural significance of the Bond phenomenon.

The Bond films were born at a precise moment in British history, a decisive period of social and cultural change – the 1960s, which simultaneously witnessed sexual liberation, Britain's global political decline and the transformation of the United Kingdom from sober and responsible superpower to swinging symbol of fashion, music, youth and consumerism. Chapman perceptively charts the ways in which the Bond films negotiated a path through these massive changes.

The films achieved an unbeatable blend of conspicuous consumption, brand-name snobbery, technological gadgetry, colour supplement chic, exotic locations and comic-strip sex and violence. But they have continually and cannily repositioned themselves as times have changed, the balance of world power has shifted, cultural norms have been transformed, and new cinematic genres have emerged to challenge the former pre-eminence of the secret agent action adventure.

With skill, wit and erudition, James Chapman examines the literary and cinematic precursors of the Bond films, their production strategies, their visual style, their attitudes to sex, violence and heroism and their distinctive Britishness. The whole adds up to an exciting, insightful and original study which throws new light on a cinematic phenomenon too often taken for granted.

Jeffrey Richards

Acknowledgements

Film historians, just as much as our colleagues in other branches of the historical sciences, are frequently concerned with identifying origins (of films, genres, trends, movements, etc.). In the long term, the origins of this book can be traced back to a family holiday in the summer of 1977 when, at the age of eight, I was taken on my first ever visit to 'the pictures'. The cinema in question was the massive and sumptuous Odeon in St Peter Port, Guernsey (sadly no longer extant). The film, equally massive and sumptuous, was *The Spy Who Loved Me*. In hindsight that evening marked the beginning of my fascination with James Bond. And, over twenty years later, *The Spy Who Loved Me* remains one of my three favourite Bond films (along with *From Russia With Love* and *On Her Majesty's Secret Service*).

However, as all historians know, long-term origins are only part of the equation. In the short term, this book is indebted in large measure to two people. Jeffrey Richards first suggested that I should turn my knowledge of James Bond into a book, over lunch at Pierre Victoire in Lancaster in late September 1995, shortly after I had completed a doctoral thesis (on a different subject) under his supervision. Philippa Brewster, my editor at I.B. Tauris, gave more concrete form to the idea by suggesting that I write a cultural history of the James Bond films, over another lunch, at the Spaghetti House in Bloomsbury Square in May 1997. Both of them have supported this project wholeheartedly from the outset, and my grateful thanks are due, therefore, to each of them in turn – even more so because they bought me lunch on each occasion ('Hearts and stomachs good comrades make').

My colleagues in the History Department of the Open University have endured my obsession with all things 'Bondian' with tolerance and good humour ('Oh, grow up, 007!'). In particular, my thanks to Tony Aldgate, who has provided much valuable encouragement as well as lending various source materials. Other colleagues, both home and away, as it were, on whom I have tried out my ideas ('And this one I'm particularly proud of!') include Rowana Agajanian, Ian Conrich, Sue Harper, Matthew Hilton, Peter Krämer, Derek Matravers, Arthur Marwick and Vincent Porter. All faults and flights of fancy in the book, I hasten to add, are entirely mine.

A special note of thanks must be recorded for all those friends past and present with whom I have viewed and/or discussed Bond films over the years, including Philip Adcock, Paul Bennett, Philip Chaston, Sarah Cobby, Bogdan Costea, Michael Coyne, Ian Darbyshire, Neil Harrison, Cathy Laing, Salim Mohammed, Eric Peterson, Thomas Ribbits, Melanie and Reg Ruse, Line Sevaldsen, Jimmy Storey, Andy Walker and George White.

Research for this book was carried out primarily at the National Library of the British Film Institute and at the British Newspaper Library, Colindale. My thanks to the staff of these institutions for their assistance. Mention must also be made of the inter-library loans service provided by the Open University Library, without which the process of tracking down so many journal and magazine articles would have been a much more laborious task.

Most of the illustrations in this book were provided by the Stills, Posters and Designs Division of the British Film Institute; others are from the author's private collection. They are from films originally distributed in the United Kingdom by Columbia-EMI-Warner, Exclusive Pictures, Metro-Goldwyn-Mayer (MGM), Radio Pictures (RKO), United Artists (UA) and United International Pictures (UIP).

The 'official' James Bond films (excluding *Casino Royale* and *Never Say Never Again*) are produced by Eon Productions Ltd. Copyright in these films is controlled by Danjaq SA. Copyright in the James Bond novels is controlled by Glidrose Productions Ltd. Grateful acknowledgement is extended to these organisations for the use of production stills from the James Bond films and for permission to quote from the James Bond novels. However, if, for any reason, I have inadvertently included any copyright material without proper acknowledgement to the owners, I offer my apologies to all concerned and will be happy to make the appropriate amendment to any future edition of the book.

Finally, my thanks to my parents, whose loyalty to the cause extends far beyond the call of duty.

Author's Note

I argue in this book that the enormous popularity of the James Bond films is more than just the sum total of their box-office receipts, that it has to do with questions of film culture in a wider sense. However, in dealing with a series of such commercially successful films, some indication of how they performed at the box-office becomes inevitable. Box-office statistics can be a minefield for the unwary. They are almost invariably quoted in US dollars, even for the Bond films which are British-made but which are financed and distributed by an American company. Moreover, there is a crucial distinction to be made between the *gross* (or *gross revenues*) of a film, which refers to the total amount of money paid by customers at the box-office, and its *rentals* (or *rental receipts*), which is the amount received by the distributor. For films made before the 1970s the rentals (compiled annually by *Variety* from information provided by distributors) provide the most reliable guide to box-office performance, while it is usually possible only to estimate their overall grosses. In more recent years, as more reliable mechanisms have become available for calculating gross revenues, it has become more common to speak in terms of grosses rather than rentals. I have used both rental and gross figures in this book, while ensuring that where comparisons are made like is compared with like. According to *Variety*, the 'domestic' (i.e. in the United States and Canada) rental receipts of the Bond films have amounted to 47.5 per cent of their gross revenues.

Another caveat regarding raw box-office statistics is that they do not take account of inflation. A more useful indication of popularity is the number of paid admissions to see a film, though unfortunately such statistics are available only for the United States throughout the entire period covered by the Bond films. As an example, there were some 74.8 million paid admissions to see 1965's *Thunderball* compared to 29 million to see 1995's *GoldenEye*. If judged by the number of people who went to see the films, therefore, *Thunderball* attracted a considerably larger audience than *GoldenEye*. However, this fact would be disguised by a straightforward comparison of their US grosses, which amount to an estimated $63 million for *Thunderball* and $107 million for *GoldenEye*. The more recent the films are, the more inflated their grosses have become, though in real terms the most successful Bond films were those released in the mid-1960s (*Goldfinger, Thunderball, You Only Live Twice*).

Finally, all quotations from the James Bond novels are referenced in the main text by the page numbers of the current Coronet paperback editions of the books. The original publication details of the books can be found in the Bibliography.

For Wendy

('decidedly un-Bond girl and
very *Star Trek* alien girl')

Introduction: Taking James Bond Seriously

W hy should we take James Bond seriously? The question is worth asking, for, to judge by the pronouncements of his creator, James Bond was never intended to be taken seriously at all. Ian Fleming liked to give the impression that the Bond novels were nothing more than entertainments which he had started writing for his own amusement. He was fond of saying that he took up writing fiction on the eve of his wedding as an 'antidote' to his alarm at facing up to marriage at the age of forty-three. He disavowed any deep meaning in his books of either a psychological or a political nature. In an article entitled 'How To Write A Thriller' in 1963, Fleming was at pains to distance himself from the so-called 'angry young men' who had emerged in post-war English literature:

> I am not an angry young, or even middle-aged man. I am not 'involved'. My books are not 'engaged'. I have no message for suffering humanity and, though I was bullied at school and lost my virginity like so many of us used to do in the old days, I have never been tempted to foist these and other harrowing personal experiences on the public. My opuscula do not aim at changing people or making them go out and do something. They are not designed to find favour with the Comintern. They are written for warm-blooded heterosexuals in railway trains, airplanes or beds.[1]

It was characteristic of Fleming that he should dismiss his own books in such terms, as minor or insignificant works. It was equally characteristic that when he submitted the manuscript of his first novel, *Casino Royale*, to his publisher Jonathan Cape in 1952, it was accompanied by a self-deprecatory note describing it as 'dreadfully banal' and a 'miserable piece of work'.[2]

The James Bond books, with their improbable plots and their descriptions of fast cars, high-stakes gambling and gunplay, were set in a very different world from the gritty 'northern realism' of contemporary novelists such as John Braine or Alan Sillitoe. Fleming had become a novelist only at the onset of middle age. He had previously tried his hand at various careers, including banking, stockbroking and journalism. During the Second World War he had been personal assistant to the Director of Naval Intelligence at the Admiralty and certainly had first-hand knowledge of espionage, if not necessarily personal experience.[3] James Bond, secret agent 007 of the British Secret Service, was a product of Fleming's vivid imagination. He said that Bond was 'the author's pillow fantasy', the sort of character he wished he could have been: 'I admit that Bond is very much the Walter Mitty syndrome – the feverish dream of the author of what he might have been – bang, bang, kiss, kiss – that sort of stuff.'[4]

Fleming's interview comments, however, were part of the self-effacing public persona of a complex man whose Old Etonian charm disguised a host of personal insecurities and contradictions. For someone who, albeit jokingly, described his own work as 'miserable' and 'banal', Fleming went to often quite extraordinary lengths to secure good reviews for his books by placing them with friends in journalistic and literary circles; and, although he was reluctant to admit it, he was highly sensitive to the criticisms which Bond attracted, particularly from his wife Anne's circle of *literati* friends such as Evelyn Waugh and W. Somerset Maugham. When he struck up a friendship with American thriller writer Raymond Chandler, whose work he greatly admired, Fleming was more candid. 'Probably the fault about my books is that I don't take them seriously enough and meekly accept having my head ragged off about them in the family circle,' he admitted to the creator of Philip Marlowe. Characteristically, however, he added the qualification: 'If one has a grain of intelligence it is difficult to go on being serious about a character like James Bond.'[5]

Critics were – indeed, still are – divided on the merits of the Bond

1. Ian Fleming, creator of James Bond: 'I write for warm-blooded
heterosexuals in railway trains, airplanes or beds.'

novels. On the one hand they have been attacked as harmful and
pernicious, particularly by critics from the left who dislike them on
ideological grounds, while on the other hand they have been disparaged
as mere entertainments which, well-written though they may be, do not
really deserve to be taken seriously. The attacks on the novels have
tended to focus on their content, with some critics reviling them for
exhibiting in excessive measure all the unpleasant 'snobbery with viol-

ence' characteristics of English crime fiction. This view is exemplified by Paul Johnson's vitriolic review of *Dr No* for the *New Statesman* in 1958, wherein he described it as 'without doubt the nastiest book I have ever read'. 'There are three basic ingredients in *Dr No*,' Johnson declared, 'all unhealthy, all thoroughly English: the sadism of a schoolboy bully, the mechanical, two-dimensional sex-longings of a frustrated adolescent, and the crude snob-cravings of a suburban adult.' As if that was not damning enough, he added that 'this novel is badly written to the point of incoherence'.[6] Other commentators, however, have accepted the Bond novels on the sort of level which Fleming would have appreciated, as superior thrillers with a sophisticated veneer. 'These books are not meant to instruct the reader or to plumb the indecipherable problem of life,' wrote R. M. Stern in the *New York Herald Tribune*. 'Their special quality consists in the fact that they answer completely to the needs of the popular novel – that is to say they amuse. Fleming is a story-teller in the classical meaning of the word.'[7]

Yet just because a writer is first and foremost a story-teller who disavows any notion of social commentary is no reason why his work should not be taken seriously, particularly when, as in Fleming's case, it was popular with the reading public. Following Fleming's death in 1964, there were signs that his books were starting to be noticed in academic circles. Kingsley Amis, novelist, critic and former university teacher, was certainly of the opinion that Fleming deserved to be taken seriously. In an affectionate but nevertheless perceptive analysis of the Bond novels, entitled *The James Bond Dossier*, Amis suggested that 'they were more than simple cloak-and-dagger stories with a bit of fashionable affluence and sex thrown in'.[8] *The James Bond Dossier* – still by far the most accessible study of the novels – was, in part, a plea for popular, generic fiction to be appreciated on its own terms. Amis argued that Fleming deserved to be ranked 'with those demi-giants of an earlier day, Jules Verne, Rider Haggard, Conan Doyle'. 'Ian Fleming', Amis continued, 'has set his stamp on the story of action and intrigue, bringing to it a sense of our time, a power and a flair that will win him readers when all the protests about his supposed deficiencies have been forgotten.'[9]

If Amis was rather impressionistic in his discussion of the narrative conventions and character types of Fleming's stories, the same could not be said of the work of Umberto Eco, the scholar who, more than any other, has brought academic respectability to the study of James

Bond. Eco set out to identify and rationalise precisely what the pleasures to be had from reading Fleming were, to which end he applied the methodology of structuralist analysis that was becoming voguish in the 1960s. Structuralism, as Terry Eagleton has observed, is 'quite indifferent to the cultural value of its object ... The method is analytical, not evaluative.'[10] According to his structuralist analysis of the Bond narratives, Eco concluded that it was the essential similarity of the novels that was their main appeal. He used the metaphor of a game of chess, whereby different characters (pieces) make certain pre-determined moves, to explain the narrative structure of the Bond novels. 'The reader's pleasure consists of finding himself immersed in a game of which he knows the pieces and the rules – and perhaps the outcome – drawing pleasure simply from the minimal variations by which the victor realises his objective,' Eco argued. 'The novels of Fleming', he went on, 'exploit in exemplary measure that element of foregone play which is typical of the escape machine geared for the entertainment of the masses.'[11]

By the time that academics had started taking Fleming seriously, James Bond had transcended his origins as the hero of a series of popular novels and had become nothing less than a cultural phenomenon. This was due in no small measure to the immensely successful series of James Bond films starring Sean Connery which had begun with *Dr No* in 1962. But while the novels have attracted their share of serious analysis, the James Bond films have not on the whole received such attention. One of the reasons for this is that admirers of Fleming – the people who have been prepared to take the literary Bond seriously – generally dislike the films, seeing the cinematic Bond as nothing more than a parody of the literary original. This attitude is perfectly ex- emplified by Anthony Burgess, who, in a short essay written as an introduction for a new paperback edition of the novels in the 1980s, was particularly disparaging. 'The films, which grew more and more gimmicky, and less and less psychologically interesting, are grotesquely parodic of the novels, and the cinema version of *Casino Royale* is a disgraceful distortion of a fine taut story which owes nothing at all to lurid fantasy,' he declared. The film of *Casino Royale* had in fact been a spoof, not of Fleming's Bond but of the series of Bond films produced by the team of Albert R. Broccoli and Harry Saltzman, who had bought the rights to all the novels except *Casino Royale*. Even in respect of the 'official' Bond films, however, Burgess contended that 'the James Bond whom Fleming created has only a nominal connection with the leering hero of the screen'.[12]

Critical reaction to the James Bond films has always been mixed. Indeed, it mirrors the reaction to the novels in that in the early days of the series the Bond films were either attacked for their excesses of sex and violence, or they were dismissed as nothing more than entertaining movies of no real importance. This was evident from the very beginning of the series, when *Dr No* polarised critical opinion. For Nina Hibbin, film critic of the communist *Daily Worker*, it was 'vicious hokum skilfully designed to appeal to the filmgoer's basest feelings'.[13] No less a moral authority than the Vatican condemned the film as 'a dangerous mixture of violence, vulgarity, sadism and sex'.[14] But while some critics despised *Dr No*, others thought it was simply good fun which was not meant to be taken at all seriously. For Penelope Gilliat, writing in the *Observer*, 'the film is full of submerged self-parody, and I think it would be as wrong to take it solemnly as it would be to worry that Sherlock Holmes's beastliness to Dr Watson encourages intellectual arrogance or the taking of cocaine'.[15] One American critic described it as 'the best bad film of the year'.[16] The film industry trade press, for its part, recognised that the Bond movies were going to win popular rather than critical acclaim. 'As a screen hero James Bond is definitely here to stay,' declared *Variety*. 'He will win no Oscars but a heck of a lot of enthusiastic followers.'[17]

Opinions of the early Bond films were split, therefore, between those who disliked them on ideological or moral grounds and those who accepted them on their own terms as popular entertainments. As the series went on, however, this division gradually disappeared, and the critics came to speak more and more with one voice – weary, resigned and despairing of the increasingly predictable and formulaic nature of the films. As the *Monthly Film Bulletin* said of *You Only Live Twice* in 1967: 'Really no better and no worse than its predecessors, the fifth James Bond is rather less enjoyable mainly because the formula has become so completely mechanical (and Bond himself so predictably indestructible) without any compensation in other directions.'[18] The longer the series continued, the more the critics lamented that the later films had lost the vitality which had made the earlier ones so fresh and exciting. Ronald Bergan, for example, considered that by the time of the fourteenth 'official' Bond film in 1985, *A View To A Kill*, 'both the hero – as interpreted by the 57-year-old Roger Moore – and the formula were beginning to look somewhat old and tired. What was fresh in the

6os and had a certain faded charm in the 7os, began to look dated and mechanical in the 8os, despite the usual technical expertise.'[19]

Even for those film journalists who do like the Bond movies, there is a tendency to assume that they should not be placed under the microscope of critical scrutiny. 'To me', writes John Brosnan, 'the James Bond films are fun, and to take them seriously would spoil the whole game.'[20] Brosnan's statement is indicative of a critical culture in which there is still great resistance to the notion that popular entertainments are legitimate objects for cultural analysis. The special qualities of the Bond films as popular cinema are, unsurprisingly, emphasised by the discourse of the film industry trade press, which exhibits a similar disinclination to engage with them on anything other than the superficial level of 'entertainment' and 'escapism'. As the *Motion Picture Herald* said of *Thunderball*:

> You, Mr Exhibitor, can just bet your Sunday buttons that your audience will come out saying they haven't had this much fun since they were kids at the movies, and the kids will come out saying they haven't had so much fun since the day school let out for the Summer. Meanwhile, the same exhibitor will be laughing hilariously – all the way to the bank! This is really entertainment 'bottled in Bond'![21]

The tone of this review is typical of the trade press, which, as is its wont, has always celebrated the box-office potential of the Bond films based on their entertainment value.

Nor has academic film study been inclined towards serious analysis of the Bond films. The tone was set by Robin Wood who, in his classic book *Hitchcock's Films*, compared the early Bond movies unfavourably with Hitchcock's celebrated spy thriller *North by Northwest*. The Bond films, in Wood's view, were mere formula pictures which lacked the thematic maturity and stylistic artistry which Hitchcock displayed in *North by Northwest*. 'If I fail to be entertained by *Goldfinger*, it is because there is nothing there to engage or retain the attention; the result is a nonentity, consequently tedious,' he declared. 'The essential triviality of the James Bond films, in fact, sets off perfectly, by contrast, the depth, the charm, the integrity of Hitchcock's film.' Unlike *North by Northwest*, which could be seen as a work of art because it was 'thematically organic', *Goldfinger* was nothing more than 'a collection of bits, carefully calculated with both eyes on the box office, put end to end with no deeper necessity for what happens next than mere plot'.[22] In the case of *From Russia With Love*, moreover, there is a direct comparison to be made between the sequence of a helicopter attack on Bond and the famous set piece in *North by Northwest* where Cary Grant is attacked by a crop-dusting plane. Wood was in no doubt which was the better of the two.

> The difference in quality will seem to some readers too great and too obvious for the comparison to be worth making; but its purpose is not to score easily off a bad film but to help us define the quality of the suspense in Hitchcock. It is worth, perhaps, pointing out that *From Russia With Love* represents precisely that pandering to a debased popular taste that Hitchcock is widely supposed to be guilty of; the most hostile commentator would find difficulty in paralleling its abuses of sex and violence in any Hitchcock film.[23]

For Wood, therefore, whereas Hitchcock's films were legitimate works of art, the Bond films were pale imitations pandering to the box-office. It has to be borne in mind, of course, that Wood had a particular agenda of his own. His book, first published in 1965, and which began with the question 'Why should we take Hitchcock seriously?', was one of the first major English-language texts to explore the notion of the film director as *auteur*, an idea that had developed mainly through the influential French critical journal *Cahiers du Cinéma* during the 1950s. Authorship theory was adopted by Anglo-American scholars in the 1960s as part of their bid to establish film studies as a legitimate academic subject. Popular film could be taken seriously, it was argued, when the presence of an *auteur* could be detected as the overall artistic intelligence behind the films. Hitchcock was held up as the example *par excellence* of an *auteur* working in mainstream commercial cinema: a master of visual narration and *mise-en-scène*, whose films were characterised by recurring stylistic and thematic motifs and which consistently set out the director's own view of the world based on a sense of the chaos lurking beneath the apparent normality of society. It is easy, in hindsight, to point out the contradiction in Wood's theoretical position: concerned with elevating Hitchcock to critical respectability, he dismissed the Bond films in precisely the same terms (commercial, insubstantial, pandering to popular taste) that had for so long been used to condemn Hitchcock himself. However, this contradiction might not have been so evident at the time Wood was writing, when the notion of authorship prevailed in film studies and when individual directors with an identifiable 'world view' were championed above mere genre films. The Bond movies, with their formula-based plots, standardised narratives and stereotyped characters, were regarded as a sort of film-making by numbers, the antithesis of the cinema of personal expression exemplified by *auteurs* like Hitchcock.

Whereas Robin Wood clearly disliked the Bond films, other scholars have tended either to ignore them or to pay them only passing mention. There has been little or no place for Bond in most standard histories of British, or indeed world cinema. A partial exception to this is Roy Armes's *A Critical History of British Cinema*, which at least pays some attention to Bond – described as the 'most potent myth of British cinema in the 1960s' – and discusses the early films in relation to others of the period such as the Hammer horror films and the cycle of 'Swinging London' films in the middle of the decade. Armes admires the early films and rates *Goldfinger* as 'perhaps the best of the series', but echoes other critics in considering that by the time of *Thunderball* and *You Only Live Twice*, 'the formula was already showing signs of becoming purely mechanical'. By the time of *The Spy Who Loved Me* in 1977, there was evidence of an 'almost inevitable decline into routine', though Armes does acknowledge that, the mediocrity of the later films notwithstanding, 'the James Bond series remains a remarkable production achievement, totally recasting the source material so that the upper-class Englishness of Ian Fleming's original gives way to the more classless virility of the Hollywood action film hero'.[24] More recently, in her book *British National Cinema*, Sarah Street discusses the Bond films in terms of their production base and generic formula:

> British and made at Pinewood, these films were backed by American dollars (United Artists) as the major component of the Hollywood, England trend – dollars which kept flowing into Bond films long after American capital was withdrawn from the rest of the British film industry at the end of the decade [the 1960s]. Like other successful British genres (Gainsborough melodramas, Ealing comedies, Hammer horror and the *Carry Ons*), a secure production base provided a long-serving technical and creative team who worked towards perfecting the Bondian formula.[25]

While the comments on the Bond films made by both Armes and Street are perceptive and suggest useful avenues of approach, in each case they are restricted to a couple of paragraphs in much wider surveys of British cinema.

It is symptomatic of the neglect of Bond by serious film historians that, while there are numerous books on the Bond films, they have all emanated from what might be termed the Bond fan culture rather than from academia. The titles of some of these books – *The Official James Bond 007 Movie Companion*, *The James Bond Bedside Companion*, *The Incredible World of 007*, *Kiss Kiss Bang! Bang!: The Unofficial James Bond Film Companion* and *The Essential Bond: The Authorized Guide to the World of 007* – are indicative of their celebratory, anecdotal and uncritical content. The usual format for these books is to recount the production histories of the films, based on interviews and behind-the-scenes information, but what they lack in scholarly apparatus they make up for in their lively style and their extensive knowledge of all things 'Bondian'. The proliferation of James Bond fan clubs and magazines, moreover – most of which focus on the films rather than the original novels – is ample testimony to the existence of an international fan culture for whom the figure of James Bond has a special significance.

It would be fair to say that those who do take James Bond seriously today are divided into two camps. On the one hand there are the Fleming purists who have little time for the films and who deplore the fact that most of the films' fans are unacquainted with the literary original. 'It is time for the aficionados of the films to get back to the books and admire their quality as literature,' Anthony Burgess declared.[26] On the other hand there is the fan culture which has grown up around the films and for whom the cinematic Bond exists in his own right and on his own terms. 'We seek to reclaim Bond from the humourless Fleming pedants who view Bond as fixed, immutable, an unalterable period antiquity', declare the authors of a recent addition to the plethora of fan histories. Alan Barnes and Marcus Hearn (respectively, a comic-strip writer and the editor of a *Star Wars* fan magazine) suggest that the mythic status of Bond 'owes everything to his incarnation on the cinema screen, and little to the novels of Fleming', whom they regard as 'tangential' to the on-going film series.[27]

The view that James Bond's status as a cultural phenomenon is attributable solely to the films is reinforced by the discourse of the trade press. 'Bond's niche in the annals of popular culture was carved out by Eon's Albert "Cubby" Broccoli', declared the trade journal *Screen*

International in 1997, going on to describe Broccoli – whose company Eon Productions is responsible for the 'official' Bond films – as 'the man whose name is synonymous with James Bond'.[28] There is, in fact, something of a discrepancy here between the trade discourse and the Bond films themselves, which, even though they have now started using non-Fleming titles, nevertheless maintain a link with the author through the main credits of each film in the series, which follow the name of the starring actor with the legend '… as Ian Fleming's James Bond 007 in …' before the title of the film proper.

So how can the neglect of the Bond series in film scholarship be explained? The most obvious explanation is the nature of orthodox film criticism, particularly in Britain, with its emphasis on 'realism' (exemplified by documentary, social-problem films and kitchen-sink dramas) and notions of 'quality' (exemplified by adaptations of classic literature, from the Dickensian films of David Lean in the 1940s to the so-called 'heritage' films of Merchant-Ivory and others in the 1980s and 1990s). The writing of British cinema history, until very recently, has been done predominantly from the perspective of a critical discourse which privileges sober, unsensational narratives, believable character-isations and a restrained visual style. In a critical tradition which favours realism and quality at the expense of fantasy and escapism, it is easy to understand why the Bond films, with their fantastic plots, their glossy visual style and their origins in a tradition of 'shocker' literature, should have been excluded from the canon of critically respectable cinema.

Since the 1980s, however, there has been a greater willingness on the part of film historians to engage with those films which had been marginalised by the dominant realist discourse. The most persistent metaphor of recent British film historiography has been that of the 'lost continent', a term coined by Julian Petley to describe the 'repressed side of British cinema, a dark, disdained thread weaving the length and breadth of that cinema, crossing authorial and generic boundaries, sometimes almost entirely invisible, sometimes erupting explosively, always received critically with fear and disapproval'.[29] Recent scholarship has been much concerned with exploring this 'lost continent', and, concomitant to that, reclaiming certain genres and cycles of films which hitherto have been neglected. The main beneficiaries of this 'new revisionism' have been critically despised but commercially successful forms such as the Gainsborough costume melodramas and the Hammer horror films. Whereas orthodox film history had marginalised these films, largely on account of their lack of serious themes or literary pedigree, the tendency now is to see them as using their ostensible fantasy ingredients as a means to explore various identities – national, class and, especially, sexual identity – which have particular resonances for audiences at historically specific moments. The Gainsborough and Hammer films are now championed for their flamboyant *mise-en-scène*, which represents an alternative to the sober realism and restrained visual style of more respectable cinema, and for their flagrant transgressions of conventionally acceptable norms of moral and sexual behaviour – precisely the qualities which orthodox criticism had either overlooked or despised. The range of this revisionist scholarship is currently being extended, exemplified by the launch in 1998 of the *Journal of Popular British Cinema* which seeks, in part, 'to make known what has been called the "unknown cinema"'. The first issue, focusing on 'Genre and British Cinema', brings together a range of articles on such diverse topics as crime films, war films, *Carry On* comedies, 'Swinging London' films and sexploitation cinema, all of which, in the words of the editors, 'contribute to the welcome trend to treat British film genres in relation to their cultural and historical conditions, as well as dealing with them as particular stylistic and thematic configurations'.[30] Admirable as its intentions are and impressive as its range of coverage is, the inaugural issue of the *Journal* nevertheless omits any consideration of the Bond films, surely one of the most popular but neglected series in cinema history.

The absence of the Bond films from the new revisionism is more difficult to explain than their exclusion from the orthodox realist historiography. One possible reason is that the Bond films do not really belong to the 'lost continent' of British cinema in the same way as other popular genre films which have recently come in for critical reappraisal. Certainly there are some similarities between the Bond series and the Gainsborough and Hammer films, both in terms of their roots in popular literature (the Gainsborough melodramas in the 'bodice-ripper' tradition of romantic fiction, the Hammer films in nineteenth-century Gothic literature) and in terms of their richly decorative set design and expressive *mise-en-scène*.[31] But there are also some important differences. The Bond movies are big-budget films with lavish production values which are filmed on locations around the world, in contrast to the modestly budgeted and predominantly studio-bound Gainsborough and Hammer films. And, on a textual level, whereas the pleasure offered by the Gainsborough and Hammer films has generally been explained in terms of their transgressive characteristics, there is nothing particularly transgressive about Bond. Indeed, the films are at best ideologically conservative, and at worst downright reactionary in their representation of, for example, race and gender.

Perhaps the main reason for the continued neglect of the Bond films at a time when other aspects of popular cinema are enjoying a long overdue critical rehabilitation is that they are, simply, unfashionable in the present intellectual climate. The character of James Bond, with his old-fashioned sense of patriotism and duty, his often contemptuous attitude towards foreigners, and, above all, his undisguised male chauvinism, is the antithesis of what is deemed 'politically correct'. The Bond films are unlikely to appeal to proponents of, say, the *Screen* school of film theory, not merely because the films are sexist, heterosexist, jingoistic, xenophobic and racist – they are all of these things, to varying degrees – but also because they seem to endorse and even celebrate those attitudes. In an age when academia is hidebound by the notion of political correctness, the Bond films are certainly beyond the pale of what is considered ideologically acceptable. And yet, despite their political incorrectness – or perhaps even because of it – the Bond films have been enormously popular with cinema-goers around the world, suggesting either that audiences do not pay as much heed to the ideological content of the films as do academics, or that the films provide a particular sort of pleasure which mediates their sexist and racist overtones.

For the evidence of the international popularity of the Bond films is overwhelming. They are, without doubt, the most successful series of films in box-office history: if the individual films have not quite achieved the super-blockbuster status of *Star Wars*, *Jurassic Park* or *Titanic*, nevertheless the cumulative grosses of the series as a whole have surpassed all other similar cycles of films.[32] Moreover, the Bond films have not been one-off successes, but have been consistently successful over a long period of time, a remarkable achievement in a period when the film industry has undergone far-reaching changes and in which film culture has been transformed out of all recognition from that which pertained when the series began in the early 1960s. The index of their success, indeed, is indicated not merely by box-office receipts, but by the fact that the films have proved so enduringly popular with audiences. They are, to borrow one of Raymond Williams's definitions of the word 'popular', evidently 'well-liked by many people'.[33] The Bond films have now won the approval of several successive generations of cinema-goers, while it has variously been estimated that between a quarter and a half of the world's population has seen a Bond film, either in the cinema or on television or video.

The international success of the Bond films is in itself worthy of particular attention, simply because it is so unusual for British cinema. Many commentators have berated the failure of the British film industry to compete in the international market. Nick Roddick, for instance, observes that Britain 'is a small country with a sometimes dispro-portionate belief in her world significance' and that this 'has fairly inescapable implications when it comes to film'.[34] The occasional high-profile international successes for the British film industry – from Alexander Korda's *The Private Life of Henry VIII* in 1933 to more recent hit movies like *Four Weddings and a Funeral* and *The Full Monty* – merely highlight how infrequent such films are. In almost all such cases, there are unique and peculiar reasons for the success of these films, while attempts to repeat them are usually doomed to failure. Those producers who have set their sights on conquering the world film market – including Korda in the 1930s, the Rank Organisation in the 1940s and Goldcrest in the 1980s – have invariably failed to sustain their ambitious production programmes and have seen their empires crumble. But while most standard film histories paint a gloomy picture of an industry unable to compete on equal terms with Hollywood, they all too often overlook the fact that in the Bond series the British cinema has produced a cycle of films which have enjoyed conspicuous and consistent success in the international market over a long period of time.

It might be argued, of course, that the Bond films are not really 'British' at all, given that the production money comes from an American company. By this token, however, films such as *Tom Jones*, *A Hard Day's Night* and *Chariots of Fire* would not qualify as British either. Ever since the 1930s, in fact, American studios have provided the financial backing for productions which are, to all other intents and purposes, British. The production base of the Bond films is British (only two so far have been made in overseas studios), most of the technical personnel are British, the generic roots of the films are British, and the ideology of national identity which the films themselves embody is British. Indeed, the Britishness of the Bond films has been one of their main selling points, a factor which differentiates them from all the other action movies which have followed in their wake.

The best academic study of the Bond phenomenon, taking into account both the novels and the films, is Tony Bennett and Janet Woollacott's *Bond and Beyond*, a book which has much to recommend it despite its heavily theorised slant and its leanings towards Marxist-based approaches to cultural studies. Bennett and Woollacott are interested 'in the figure of Bond, in the diverse and changing forms in which it has been produced and circulated, and in the varying cultural business that has been conducted around, by means of and through this figure during the now considerable slice of post-war history in which it has been culturally active'. The aim of their study, they claim, is 'to go beyond the Bond novels and films to take account of the broader range of texts and coded objects through which the figure of Bond has been put into circulation as a popular hero'.[35] Accordingly they analyse not only the books and the films, but also the images of Bond in other media – advertisements, newspapers, magazines – to show how Bond has functioned as a point of reference in popular culture. The principal theoretical assumption underlying *Bond and Beyond*, typically for cultural studies during the 1980s, is the Gramscian notion of hegemony which supposes that the relationship between popular fictional forms and ideological discourses is subject to negotiation and transformation. Conceptualising the relationship between fiction and ideology, they continue:

> The ideological work effected by both the films and the novels, we suggest, is not that of imposing a range of dominant ideologies but that of articulating the relations between a series of ideologies (subordinate as well as dominant), overlapping them on to one another so as to bring about certain movements and reformations of subjectivity – movements whose direction has varied with different moments in Bond's career as a popular hero in response to broader cultural and ideological pressures.[36]

Bond, according to this view, is not reducible to a particular ideology or a single meaning, but rather can mean different things to different people at different moments.

A more historical dimension to Bennett and Woollacott's work is evidenced by their analysis of the various 'moments of Bond' through-out his 'career' as a popular hero. They chart how 'the cultural and ideological currency of the figure of Bond has been changed and adapted to changing circumstances'.[37] They identify three particular

moments which defined Bond's place in popular culture. Pointing out
that Fleming's novels did not immediately achieve best-seller status,
Bennett and Woollacott identify 1957 – the year in which the stories
were first serialised in the *Daily Express* and when a 'James Bond' strip
cartoon began in the same newspaper – as 'the first stage in the transformation of Bond from a character within a set of fictional texts into
a household name'.[38] The second key 'moment' of Bond was the mid-
1960s when the success of the early James Bond films 'both significantly
broadened the social basis of Bond's popular appeal in Britain and
extended the horizons of his popularity internationally'.[39] The films
transformed the essentially conservative, establishment figure of
Fleming's novels into a modern, classless hero more in tune with the
social climate of the 1960s. It was during the mid-1960s that the
phenomenon of 'Bondmania', attributable principally to the success of
the films, which in turn boosted sales of the novels, was at its height.
The third 'moment' of Bond is the period since the early 1970s when
the nature of Bond's popularity changed by becoming less of a cultural
phenomenon and more of an 'institutionalised ritual' with the production
of a new film on a regular basis every two years. Moreover, from 1975
onwards, 'the transmission of a Bond film by ITV on Christmas Day
established a regular place for Bond in the "way of life" of the British
people'.[40] Bond has now become a familiar and recognisable institution,
a 'dormant signifier' which is inactive most of the time but is 'capable
of being periodically reactivated' with the release of each new film.

Bennett and Woollacott provide a thoroughgoing, stimulating, theor-
etically informed investigation of the Bond phenomenon which contains
much useful and perceptive analysis of both the novels and the films.
What *Bond and Beyond* emphatically is not, however, is a contextual history
of the James Bond films. The authors do not consider the films in the
context of British cinema history more generally. Nor do they discuss
the place of the Bond movies in *film* culture specifically (as opposed to
popular culture in general). There is much scope, therefore, for further
critical and historical analysis of the Bond films. For instance, whereas
the place of the novels within the spy thriller genre has been thoroughly
investigated by literary theorists – Michael Denning's book *Cover Stories*
is exemplary in this respect – there has been no comparable generic
analysis forthcoming from a film studies perspective.

This book arises from a desire to subject the James Bond films to the
same sort of critical scrutiny that has recently been applied to other areas

of popular cinema. This is not, I should emphasise, yet another account of the production histories of the Bond films, an angle which has been thoroughly described in the behind-the-scenes accounts already referred to. It is, rather, as the subtitle states, a cultural history of the James Bond films. I shall seek to place the Bond films in the contexts of British cinema history and film culture. This will involve, in the first place, investigating the generic roots of the films, in particular their relationship to the spy thriller genre, and, thereafter, analysing the production ideology and working practices of the film-makers. This will be followed by close analysis of the films themselves, both as text and in context. My textual analysis focuses on the narrative ideologies of the films, their visual style, their representation of gender and their construction of national identity (a problematic concept, of course, but one which is central to the Bond mythology through the notions of 'Englishness' which are attached to the central character). My contextual analysis focuses on the critical and popular reception of the films, and discusses how they have responded over time to changes both in the film industry and in society at large. The longevity of the series is due, in large measure, to the strategies which the film-makers have adopted for renewing and updating the Bond formula. Thus, the films themselves have always kept slightly ahead of the times through their displays of futuristic technology, while periodically new actors have been brought in to play the central character, who is always a contemporary rather than a period figure. The approach I have followed is to group two or three films together per chapter, in order to illustrate the generic and stylistic development of the series. For example, the first three films can be grouped together in that they came closest to the 'snobbery with violence' style of Fleming's books, while *The Spy Who Loved Me* and *Moonraker* are clearly a pair, if only in the sense that the latter is more or less a straight remake of the former. In order to locate them within film culture, I have drawn extensively on contemporary reviews of the Bond movies from a wide range of sources, embracing not only middle-brow and 'quality' publications but also the popular and trade press. Newspaper and magazine reviews are too often neglected by film theorists, perhaps because their approach to criticism seems unsophisticated in comparison to the academic jargon of most scholarly journals, but for the film historian they provide useful evidence of the cultural and intellectual climate within which the films were received, as well as providing a barometer of critical taste over a period of some four decades.

Readers will find that I do not concern myself with the question of who is the 'best' James Bond. This is a question which has been debated within the Bond fan culture for years, generally in terms of a simplistic and tedious comparison of the acting styles of Sean Connery and Roger Moore, with the former usually emerging as the fans' favourite. It is my contention, however, that there is and can be only one definitive James Bond (just as there is and can be only one definitive Sherlock Holmes), and that is the original literary character. Ian Fleming's James Bond is definitive, while all the other James Bonds – including not only the actors who have played him on screen, but also the novels by other authors who have followed Fleming in writing Bond stories – are interpretations.

Finally, I should point out that I write this book both from the perspective of a film historian and as a Bond fan. As a film historian, it is my belief that the Bond series has been too long neglected in film history and is long overdue critical rehabilitation. At the same time, as a Bond fan, I accept that the Bond films are fun and can also be appreciated on that level. Too many academic writers seem to be almost embarrassed to admit to enjoying the movies they write about, as if doing so would somehow compromise their scholarly objectivity. Part of the process of taking the Bond films seriously, however, is to recognise that they are made for purposes of entertainment, an entertainment in which we all share. Ever since *Dr No* burst on to cinema screens in 1962, James Bond has held a licence to thrill audiences all over the world. It is high time that the most successful and enduring series of films in cinema history were accorded their rightful place in the sun.

1

Bond and Beyond: the James Bond Films and Genre

The James Bond films are genre films of a unique and special kind. 'Stated simply,' writes Barry Keith Grant, 'genre movies are those commercial feature films which, through repetition and variation, tell familiar stories with familiar characters in familiar situations. They also encourage expectations and experiences similar to those of similar films we have already seen.'[1] The Bond films are genre films in that they exhibit a basic formula which remains remarkably consistent throughout the series. Audiences have become familiar with the stories, character types and narrative situations of the films, and, moreover, expect them to recur in each new film. As one critic remarked at the time of the seventeenth official Bond film, *GoldenEye*: 'We want to like most movies we pay to see but we already know the Bond formula – it has already earned our good will – so our pleasure revolves around seeing how the film-makers execute their turn.'[2]

But to which genre does James Bond belong? Locating the Bond series in the generic profile of popular cinema is not such an easy task as it might seem. Indeed, the Bond movies can be placed in various different generic contexts; relationships can be identified between the Bond movies and several other types of popular cinema both past and present. The aim of this chapter is to explore the generic and cultural roots of the Bond films, and, further, to demonstrate how the generic formula of the Bond series has been institutionalised through the development of a particular production ideology. It will be useful in the first instance, however, to outline the various generic contexts in which the Bond films might be placed. The following list is not intended to be too schematic, but rather to suggest a general framework for critical investigation.

1. *The British imperialist spy thriller.* On one level the Bond films represent the last, glorious, big-budget flowering of the old-fashioned British imperialist spy thriller. The link here is foremost a literary one in that Ian Fleming is widely regarded as having inherited the mantle of a previous generation of British thriller writers, particularly John Buchan and 'Sapper' (H. C. McNeile), whose fictional heroes – Richard Hannay and Bulldog Drummond – have been seen as the literary predecessors of James Bond. Fleming's Bond is undoubtedly one of 'the Breed', that group of instinctively competitive, patriotic, honest and square-jawed defenders of the realm so memorably evoked in Richard Usborne's nostalgic tribute *Clubland Heroes*. But the imperialist spy thriller also successfully made the transition to the cinema, enjoying its heyday with the films of Alfred Hitchcock, and others, during the 1930s: *The Man Who Knew Too Much*, *The 39 Steps*, *The Secret Agent*, *The Lady Vanishes*, *The Return of Bulldog Drummond*, *Bulldog Drummond at Bay*, *Sexton Blake and the Hooded Terror*, *Q-Planes* and *The Four Just Men* were among the films which made the decade the golden age for the genre in British cinema. Subsequently the spy genre was modified, first through the secret mission narratives of the Second World War, then through the espionage films of the Cold War. The Bond films, in this sense, can be placed in a generic lineage of British popular fiction. The film critic of *The Times*, in reviewing *From Russia With Love* in 1963, described the screen Bond as 'the Four Just Men, 1960s style, all rolled into one'.[3] But already, by the time that Bond made his cinema debut, the values and ideologies of the imperialist spy thriller had been overtaken by events. Bond himself was an anachronism, a defender of empire in a post-colonial age. Raymond Durgnat certainly saw him in these terms, employing a typically British metaphor in suggesting that 'Bond J. is the last man in of the British Empire Superman's XI. Holmes, Hannay, Drummond, Conquest, Templar *et al* have all succumbed to the demon bowlers of the twentieth century, while The Winds of Change make every ball a googlie'.[4]

2. *The cliff-hanger adventure serial.* 'If any cinematic genre inherited the mantle of the Saturday matinee serials and Pearl White tied to the rails,

it was James Bond,' remarks film critic Andrew Rissik.[5] The film serial, or 'chapter play', can be seen as an alternative mode of film practice to the dominant classical cinema of Hollywood between the mid-1910s and the early 1950s, representing the continued existence of a cinema based on 'attractions' (stunts, chases, fights, death-defying escapes) and on the non-closure of narrative (at least until the final chapter). While the serials ranged across various genres, including westerns, adventure melodramas, science-fiction and crime-fighter serials, in the collective consciousness of cinema-goers they have come to represent a cinema of thrills, spills, master criminals and imperilled heroines. The Bond films have frequently been compared to the old movie serials, the only major difference being that they are made on a bigger and more ex-pensive scale. 'Certainly, the James Bond films and all the imitations of them were only movie serials made acceptable to adults,' write serial historians Jim Harmon and Donald F. Glut. 'The mad scientists were better characterized to make them more believable; their inventions were made to look more convincing; sexy girls were added; the week-to-week continuation was subracted [*sic*] for a jaded, impatient audience.'[6] Furthermore, it is not only through the cinema that the influence of the serial on the Bond films can be detected. The British radio serial *Dick Barton*, for example, might be seen as another forerunner of James Bond: a 'special agent' who, complete with his own distinctive theme tune, defended Britain against the fiendish plots of diabolical criminal masterminds.

3. *The modern Hollywood action movie.* If the links to the imperialist spy thriller and the serial suggest that the Bond films are best located in relation to genres and modes of the past, their influence on the modern Hollywood action movie illustrates that they can also be placed in the context of one of the most popular and characteristic genres of contemporary American cinema. The Bond series can be seen as the progenitor of the high-tech action film – a genre which one com-mentator has dubbed the 'big loud action movie' (the acronym is so obvious that it does not need spelling out) – that is now a staple of Hollywood film-making. In the view of screenwriter Larry Gross, the Bond films represented 'an entirely new super-kinetic cartoon-type action movie'.[7] The characteristics of the modern Hollywood action thriller – the emphasis on (usually violent) action over plotting and characterisation, the reduction of narrative complexity to a series of set pieces and chases, the foregrounding of technology and firepower,

and, perhaps above all, the hero who never dispatches a villain without a 'witty' one-liner – can all be traced back to the Bond films. The starring vehicles of Hollywood action-men such as Mel Gibson, Arnold Schwarzenegger, Sylvester Stallone, Bruce Willis *et al.* are nothing if not Americanised reworkings of the James Bond formula. Even the Indiana Jones films, in which the hero is characterised in contrast to James Bond (scruffy and crumpled rather than suave and sophisticated, relying on a bullwhip rather than technological gadgetry), owe as much to Bond as they do to the serials which inspired them. Bond, the first of the cinema's dark, saturnine, cynical superheroes might be seen as the 'father' of Indiana Jones – and, indeed, when Sean Connery was cast as Harrison Ford's father in *Indiana Jones and the Last Crusade*, the inter-textual link became explicit.

4. *The 'Bondian'*. For all the similarities which the Bond films share with other genres, the Bond series itself is nevertheless unique in cinema history. In this sense it might be argued that the Bond series is a genre (or at the very least a sub-genre) in its own right. The Bond series is differentiated from other action movies through the character of James Bond himself. 'There is no other romantic anti-hero in existence at the moment,' remarked *GoldenEye* director Martin Campbell in 1995. 'They are all blue collar – Arnold Schwarzenegger, Bruce Willis, Sylvester Stallone. There are no sophisticated or British comparisons to Bond.'[8] The Bond film-makers have developed their own production ideology based on the notion of what is and what is not 'Bondian'. This production ideology constitutes a set of expectations about what a Bond movie should be like, what it should contain, how it should be made, and so on. This was a recurring theme in a series of interviews with production personnel conducted for an Open University case study of the making of *The Spy Who Loved Me* in 1976–77 and which is the basis of an essay on the production of the Bond films by Janet Woollacott. '"Bondian" was the phrase used by Broccoli and other members of the production team to mean "in the spirit of James Bond",' she writes. 'To a certain extent the term "Bondian" was used to describe the Bond films, which were seen as a distinctive formula, a specific genre of film.'[9]

It is evident, even within these brief schemata, that the Bond series marks the convergence of a number of different generic forms and traditions. The Bond films are unique in so far as there is no comparable group of films which can be located at precisely the same point of convergence between genres. It can further be argued that the Bond films are not only *generically* unique, but they are also *historically* unique within the genres to which they belong: while they are the last of the imperialist spy thrillers, they are at the same time the first of the 'big loud action movies'. Furthermore, the generic traditions which come together in the Bond series encompass different national cinemas (Britain and Hollywood), which not only adds to their uniqueness but also goes some way towards explaining their international popularity. A distinction should be made, however, between the generic *influence* of the Bond films, which extends not only to Hollywood but beyond (think, for example, of the popular Hong Kong action cinema) and their generic *origins*, which are to be found in a particularly British context. Given that the Bond films were based, initially at least, on the novels of Ian Fleming, then his work is the most appropriate starting point for exploring the generic and cultural origins of the Bond phenomenon.

The first James Bond novel, *Casino Royale*, was published by Jonathan Cape in April 1953. Thereafter Fleming published another eleven Bond novels, and two collections of Bond short stories, writing a book each year until his death in 1964 (the last novel, *The Man With the Golden Gun*, and the short story volume *Octopussy and the Living Daylights*, were published posthumously). Although Fleming was eventually to fulfil his ambition of entering the best-seller stakes, it was not until near the end of his life that he really enjoyed the fruits of his labours. Sales of the early hardbacks were respectable if not spectacular, though the print runs at first were not very large (the first edition of *Casino Royale* – now a highly-prized item for book collectors – had a print run of only 4,750). It was the publication of paperback editions of the books by Pan from 1955, and the serialisation of *From Russia, With Love* in the *Daily Express* in 1957, that saw the popularity of James Bond take off. Paperback sales of the novels increased during the late 1950s and reached their peak in the mid-1960s, when the first films were released. In each year between 1962 and 1967 inclusive, over a million James Bond paperbacks were sold in Britain. The Bond novels marked an important moment in publishing history, according to literary historian John Sutherland, who describes them as 'a breakthrough comparable in some ways to [Allen] Lane's, thirty years earlier'. 'The importance of the Bond books', he continues, 'was that they revealed a new reliable market for a certain kind of book that was not trash and could be marketed as a "brand name" (i.e. "the latest Bond").'[10]

'I think it is safe to say that James Bond has the stuff of immortality in him,' Anthony Burgess remarked.[11] Writing in 1987, Burgess considered that Bond 'has been around long enough to have taken on some of the quality of a classic character', and, like many other commentators, compared Bond to that other great immortal of popular fiction, Sherlock Holmes: 'He [Bond] is not, true, as universal as Sherlock Holmes, for the Soviet bloc very naturally rejects him, but he intrigues us as Sherlock Holmes does: he is tough, ingenious, and not lacking in contradictions.' Like the literary Holmes, the literary Bond has attracted much critical attention, ranging from the scholarly studies of Umberto Eco and others to trivial discussions of his personal habits and character traits. Just as 'Sherlockians' discuss endlessly the world of their hero, so too the game of 'Bondology' is played by aficionados who seek to identify the literary influences on Fleming and highlight the various factual and technical inaccuracies of his work. Furthermore, like Holmes, Bond has become part of popular culture in a wider sense, a figure which is recognisable and which has certain cultural associations beyond the original texts themselves.

Where does James Bond stand in the generic lineage of popular fiction? Although Kingsley Amis argued that Bond himself is properly described as a secret agent rather than a spy ('It's inaccurate, of course, to describe James Bond as a *spy*, in the strict sense of one who steals or buys or smuggles the secrets of foreign Powers'),[12] the spy thriller is nevertheless the most appropriate generic context in which to place his adventures. Academic work on the spy thriller genre has focused almost exclusively on its literary form. This is explicable in that the genre began as popular literature and that most spy films have tended to be adapted from novels (Hitchcock's *North by Northwest* stands out as perhaps the only major spy film which was not based, however loosely, on a literary original). In order to place the Bond films in the spy thriller genre, therefore, it is necessary in the first instance to consider where in the generic lineage of spy fiction the original books can be located.

On one level the spy thriller is a sub-genre of the thriller, a broad category which covers a range of forms and narrative types. The term 'thriller' (along with 'shocker') came into widespread use in the late nineteenth century to describe a new type of sensational fiction which proliferated at the time, due largely to the emergence of cheap circulation libraries and serialisation in newspapers and magazines. The imperial adventure stories which had been the favourite reading of the late Victorian period – from the heroic boys' stories of G. A. Henty and

R. M. Ballantyne to the more 'literary' novels of Robert Louis Stevenson and Henry Rider Haggard – were superseded around the turn of the century by the thrillers of writers like E. Phillips Oppenheim and Edgar Wallace. A thriller is usually taken to indicate a story where sensational plot elements, action, mystery and intrigue predominate. In his book *Thrillers*, Jerry Palmer argues that the two essential ingredients of the thriller are the hero, who is characterised by an instinctively competitive personality, and the conspiracy, which represents a threat to the hero and the values he stands for. 'This pair – conspiracy and hero – constitute the most fundamental layer of the thriller,' Palmer writes. 'The plot – the story – is the process by which the hero averts the conspiracy and this process is what provides the thrills that the reader seeks.'[13]

Within the broad category of the thriller, the spy thriller is a particular variation in which certain themes and narrative ingredients are fore-grounded. As Tom Ryall observes: 'The distinct status of the spy thriller is partly a matter of the specific subject matter of espionage and partly a matter of the precise weight allocated to the elements which it shares with adjacent literary currents within the general sphere of crime fiction.'[14] So, for example, although the stealing of secret papers was the subject of several of the Sherlock Holmes stories ('The Naval Treaty', 'The Second Stain', 'The Bruce-Partington Plans'), these would not be considered spy thrillers because the narrative follows the process by which the thefts are discovered and the thieves captured. Whereas in the detective story the narrative focuses on unravelling the mystery and solving the crime, in the spy thriller such elements as murder and theft are background to the plot rather than its *raison d'être*.

Perhaps the main distinguishing characteristic of the spy thriller which sets it apart from other variants of the thriller is its political content. This does not mean that the spy thriller necessarily expresses a particular political viewpoint, though quite frequently it does, but rather that politics – usually international politics – provide the topical background to the genre. In his excellent book on the British spy thriller, Michael Denning writes:

> Since the turn of the century, spy thrillers have been 'cover stories' for our culture, collective fantasies in the imagination of the English-speaking world, paralleling reality, expressing what they wish to conceal, and telling the 'History of Contemporary Society'. Thrillers use cover stories about assumed identities and double

agents, and take their plots from cover stories of the daily news; and their tales of spies, moles and the secret service have become a cover story, translating the political and cultural transformations of the twentieth century into the intrigues of a shadow world of secret agents.[15]

The political content of the spy thriller, Denning argues, is 'a pretext to the adventure formulas and the plots of betrayal, disguise and doubles which are at the heart of the genre'. These formulas and plots, in turn, provide the means by which 'the spy thriller narrates the crises and contradictions in ideologies of nation and Empire and of class and gender'. While the tensions which provide the topical background for the spy thriller change over time – imperialism, communism, fascism, the Cold War, political terrorism – the genre itself remains tied to its national roots. As Denning observes: 'The spy thriller has been, for most of its history, a British genre, indeed a major cultural export.'[16]

It is pointless to try to identify the first spy story, as to do so would be to attribute the origins of the genre to a particular individual, whereas genres are better understood as evolving over time, drawing on and modifying other forms and traditions. At particular points in the history of the spy thriller, however, certain authors have stood out as representative of the various trends and phases in the genre's evolution. Broadly speaking, most British spy thrillers since the Edwardian period have followed one of two lineages. Denning posits a difference between, on the one hand, what he terms 'magical thrillers where there is a clear contest between Good and Evil with a virtuous hero defeating an alien and evil villain', and, on the other hand, 'existential thrillers which play on a dialectic of good and evil overdetermined by moral dilemmas, by moves from innocence to experience, and by identity crises, the discovery in the double agent that the self may be evil'.[17] The difference between these two forms might also be described as that between the 'sensational' spy thriller and the 'realist' spy thriller. The 'magical' or 'sensational' spy thriller is characterised by an emphasis on action and adventure, by narratives of movement and pursuit, and by a public-school notion of espionage as a game or sport. It is exemplified on either side of the First World War by the stories of William Le Queux and E. Phillips Oppenheim, with their tales of intrigue and conspiracies in the courts and governments of Europe, and thereafter by the work of Sax Rohmer (whose fiendish oriental master criminal Fu Manchu, and his Holmes-like nemesis Nayland Smith, first appeared in 1913), John Buchan (particularly the Richard Hannay novels, beginning with *The Thirty-Nine Steps* in 1915) and 'Sapper' (whose Bulldog Drummond first appeared in 1920). The 'existential' or 'realist' spy thriller, by contrast, tends to use spying as a metaphor for probing the psychology of the human condition. It explores the seedier side of espionage and is characterised by greater moral ambiguity over what is right or wrong. It is exemplified by Joseph Conrad's *The Secret Agent* (1907), W. Somerset Maugham's Ashenden stories (appearing in 1928), the novels of Graham Greene and Eric Ambler on both sides of the Second World War, and the work of John le Carré and Len Deighton in the 1960s and after.

So where does James Bond belong in the lineage of the spy thriller? Just as the Bond films occupy a point of convergence between several different genres, so, too, the Bond novels exist at the meeting point of different trends within the literary spy thriller. On the one hand Fleming's Bond might be seen as a throwback to the world of Richard Hannay and Bulldog Drummond, but on the other hand some commentators have interpreted him as a modernising hero, with the novels anticipating the more realist spy thrillers of the Cold War. Identifying the specific influences on Fleming from other practitioners of spy fiction has become part of the game of 'Bondology' which is played by many critics. 'Fleming, by design, instinct or great good luck, repeated every prescription in the pharmacopoeia of crime and spy fiction,' wrote Colin Watson. 'His thirteen [*sic*] James Bond novels can be seen as a potted history of the twentieth-century thriller.'[18]

In most respects, the Bond stories belong to the sensational lineage of spy fiction. Fleming, who was born in 1908, had grown up during the golden age of the imperialist spy thriller, and is known in his boyhood to have been an avid reader of that type of fiction. Many commentators, indeed, have seen James Bond as an updated version of Bulldog Drummond. *The Times Literary Supplement*, for example, considered that *Casino Royale* 'is an extremely engaging affair, dealing with espionage in the "Sapper" manner, but with a hero who, although taking a great many cold showers and never letting sex interfere with work, is somewhat more sophisticated'.[19] Created by Herman Cyril McNeile, a former officer of the Royal Engineers (hence his pen-name of 'Sapper'), the character of Captain Hugh 'Bulldog' Drummond was a retired army officer who, finding civilian life dull, placed a newspaper advertisement seeking adventure and became embroiled in a contest against the villainous Carl Peterson, head of a crime syndicate attempting to bring about a revolution in Britain. Drummond and his pals Algy, Peter and Toby fought four 'rounds' against Peterson (*Bulldog Drummond, The Black Gang, The Third Round* and *The Final Count*), and another two against Peterson's vengeful mistress Irma (*The Female of the Species, The Return of Bulldog Drummond*). Hugely popular in his day, particularly with boys, Drummond is now among the most unfashionable of popular fictional heroes, on account of his aggressive nationalism, xenophobia and anti-Semitism. Although described as 'a sportsman and a gentleman', he seems, to modern eyes, more like a thuggish, authoritarian vigilante with fascist tendencies. But to what extent was he a model for James Bond? According to Richard Usborne, a schoolboy fan of the Drummond stories later to become an author himself:

> Among other enthusiastic readers of Drummond's exploits, from the start shortly after World War I, was an exact contemporary of mine, Ian Fleming. Fleming, shortly after World War II, remembered the Drummond books shrewdly in planning his James Bond. He gave Bond a sex-life more in keeping with the demands of the fiction of the 1950s and '60s. But he went, professionally and gratefully, for the essentials of the Sapper plot, movement and supra-national villainy.[20]

However, Fleming denied that he based Bond on Drummond at all, suggesting instead that the hard-boiled detectives of American crime fiction were his models. 'I didn't believe in the heroic Bulldog Drummond types. I felt these types could no longer exist in literature,' he told one interviewer. 'I wanted my lead character to more or less follow the pattern of Raymond Chandler and Dashiell Hammett's heroes, who are believable people, believable heroes.'[21]

But if Fleming wanted to create a believable hero, then his villains were undoubtedly out of the sensational school of the thriller. Bond's arch-enemy Ernst Stavro Blofeld bears comparison not only to Carl Peterson, in that he was the head of an international crime syndicate and featured in three of the books (*Thunderball, On Her Majesty's Secret Service, You Only Live Twice*), but also to Sherlock Holmes's nemesis Professor Moriarty (at the end of *You Only Live Twice* Bond is presumed dead, just as Holmes had been in 'The Final Problem'). Furthermore, during the course of his adventures Bond faced a veritable gallery of grotesques – Le Chiffre, Mr Big, Sir Hugo Drax, Dr No, Goldfinger,

Scaramanga – who would have been recognisable to anyone versed in the stories of Edgar Wallace and Sax Rohmer. The megalomaniac villains of the sensational thrillers were larger-than-life, caricatures rather than characters, often of bizarre physical appearance, invariably bent on the acquisition of wealth and power, and with a tendency to devise ingenious death scenarios for the hero (from which he would, of course, contrive to escape). As John G. Cawelti points out, moreover, there was also an explicitly racial and cultural dimension to their villainy: 'The British Empire and its white Christian civilization are constantly in danger of subversion by villains who represent other races or racial mixtures. Saxe [*sic*] Rohmer's Fu Manchu and his hordes of little yellow and brown conspirators against the purity and safety of English society are only an extreme example of the pervasive racial symbolism of this period.'[22]

'With Mr Fleming,' Kingsley Amis observed, 'we move beyond the situation in which you only had to scratch a foreigner to find a villain, but you still don't need to scratch a villain to find a foreigner.'[23] Thus Sir Hugo Drax in *Moonraker*, ostensibly an English patriot, is really Graf Hugo von der Drache, a fanatical German nationalist who is plotting to destroy London with a nuclear missile. The 'racial symbolism' identified by Cawelti was no less pronounced in Fleming's thrillers than in his pre-Second World War counterparts. His villains included not only the usual Russians and Germans, who had always been presented as the enemies of Britain in the imperialist spy thriller, but also black American gangsters (Mr Big in *Live and Let Die*) and Chinese mad scientists (Dr No's physical appearance is strongly reminiscent of the 'devil doctor' Fu Manchu himself).

Another aspect of the old-fashioned imperialist spy thriller which features strongly in the Bond novels is the ideology of national identity which is overlaid on the contest between Bond and the villain. Fleming's Bond is an essentially conservative hero, a defender of the realm, committed to preserving the institutions and society of his country, which typically is referred to as 'England' rather than 'Britain'. The threats to those institutions and society generally come from foreign villains who are contemptuous of England and English values. When Bond thinks of his country, it is characterised in rosy, picture-postcard terms:

> His mind drifted into a world of tennis courts and lily ponds and
> kings and queens, of London, of people being photographed with

pigeons on their heads in Trafalgar Square, of the forsythia that would soon be blazing on the bypass roundabouts, of May, the treasured housekeeper in his flat off the King's Road, getting up to brew herself a cup of tea ... of the first tube trains beginning to run, shaking the ground beneath his cool, dark bedroom. Of the douce weather of England: the soft airs, the heat waves, the cold spells – 'The only country where you can take a walk every day of the year.' (*Dr No*, p. 182)

Bond's England, as Amis points out, is 'substantially right of centre'.[24] It is one in which the monarchy is at the head of things, a point made explicit in the title of the eleventh volume, *On Her Majesty's Secret Service*; Bond's work is carried out in the name of the sovereign, and he has official legitimation to destroy the enemies of his country (a 'licence to kill'). Bond himself is frequently constructed through imagery which enforces notions of patriotism and duty. The contest between Bond and one of his enemies, for example, is described through a mixed metaphor redolent with cultural and mythical overtones:

> Bond sighed wearily. Once more into the breach, dear friends! This time it really was St George and the dragon. And St George had better get a move on before the dragon hatched the little dragon's egg he was now nesting so confidently. (*Goldfinger*, p. 180)

While perhaps ironic in intent, all the same the metaphor is a powerful one: Bond is compared to two of the great English folk heroes, Shakespeare's Henry V and St George, warrior-king and saintly protector of damsels in distress.[25]

The ideologies of national identity and patriotism in the Bond novels, therefore, link them to the pre-war imperialist spy thriller. But in other respects the Bond novels also illustrate certain tendencies in the post-war development of the genre. Most obviously, Fleming's Bond was a product of the historical and ideological conditions of the Cold War. The emergence of politically and militarily opposed power blocs in Europe after 1945 provided the background for the post-war spy thriller, in which the enemy was the Soviet-dominated Eastern bloc; an enemy which was no longer just a country (Russia) but an ideology (Communism) which presented a very real threat to the 'free' West. In all but one of the books written during the 1950s (from *Casino Royale* to *For Your Eyes Only*) Bond's enemy is either Soviet or Soviet-backed, usually a member of SMERSH (a contraction of *Smiert Spionam* – 'Death to Spies'). The one exception is *Diamonds Are Forever*, in which Bond combats American gangsters. However, from the ninth book, *Thunderball*, published in 1961 (wherein Bond reflected that 'with the cold war wearing off, it was not like the old days'), Fleming introduced an international terrorist organisation called SPECTRE (Special Executive for Counter-Intelligence, Terrorism, Revenge and Extortion) which was apolitical in so far as it was not motivated by ideology, but was rather a freelance organisation bent on the acquisition of wealth and power through terrorism.

One of the important differences between Fleming's work and the pre-war thrillers of Buchan and Sapper is that although espionage is still described in terms of a game, there is a recognition that it is a game which is being played in deadly earnest and in which there is no place for amateurs. As Bond's first enemy, Le Chiffre, tells him (before torturing him nearly to death), 'the game of Red Indians is over, quite over. You have stumbled by mischance into a game for grown-ups and you have already found it a painful experience' (*Casino Royale*, p. 120). Fleming constantly emphasises Bond's professionalism, describing his careful and detailed preparations before embarking on a mission and giving him no life of his own outside the secret service. Bond differs from those talented amateurs Hannay and Drummond in that his secret life is his job, not an amusing diversion between rubbers of bridge or hearty games of rugger. Bond lives solely for his job, and frequently succumbs to periods of *ennui* (which he refers to as his 'dog days') between missions.

While Fleming is clearly very different from 'existential' thriller writers such as Greene and Ambler, there are nevertheless some indications in the Bond novels of a certain sense of ambiguity about the practice of espionage. Although the patriotic basis of Bond's character is never seriously called into question, there are moments of introspection in the novels where he questions the nature of his profession. This is evident from the outset, in *Casino Royale*, when, after being tortured by Le Chiffre, Bond suggests that 'this country right-or-wrong business is getting a little out of date' and remarks that 'I'm wondering whose side I ought to be on' (pp. 143–4). The first of the novels is also significant in that, for the only time in the series, it transpires that the woman for whom Bond has fallen is a double agent. Published only two years after the embarrassing revelation that British intelligence agents Guy Burgess and Donald Maclean had been Soviet moles, the revelation that Vesper Lynd is 'a double, working for Redland' had obvious topicality. *Casino Royale*, in fact, is a taut, spare story in which there is no far-fetched plot: Bond's mission is to discredit a Soviet agent, who has been swindling funds from his paymasters, by defeating him at the gambling table. It is by far the most 'realistic' of the novels, and the one which is most removed from the sensational school of spy fiction. In the opinion of Fleming's biographer Andrew Lycett, 'there was ample evidence that at the start, at least, Ian attempted something more ambitious than simply updating the swashbuckling secret service adventure stories of his childhood'. He continues:

> What raised *Casino Royale* out of the usual run of thrillers was Ian's attempt to reflect the disturbing moral ambiguity of a post-war world that could produce traitors like Burgess and Maclean. Although Bond is presented like Bulldog Drummond with all the trappings of a traditional British fictional secret agent (such as his Bentley), in fact he needs 'Marshall Aid' from Leiter to enable him to continue his baccarat game with Le Chiffre. Bond is rescued from his kidnapper not by the British or the Americans but by the Russians, who complete the job he should have done of eliminating Le Chiffre. Bond does not even get the girl: she has been duplicitous throughout, betraying not only him personally but all Western intelligence's anti-Soviet operations. No wonder, feeling let down and abandoned, he fails to conceal his bitterness at the end and spits out, 'The bitch is dead now'.[26]

In this respect, *Casino Royale* anticipated the stories of internal treachery and deceit by John le Carré (*Tinker, Tailor, Soldier, Spy*) and Len Deighton (*The Ipcress File*).

The Bond novels, therefore, while having most in common with the sensational lineage of spy fiction through their (usually) fantastic plots and bizarre villains, also shared some of the characteristics of the realist spy thriller in reflecting (occasionally) on the seamier side of the secret world of spies and espionage. Other critical approaches to the Bond novels, however, have been less concerned with genre than with narrative. Umberto Eco, as part of his chess analogy, argues that the narrative construction of all the Bond novels is the same and can best be understood as a series of 'moves' in which characters play out familiar situations: Bond is given a mission by M (Head of the British Secret

Service); Bond gives first check to the villain, or the villain gives first check to Bond; Bond meets the heroine and seduces her, or begins the process of doing so; Bond and the heroine are captured by the villain; the villain tortures Bond; Bond conquers the villain and possesses the heroine; and so on. Furthermore, interwoven with the plot structure is a set of structural oppositions: oppositions between characters (Bond/ M, Bond/villain, Bond/girl), between opposing ideologies (Soviet Union/Free World, England/non Anglo-Saxon countries) and between different values (duty/sacrifice, luxury/discomfort, excess/moderation, loyalty/disloyalty).[27]

Tony Bennett modifies Eco's analysis by arguing that the Bond novels can be understood through a set of narrative codes which regulate the relationships between characters. He identifies three particular narrative codes – the 'sexist code', 'imperialist code' and 'phallic code' – which are all present in the Bond novels. The 'sexist code' regulates the relationship between Bond and the 'girl' (the heroine in a Bond story is almost invariably described as a 'girl'). The girl is usually out of place, either sexually, in the sense that she is initially resistant to Bond, or ideologically, in that she is in the service of the villain, or both. Bond's seduction of the girl therefore serves an ideological purpose in that he 'repositions' her by putting her back into the 'correct' place. 'In thus replacing the girl in a subordinate position in relation to men,' Bennett argues, 'Bond simultaneously repositions her within the sphere of ideology in general, detaching her from the service of the villain and recruiting her in support of his own mission.'[28] The 'imperialist code' regulates the relationships between Bond and his allies, who are usually loyal colonial or pro-British characters, who defer to Bond and who are in a subordinate power relationship to him. And the 'phallic code' regulates the relationship between Bond and M, a symbolic father-figure who endows Bond with power and authority (his 'licence to kill'), and between Bond and the villain, who threatens Bond with symbolic castration through torture.

While Bennett provides a useful theoretical interpretation of the novels, his reading is noticeably lacking any historical dimension. His analysis of narrative codes – as with Eco's analysis of narrative structure – does much to explain the ideological processes at work within the novels, but those ideological processes cannot be detached from their historical context. It is not just that the Bond novels rehearse a set of ideologies about gender and national identity, but also that they express those ideologies in a manner that has specific historical resonances within the period during which they were written. In other words, Bond's attitude towards women and towards England makes sense only when it is understood in the context of the social and political conditions of the 1950s and early 1960s.

Like so many works of popular fiction, the Bond novels are tracts for their times. In his essay 'James Bond and the Decline of England', historian David Cannadine suggests different ways in which the books reflected, or were perceived to reflect, the state of the nation:

> The period during which the Bond books appeared, from 1953 to 1966, was one in which Britain was often described as being 'in decline'. At home, a changing conventional morality was accompanied by an unprecedented rise in living standards, which encouraged the most puritanical critics of 'decline' to liken England to the later Roman Empire or early 17th-century Spain – obsessed with sex and self-indulgence, and turning its back on the more Spartan modes of life which had been the foundation of former greatness. And moral 'decline' at home was mirrored in international 'decline' abroad, as the tropical African empire was wound up, the white Commonwealth was severely shaken by the departure of South Africa, and Britain's standing in the eyes of the world was irretrievably damaged as a result of the Suez fiasco. Elizabeth's coronation, at the time of the first full-length novel, was a retrospectively unconvincing reaffirmation of Britain's continued great-power status. But the Churchill funeral, at the time of the last, was not only the last rites of the great man himself, but was also self-consciously recognised as being a requiem for Britain as a great power.[29]

Cannadine discusses Fleming's novels in relation to this widely perceived national decline, a decline in both social and moral standards at home and in Britain's standing abroad. He suggests that Fleming's attitude towards the changes which were taking place was equivocal in that while he welcomed some of them, especially the greater sexual freedom of the post-war years, he regretted some of the others, particularly the passing of the public-school ethic of duty, competitiveness and elitism, qualities which he believed had made Britain great. It was this equivocation in the books, Cannadine argues, which accounted for the different critical reactions to them, for 'while some critics saw his work as an unpleasant embodiment of reality, others acclaimed it as a welcome escape'.[30]

On one level, certainly, the Bond novels can be read as a reflection of Britain emerging from the drab world of post-war austerity and entering a new age of affluence in the 1950s. Bond's, and Fleming's, obsession with expensive brand-name goods, fine wines and elaborate meals, rather than being included merely for the snob-value which some critics have alleged, should be seen in the context of a country which had recently emerged from years of austerity and rationing and which, during the 1950s, was beginning to enjoy the consumer affluence promised by glossy magazines, television advertising and Hollywood. 'Despite recurrent economic crises,' Arthur Marwick asserts, 'the reality for the vast majority of British people was that at last the country seemed to have emerged into the kind of high-spending consumer society long familiar from American films.'[31] Bond's brand-name trappings, to be fair, were still rather more extravagant than most people could afford (he wears a Rolex Oyster Perpetual wristwatch and has his cigarettes made specially for him by Morlands of Grosvenor Street), but many British people were now able to aspire, albeit in their more modest ways, to a more affluent lifestyle than they had enjoyed before.

Closely related to the conspicuous consumption of the Bond novels was the increased prominence of sex, certainly in comparison to pre-war fiction. Bond is a hedonist who enjoys sexual relationships with his various girlfriends without (usually) any suggestion of long-term commitment or any feelings of guilt. In this respect, the novels again reflected the *Zeitgeist*: they need to be understood in the context of a period when British society was gradually breaking free from the prurient Victorianism which had, depending on one's view, acted as either a straitjacket or a safety-valve for the past century. Although the 1960s are generally labelled the age of 'permissiveness', changes in sexual attitudes were gradual and can be traced back into the 1950s. As Christopher Booker observed in his classic survey of the period, *The Neophiliacs*:

> the new prominence of sex in the late Fifties was not just a concern with the realities of sex; even more, it was a preoccupation with the idea of sex, the image of sex; the written word, the visual image, the image that was promulgated in advertisements, in increasingly 'daring' films, in 'controversial' newspaper articles and

'frank' novels; the image purveyed by the strip-tease clubs and pornographic book shops that were springing up in the back streets of Soho and provincial cities; and the image that, mixed with that of violence, was responsible in the years after 1956 for the enormous boom in the sales of Ian Fleming's James Bond stories.[32]

One of the charges levelled against Fleming was that his books amounted to a kind of pornography, a view apparently endorsed by the author's own remark that 'the target of my books ... lay somewhere between the solar plexus and, well, the upper thigh'.[33]

Denning suggests that 'the James Bond tales can rightly be seen as an important early form of the mass pornography that characterizes the consumer society, the society of the spectacle, that emerges in Western Europe and North America in the wake of post-war reconstruction'.[34] It is often pointed out that the year in which the first Bond novel was published also saw the launch of *Playboy*, the first mainstream pornographic magazine. Although it was not until the 1960s that the links between Bond and *Playboy* were institutionalised when the magazine serialised some of the later Bond stories, in addition to running photo-features on starlets from the Bond films, even beforehand there was an obvious similarity between Bond's attitude towards women and the *Playboy* ethos of easy, free, open sexuality. The type of pornography represented by *Playboy* was not so-called 'hard core' (meaning the graphic depiction of sexual acts) but rather 'soft core' (a term usually used to refer to visual representations of women in various stages of undress). Fleming's descriptions of women tend to construct them as erotic objects, emphasising their physical characteristics. Often there is a scene in which Bond looks at a girl in a state of nudity or near-nudity:

> It was a naked girl, with her back to him. She was not quite naked. She wore a broad leather belt round her waist with a hunting knife in a leather sheath at her right hip. The belt made her nakedness extraordinarily erotic. She stood not more than five yards away on the tideline looking down at something in her hand. She stood in the classical relaxed pose of the nude, all the weight on the right leg and the left knee bent and turning slightly inwards, the head to one side as she examined the things in her hand. (*Dr No*, p. 67)

Once in the bedroom, stereotyped male assumptions about female sexuality and sexual behaviour take over. Fleming's views on what women really want from sex would be enough to leave some feminists apoplectic with rage:

> All women love semi-rape. They love to be taken. It was his sweet brutality against my bruised body that had made his act of love so piercingly wonderful. That and the coinciding of nerves so completely relaxed after the removal of tension and danger, the warmth of gratitude, and a woman's natural feeling for her hero. (*The Spy Who Loved Me*, p. 154)

> [T]he girl reached up a swift hand that smelled of Guerlain's 'Ode' and put it across his lips. 'I said "no conversation". Take off those clothes. Make love to me. You are handsome and strong. I want to remember what it can be like. Do anything you like. And tell me what you like and what you would like from me. Be rough with me. Treat me like the lowest whore in creation. Forget everything else. No questions. Take me.' (*On Her Majesty's Secret Service*, p. 36)

Nor would some feminists be amused by the sort of overtly sexual names which Fleming invented for his heroines – Pussy Galore, Honeychile Rider, Kissy Suzuki, Mary Goodnight – though they should probably be taken as nothing more than an elaborate joke.

There is no doubt that the ingredients of sex, high-living and conspicuous consumption in the Bond novels account in large measure for their appeal. Hugh Gaitskell, a close friend of Fleming's wife Anne, summarised it thus: 'The combination of sex, violence, alcohol and – at intervals – good food and nice clothes is, to one who leads such a circumscribed life as I do, irresistible.'[35] For male readers in particular, the Bond novels offered a fantasy which provided scope for the gratification of repressed desires, whether they be focused on fast cars, food, drink, women, or all of those. One critic described Fleming's style as 'the technique of the erotic distraction'. His stories were written for the total stimulation of the reader, encouraging the reader to share by proxy in Bond's sexual encounters and expensive lifestyle. Andrew Bear argues that Fleming 'managed to write his sensual titillation into the very texture of the stories, and this is what can be called the technique of the erotic distraction – the Fleming Effect itself'.[36]

It was precisely those qualities, however, which drew such fierce criticism from Fleming's detractors, who objected to the high-living and

culture of self-indulgence described in his stories. Attacks on the perceived immorality of the books reached a peak in the late 1950s. In
1958, the same year that Paul Johnson accused Fleming of 'Sex,
Snobbery and Sadism' in the *New Statesman*, a similar broadside was
launched by Bernard Bergonzi in *Twentieth Century*. Bergonzi compared
Fleming unfavourably with previous thriller writers, considering that
the Bond books 'have an air of vulgarity and display which contrast
strongly with those subdued images of the perfectly self-assured gentle-
manly life that we find in Buchan or even Sapper'. Bergonzi deplored
the 'strongly marked streak of voyeurism and sado-masochism in his
books' and 'the total lack of any ethical frame of reference'. The success
of the Bond novels, Bergonzi believed, was a sure sign of a society in
moral decline. 'Mr Fleming, I imagine, knows just what he is doing,' he
concluded, 'but the fact that his books are published by a very reputable
firm, and are regularly reviewed – and highly praised – in our self-
respecting intellectual weeklies, surely says more about the present state
of our culture than a whole volume of abstract denunciations.'[37]

The other aspect of decline identified by Cannadine and addressed
in the Bond novels is the decline of a great power in the international
arena. The novels spanned a period during which Britain suffered a
crisis of national identity as its role in international affairs had to be
redefined. The humiliation of the Suez Crisis in 1956 showed that
Britain's imperial power was waning: it was no longer militarily or
economically capable of acting independently to protect its strategic
interests without the support of the United States of America.
Furthermore, the dismantling of the British Empire and the exclusion
from the Common Market (through the French veto placed on Britain's
application to join in 1963) left Britain with little role to play on the
world stage beyond that of a junior ally of the United States. The long-
held assumption that Britain was a leader in international affairs, an
assumption which informed the world of the imperialist spy thriller, no
longer had a basis in reality. Moreover, embarrassing revelations of
moles in the British intelligence services – the Burgess and Maclean
affair of 1951 was followed by the defection of Kim Philby in 1963 and
by the imprisonment, and subsequent escape in 1966, of George Blake
– fatally weakened the prestige of the real-life equivalent of Fleming's
fictional secret service.

It can be argued that, just as on one level the Bond novels represent
a hedonistic male fantasy, on another level they represent a nationalist

fantasy in which Britain's decline as a world power did not really take place. One of the ideological functions of the Bond narrative is to construct an imaginary world in which the *Pax Britannica* still operates. Thus, Britain is presented as being in the front line of the conspiracies directed against western civilisation, whether they originate with SMERSH or SPECTRE. For example, in *From Russia, With Love* SMERSH's plot is 'aimed at the heart of the Intelligence apparat of the West', while the British secret service is 'the most dangerous and [that] which we would most wish to damage' (p. 36) – an assumption which in hindsight, given Soviet penetration of the British intelligence services, seems highly ironic. And in *Thunderball*, SPECTRE's nuclear threat is directed against both Britain and the United States, which are regarded as equals. The Bond novels, therefore, both deny and redress the fact of Britain's decline. The closest that Fleming comes to accepting decline is in *You Only Live Twice*, wherein Bond's mission is undertaken to prove to the Japanese that the British are still a nation to be reckoned with.

Bennett and Woollacott suggest that 'Bond can be read as a hero of the NATO alliance'.[38] The first Bond novel appeared a few years after the formation of the North Atlantic Treaty Organisation (NATO) in 1949 and shortly before the end of the Korean War (1950–53). Bond is assisted by NATO allies, most usually by an American, Felix Leiter of the Central Intelligence Agency (CIA), who appears in six of the novels. The professional and personal friendship between Bond and Leiter represents the 'special relationship' which has supposedly existed between Britain and the United States since the end of the Second World War, though, in a quaint reversal of the real balance of power, it is the American Leiter who is the subordinate partner to the British Bond. As Amis astutely observes:

> The point of Felix Leiter, such a nonentity as a piece of characterization, is that he, the American, takes orders from Bond, the Britisher, and that Bond is constantly doing better than he, showing himself, not braver or more devoted, but smarter, wittier, tougher, more resourceful, the incarnation of little old England with her quiet ways and shoe-string budget wiping the eye of great big global-tentacled multi-billion-dollar-appropriating America.[39]

In this respect, the Bond stories again represent a denial of the decline of British power and construct an imaginary arena in which Britain still occupies centre-stage in world affairs.

The power relationship between Britain and America presented by the novels is significant when it comes to an evaluation of the first screen adaptation of a Bond story. Given that the literary and cultural roots of James Bond are to be found in a specifically British generic tradition, it is rather surprising that Bond's first screen incarnation was in a very different medium and idiom. In 1954 Fleming had sold the television rights for his first novel to the American television network CBS (Columbia Broadcasting System) for $1,000.[40] On 21 October 1954, a one-hour adaptation of *Casino Royale* was broadcast live by CBS as part of its weekly thriller series, *Climax!* Long thought to be 'lost', like so much live television drama of the time, it has since transpired that *Casino Royale* was in fact telerecorded, and its release on video in the 1990s provides a fascinating opportunity to analyse the first adaptation of one of Fleming's novels.[41] Although dismissed as a curio by most commentators on the grounds that it is so different from the much more successful incarnation of James Bond in the cinema, the television *Casino Royale* is nevertheless worthy of attention, not only for the fact that it is the first Bond 'film' (albeit a telefilm), but also for the way in which it offers an alternative to the more familiar cinematic version of Bond, particularly in the configuration of the Anglo-American relationship.

Climax! was one of the dramatic anthology series which proliferated on American television during the mid-1950s. Before filmed series with recurring characters became dominant towards the end of the decade, the usual form of television fiction was the live, self-contained play. Sponsored by the Chrysler Corporation, and broadcast on Thursday evenings at 8.30 p.m., *Climax!* focused on stories of adventure and action, often adapted from well-known thrillers. Its first broadcast, on 7 October, was an adaptation of Raymond Chandler's *The Long Goodbye*, starring Dick Powell as Philip Marlowe (Powell had previously played Marlowe in RKO's *Murder, My Sweet*, a film version of Chandler's *Farewell, My Lovely*, in 1944). The third *Climax!* presentation was *Casino Royale*, based on what host William Lundigan described, with some exaggeration, as 'the best-seller by Ian Fleming'. The book was adapted by Antony Ellis and Charles Bennett. The latter had been a regular collaborator with Alfred Hitchcock between 1929 and 1940, working on the screenplays of *Blackmail* (adapted from his own play), *The Man Who Knew Too Much*, *The 39 Steps*, *The Secret Agent*, *Sabotage*, *Young and Innocent* and *Foreign Correspondent*. It was produced by Bretaigne Windust, a theatre producer who had turned his hand to film and television, his best-known film as a director being the Humphrey Bogart crime thriller *The Enforcer* (1950). American actor Barry Nelson, best known for his starring roles on Broadway, was cast as James Bond. While an American Bond marked a substantial departure from the novel, the casting of the other two principal parts was more propitious. Hollywood starlet Linda Christian was certainly the right physical type for a Fleming heroine: beautiful, elegant and cool. The master stroke, however, was the casting of Peter Lorre as Le Chiffre. A veteran of German, British and American cinema, Lorre had first made his mark playing the psychopathic child-murderer in Fritz Lang's *M*, had been well used by Hitchcock in *The Man Who Knew Too Much* and *The Secret Agent*, and had then carved out a niche as a character actor in Hollywood, including highly memorable appearances in *The Maltese Falcon*, *Casablanca* and *The Mask of Dimitrios*. By the time of his appearance in *Casino Royale*, the once slightly-built Lorre had ballooned in weight to such a degree that his short, bulky physique made him the perfect visualisation of the villain Fleming had described.

While the telefilm of *Casino Royale* is necessarily condensed from the novel, and has been adapted to meet the logistics of live television production with a minimum of sets (interiors only) and no costume changes, it maintains Fleming's basic plot. The main difference is that Bond is an American agent, referred to as 'card-sense Jimmy Bond'. The production begins with someone taking pot shots at Bond outside the front door of the casino as he arrives. As in the novel, Bond has been sent to beat Le Chiffre at baccarat. Le Chiffre is referred to as the 'chief Soviet agent for this area – controlled by Leningrad through Paris', thus locating the television *Casino Royale* within the Cold War context of the early novels. Le Chiffre needs to make up some eighty million francs that he has embezzled from the funds of the French Communist Party. Bond makes contact with Clarence Leiter (Michael Pate) of the British Secret Service. He also finds that his old girlfriend Valerie Mathis is now with Le Chiffre (in the novel the heroine had been called Vesper Lynd; René Mathis was an agent of the Deuxième Bureau, the French Secret Service). The following evening Bond plays baccarat against Le Chiffre and, after a long drawn out game which swings both ways, Bond wins. He survives an assassination attempt by one of Le Chiffre's henchmen armed with a gun disguised as a walking stick (an incident from the novel). He converts his winnings into a cheque, which, as in the novel, he hides behind the number plate on the front of his hotel room door. Whereas in the novel the girl had been kidnapped and Bond had given chase in his car, here Le Chiffre and his men simply arrive at Bond's room, along with Valerie, whom Le Chiffre has discovered is an agent of the Deuxième Bureau. The notorious torture sequence of the novel, in which Le Chiffre beats Bond's genitals with a carpet-beater, is changed to Bond being tied in the bathtub of his hotel suite and Le Chiffre pulling out his toenails with pliers. But Le Chiffre leaves his cigarette case, which Bond knows contains a razor blade, on the side of the bath, allowing Bond to escape while Le Chiffre and one of his heavies are searching the room. Bond knocks out the heavy, takes his gun and shoots Le Chiffre, who collapses in a chair, before jumping up again, grabbing Valerie and threatening her with another razor. Bond shoots him and this time kills him, before collapsing in Valerie's arms.

The James Bond fan culture has little time for the television *Casino Royale*. Steven Jay Rubin considers it 'feeble', while Barnes and Hearn describe it as 'a creaking adaptation of the story'.[42] Such dismissive judgements seem more than a little unfair, however, for if judged on its own terms rather than in comparison to the films, *Casino Royale* stands up very well indeed. In the first place, quite apart from any intrinsic merits, it is a historically valuable example of a particular kind of television drama technique. This apart, the telefilm itself has a particular aesthetic quality of its own: with its spare, economical narrative, its necessarily claustrophobic sets, its precise and fluid camera movement and its effective use of close-ups at heightened moments of tension, it is more successful than any of the films have ever been in capturing the mood and suspense of the original novel. Two sequences in particular stand out, as they do in the novel: the baccarat game and the torture scene. The baccarat game, while inevitably condensed from the novel, still takes up fully seven minutes of screen time, gradually building the tension by its insistent pans and cuts between the silent, smirking Le Chiffre and, in direct contrast, an increasingly tense and agitated Bond (Nelson repeatedly frowns, sighs heavily and rubs his brow) as the game drifts away from him. And the torture scene is quite harrowing, with the camera, at Bond's eye-level in the bathtub, looking up at the menacing figure of Le Chiffre, Lorre's sheer physical bulk dominating the frame. While the act itself is not shown, for obvious reasons, the reaction shot on the contorted faces of Bond and Valerie gives a vivid indication of the pain which is being inflicted. Although the telefilm ends with Bond and Valerie together, not with her suicide as in the novel, it is still something less than a conventional happy ending, as Bond is obviously in great pain from the injuries he has suffered. It is, in short, more bleak and downbeat than the films, and certainly does not warrant Peter Haining's remark that 'the whole production had an element of comedy about it'.[43]

The most significant difference from the novel, obviously, is that Bond has become an American agent. The Americanisation of Bond – and, at the same time, the Anglicisation of Leiter – symbolically reverses the power relationship of the novel. In line with political reality, it is America which is the leading power and Britain which is the subordinate partner in the 'special relationship'. But while the Americanisation of James Bond may offend the purists, it is entirely explicable (and, dare one say, acceptable) in its own terms. Given that *Casino Royale* was made by an American television company for American audiences, then it is perfectly understandable that the hero should be an American. At this time, moreover, James Bond had not yet developed into the cultural phenomenon that he was later to become. An American hardback edition of *Casino Royale* had been published by Macmillan in 1954, but had excited little interest. Bond simply did not exist in the popular consciousness at this time, certainly not in America. Unlike today, when Bond is regarded all over the world as a quintessentially British hero, for American television viewers in 1954 there was no predetermined association of Bond as British, simply because so few of them would have heard of him.

For all its merits, however, *Casino Royale* is more interesting in hindsight, given knowledge of what James Bond was later to become, than it was for either critics or public at the time. Critical reaction focused on the violent and unpleasant aspects of the story. *Daily Variety*, for example, expressed concern whether it was suitable viewing for children:

> Violence, gunplay, gambling and other dark deeds associated with Continental spy rings is tied here with Chrysler's 'Forward Look', and providing further ammunition for crusaders against grisly crime in the early evening hours while the small fry is still wide-eyed and setside. The dose is a heavy one, with torture thrown in to intensify the melodramatics. Even the elders might have found it a little strong to take.[44]

'The torture scene', the reviewer went on, 'was hideous enough without the actual horror instrument being shown at its grisly work.' While on one level this provides another example of how Bond in various forms has been criticised for violence, on another level the reaction also needs to be seen in the light of concerns which were arising in America about the depiction of violence on television. These concerns (to which the *Variety* reviewer alludes) grew during the 1950s as television crime drama became more and more violent, reaching an apogee of sorts with ABC's *The Untouchables*, which ran from 1959 to 1963 and which is often held to be, for its time, the most violent series shown on television.

Although *Casino Royale* proved to be a one-off, Fleming himself remained interested in the possibility of transferring James Bond to either the big or the small screen. However, his attempts to interest film and television producers during the 1950s came to nothing. Sir Alexander Korda, the flamboyant Hungarian-born producer who had made his base in Britain, read a proof of *Live and Let Die* early in 1954, but while he claimed to have found it exciting, telling Fleming that 'I really could not put it down until I had finished it', he did not think it would translate well to the screen, observing that 'the best stories for films are always the stories that are written specially for films'. Fleming, neverthless, was excited by Korda's interest, and replied that his next novel, *Moonraker*, would make more appropriate film material: 'It is an expansion of a film story I've had in mind since the war – a straight thriller with particularly English but also general appeal, set in London and on the White Cliffs of Dover, and involving the destruction of London by a super V-2, allowing for some wonderful film settings in the old Metropolis idiom.'[45] No further interest was forthcoming from Korda, however. In 1955 the American actor John Payne was involved in negotiations for an option on *Moonraker*, which broke down after complicated wrangling about rights between Fleming's British and American agents. *Moonraker* was also touted to the Rank Organisation, which bought an option on the film rights but did not persevere with the project beyond that stage.

In 1958 Fleming was involved in negotiations with CBS about writing a James Bond television series. He wrote treatments for thirteen episodes, and made some suggestions as to how Bond should be played. He was particularly concerned about there being 'too much stage Englishness' about the series. 'There should, I think, be no monocles, moustaches, bowler hats, bobbies or other "Limey" gimmicks,' he said. 'There should be no blatant English slang, a minimum of public-school ties and accents, and subsidiary characters should generally speak with a Scots or Irish accent.'[46] Fleming's aversion to 'stage Englishness' is interesting in so far as a British series which began a few years later, *The Avengers*, would deliberately highlight bowler hats and other 'Limey gimmicks' in asserting its sense of Englishness in contrast to the many American crime series of the time. The James Bond television series did not proceed beyond the development stage, so Fleming used several of the treatments he had prepared as the basis for the short story collection *For Your Eyes Only*.

A rather more significant initiative in the late 1950s was the development of a film project based on an original Bond story. In 1958 Fleming was introduced through his friend Ivar Bryce to Kevin McClory, an Irishman who was involved in the film industry as an associate producer and who had been foreign location director for Mike Todd's production of *Around the World in 80 Days* (1956). Bryce had co-produced, and financed, McClory's first film as a director, *The Boy and the Bridge* (1959), a whimsical fable about a small boy who runs away from home and hides in the ramparts of Tower Bridge. Fleming and McClory worked on various screen treatments during 1959, with McClory particularly keen on setting the film in the Bahamas so that his production company, Xanadu, would benefit from the Eady Levy, a fund raised from sales of cinema tickets which was divided between producers of British-made films on the basis of their box-office takings. On 1 October 1959, the trade paper *Kinematograph Weekly* announced that McClory was developing 'an underwater adventure story with the working title of *James Bond of the Secret Service* ... from an original script by Ian Fleming. It will be shot in colour and in a wide-screen process – either Todd-AO or Technirama.'[47] Fleming's interest in the project waned as the financial and logistical problems inherent in such an ambitious undertaking mounted. McClory continued working on the story with British screenwriter Jack Whittingham, the title being changed to *Longitude 78 West*, but was unable to raise the finance to make the film. As he had done several times before, Fleming used the story of the aborted project as the basis for his next novel, *Thunderball*. However, McClory and Whittingham objected to this and launched legal action against Fleming. In March 1961 they issued a writ alleging breach of copyright and petitioned the High Court to issue an injunction to prevent publication of the novel. The injunction was refused, but the legal action was to drag on for over two years.

Throughout the 1950s, therefore, various initiatives to transfer James

Bond to the screen had failed. The resistance of film companies can probably be explained in terms of the status which the spy thriller held in film culture at this time. With the exception of the films of prestigious, 'name' directors like Alfred Hitchcock, thrillers were widely regarded as nothing more than B-movie fodder. This was especially the case with films based on the adventures of detectives, secret agents and other crime-fighters, and it was equally true of British and American cinema. Characters such as Bulldog Drummond, The Saint and Dick Barton had all featured in series films during the 1930s and 1940s which almost invariably occupied the bottom half of a double bill. Terence Young, who was to direct three of the first four Bond films, made the point that the Bond stories were the sort of material usually associated with the smaller studios of Hollywood's 'Poverty Row'. 'Well, when you analyse it, and this is no disrespect to Ian, they were very sophisticated "B"-picture plots,' he said. 'If someone tells you, "A James Bond film", you'd say, "My God, that's for Monogram", or Republic pictures, who used to be around in those days. You would never have thought of it as a serious "A" film.'[48]

In order to locate the Bond films in the generic lineage of the thriller, it is useful, as with the literary Bond, to consider their relationship to what had gone before. In so far as Bulldog Drummond has been seen as a literary predecessor of James Bond, then the films made of his adventures might be seen as cinematic precursors of the Bond movies. Drummond was the one hero of sensational crime fiction who had appeared in something at least approximating an A-class feature film. Ronald Colman had played Drummond in a successful early talkie, *Bulldog Drummond* (1929), produced by Samuel Goldwyn. Although rather primitive in technique (like most early talkies it suffers from a static camera), it nevertheless captured successfully the thick-ear melodrama of the original 'Sapper' story. With his suave, debonair persona and highly resonant speaking voice, Colman came closer than any other actor to capturing the Drummond character: he was tough, but the more brutal character traits were filtered out by his charm and sophistication. His style of performance might be said to fall halfway between the different interpretations of James Bond offered by Sean Connery (tough and cynical) and Roger Moore (suave and sophisticated). Colman played Drummond once more in *Bulldog Drummond Strikes Back* (1934), a more slick and polished thriller with a greater emphasis on comedy than the first. Otherwise, there were a couple of British films during the

2. The gentleman hero: Ronald Colman as *Bulldog Drummond* (1929),
a character widely regarded as a prototype for James Bond; silly ass
Algy (Claud Allister) looks on.

1930s – *The Return of Bulldog Drummond* (1934), starring Ralph Richardson
and based on Sapper's *The Black Gang*, and *Bulldog Drummond at Bay*
(1937), starring the long-forgotten John Lodge – and a series of eight
adventures made in Hollywood by Paramount Pictures in the late 1930s.
The Paramount series were undeniably supporting features, running

3. The suave and unruffled George Sanders as Simon Templar in *The Saint in London* (1939), a debonair British hero who preceded Bond in his own film series.

just over an hour and featuring a recurring cast of supporting actors, but they were brisk entertainment which again foregrounded comedy (John Barrymore appeared in three of them as a Scotland Yard detective who wears a variety of disguises) and were set in a quaintly unrealistic Hollywood studio version of England. Ray Milland played Drummond in the first, *Bulldog Drummond Escapes* (1937), while American John Howard took over for the rest of the series.[49] Finally, an ageing Drummond was portrayed by Canadian actor Walter Pidgeon in *Calling Bulldog Drummond* (1951), a British-made picture which transposed the original Drummond story to the aftermath of the Second World War.

RKO Radio Pictures enjoyed a similarly successful series of eight films based on Leslie Charteris's Simon Templar stories. Simon Templar, alias The Saint, was characterised as the 'Robin Hood of Modern Crime', a crusader who takes vengeance on criminals the law cannot touch. As with Bulldog Drummond, there is a vigilante aspect to his character, which is prominent in the first film, *The Saint in New York* (1938), in which Templar is hired to kill off the members of the metropolitan underworld. In this film Templar was played by South African-born Louis Hayward, though his mid-Atlantic accent and insouciant charm made him the closest screen approximation of Charteris's character. Hayward was replaced by the English George Sanders for the next five films, who was less like Charteris's original but whose screen roles always had a touch of villainy about them, even when playing the hero. Sanders was suave but also something of a bully; he could turn on the charm for his leading ladies, but was also capable of being surly and nasty as required. It is interesting to conjecture what kind of James Bond he would have made had he been the right age when the films came to be made, for, although Fleming reckoned that David Niven would have been his ideal choice as Bond, Sanders had a cynical edge to his screen persona that Niven did not. Sanders in turn gave way to Hugh Sinclair, who lacked the polish and whose upper lip proved too stiff for American audiences, making only two films before the series ended.[50]

The nearest equivalent to James Bond, however, was a British radio character who made the transition to the cinema in the late 1940s. *Dick Barton, Special Agent* was an action-packed thriller serial, created by Edward J. Mason, which ran between 1946 and 1951. Barton (played on radio by Noel Johnson), along with his sidekicks Jock and Snowy, was usually to be found battling against machiavellian master criminals with sinister conspiracies designed to undermine Britain. Barton was comparable to Bond in several ways: he was a 'special agent'; his adventures were characterised by action and chases rather than cerebral detection; and he had his own highly distinctive theme tune, 'The Devil's Gallop', a whirlwind of furious strings, blaring horns and clashing cymbals, which perfectly captured the pace and urgency of the serial. Three low-budget movies were made by Hammer Films, of which the first, *Dick Barton – Special Agent* (1948), was the best. The plot pre-figures not only James Bond but also *The Avengers*: Barton travels to Echo Bay, a small fishing village, to investigate a smuggling ring and discovers that the sinister Dr Caspar is plotting to destroy Britain by germ warfare. Barton was played by Don Stannard, a square-jawed, muscular, personable leading man who would have made an excellent James Bond. The *Monthly Film Bulletin* said:

Though somewhat lacking in intentional humour, the film is packed with every imaginable adventurous situation, both of the

4. Another proto-James Bond: Don Stannard stars as *Dick Barton – Special Agent* (1948), here facing the sort of bizarre predicament that would have tested even Bond's ingenuity.

credible and the distinctly incredible kind, and if most adult audiences find it hard to take it seriously, it is sure of a riotous success with schoolboys. Don Stannard makes a manly and dashing hero as Dick, and it is largely due to his magnificent physique that some of the incidents in the film are less ludicrous than they might otherwise appear.[51]

Another two films followed – *Dick Barton Strikes Back* (1949) and *Dick Barton at Bay* (1950) – until the series was curtailed following Stannard's tragic death in a motor accident.

The Dick Barton trilogy was among the last flowering of the low-budget crime-fighter film series. In the 1950s television proved that it could do the same sort of thing even cheaper; by the end of the decade the B-movie was, if not quite a thing of the past, certainly on its last legs. Led by Hollywood, the response of the film industry to the rise of television was to make fewer but bigger films. Film historians Kristin

5. *North by Northwest*: Cary Grant and Eva Marie Saint enjoy a romantic interlude in Hitchcock's classic thriller which anticipated the Bond movies with its glossy sophistication, luxury, consumerism and sex.

Thompson and David Bordwell identify a process of what they term the 'upscaling' of genres during the 1950s. Genres such as the western, the musical and the historical epic were at the forefront of Hollywood's obsession with more expensive production values, colour and widescreen, but other genres which had previously been regarded as essentially low-budget fare, including horror, science-fiction and the thriller, also benefited from the tendency to lavish A-class production values on B-movie scripts. 'The effect of amplifying B-film material was perhaps most visible in the rise of the big-budget espionage film,' Thompson and Bordwell suggest, citing Hitchcock's *North by Northwest* as an important individual film before declaring that 'the catalyst for genre upscaling was Ian Fleming's fictional British agent James Bond'.[52]

The Bond films, then, occupy a significant place in cinema history in that they mark the transition of the spy thriller from the netherland of the B-movie to the glossy, big-budget world of the A-feature. They were not alone in this, for, as Thompson and Bordwell suggest, *North by Northwest* (1959) can be seen as part of the same process. In so far as it came shortly before the Bond films, it is relevant to consider Hitchcock's film in the same generic context. *North by Northwest* is undoubtedly an important film in an *auteurist* context. It is essentially an Americanised reworking of the sort of spy story that Hitchcock had made his own in his British films of the 1930s, particularly *The 39 Steps* (1935). Both these films feature innocent bystanders being caught up in a web of conspiracy and intrigue and who find themselves hunted by both the police and the real criminals; both are narratives of flight and pursuit in which the hero travels across the country; both reduce plot explanation to a minimum through their elusive 'McGuffin' (Hitchcock's term for the object that all the fuss is about); and both feature the same three character types of debonair leading man (Robert Donat, Cary Grant), cool blonde heroine (Madeleine Carroll, Eva Marie Saint) and outwardly respectable villain (Godfrey Tearle, James Mason).

But where does *North by Northwest* stand in the generic lineage of the thriller? Although the setting and idiom are American, the film's generic roots would seem to lie somewhere between the two main traditions of the British spy thriller. From the sensational lineage it borrows the narrative of fast movement, the action set pieces and the self-assured hero. From the realistic lineage, however, it borrows a certain sense of moral ambiguity: learning that the heroine has been persuaded to sleep with the villain in order to discover his secrets, Grant's character Roger Thornhill is outraged with the American intelligence chiefs ('If you fellows can't lick the Vandamms of this world without asking girls like her to bed down with them and fly away with them and probably never come back, perhaps you ought to learn to lose a few cold wars'). Its place within the spy genre is identified by James Naremore:

> At the level of generic conventions, for example, *North by Northwest* is symptomatic of a transitional moment in the evolution of spy fiction: it draws many of its best effects from an extensive (and mostly British) tradition of narratives about international intrigue to which Hitchcock himself had been a major contributor; at the same time it predicts certain features of the sleekly commodified James Bond films that followed in its wake.[53]

To what extent might *North by Northwest* be described as a proto-James Bond film? With its glossy visual style, its witty dialogue and its spectacular set pieces such as the famous crop-duster sequence and the

6. *North by Northwest*: Suited hero Cary Grant flees a death-dealing aeroplane in a famous sequence that again anticipates the stunts and set pieces of the Bond movies.

climax on the presidential heads of Mount Rushmore (albeit reconstructed in a studio), there is certainly much in Hitchcock's film that is comparable to the Bond movies. It constructs a very similar consumerist and sexual fantasy world. Cary Grant's character is a successful Madison Avenue advertising executive whose handsome good looks and slightly dangerous charm make him irresistible to women. At one point Grant and Eva Marie Saint travel on the Twentieth Century Limited from New York to Chicago, a refined setting where they eat brook trout before making love. Grant's seduction of her – she is the villain's mistress who is now working as an agent for the American government – might be seen as a partial working through of the process of 'ideological repositioning' which Bennett identifies in the Bond narrative. On a visual level, the sleek, modernist set design of the film, exemplified by the villain's mountain-top eerie with its angular beams and large windows, anticipates Ken Adam's work for the Bond films. Finally, it also has, in Cary Grant, a suave, suited hero who moves through the twists and turns of the plot with a bemused and slightly detached air.[54]

It may have been the popular success of *North by Northwest* (Fleming mentions the film in *Thunderball*) that finally made film-makers interested in James Bond. The story of how Albert R. Broccoli and Harry Saltzman came together to produce the Bond films has been told at length elsewhere, so there is no need here for anything more than a reminder of the salient facts.[55] Early in 1961, Fleming had sold an option on all the available Bond titles (excluding *Casino Royale*) to Saltzman, a Canadian producer based in Britain. Saltzman had been a co-founder, along with director Tony Richardson and playwright John Osborne, of Woodfall Films, the company which produced some of the key British 'New Wave' films of the late 1950s and early 1960s such as *Look Back in Anger* and *Saturday Night and Sunday Morning*, but had left the company following creative differences. Saltzman was unable to raise the financial backing to produce the Bond films and his option had almost expired when Broccoli entered the scene. Broccoli was an American producer, also based in Britain, who in the early 1950s had set up Warwick Pictures in partnership with Irving Allen, producing a string of successful medium-budget action movies such as *The Red Beret*, *Cockleshell Heroes*, *Safari* and *The Killers of Kilimanjaro*. According to screenwriter Richard Maibaum, Broccoli had considered filming the Bond books in the mid-1950s:

> In 1956 or 1957, when I was in England writing for Cubby and Irving Allen, Cubby gave me two of the James Bond books to read. I read them and liked them enormously. Cubby was very excited, too, but Irving Allen didn't share his enthusiasm. So Cubby put them aside. It's my personal opinion now that that was a wise thing to do, because with the censorship of pictures that existed

then, you couldn't even have the minimal sex and violence that we eventually put into the pictures. They just wouldn't have been the same.[56]

Following the end of his partnership with Allen, Broccoli renewed his interest in the Bond books and, learning that Saltzman had an option but no financial backing, agreed to go into partnership. They approached Columbia Pictures and asked for $1 million to produce either *Thunderball* or *Dr No*, but the studio baulked at the budget. 'They saw it as just a low-budget film and wanted us to consider making it for $300–400,000,' Broccoli told Alexander Walker. 'I said the cheapest film we'd made for Columbia at Warwick had been *The Red Beret* and that had cost $700,000 and made eight million worldwide.'[57] But Broccoli convinced Arthur Krim, one of the chief executives of United Artists, to give them a sympathetic hearing. On 20 July 1961, *Kine Weekly* announced that 'Saltzman's project with Albert Broccoli to film the Ian Fleming spy-thriller books is maturing nicely. They have clinched a deal with United Artists for 100 per cent financial backing and distribution of seven stories which will be filmed here and on foreign locations.'[58]

The deals which were concluded in the summer of 1961 were complicated, but were to provide the production base of the Bond films for decades to come. Broccoli and Saltzman went into partnership and set up a production company, which they named Eon Productions ('Eon' stood for 'Everything Or Nothing'). Another company, Danjaq (from the names of Broccoli and Saltzman's wives, Dana and Jacqueline), was formed to control the copyright of the films. United Artists agreed to provide the finance and distribute the films, which were to be made at Pinewood Studios in Britain with a predominantly British crew. In this way the producers would be eligible for a subsidy from the Eady Levy, provided the films were successful at the domestic box-office. The budget for the first film, which it had been decided would be *Dr No* due to the on-going legal dispute over *Thunderball*, was set in the region of $800–900,000, though in the event the negative cost came in at slightly more than that. For his part, Fleming was not to be involved in the script-writing process but would receive a fee of $100,000 per film, plus a percentage of the profits.

Fleming himself lived long enough to see only the first two Bond movies, *Dr No* and *From Russia With Love*, before his death from his second heart attack in August 1964. Although the relationship between the films and his novels was to become increasingly tenuous as the series progressed, at the outset this was not the case. Indeed, Fleming's name was privileged in the advertising and marketing of the early films, which emphasised the best-seller status of his novels. The theatrical trailer of *Dr No*, for example, featured this on-screen caption: 'Announcing an exciting new motion picture ... from Ian Fleming whose brilliant action filled books have entertained millions of readers ... now for the first time on the screen ... [cut to] Ian Fleming's *Dr No.*' The popularity of the novels was seen as an important factor in the likely box-office success of the films. Thus, in reviewing *Dr No*, the *Motion Picture Herald* declared: 'The vast numbers of people in this country, not to mention those overseas, who have read avidly, hungrily and expectantly every story of intrigue and excitement written by Ian Fleming ... form a wide, waiting, and ready audience for the first of the films based on the James Bond stories.'[59] What this illustrates is that there was believed to be an audience for the films due to the popularity of the literary Bond. It certainly provides evidence that Bond's popular appeal pre-dated the production of the films.

Having said that, the success of the films certainly boosted readership of the novels to even greater heights. Anecdotal evidence of this was provided by Harry Saltzman. 'The *Dr No* book had sold virtually nothing when we made the film,' he said. 'Then I went to Pan and suggested they print an extra 500,000 copies. They laughed at me. And, do you know, in the next seven months, they sold one and a half million copies.'[60] While the precise statistics do not quite bear out Saltzman's figures, they do nevertheless demonstrate that paperback sales of *Dr No* did increase significantly following the release of the film in 1962: in Britain the title sold 115,000 paperback copies in 1960, falling to 85,000 in 1961, but increasing to 232,000 in 1962, 437,000 in 1963, 530,000 in 1964 and 476,000 in 1965.[61]

For all that Fleming's saleability as an author was an important factor in getting the Bond films off the ground, however, the film-makers did not transfer his books wholesale. 'I think the mere fact that we were lucky to stumble upon Ian Fleming and Bond was a bit of good fortune,' Broccoli told the Open University in 1976. 'The rest was all hard work.'[62] The novels posed some problems for screen adaptation. For example, one of Fleming's strengths lay in his descriptive powers, but prose style cannot be conveyed in the cinema. Richard Maibaum believed there was an 'untransferable quality' in Fleming's writing: 'It's all very well; Fleming writes two and a half pages describing the fish underwater, the beautiful waving weeds, the colours – but, what the hell, it's just a pretty piece of celluloid when you see it on the screen.'[63] Film critic Penelope Houston made a similar point:

> If the books are compellingly readable, it's for all sorts of non-adaptable reasons. Ian Fleming was not, like Graham Greene in the mood of his 'entertainments', a master of the almost self-consciously cinematic image. The things he did best were mainly things that the cinema does badly. ... He was very good on the sensations of fast driving: the cinema can't cope with this, perhaps because of the problem of just where to fit the camera, so that you are liable to end up with no more than screaming tires on the sound track, close-ups of hands on the wheel, and windscreen views of the road. You can do all sorts of things with cars in the cinema, except communicate the sensation of actually driving one. He was knowing and exact about travel – the cinema prefers the generalities. He wrote greedily about food – film-makers are cautious about what actors eat, presumably since there's felt to be a risk of hungry audiences stampeding from the cinemas.[64]

Whereas Fleming had a knack for describing sensations, the films had to rely instead on visual spectacle – hence their emphasis on extravagant sets and technological gadgetry.

The most significant difference between the films and the books, however, is that the films added a sense of humour that had been lacking in the novels. There is no evidence of any humour with Fleming's Bond; the filmic Bond, by contrast, is always ready with a witty quip. 'That was the thing we changed most about his books as far as the pictures were concerned,' Maibaum said. 'We made Bond more humorous, throwing away those one-liners that are now obligatory in Bond films.'[65] From the beginning the films were played in a slightly tongue-in-cheek fashion, so that instead of the rather dour and humourless character of the novels the screen Bond made droll asides, usually after moments of violence, which gave the impression that he was not taking the bizarre situations in which he found himself entirely seriously. Although critics would complain that in some of the later films the humour became too broad and vulgar, particularly during the 1970s, it was received as a breath of fresh air in the early films. Penelope Houston saw the injection of humour as a deliberate strategy on the part of the film-makers to overcome some of the problems of the books. In Fleming's novels, she suggested, 'the film-makers found themselves with a brand-name hero, a conventional line in criminal master-minds ... a lot of skilful, unassimilable detail, and the legend of sex, violence, etc., which they had to steer past the censor'. What they did, whether by accident or design, was to 'hit on the entirely contemporary solution to an otherwise insoluble problem – to turn it into a frantic joke'.[66]

The Bond films depend for their effect on what is generally described as a 'willing suspension of disbelief'. As well as the humour, another strategy they employ to this end is to emphasise movement and action over narrative logic. In terms of their narration, the early Bond movies were quite innovative. 'One wanted the films to have a very slick quality,' said Terence Young. 'We wanted to make them as sophisticated as we could, and above all I gave the picture [Dr No] an enormous sense of tempo, in fact, it changed styles of filmmaking.'[67] The Bond films are notable for the pace of their editing, which is faster than usual in mainstream cinema. Although Young was not slow to take the credit, the contribution of editor Peter Hunt to the early Bond movies cannot be underestimated. Hunt's editing techniques broke some of the conventional rules of film 'grammar', for example by cutting in the middle of pans and not always matching precisely on action, a style that was to be particularly influential on television action series. The narration of the Bond movies bears comparison to the style of the comic strip – exemplified by the 'James Bond' strip cartoon which ran in the *Daily Express* between 1957 and 1963 – in which information has to be conveyed quickly and as far as possible by the visual image alone. The short shot lengths of the Bond films, particularly in the action sequences with their fast close-ups of fists, feet and guns thrust into the frame, are the filmic equivalent of the panels of the comic strip.

The kinetic style of the Bond films is such that it disguises the absence of narrative logic. Young remarked that 'there were an awful lot of plot holes, in *Dr No*, but I worked out that if you could entertain an audience for a couple of hours, they wouldn't really start being difficult about the story till they were on the way home'.[68] Of course, there was nothing new about this realisation, which had been one of Hitchcock's guiding principles for some thirty years or more. Hitchcock's films were full of what he called 'swift transitions'. 'The rapidity of those transitions heightens the excitement,' he told François Truffaut. 'It takes a lot of work to get that kind of effect, but it's well worth the effort. You use one idea after another and eliminate anything that interferes with the swift pace.'[69] Maibaum admitted that the narrative construction of the Bond films owed something to Hitchcock:

Hitchcock once said to me, 'If I have 13 "bumps" I know I have a picture.' By 'bumps', he meant, of course, shocks, highpoints, thrills, whatever you choose to call them. From the beginning ... Mr Broccoli and Mr Saltzman, the producers, and myself have not been content with 13 'bumps'. We aim for 39. Our objective has been to make every foot of film pay off in terms of exciting entertainment.[70]

What is most memorable about the Bond movies, indeed, is not so much the plots of the individual films as the many outstanding moments: the vicious fight on the Orient Express in *From Russia With Love*, the golf game in *Goldfinger*, the underwater climax of *Thunderball*, the moonlit ski chase in *On Her Majesty's Secret Service*, the breathtaking ski-parachute jump in *The Spy Who Loved Me*, the outer-space climax of *Moonraker*, the airborne fight on the cargo net in *The Living Daylights*, and dozens of other set pieces.

From the point of view of the film-makers, the stunts and set pieces are an essential part of the 'Bondian' production ideology. Along with this goes an emphasis on production values – those aspects of a film designed to appeal to the audience independently of the story, such as sets, set dressings, costumes, special effects, and so on. The advertising slogans for the films emphasise their sheer size and spectacle: *Thunderball* ('Here Comes the Biggest Bond of All!'), *On Her Majesty's Secret Service* ('Far Up! Far Out! Far More!'), *The Spy Who Loved Me* ('It's the Biggest. It's the Best. It's BOND – and B-E-Y-O-N-D'), *Moonraker* ('Where all the other Bonds end ... this one begins!'). Furthermore, with each new film there is an imperative to make it even more spectacular and exciting than its predecessors. This aspect of the production ideology was explained by Broccoli in an interview with *Screen International* in 1979:

With each new Bond picture we *have* to be bigger, better, more spectacular, more exciting, more surprising than the previous ones. Dreaming up new stunts, new twists, original gimmicks, new ways to entertain and thrill audiences can take months of discussions and meetings with scriptwriters, stunt co-ordinators, production personnel and those who take care of the mounting costs of each new picture. Costs are a big headache. But all the James Bond films have been very profitable. So I guess you have to be philosophical about it and lay out money to make money.[71]

While *Dr No* was made on a relatively modest budget, the negative costs of the subsequent films increased. It was a direct consequence of the success of the films that more money would be lavished on the next one in the belief that bigger (meaning more expensive) production values would reap even greater rewards. So, whereas *Dr No* had cost $950,000, *From Russia With Love* cost $2 million and *Goldfinger* $3 million. From the mid-1960s until the mid-1970s the costs of the Bond films usually came in at between $6 and 7 million, followed by a dramatic inflationary rise in the late 1970s. Throughout the 1980s most of the films cost between $30 and 35 million.[72] Broccoli's policy to 'lay out money to make money' is a typical statement of the commercial logic of the film industry, particularly Hollywood. Indeed, despite the production base of the Bond series in Britain, Broccoli himself, who continued as sole producer of the films following his break with Saltzman in 1975, belongs to the tradition of big-thinking 'showmen' and the cinema of spectacle associated with American film-makers such as Cecil B. De Mille and David O. Selznick.

Another aspect of the production ideology of the Bond series is the emergence of a core production team. While there have been changes in personnel over the years, many of the creative and technical personnel have worked on the Bond movies over a period of time. Among those who became key members of the Bond 'team' are title designer Maurice Binder (fourteen), screenwriter Richard Maibaum (thirteen), composer John Barry (twelve) and production designer Ken Adam (seven). Although the Bond series institutionalises the practice of film-making by committee, there are certain members of the production team who have made their own distinctive individual contribution to the 'Bondian' style.

In so far as they foreground visual style and spectacle over narrative, the Bond films offer unique scope for set design and art direction. The distinctive 'look' of the films owes a great deal to the work of designer Ken Adam. The Bond films are noted for their lavish, modernist sets: Adam's designs emphasise large, airy interiors, smooth surfaces of polished metal and glass, gleaming colours, and a dazzling array of technological gadgetry. The effect is to create a futuristic look which provides the perfect visual arena for Bond's highly fantastic adventures. Clearly influenced by the work of William Cameron Menzies, the designer of films like *Things to Come* (1936), Adam eschewed any notion of conventional realism and enjoyed creating a visual world which is as distinctive in its own way as the cinema of German Expressionism. 'I found I could create more sense of cinema "reality" by abandoning naturalism, finding a concept to match a film's content and then extending it into the imagination of the audience – however irrational it might be in real life,' he told Alexander Walker.[73] The visual spectacle of the Bond films reaches its fullest expression through the sets: the gleaming interior of Fort Knox in *Goldfinger*, the rocket launch pad hidden inside a volcano in *You Only Live Twice*, the submarine-swallowing supertanker in *The Spy Who Loved Me*, the space station in *Moonraker*, all of which create an overwhelming sense of space and size.

The unique visual style of the Bond films is also exhibited in their title sequences. The short sequence which opens each film has become a trademark: Bond, seen through the barrel of a gun, strides across the screen to the strains of the 'James Bond Theme', then turns and fires at the camera, whereupon a red wash runs down the screen. Designed by graphic artist Maurice Binder, the gun barrel sequence foregrounds the motif of looking which is central to the spy genre, as well as recalling the gun fired at the audience at the end of *The Great Train Robbery* (1903), while the red wash represents an assassin's blood. Binder went on to design most of the main titles of the Bond films, self-contained three-minute sequences which have again become one of the defining elements of the series. Usually revolving around images of scantily clad or naked girls swimming or performing acrobatics around the barrels of massively phallic guns, Binder's title designs encapsulate the themes of sex and death which are so prominent in the Bond films. Their matching of abstract images to song lyrics has been hugely influential on the development of the pop music video since the 1980s.

The distinctive look of the Bond films is complemented by their equally distinctive sound. The 'James Bond Theme' is always credited to Monty Norman, though it was a more up-tempo arrangement performed by John Barry's orchestra that was used in *Dr No* and which has provided the basis for the familiar recurring theme in all the subsequent films: with its twanging electric guitar and strident brass, the energetic melody has become integral to the identity of the Bond films and to the character of Bond himself. In the early films in particular it is used at moments when 'action' music would not normally be used, such as shots of Bond walking across an airport concourse or prowling around a hotel room, creating a sense of urgency and movement. Barry, who scored most of the films until the mid-1980s, is an extraordinarily versatile composer, equally at home with jazz as with orchestral composition, and his Bond scores use different styles to complement the visuals: insistent brass for the action sequences, lush strings for the love scenes, and upbeat jazz motifs (virtually amounting to parodic lounge music) to highlight the excess of Bond's world.

What about the role of the director in the Bond movies? Lewis Gilbert suggested that they were unlike any others because of the logistics involved. 'I suppose it's like being a field marshal in charge of the troops,' he said. 'It isn't really like an ordinary film, because there is so much that has to be co-ordinated, but the actual directorial part is really quite a small part of the game.'[74] But while the Bond films are the last place to look for evidence in support of the *auteur* theory, this is not to say the directors themselves remain totally anonymous. The sixteen Bonds made between *Dr No* in 1962 and *Licence To Kill* in 1989 were all directed by one of five men: Terence Young (who made three), Guy Hamilton (four), Lewis Gilbert (three), Peter Hunt (one) and John Glen (five). All these men were of roughly the same generation: Young was the oldest (born 1915), Glen the youngest (born 1932). Young, Hamilton and Gilbert had all worked their way up through the ranks of the British film industry, directing mainstream genre pictures during the 1950s before joining the Bond team, whereas Hunt and Glen were highly experienced editors who cut their directing teeth on the Bond films. None of them would be likely candidates for construction as *auteurs*, but rather would be placed within the duffle-coated brigade of proficient, British journeymen directors whose greatest asset was their ability to transfer the script to the screen in a straightforward way without any self-conscious tricks (for this reason it is highly unlikely that directors such as Michael Powell, Richard Lester or Ken Russell would have made good Bond directors). That having been said, however, there are certain stylistic differences between their Bond films: Young's have a harder edge to the action scenes and a greater urgency of movement within the frame, Hamilton's visual style is more glossy and sophisticated, Gilbert is the master of handling the really massive sets, while Hunt and Glen, as befits former editors, are crisp storytellers whose films are stronger on action sequences than characterisation.

In so far as the Bond series has involved, until recently, a relatively small number of directors who worked within a certain production ideology, but who nevertheless managed to provide subtle variations on the style, it is useful to draw a comparison with another instance of a particular group of people being responsible for a distinctive group of films in British cinema. In his book *Ealing Studios*, Charles Barr shows how the development of a distinctive studio style was due to the creation of a relatively small and tightly knit group of personnel who between them were responsible for the bulk of the studio's output.[75] On the face of it, Ealing would seem to have little in common with the Bond series: the former was a critically respectable, small-scale and essentially domestic cinema, whereas the latter has been neglected by the critical establishment, and is massive and international in its scope. But there is a comparison in that both Ealing and the Bond series have projected their own particular ideology of 'Englishness' or 'Britishness' – different ideologies, certainly, but ideologies which are recognisable and distinctive in each case.

To conclude, the Bond films are the result of a production ideology which has institutionalised a certain style and formula. The formula was originally based on the novels of Ian Fleming but has now evolved far beyond its source, even though the films continually purport to feature 'Ian Fleming's James Bond 007'. This chapter has considered the place in various generic lineages of both the Bond novels and the Bond films. The relationship between the novels and the films is a complex one which raises intriguing questions about which set of texts should be regarded as definitive. Bennett observes that while the literary Bond was the original source, most people's first taste of Bond came through the films:

> The novels are undoubtedly privileged in the sense that, historic-ally, they came first. They function as a textual source for the film, and as legitimators – both culturally (an authentic Bond film must, however loosely, be based on a Fleming source) and legally (Eon Productions owns the film rights to all the Bond titles except *Casino Royale*). From this point of view, the films are secondary and derivative in relation to the novels. From the point of view of their role in the construction and circulation of the figure of Bond, however, the films are clearly privileged in relation to the novels. This is not merely to say that many more people have seen

the films than have read the novels; rather more important is the fact that, for most readers, the films came first and the novels second.[76]

The longer the films have continued, furthermore, the more privileged they have become. For one thing, the film-makers have now run out of source novels and have started using non-Fleming titles, thus extending the career of James Bond beyond the original set of texts in which he appeared. And for another thing, while the original novels remain rooted in the social and political contexts of the 1950s, the films have sought to modernise and keep pace with the times. In order to demonstrate how the Bond series has responded to changes in the film industry, and to broader social and cultural changes, it becomes necessary to chart the development of the series on a film-by-film basis.

2

Snobbery with Violence:
Dr No, From Russia With Love,
Goldfinger

The first three James Bond films – *Dr No* (dir. Terence Young, 1962),
From Russia With Love (dir. Terence Young, 1963) and *Goldfinger* (dir.
Guy Hamilton, 1964) – may be grouped together in various ways. They
are the closest of all the films to the snobbery-with-violence ethic of
the British spy thriller in general and the work of Ian Fleming in
particular. While later films deviated further and further from the books,
the first three Bond movies all bear a close enough resemblance to their
literary originals to be considered as genuine adaptations of Fleming.
Furthermore, it was during these three films that the generic formula
of the Bond series was established. The narrative structure and film
style were developed over the course of these three to the extent that
by the time of *Goldfinger*, regarded by many as the best film of the entire
series, all the now familiar ingredients were squarely in place. In an
economic context, moreover, the box-office success of the films snow-
balled. The success of *Dr No* took all but the film-makers themselves
by surprise, but it was quickly surpassed by *From Russia With Love* and
Goldfinger, each of which was the biggest attraction of its year in Britain,
breaking all existing box-office records. The critical reception of the
films was mixed, but, while *Dr No* passed some critics by, the next two

films were sufficient to convince even those who demurred that, whatever they thought of the films themselves, Bond had emerged not only as the most popular screen hero in memory but also as a cultural phenomenon of the first order.

In order to understand the impact which the early Bond movies made, particularly in Britain, it is necessary to consider them in the context of the film culture of the time. The 1950s has generally been characterised as the 'doldrums era' of British cinema, the dull decade between the 'golden age' of the 1940s and the vibrant, new, youth-oriented film culture of the 'swinging sixties'. The dominant genres of 1950s British cinema – the war film, the comedy, the crime thriller – are widely regarded as backward-looking and unimaginative. In 1957, for example, Lindsay Anderson lamented 'the rather tepid humanism of our cinema', which he considered was 'snobbish, anti-intelligent, emotionally inhibited, wilfully blind to the conditions and problems of the present, dedicated to an out-of-date, exhausted national idea'.[1] It was also a decade when cinema-going as a social habit was in decline: annual cinema admissions fell from some 1,365 million in 1951 to 500 million by 1960.[2] And, although some British films were very successful, this has to be set against the fact that Hollywood movies continued to dominate British screens.

Towards the end of the 1950s, however, there were signs of a revival in the fortunes of British cinema. The popular success of Hammer's *The Curse of Frankenstein* (1957), particularly in overseas markets, paved the way for a cycle of colourful, full-blooded Gothic horror films which became synonymous with the studio's name. Despised by the critical establishment for their sensational subject matter and visceral excess, the Hammer horror films were, for a decade or more, successful at the box-office, winning the popular acclaim of increasingly youth-dominated audiences. In Peter Cushing's Baron Frankenstein and Christopher Lee's Count Dracula, Hammer created two of the great anti-heroic characters of British cinema, whose defiance of authority and social convention in the pursuit of perverse science (Frankenstein) and lustful desire (Dracula) might be seen, in retrospect, to anticipate the emergence of the sub-cultures of the 1960s which celebrated personal gratification and sexual licentiousness. The amorality of the Hammer 'heroes' has drawn comparison to James Bond. To quote Robert Murphy: 'Cushing's Frankenstein, sexually active and almost Bond-like in his casual use (and disposal) of women, sets a tone altogether new to the horror film and to British cinema.'[3] There was a significant difference, however, in that whereas the Bond films were to be thoroughly modern in their foregrounding of technology, the Hammer horrors were usually set safely in the past.

If Hammer represented the commercially successful but critically disreputable end of British cinema in the late 1950s and early 1960s, the 'New Wave' films of the same period occupied the other end of the spectrum: critically acclaimed, serious and respectable cinema with the emphasis very much on realism and social relevance. The core of New Wave films is relatively small – *Look Back in Anger* (1959), *Room at the Top* (1959), *The Entertainer* (1960), *Saturday Night and Sunday Morning* (1960), *A Taste of Honey* (1961), *A Kind of Loving* (1962), *The Loneliness of the Long Distance Runner* (1962), *Billy Liar* (1963) and *This Sporting Life* (1963) – but, taken together, they are usually held to have brought a new vitality and social awareness to British cinema. Most of these films were adapted from the work of the so-called 'angry brigade' of dramatists (John Osborne, Keith Waterhouse, Shelagh Delaney) and the novels of the 'northern realists' (John Braine, Alan Sillitoe, David Storey); they utilised the talents of a new generation of younger, naturalistic actors (Albert Finney, Tom Courtenay, Alan Bates, Richard Harris); and they were characterised by the gritty realism of their visual style, by their stark black-and-white photography, and by their use of natural lighting and real locations, most often in the back streets, canals and workshops of grim northern industrial towns. They were also rather more frank in their acknowledgement of class divisions and their treatment of sex (most of them were awarded an 'X' certificate) than had hitherto been common in British cinema.

While not denying the importance of the New Wave in British cinema history, it must be considered that it was relatively short-lived, flowering and disappearing within the space of four or five years. Certainly by 1963, there were strong indications that the tides of critical and popular taste had turned. Lindsay Anderson's *This Sporting Life*, generally regarded as the last of the New Wave films, had a mixed press and was a commercial failure, prompting Sir John Davis, managing director of the Rank Organisation, which had financed it, to observe that the days of this new type of realist drama had come to an end. 'I do feel that independent producers should take note of public demand and make films of entertainment value,' he told the Rank Theatre Division's Annual Showmanship Luncheon in December 1963. 'The public has clearly shown that it does not want the dreary kitchen sink dramas.'[4] Although Davis's comments were probably inspired as much by the reluctance of the major cinema circuits to show 'X'-certificate films, the timing of the speech is significant in that *From Russia With Love*, which surely ex-emplified the sort of 'entertainment value' which he mentioned, had recently broken circuit records for the Rank-owned Odeon cinemas.

It is tempting, though perhaps a little too simplistic, to suggest that the impact of the James Bond films arose from a film culture in which popular taste was already turning against the New Wave. To some extent, of course, this is probably true, and it is reflected in the career trajectory of Harry Saltzman, who left Woodfall Films in 1960, declaring in hindsight that he was tired of social realism. 'All the films were designed to show how the other half lives, but for God's sake, we *are* the other half,' he later said. 'I thought it was time to go back to big entertainment and I saw in the Bonds the bigger than life thing.'[5] Terence Young, director of *Dr No*, endorsed this view. 'It fitted the mood of the people, anyway in Britain,' he told *Films and Filming* in 1967. 'I think people were getting tired of the realistic school, the kitchen sinks and all those abortions.'[6]

Obviously, with their far-fetched plots, exotic foreign locations and colourful visual style, the Bond films created a fantasy world which was far removed from the kitchen sink realism of the New Wave. If, as Arthur Marwick suggests, *Room at the Top* 'could have been photographed to illustrate certain passages in Hoggart's *The Uses of Literacy*', then the Bond films, as Jeffrey Richards remarks, were the equivalent of 'colour supplement chic'. [7] Yet for all these differences in style, it is possible to trace some thematic links between New Wave cinema and the Bond films. In certain respects the character of Bond can be compared to Joe Lampton, the protagonist of *Room at the Top*. Lampton (Laurence Harvey) is a northern working-class hero with a chip on his shoulder and a burning ambition for money and status: what he wants is 'a clerk's dream – a girl with a Riviera tan and a Lagonda'. James Bond, it might be argued, is Joe Lampton's fantasy *alter ego*. The glossy, materialist world of the Bond films is what Lampton aspires to. In the persona of Sean Connery, Bond has all the abrasiveness of Lampton, but he inhabits a very different world of elegant Mayfair clubs and Whitehall offices. He enjoys social mobility, has money and social status without having been born into the privileged classes, has plenty of girls with a suntan and a sports car, and, moreover, can indulge his sexual appetite without having to marry any of them. 'In terms of ideology, the Bond films were not escapist aberrations,' remarks Sarah Street. 'Bond's globetrotting and proven success with women reveals another, fantasy aspect of the social realist films' masculine nightmare of being trapped in the provinces with a wife and family.'[8]

There is a thematic link of sorts, therefore, between the Bond films and the New Wave, suggesting that the success of the early Bond movies should not be attributed solely to their stylistic differences from the social realist films. Nor were the Bond movies the only non-realist genre of the 1960s: horror films, pop musicals and 'Swinging London' films also foregrounded fantasy and escapism. In this sense the Bond films, again, were not an aberration, but rather the most extreme manifestation of a trend towards colourful fantasy in 1960s British cinema after the sober black-and-white aesthetic of the 1950s.

So why did the Bond films make such an extraordinary impact? Young thought that *Dr No* was 'the most perfectly timed film ever made'. 'I think we arrived [in] not only the right year, but the right week of the right month of the right year,' he said.[9] But while this might be sufficient to account for a one-off success, it does not explain the phenomenal and on-going success of the Bond series. The reason why the early Bond films were so successful in Britain is tied to deeper, longer-term developments in film culture and the film industry. There are two interrelated factors which, it seems reasonable to suggest, provided the conditions in which the Bond movies could make the impact they did. The first is that they offered a very different entertainment pattern from anything else in popular cinema at the time. The second is that at a time when cinema attendances were in decline, the Bond films succeeded in tapping the diverse constituents of an increasingly fragmented cinema audience.

That the Bond films stood out from the rest of popular cinema can be demonstrated by considering the type of films which had been most successful at the box-office in the years immediately preceding their arrival. Although precise box-office statistics are not available for this period, the trade press provided annual surveys of the top attractions, which, if inevitably somewhat impressionistic, were regarded within the trade as a reliable guide to which films had been most successful.[10] What the trade press surveys between 1955 and 1960 reveal is that British audiences preferred big-budget Hollywood productions alongside smaller-scale home-grown products. The most successful Hollywood movies of the late 1950s and early 1960s included biblical/historical epics (*The Ten Commandments, Ben Hur*), adventure spectaculars (*Around the World in 80 Days*), musicals (*The King and I, South Pacific*) and westerns (*The Big Country, The Magnificent Seven*). Taken together, this would seem to indicate a preference for widescreen, colour spectaculars with high production values and big-name stars. At the same time, however, certain British genres also did very well domestically, particularly war films (*The Dam Busters, Reach for the Sky, The Bridge on the River Kwai, Dunkirk, Sink the Bismarck!*) and comedies (especially the 'Doctor' series, which had started with *Doctor in the House* in 1954, and the 'Carry On' series, starting with *Carry On Sergeant* in 1958). Most of these films were concerned with peculiarly British themes and subject matter. Certainly in the case of the 'Carry On' films (*Carry On Nurse* was *Kine Weekly*'s 'biggest box-office attraction' of 1959) they were rooted in an indigenous cultural tradition of low-brow, vulgar comedy which appealed uniquely to British audiences. The Bond films, therefore, filled a gap in the prevailing film culture in that they combined a particularly British generic tradition (the spy thriller) with the sort of production values, colour and spectacle more usually associated with Hollywood movies.

It was realised at the time that the Bond films did not fit easily into the existing generic profile of popular cinema. Veteran trade journalist Josh Billings, in his annual survey of the box-office winners for *Kine Weekly* in 1962, seemed unsure precisely how to account for *Dr No*. Selecting the Cliff Richard musical *The Young Ones* as the top money-maker ('typically English light entertainment put over with tremendous zing'), he identified *Dr No* as the 'second biggest winner', but was unsure how to categorise it, describing it rather uneasily as 'a bizarre comedy melodrama'.[11] Anecdotal evidence for the popular appeal of the Bond films is provided by future James Bond star Timothy Dalton: 'The first Bond movie I saw was *Dr No*, in my local cinema in a place called Belper in Derbyshire. I must have been about 13 or 14 years old … The only movies we'd seen were war pictures, or drawing room comedies, or westerns, and here was something right up to date and really terrific.'[12] Dalton's comment is particularly interesting in that he emphasises Bond's appeal for youth audiences, a point which is linked to the second factor in explaining the movies' success.

The 1950s had witnessed not only the decline of the regular cinema-going audience, but also the start of the various processes whereby the cinema audience became more fragmented. It was not only the rise of television which drew audiences away from the cinema. The regular cinema-goers of earlier decades now had homes and families of their own, while post-war youth had other leisure interests, particularly rock'n'roll, which competed with the cinema for their patronage. By the late 1950s the family audience for films was dwindling, while teenagers and young adults comprised the majority of cinema-goers. The film industry, in Britain as in America, tried to adapt to the changing composition of its audience by making films aimed at particular groups. One manifestation of this was the emergence of the pop musical. British youth audiences responded in particular to Bill Haley and the Comets (*Rock Around the Clock*), Elvis Presley (*Jailhouse Rock*, *King Creole*) and the home-grown British equivalent, Cliff Richard (*Expresso Bongo*, *The Young Ones*, *Summer Holiday*). Another manifestation was the horror film, which appealed primarily to a young adult male audience, and which was reflected in the box-office success enjoyed by Hammer in the late 1950s and early 1960s. The Bond films, as Timothy Dalton observes, were modern and up-to-date in a way that other genres such as the war film and the western were not. Their immediacy and contemporaneity, their use of popular recording artistes to perform the title songs, and their calculated inclusion of elements of sex and violence, surely account in large measure for their popular appeal.

The decline and fragmentation of the cinema audience obviously had important consequences for the film industry. From the 1950s, Hollywood had ceased to be the 'film factory' that it had been during the 1930s and 1940s, when each of the major studios produced about fifty films a year which, taken together, would ensure an overall profit. Instead, the tendency was to concentrate on producing fewer but bigger films intended to reap individual profits. This was the origin of the 'blockbuster' syndrome: the production of big-budget, high-profile films which it was hoped would prove spectacularly successful at the box-office. The Bond films arrived at precisely the moment when the British film industry was beginning to follow the pattern established by Hollywood. As Bill Altria, replacing Josh Billings as *Kine Weekly*'s chief reviewer, observed in 1963: 'The really big pictures – big at the box-office that is – are attracting larger audiences and more money to cinemas then ever before, but the run-of-the-mill films, the type that only a year or so ago were the bread and butter of the business, are barely yielding a crust.'[13] Following *Dr No*, which was something of a surprise success, all the Bond films were treated by producers, distributors and exhibitors alike as 'big' films which had great box-office potential. *From Russia With Love*, Altria observed, was 'a natural', and by the time of *Goldfinger* it was taken for granted that the Bond film would be the top money-maker of the year. Within a very short space of time, the Bond series had established itself as an annual institution of the British film industry.

The quite extraordinary success of the Bond movies in the early 1960s was due, therefore, to changes both in film culture and in the film industry. Far from being a mere accident of timing, the impact of the Bond films arose from a combination of circumstances and trends which had been on-going for some time. But what of the films themselves? What was the formula which proved so successful? And what were the narrative and stylistic ingredients which established the Bond series virtually as a new genre in its own right?

Terence Young liked to give the impression that the style of the films came together almost by accident. 'I don't think when I took on *Dr No* I had a very clear conception of what I was going to do,' he said. 'The original Ian Fleming story was diabolically childish, something straight out of a Grade B thriller ... The only way I thought we could do a Bond film was to heat it up, to give it a sense of humour, to make it as cynical as possible.'[14] Childish it may have been, but what is most remarkable about the adaptation of *Dr No* from page to screen is just how cinematic Fleming's novel actually was. In part this was due to the fact that, like *Thunderball*, the origins of *Dr No* lay in a screen treatment. In 1957 Fleming had been approached by budding producer Henry Morgenthau III (son of the wartime US Treasury Secretary) to devise a treatment for a television series based on the adventures of an American secret agent, variously referred to as *Commander Jamaica* or *James Gunn, Secret Agent*. Fleming's story revolved around an on-going battle between the titular hero and his enemy Dr No, 'an international freelance spy of Chinese–German extraction', who attempted to sabotage an Anglo-American missile test station in the Caribbean. The projected series failed to materialise, but Fleming used the basic storyline for his sixth Bond novel.[15]

Dr No has Bond investigating the disappearance of Commander Strangways, the British Secret Service Head of Station in Jamaica. He is assisted by loyal Cayman Islander Quarrel (who had previously appeared in *Live and Let Die*), while attempts are made to kill Bond with poisoned fruit and with a deadly tropical centipede which is left in his hotel bed. Bond pursues a link to Dr No, a Chinese German who owns a guano (bird dung) refinery on the island of Crab Key. Bond and Quarrel sail out by night to the island, where they meet Honeychile Ryder, a wild, beautiful young woman diving for valuable sea shells who tells them Dr No has a dragon. They are hunted by Dr No's men: Quarrel is killed by the 'dragon' (a marsh-buggy armed with a flame-thrower), while Bond and Honeychile are captured and taken to Dr No's headquarters. Dr No, a scientific mastermind backed by the Russians, is using a specially developed radio beam to interfere with American test rockets launched from a nearby base on Turks Island. Bond endures a horrifying obstacle course, involving crawling through a series of small ducts and tunnels, a cage of tarantulas and finally plunging into the sea where he faces a giant squid. But he negotiates it successfully, kills Dr No by burying him under a pile of guano and makes his escape with Honeychile.

Of all Fleming's books, *Dr No* attracted most criticism for its 'sex, snobbery and sadism'. Unlike the previous novel, *From Russia, With Love*, which had been a taut, suspenseful espionage story, *Dr No* is closer to the world of Edgar Wallace and Sax Rohmer with its megalomaniac criminal mastermind and its fast-paced narrative with the emphasis on action rather than exposition. The science-fiction elements were to be developed in the film, which, nevertheless, is a reasonably faithful adaptation of Fleming's story.

According to the stories which circulate about the preparation of *Dr No*, however, this was not always the case. 'We had at one time, I think, five different scripts on *Dr No* including one in which Dr No was a monkey,' Young recalled.[16] Several writers worked on the film, and it is difficult to ascertain who made the most significant contributions. 'The prolific pen of Wolf Mankowitz has been signed by Harry Saltzman and "Cubby" Broccoli to do the screenplay of *Dr No*, first of the James Bond series which the producers are making for United Artists,' *Kine Weekly* reported in July 1961.[17] Mankowitz was a British writer, author of several novels including *A Kid for Two Farthings* (which he had adapted for the screen in 1955) and screenwriter of British films including Hammer's *The Two Faces of Dr Jekyll* (1960), the Peter Sellers comedy *The Millionairess* (1961) and the science-fiction drama *The Day the Earth Caught Fire* (1961). According to Richard Maibaum, however, he had already been working on a Bond script before Mankowitz came on board:

Thunderball was actually the first; we decided it was the one to start with. I'd finished a first draft, and then Kevin McClory jumped up with a lawsuit against Ian Fleming ... So we put *Thunderball* aside until that was settled and decided to do *Dr No*. I was then in London, after having finished the first draft of *Thunderball*, so I began to write *Dr No* with Wolf Mankowitz. Cubby and Harry didn't like our first treatment, so Wolf bowed out; and I went on to do the first draft of the screenplay. Later, after I left, a novelist named Aubrey [*sic*] Mather (Jasper Davis is his real name) did some work with a girl playwright, Joanna Harwood.[18]

Young gave a slightly different account again of the completion of the script, saying that he polished it up with his script girl: 'That's how this girl, Joanna Harwood, who was my continuity girl on a previous picture, got in it with me. We took a room at the Dorchester Hotel and we worked day and night.'[19] On the titles of the film itself, the screenplay is credited to Maibaum, Harwood and Berkeley Mather (whose name is misspelt as 'Berkely').

While the various contributions by the different writers may be impossible to disentangle, it seems likely that Maibaum and Mankowitz between them were most responsible for the final shape of the story. The 'fourth draft screenplay', dated 12 December 1961, bears both Maibaum's and Mankowitz's names.[20] It follows the general storyline of the novel and transposes many scenes directly: the opening with the three 'blind' beggars who gun down Strangways, Bond's interview with M and his re-equipping with a new gun (a Walther PPK 7.65-millimetre instead of the old Beretta .25), the night-time canoe expedition, the first appearance of the girl on the beach, the battle with the marsh-buggy and Quarrel's death, and the scene where Bond and his companion are wined and dined by Dr No while he lectures them on the nature of power. The main changes made in the screenplay were due to the need to flesh out the story, rather than alter it in any drastic way. So, for example, as this was to be the first film of a series, a scene was fashioned to introduce James Bond to the audience: this takes place in a London gambling club (perhaps deriving from the introduction of Fleming's Bond in *Casino Royale*), where Bond meets and flirts with Sylvia Trenchard over a game of baccarat. Sylvia (whose surname in the film is Trench) was an additional love interest who was not in the novel, suggesting that even from the beginning the film-makers intended to increase the number of sexual partners for Bond. The screenplay also lengthened the section of the story in Jamaica before Bond and Quarrel set out for Dr No's island. Bond's American colleague Felix Leiter, who does not appear in the novel, was written into the screenplay, and the character of Miss Taro, Dr No's spy inside Government House, was developed to provide another sexual encounter for Bond. An incident alluded to in the novel whereby Bond learns that his car, being driven by someone else as a decoy, has been caused to crash, was developed into a chase sequence with Bond at the wheel of his car pursued by a hearse which tries to force him off a mountain road. The script also changed the centipede in Bond's bed to a tarantula. When Bond and Quarrel arrive on Crab Key, the screenplay follows the novel quite closely until the climax, though the girl whom Bond and Quarrel encounter is known simply as Honey rather than Honeychile and has her own personal grudge against Dr No, whom she believes responsible for the death of her marine zoologist father. The object of Dr No's 'toppling' radio beam are now American space rockets launched from Cape Canaveral – a topical touch in so far as there had been a number of misfires in the early days of the American space programme. Bond's ordeal in Dr No's obstacle course is simplified, the episode of the giant squid is omitted, and instead of having Bond kill Dr No by burying him under a pile of guano, the screenplay substituted a fight to the death between Bond and the doctor in the reactor room ('Dr No is tearing and slashing with his claws. Bond's suit and headpiece are now in tatters and fall away, finally disclosing him'). Honey's ordeal from the book, wherein she is staked out in the path of giant crabs, was omitted from the screenplay, though such a scene would later be filmed.

While most of the differences between novel and screenplay were fairly cosmetic, reflecting the necessity of a different structure and tempo for a film, one particularly significant alteration was made at this stage which was to determine the future direction of the Bond series. Whereas in the novel Dr No's operations were backed by the Russians, in the screenplay he became a member of SPECTRE. Given that Maibaum had previously worked on a screenplay of *Thunderball*, the novel in which Fleming had introduced SPECTRE, this change may well have been his idea. The draft screenplay of *Dr No* contained more details about SPECTRE than does the finished film:

> BOND: With your sort of disregard for human life you can only
>   be working for the East.

DR NO (*contemptuously*): East? West? Points of the compass, Mr Bond. Each as brutishly stupid as the other. *I* work for SPECTRE.

BOND: Spectre? Never heard of them ... and I thought I knew all the nuts.

DR NO: Special Executive for Counter-Intelligence, Terrorism, Revenge and Extortion.

BOND: They sound a pleasant bunch. (*He looks round and shrugs*). Albeit a little theatrical ... if this is their headquarters.

DR NO: Headquarters? Don't talk like a fool, Bond. Or are you trying to make me lose my temper? No, this is not their headquarters. Crab Key is but a microcosm of the organisation, syndicate, call it what you will. Do you think that the diversion of a few miserable rockets is the be-all and end-all of our efforts?

BOND (*looking at him levelly*): I'm calling your bluff. What is?

DR NO (*after slightest pause, looking at him levelly*): Ultimate Control ... Complete ... All-Powerful ... of the world ... and beyond.

BOND looks at him for a further few minutes in silence. Then throws his head back with a shout of laughter.

BOND: I see. Doctor, I said 'nuts' just now. I apologise for the coarseness of my speech. The psychiatric term, I believe, is paranoia ... illusions of grandeur.

The reference to SPECTRE's long-term ambitions suggests that from the beginning the film-makers anticipated there would be more screen adventures to follow.

The introduction of SPECTRE, as various commentators have suggested, marked an important ideological shift which differentiated the films from the books. Bennett and Woollacott argue that 'the primary impetus for this ideological readjustment came from the requirements of the film industry'.[21] The films were deliberately de-politicised and detached from the Cold War background of the novels, a point which is made explicit through Dr No's reference to East and West as nothing more than 'points of the compass'. The argument that this de-politicisation accounts for the success of the Bond films in the international marketplace, however, seems a spurious one given that other successful films – including Hitchcock's *North by Northwest* – had made direct reference to the Cold War. And it should also be borne in mind that in adopting the SPECTRE formula, the films were still following the narrative strategy established by Fleming himself with *Thunderball*.

Dr No introduced most of the generic ingredients that have come to define the Bond films. These can be identified at various levels, including narrative structure, visual style and characterisation. In the first place, *Dr No* encapsulates the narrative formula which was to be followed in most other Bond movies: a villainous conspiracy is plotted; Bond is assigned by M (played by Bernard Lee) to investigate; Bond travels abroad and meets up with allies; various attempts are made to kill Bond; Bond seduces a woman in the service of the villain; Bond meets 'the girl' who is destined to be the principal heroine; an ally meets a grisly death; Bond and the girl are captured by the villain and taken inside his headquarters; the villain reveals his plot to Bond; Bond then foils the plot, kills the villain and escapes with the girl.

While, on the surface, this may seem nothing more than a *Boy's Own* adventure story, at a deeper level certain ideological structures are apparent. Most obviously, Bond functions as an agent of British imperialism. This is more explicit in *Dr No* than in the later films, due in large measure to the Jamaican colonial settings, including Government House and the Queen's Club. Some commentators, indeed, regard it as a reactionary film. Raymond Durgnat posits a reading which dismisses the notion of Bond as a modernising hero and instead stresses the racial undertones in the representation of British imperialist ideology:

> Whatever Brand X critics may have written, Bond isn't just an Organization Man, but a rigid jingoist, almost loveably archaic. If you have forelocks, prepare to touch them now, in fond farewell to the Edwardiana in modern drag lovingly panoplied forth in the first half of *Dr No* (1962) as Bond glides along the Establishment's Old Boy Net. The British Raj, reduced to its Caribbean enclave, lords it benevolently over jovial and trusting West Indians and faithful coloured police-sergeants, the Uncle Toms of Dock Green. We might almost be back with Lieutenant Kenneth More on the North-West Frontier. Meanwhile out on Crab Key lurks Dr No, last of the war lords, whose 'chigro' minions ... blend of the Yellow Peril and the Mau-Mau, battle it out with his English co-anachronism.[22]

Durgnat can be the most idiosyncratic of writers, but it is hard not to agree with his interpretation here. The film does seem explicitly racist, not only in the characterisation of its villains (all Chinese or black, with the exception of Anthony Dawson's Professor Dent), but also in the diminution of the character of Quarrel: in the novel treated by Bond with respect, but in the film little more than a lackey ('Fetch my shoes', Bond orders him at one point) played in stereotypical eye-rolling fashion by John Kitzmiller. Bond's intervention in Jamaica saves this colonial outpost from the potentially subversive threat of a sinister secret organisation – a reaffirmation of white, British superiority at a time when, in reality, Britain was beating a hasty retreat from empire (Jamaica became independent on 6 August 1962).

On another level, however, Bond can be seen as more than just the last imperial hero. As Britain reluctantly faced up to the decline of its power in the 1950s, the conviction grew among British politicians and diplomats that the country could still play a role on the world stage through its 'special relationship' with the United States. In *Dr No*, Bond functions as an index of Anglo-American relations. The threat is directed at American space rockets, but as the interference originates in the Caribbean the Americans have passed the investigation over to the British ('You Limeys can be pretty touchy about trespassing,' remarks Jack Lord's Felix Leiter). It is Bond, rather than Leiter, who sails out to Crab Key ('it's my beat'). At the end of the film Leiter turns up on a Royal Navy motor launch with a detachment of Royal Marines (a scene not in the Maibaum–Mankowitz screenplay). But Bond has already saved the day: 'Where were you when I didn't need you?' he asks Leiter, thus reasserting his ability to sort out the crisis without American help. American involvement, therefore, is marginal and is legitimised through co-operation with the British. In reality, of course, the Americans have rarely shown such deference to the remnants of British colonialism in the Caribbean, a fact dramatically demonstrated in 1983 by their military intervention in the Commonwealth island of Grenada following a Marxist coup – against the wishes of the British government. In the Bond films, as in the novels, the 'special relationship' was rather more equal than *realpolitik* would allow.

But if *Dr No* harks back to the glories of Britain's imperial past, why was the film received as something so fresh and new? The answer lies not in the narrative ideology of the film, but in its visual style. *Dr No* established the look of the Bond films with its glossy surface and highly detailed *mise-en-scène*. The film is at pains to distance itself from the sober, restrained visual style which was so prevalent in British cinema, especially through its insistence on colour. Everything in *Dr No* emphasises colour, from the pop-art title sequence – a kaleidoscope of brightly coloured dots which flash on and off in rapid succession, suggesting that the film is going to be fast, fun and frenetic – to the high-definition Technicolor cinematography which creates a travel brochure image of Jamaica, all sunshine and bright primary colours. There is only one disappointingly slack and old-fashioned sequence: the car chase, with its repeated shots of two cars driving along the same piece of road and its highly obvious back-projection, is reminiscent of so many B-movie thrillers.

The most distinctive aspect of the look of the Bond films, however, has always been their set design. *Dr No* provides an early indication of the complex design work of Ken Adam which was to become one of the distinguishing features of the series. In his designs for *Dr No*, Adam employs different styles, contrasting the traditional with the exotic. Bond is introduced in the refined surroundings of an elegant London gambling club (supposedly 'Les Ambassadeurs' in Park Lane), while his briefing takes place in M's reassuringly traditional office, with its wood panels, naval paintings and leather-bound furniture. Dr No's lair, by contrast, mixes Adam's characteristically modernist aesthetic with designs which are strongly reminiscent of the cinema of German Expressionism. Perhaps the most visually striking set in the film is the eerie chamber where Professor Dent (Anthony Dawson) receives his orders from the voice of the unseen Dr No: with its grey walls, low ceiling and a large grille which casts cross-patterned shadows over the floor, the design foregrounds visual style over narrative logic and marks the moment at which the film breaks decisively from any pretence of realism. Adam's *tour de force*, however, is Dr No's bizarre underground dining room, with its Gothic candelabras and an aquarium built into the wall, a set which locates Dr No visually in the lineage of criminal masterminds such as Fritz Lang's Dr Mabuse. Finally, the atomic reactor room, all gantries and banks of instruments, is the first of the futuristic science-fiction sets which would become increasingly familiar in later films.

As well as establishing the narrative formula and style, *Dr No* also introduced the basic character types of the Bond series. The most important of these, of course, is Bond himself. Connery's performance in *Dr No* did much to define Bond's screen persona. Introduced in a sequence which both parodies and pays homage to the classic Hollywood star build-up – Young is said to have modelled it on Paul Muni's

7. *Dr No*: 'I admire your luck, Mister — ?' 'Bond. James Bond.'
Sean Connery's classic introduction.

appearance in *Juarez* (1939) — Connery displays remarkable confidence
in his first major starring role. '*Dr No* effectively marked the end for the
kind of arid stardom that actors like Leslie Howard had epitomised,
and in which Britain had persistently traded,' writes Andrew Rissik. 'It
declared a whole tradition obsolete, a tradition that had associated
chivalry with polite vowels and a decorous repression of passion, overt

8. *Dr No*: Bond meets 'the girl', Ursula Andress wearing *that* bikini.

sexuality and any real kind of spontaneous physical action.'[23] Although trailers for the early films described Bond as 'the gentleman agent with a licence to kill', he had less in common with the traditional image of the English gentleman hero personified by actors like Ronald Colman, Robert Donat and David Niven, than he did with the rugged masculinity, physical presence and virile sexuality more often associated with American stars such as Clark Gable or Gary Cooper. Connery (whose ability as an actor has consistently been under-rated by critics) should be credited with having established a new style of performance: a British screen hero in the manner of an American leading man. In *Dr No*, admittedly, his interpretation of Bond is not yet complete: the rough edges are still apparent, some of the polish is lacking. He gives the impression of being on edge; there is an abrasiveness in his performance, demonstrated in his exchanges with other actors where he is often curt and impatient. There are early indications, however, of the snobbery which was such an essential part of the Bond character. This is best exemplified in the dinner sequence when Dr No orders his guards to take Honey away and Bond picks up a champagne bottle as a weapon.

'That's a Dom Perignon '55, it would be a pity to break it,' Dr No remarks, to which Bond replies, 'I prefer the '53 myself' – both a snobbish assertion of his superior taste in champagne, and an indication that he is not taking the situation entirely seriously.

Along with the snobbery, of course, goes the violence. Few spy thrillers, with the notable exception of Hitchcock's *The Secret Agent* (1936), had ever focused on the secret agent's role as assassin. *Dr No* included one important sequence which defined the nature of Bond's job as a professional killer. The Maibaum–Mankowitz screenplay introduced a scene in which Bond waits for Professor Dent at Miss Taro's apartment (Miss Taro herself having already been handed over to the police). Scene 135 in the screenplay is as follows:

> FIGURE *glances round – sees bedroom door ajar – creeps over – listens – pushes door gently open – peers round door – sees barely visible dark forms under sheet –* KICKS DOOR OPEN *– raises gun and fires four times into forms (silenced 'coughing' shots which done properly can sound horrible).*
>
> BOND (*out of darkness*): Good evening ... Professor.
>
> *The room springs to life as light goes on.* BOND *is seated in chair, one leg over the arm – left hand on table light switch – Walther in right.* DENT *swings on* BOND, *snarling. Two 'plunks' are drowned in roar of* BOND's *unsilenced gun. The* PROFESSOR *does* NOT *stagger forward – he spins backwards as if somebody has kicked him in the chest – slamming up against a flimsy Chinese table and crushing it as he collapses. He rolls right over onto his back ... brings his legs up under his chin in an agonised convulsion ... shoots them straight out ... and then lies still.*
>
> BOND *rises and crosses to him. He doesn't need to examine him closely – he knows exactly where he's hit him – right between the two nipples. He blows fumes away from his gun and replaces it carefully in shoulder holster. He then goes to bed where we see two interlaced 'forms' are bolster and pillow. They are ripped by shots – (charred round edges of holes) – and feathers are scattered.* BOND *takes up phone and dials. His eyes are hard.*

The description of Dent's death is graphic enough in the screenplay, though as the scene is played in the film Bond is even more cold-blooded. Dent fires six shots into the bed, whereupon Bond, holding a silenced pistol, switches on the light and orders him to drop the gun. As Bond quizzes Dent, the professor pulls the rug on which he has dropped his gun towards him with his foot, apparently unnoticed by Bond, and then suddenly picks the gun up, only to find that it is empty.

9. *Dr No*: The megalomaniac villain Dr No (Joseph Wiseman) politely entertains his captives to cocktails before trying to kill them.

'That's a Smith and Wesson – and you've had your six,' Bond says coldly. He then shoots Dent in the chest, with the professor spinning around as in the script to lie face-down on the floor, whereupon Bond fires another bullet into his back. Whereas in the script Bond had killed Dent while the professor was shooting at him, in the film it is a cold-blooded act because Bond knows Dent's gun is empty. The additional shot which Bond fires into the dead man's back is unnecessary, therefore gratuitous. The scene was controversial and apparently caused some problems with American film executives. 'That caused a lot of heartache; United Artists were not happy about it,' said Young.[24]

Dr No also established the prototypes for the Bond villain and the Bond girl. Joseph Wiseman's Dr No, with his expressionless face and monotone 'voice of doom' delivery, set the standard for all the later megalomaniacs bent on world domination. And Ursula Andress's celebrated appearance, walking out of the ocean wearing a clinging white bikini – Young thought it 'the greatest woman's entrance in a picture'[25] – established the enduring visual image of the 'Bond girl'. The film follows the novel in introducing Honey in a voyeuristic manner whereby Bond gazes at her before she is aware that she is being watched. Indeed, the sequence can be seen as a textbook example of certain feminist theories of the representation of women in mainstream cinema. Laura Mulvey has argued that women function as fetishised 'objects of to-be-looked-at-ness'. Visual pleasure in the cinema, she suggests, is linked to an explicitly male point-of-view, in which women are objects of the male gaze, providing sexual stimulation not only for the male protagonist, but also for the male spectator through the way in which filmic narration identifies with the male point-of-view.[26] While this interpretation of the ideological processes of mainstream cinema has since been modified by other writers, the Bond films do lend credence to Mulvey's thesis. Indeed, the predominance of the male gaze is institutionalised: in the screenplay Honey's first appearance is described from Bond's point of-view ('Bond's Eyeline … What He Sees'). That women in the Bond films were there purely for decoration is reinforced in so far as Andress (along with other early Bond girls Eunice Gayson, Daniela Bianchi, Shirley Eaton, Tania Mallet and Claudine Auger) was dubbed; denied her own voice, the girl is, literally, reduced to the level of an object only to be looked at.[27]

As the first of the James Bond films, the reception of *Dr No* is worth considering in some detail. The critics were divided, with the film finding admirers and detractors among both the popular and the quality press. What most critics recognised from the outset, however, was that it was likely to be the first of a series of screen adventures for Fleming's hero. Many accepted it as undemanding entertainment and believed it was likely to be successful on that basis. One of the film's biggest admirers was Dilys Powell, one of the two 'Sunday ladies' (along with

C. A. Lejeune) who had dominated middle-brow British film journalism for over two decades. She compared it favourably to the classic days of British Hitchcock, and considered that the humour hit just the right note:

> Efficiency: perhaps that doesn't sound high praise for *Dr No*, but I mean it as high. The first of the James Bond films (I trust there will be others) has the air of knowing exactly what it is up to, and that has not been common in British thrillers since the day when Hitchcock took himself off to America. The jokes (one of them, a beauty, has been buzzing round London all the week) are tossed away with exactly the right carelessness. The excitements have a right little skin-crawling effect, but they aren't over-emphasised; the hair's-breadth escape from the ambush is handled with the nonchalance proper to agent 007; all in the day's work, now for the next, please. [28]

The joke which most amused the critics, incidentally, was that a painting which Bond notices in Dr No's headquarters was Goya's portrait of the Duke of Wellington, which had recently been stolen from the National Gallery – the first of many such topical references in the films.

Other critics, however, were less enthusiastic. The *Monthly Film Bulletin* thought that it did not stand comparison even to lesser Hitchcock or Lang:

> Once the cluttered preliminaries are out of the way – for instance the film is obviously destined to be the first of a James Bond series, so M must be glimpsed at his London desk – the story proceeds in traditional thick-ear fashion from vamps and violent death to the fitting grandeur of a final holocaust. One by one Bond's enemies are rendered brutally *hors-de-combat*, while Bond himself survives tarantulas and cliff-side car collisions at the expense of little more than a few bruises and a lot of perspiration. And yet strangely enough excitement, and humour, and the glamour of corruption, are all rather lacking. Just as, say, *The 1,000 Eyes of Dr Mabuse* seemed to wander anachronistically through the motions of once splendid (and why not still?) devices that Lang no longer retained much apparent faith in, *Dr No* misses the genuine sadistic, sybaritic relish attributed to Fleming's novels, and the narrative invention of even second-rate Hitchcock. Something really new is

needed, if not in the incidents then in the telling of them. Terence Young's direction has pace but little real vigour; the tortures and the killers are comparatively tame, nowhere near bizarre enough; the women, apart from Dr No's ultra-polite Chinese receptionist, are sexless and dull; and Sean Connery is such a disappointingly wooden and boorish Bond that the script's touches of grim humour go for less than they need.[29]

Ian Cameron, in the *Spectator*, was rather more abrupt: '*Dr No*: no, no. Too inept to be as pernicious as it might have been. Costly gloss flawed by insidious economy on girls. Superannuated Rank starlet tries to act sexy. Grotesque.'[30]

Just as they were divided on the film itself, the critics were also split on how suitable Connery was for the role of Bond. Derek Hill, himself no fan of the Bond character, thought he was 'played with exactly the right mixture of strong-arm fascist and telly commercial salesman by Sean Connery'.[31] *The Times* compared the screen Bond unfavourably with Fleming's Bond, opining that 'it is doubtful whether either his admirers or his detractors will recognize him' on the grounds that he exhibited an 'Irish-American look and sound, which somehow spoils the image'. It reserved judgement on Connery, suggesting that 'perhaps Mr Sean Connery will, with practice, get the "feel" of the part a little more surely than he does here'.[32] Many critics, confronted with Connery's Scots burr, clearly had some difficulty in placing his accent, which was widely described as Irish-American.

Other critics were less concerned with how appropriate Connery was to play Bond than with the question of whether Bond was an appropriate character to transfer to the screen at all. 'I find it disturbing that we should be offered as a hero – as someone we are supposed to admire – a man whose methods and morals are indistinguishable from those of the villains,' said Thomas Wiseman in the *Sunday Express*.[33] Nina Hibbin, film critic of the communist *Daily Worker*, saw in *Dr No* evidence of all the snobbery-with-violence ethics that other left-wing critics had found so repulsive in the novels. She disliked its 'sinister racialist implications', considered it 'a brutalised film' and thought it even nastier than the Hammer horrors (which she also disliked): 'It doesn't wallow, as horror films do, in blood and torture and slow death. It goes a stage further – by asking you to take such things for granted, playing for a laugh whenever the sardonic Mr Bond makes a new joke.'[34] Hibbin was to be the most outspoken critic of the early Bond movies, but hers was by no means an isolated voice. Richard Whitehall of *Films and Filming* compared Bond to Mike Hammer, the thuggish Red-bashing American private eye created by Mickey Spillane and brought to the screen in a couple of low-budget thrillers, *I the Jury* (1953) and *Kiss Me Deadly* (1955):

> There hasn't been a film like *Dr No* since … when? The Mickey Spillane thrillers of the middle 'fifties? *Dr No* is the headiest box-office concoction of sex and sadism ever brewed in a British studio, strictly bath-tub hooch but a brutally potent intoxicant for all that. Just as Mike Hammer was the softening up for James Bond, so Bond is the softening up for … what? A fascist cinema uncorrupted by moral scruples? The riot of a completely anarchist cinema? *Dr No* could be the breakthrough to something … but what? At one point Bond nonchalantly fires half a dozen shots into the *back* of a helpless opponent – the British cinema will never be the same again. [35]

It was, Whitehall considered, 'the perfect film for a sado-masochistic society', and he even went so far as to compare it to Michael Powell's notorious *Peeping Tom* (1960), which had drawn howls of outraged protest from the critics. He believed it should have been given an 'X' certificate, and wondered why the British Board of Film Censors had let it through with only an 'A'. 'Oh, Trevelyan, art thou sleeping in Soho?' he asked. 'This is surely one of the X'iest films imaginable, a monstrously over-blown sex fantasy of nightmarish proportions.'

For all the criticisms levelled against its sex and violence, however, *Dr No* had been passed by the BBFC with nothing more restrictive than an 'A' certificate, and was therefore considered appropriate for general audiences in a way that horror films, with their sensationalist crimes and visceral gore, and New Wave films, with their adult discussion of sexual issues, were not. BBFC secretary John Trevelyan said that he had discussed the representation of sex and violence in the Bond films with the producers and they had agreed what was necessary for the films to be suitable for an 'A' certificate:

> When we had the first of these films, *Dr No*, I had a discussion with Harry Saltzman and we agreed that since he intended to make a series of these films we should aim to get them all suitable for the 'A' category since 'X' certificates would reduce his viewing

audiences. These films were essentially fantasies, Bond being the 'Superman' of the 1960s who could not only get all the girls to bed without any difficulty but could escape from any perilous situation, using violence and being quite callous about it even to the point of joking about it. The agreement resulted in keeping the sex to a reasonable level, but we had some problem with the violence and in most of the films we asked for some modifications. We were anxious to avoid anything that was realistic or nasty. It is of course arguable that by doing this we were encouraging people to avoid facing up to the realities of violence by making them laugh when Bond killed an enemy and made a joke about it. However, although I have some sympathy with this argument, I think our category decision was right.[36]

While clearly sensitive to the criticisms of the films, Trevelyan believed that their fantasy aspect had the effect of rendering the violence less realistic. It would seem that, as was his policy, Trevelyan had consulted with the producers to avoid any conflict between them and the BBFC over the content of the Bond films. It is unclear, however, whether the script of *Dr No* had been presented for pre-production scrutiny by the BBFC (a procedure which film-makers were encouraged to follow, though it was not compulsory), or whether the film had been viewed by the censors in a rough cut.[37]

Ian Fleming's own opinion of the first James Bond film, publicly at least, was that it was good, though not as good as the novel. 'Those who've read the book are likely to be disappointed, but those who haven't will find it a wonderful movie,' he told the press. 'Audiences laugh in all the right places.'[38] As with his novels, however, he had to endure the scorn of his wife's *literati* friends who thought it low-brow and vulgar. Evelyn Waugh described the premiere of *Dr No* as a 'preposterous event' and thought the film itself 'was totally fatuous and tedious, no mystery, not even erotic'.[39]

Dr No opened at the London Pavilion on 5 October 1962 and was soon reported to be attracting large and enthusiastic audiences.[40] By chance, it happened to be showing in cinemas during the period of the Cuban Missile Crisis, which was at its height in the fourth week of October, and it is quite possible that international events, and the very real danger of nuclear war between the Superpowers, created the sort of atmosphere in which a film about the 'toppling' of American space rockets acquired a sudden topicality. As one recent commentator has observed: '*Dr No* was not the most extravagant of Bond novels, but it was surely the most timely in its concern with a malevolent island despot and secret missile base in the Caribbean.'[41] Coincidentally, it was also in October 1962 that arguably the greatest Cold War spy thriller opened in America. John Frankenheimer's *The Manchurian Candidate* bears some comparison to the Bond movies through its brainwashed assassin, sinister orientals and bruising karate-fight, though Frankenheimer's black-and-white film creates a much more claustrophobic atmosphere of conspiracy and paranoia than any of the Bonds have ever achieved.

By the time *Dr No* was released in America in May 1963, it would no longer have benefited from the topicality which the Cuban Missile Crisis had engendered. Its critical reception was again mixed. Some reviewers admired it as undemanding hokum. Bosley Crowther, the senior film critic of the *New York Times*, thought it a 'lively, amusing picture' which 'is not to be taken seriously as realistic fiction or even art ... It is strictly a tinseled action-thriller, spiked with a mystery of a sort. And, if you are clever, you will see it as a spoof of science-fiction and sex.'[42] But others were less enthusiastic. *Time* magazine was particularly disparaging, considering that the filmic Bond would disappoint fans of the books: 'Is it possible to make a good movie out of a James Bond thriller? Fleming fans probably won't take *No* for an answer.'[43] The American trade press, however, were unanimous that the film was an excellent box-office prospect. And, given that by the time *Dr No* opened in America the second Bond film had already gone into production, the trade journalists knew there would be more to follow. 'There is every reason to suppose, and expect, that Harry Saltzman and Albert R. Broccoli, the producers, have here the first of what could become the most successful series of films of its kind since the happy days of the Charlie Chan pictures and the Thin Man films,' declared the *Motion Picture Herald*, adding that 'the film is said already to have recouped its negative cost in its initial engagements in England and on the Continent alone'.[44]

In the long term, of course, the predictions of success for the series were to be fulfilled, but what is sometimes overlooked is that *Dr No* itself was not especially successful, initially at least, at the American box-office. According to the *Hollywood Reporter*, by 1976 the total domestic (North American) rentals amounted to $6.4 million, a healthy total in itself, but one which includes several profitable re-releases as well as the all-important first run, and certainly one which pales in comparison with the $15.7 million of foreign rentals.[45] United Artists, Broccoli recalled, 'expressed some doubt that they could sell a picture in the major US cities with "a Limey truck driver playing the lead"'.[46] *Dr No* was not accorded the prestigious, high-profile release that came to characterise later Bond films. It was released in what was traditionally a 'low' season; in New York it played at only a few locations (the Astor Theater on Broadway and several cinemas on the East Side); and across the country it was generally shown in smaller neighbourhood movie theatres and at the drive-ins, where it did reasonable business through good word-of-mouth. Although Bond would eventually conquer America, the films' success in that market did not come about immediately.

It was the British and European success of *Dr No*, therefore, which allowed for the production of a second James Bond film. *From Russia With Love* was budgeted at $1.9 million (twice the cost of *Dr No*). The choice of this particular novel as the second film has often been attributed to the fact that President Kennedy had named it as one of his ten favourite books in an article for *Life* magazine, so therefore the title already had a degree of public recognition and kudos from Kennedy's endorsement. But this seems an unlikely explanation given that the *Life* article had been in March 1961, a full two years before the start of production on *From Russia With Love*, and also before production had started on *Dr No*. A more likely explanation for the decision to make *From Russia With Love* the second film was that it offered the opportunity to exploit Bond's popularity in Europe: it is the most 'European' of all the films in its content and style.

From Russia, With Love is one of Fleming's strongest stories, a richly detailed and tightly plotted narrative of intrigue and suspense. The plot concerns SMERSH's plan to destroy the reputation of the British Secret Service by luring its most celebrated agent to a humiliating death. SMERSH concocts a plan whereby a Russian cypher clerk in Istanbul claims that she has fallen in love with Bond from a photograph, and that she is willing to defect if Bond will personally come to rescue her. The bait for the trap is a brand-new 'Spektor' cypher machine. The first third of the novel details the planning of the trap by SMERSH, whose personnel include chess master Kronsteen, the notorious Rosa Klebb, Head of Operations and Executions, and the chief executioner Donovan 'Red' Grant. Bond duly travels to Istanbul, where he teams up with Darko Kerim, Head of the Turkish Section. Bond meets the girl, Tatiana Romanova, who steals the cypher machine from the Russian Embassy, and along with Kerim they make their getaway on the Orient Express. Kerim is killed by a Russian security man, while Bond is successfully deceived by Grant, masquerading as British agent 'Captain Nash'. Grant reveals that he is to kill Bond and Tatiana, leaving their bodies together on the train, but Bond gets the better of Grant and kills him. Arriving at the Ritz Hotel in Paris, Bond finds Rosa Klebb waiting, disguised as an old woman. Bond overpowers her and hands her over to the French authorities, though not before she has managed to kick him with a poisoned steel spike concealed in her shoe.

The screenplay of *From Russia With Love* was again a collaborative venture, though Richard Maibaum would seem to have had the greatest input. Maibaum said that another distinguished thriller-writer was involved in the early stages:

> On *From Russia With Love* they had Len Deighton start, and he did about thirty-five pages; but it wasn't going anywhere, so they brought me in. I did the screenplay and got a solo credit on it. Joanna Harwood got an adaptation credit, because she worked some with the director, Terence Young, and made several good suggestions. I was a little put out that she was given an adaptation credit because I didn't think she deserved it, but there are always politics in these things.[47]

While the screenplay followed the general narrative structure of the novel, there were again some changes to the details of Fleming's story. The most important of these, as in *Dr No*, was the substitution of SPECTRE for SMERSH as the principal villains of the piece. Klebb, Kronsteen and Grant all become agents of SPECTRE (Klebb having recently defected), and the character of Blofeld – the head of SPECTRE introduced by Fleming in *Thunderball* – was written in to the story. The lengthy planning sequence in the first third of the book was condensed, though Maibaum added two new scenes. The first of these was an opening where Grant stalks 'Bond' through a 'Renaissance Garden' and kills him ('Bond', of course, turns out to be another man entirely). The second was a scene to introduce Blofeld, which took place on the SPECTRE yacht – described in the screenplay as 'a large, beautiful boat similar to one owned by a well-known Greek shipping tycoon', suggesting an intriguing real-life model for a Bond villain. Maibaum also opened up the last quarter of the story, adding two more action sequences following Bond's fight with Grant on the Orient Express – a helicopter

10. *From Russia With Love*: Bond's playful flirtation with Miss Moneypenny (Lois Maxwell) is not appreciated by his boss M (Bernard Lee).

attack and a motorboat chase – before the final confrontation between Bond and Klebb, which now took place in Venice rather than Paris.[48]

Broccoli later nominated *From Russia With Love* as his favourite Bond movie, 'as I feel it was with this film that the Bond formula and style were perfected'.[49] Many Bond aficionados share Broccoli's view, but it seems rather odd that he should have considered the formula and style to have been perfected in *From Russia With Love* when the film is compared to all the others in the series. The second Bond movie, indeed, adopts a different narrative structure and exhibits a different visual style than the films which came before or after it. What this illustrates is that at this early stage of the series the Bond formula was not yet absolutely fixed: variations were possible, other directions could be explored, the generic evolution was not an entirely linear process. *From Russia With Love* is the nearest of all the films to a 'straight' espionage story, which has resulted in it being claimed as the most 'realistic' Bond film within the fan culture. While it is hardly realistic in comparison to, say, *Saturday Night and Sunday Morning*, it certainly eschews the science-fiction trappings that had been foregrounded in *Dr No* in favour of a less spectacular espionage narrative. The set pieces are still there, of course, but the conspiracy in *From Russia With Love* is a relatively small-scale affair by Bond standards, and the threat is directed more against Bond personally than against the whole of civilisation as we know it. Many of the incidents in the film – the secret meetings between spies, the exchange of recognition codes, the train journey, the problem of a border crossing – are standard narrative devices of spy fiction. Unlike the later films, where such generic clichés would be parodied, here they are played entirely straight. *From Russia With Love*, therefore, represents not so much the perfection of the Bond formula as an aberration from it, an excursion into a more traditional sort of spy story which was not to be repeated.

From Russia With Love is the most political of the early Bond movies. Partly this is due to the title, with its specific resonances within the spy genre. Although the film is at great pains to stress that SPECTRE is playing Britain and the Soviet Union off against each other for its own gain, nevertheless it is not as completely detached from the ideological context of the Cold War as *Dr No* had been. For the first two-thirds of the film, Bond believes that he is up against the Russians, and the film draws explicitly upon Cold War tensions. Klebb only has to have Grant kill a Russian agent in order to ignite those tensions ('Who can the Russians suspect but the British? The Cold War in Istanbul will not remain cold very much longer'). The fact that another enemy is behind the conspiracy does not mean that the incidents in the film – a pitched battle between Kerim's gypsy associates and their Bulgar enemies, the assassination by Kerim and Bond of the agent Krilencu, and Bond's raid on the Russian Embassy – are devoid of any political meaning of their own. In locating part of its action in Cold War conflict, *From Russia With Love* again represents a deviation from the usual narrative formula of the films. Not until the 1980s was the Bond series to refer so explicitly to the Cold War as its political background.[50]

For all its political content, however, there is a sense in which *From Russia With Love* is the most old-fashioned of the Bond films. In particular, the Orient Express sequence is a link to the past, its steam locomotive and elegant Pullman carriages harking back to the refined days of continental travel in refined luxury before the advent of the jet airliner. The setting, in fact, is reminiscent of 1930s fiction, from Graham Greene's *Stamboul Train* (1932) and Agatha Christie's *Murder on the Orient Express* (1934) to Hitchcock's film of *The Lady Vanishes* (1938), which,

11. *From Russia With Love*: Villainess Rosa Klebb (Lotte Lenya) prepares the unwitting Tatiana Romanova (Daniela Bianchi) for 'a real labour of love'.

if not actually on the Orient Express, nevertheless is set on a train in a vaguely defined Middle Europe. The Orient Express sequence, moreover, which takes up almost a quarter of the film, exhibits a quaintly dated style of narration with its montages of engine wheels and speeding carriages superimposed over a map which charts the train's progress through the Balkans. The old-fashioned look of the film is also apparent in its visual style, which eschews the technological modernism of *Dr No* and instead foregrounds authentic locations (Istanbul, Venice) and elegant interiors. Penelope Gilliat observed that the chess tournament 'seems to be being played in somewhere like the Doge's Palace in Venice'.[51] It may be significant in this respect that *From Russia With Love* was designed not by Ken Adam, but by Syd Cain, who had been the art director on *Dr No*.

The distinctly old-fashioned look of *From Russia With Love* is one of the factors which makes it stand out among the films, but there are many other reasons why it is so highly regarded by aficionados. Connery looks much more at ease, with the nervous, edgy quality he had shown in *Dr No* replaced by a relaxed, wry performance of subtle wit and style. It was in *From Russia With Love* that his interpretation of Bond really took shape, acquiring the exterior polish to complement the hardness. Altogether it is the most perfectly cast of the films, with Lotte Lenya (Klebb), Robert Shaw (Grant) and Pedro Armendariz (Kerim) all turning in memorable performances. Lenya, widow of composer Kurt Weill and star of G. W. Pabst's film of *The Threepenny Opera* (*Die Dreigroschenoper*, 1931), is the perfect visualisation of Fleming's toad-like lesbian villainess who terrifies Tatiana (Daniela Bianchi) and tries to kick Bond to death with her poisoned shoe-spikes.

From Russia With Love is also the most atmospheric and suspenseful of the films. The pre-title sequence, as 'Bond' is stalked by Grant through moonlit, ornamental gardens, is an eerie, almost dreamlike piece of visual story-telling which Young said he modelled on Alain Resnais's *Last Year at Marienbad* (*L'Année dernière à Marienbad*, 1961): a deliberate reference to European art cinema which establishes the very European style of the film. The sequence in the San Sofia Mosque recalls Hitchcock's habit of using famous landmarks as atmospheric background for important scenes, while the helicopter sequence, as many critics remarked, seemed to have been borrowed directly from *North by Northwest*. On a rather different level, *From Russia With Love* also included the first of the instances of inter-textuality that were to become increasingly common in the series in later years. In this instance it takes the form of a visual in-joke: the escape route from Krilencu's hideout is disguised by a giant billboard advertising the film *Call Me Bwana* – a Bob Hope–Anita Ekberg comedy produced by Broccoli and Saltzman between the first two Bond movies.

The snobbery-with-violence ethos is again much in evidence. Only in a Bond film could a villain give himself away by his choice of red Chianti to accompany grilled sole ('Red wine with fish – that should have told me something,' Bond remarks). In this instance, snobbery is followed immediately by violence as Bond and Grant fight to the death in a confined train compartment. What makes the Bond/Grant confrontation so effective is that in the sequence preceding the actual fight Grant has held the upper hand, holding Bond at gunpoint, while Bond desperately tries to trick Grant into opening his booby-trapped attaché case (primed with a tear-gas canister ready to explode). A long drawn-out suspense sequence is therefore followed by an explosion of violent

12. *From Russia With Love*: Bond fights with Grant (Robert Shaw) after the assassin has given himself away by ordering red wine with fish.

mayhem as Bond and Grant grapple with each other, exchanging blows, bouncing off the walls and doors of the compartment, a frenzy of movement and noise, before Bond kills Grant with his own garotte. Unlike most movie fight sequences, which were often filmed in long takes, the Bond/Grant struggle is a montage of fast shots, with hand-held cameras being used to cut into the screen space and exaggerated sound effects emphasising the violence. The potential of using sound in this way was not unique to Bond films, however, for in the same year Lindsay Anderson had used non-naturalistic sound to great effect in the rugby-scrum sequences of *This Sporting Life*.

From Russia With Love also furthers the voyeuristic tendencies that had been evident in *Dr No*. Indeed, the act of looking is central to the narration: Bond's first glimpse of Tatiana is the sight of her legs through a periscope hidden beneath the Russian Embassy; Klebb and Grant film Bond and Tatiana making love through a one-way mirror in Bond's hotel suite; and they are again filmed by tourists with a cine-camera at the end of the film. Furthermore, the film explicitly presents the female body as a fetishised erotic object. Thus, the main title sequence (designed in this instance by Robert Brownjohn) presents the cast and credits by superimposing them on the body of a belly-dancer. And one sequence in particular foregrounds the female body as erotic spectacle: the catfight between two gypsy girls, which occurs immediately prior to the Bulgars' attack on the gypsy camp. The two combatants, both skimpily dressed (one in green, the other in red – the visuals again emphasise primary colours), claw and scratch viciously at each other, while Bond, Kerim and the other gypsies sit and watch. The girl-fight is irrelevant to the main narrative; the purpose it serves is entirely for the erotic gratification of the spectators (both the characters in the film who are watching and the spectator in the cinema).

From Russia With Love was released in Britain in October 1963 to immediate popular acclaim. Whereas *Dr No* had opened at the London Pavilion, the second Bond movie was premiered at the Rank Organisation's flagship cinema, the Odeon, Leicester Square, where it broke the house record by taking £14,528 in its first week. 'The Most Sensational Business in the History of the Film Industry', trumpeted *Kine Weekly*.[52] It went on to become not only the biggest box-office attraction of the year in Britain, beating *Tom Jones* and *The Great Escape*, but also the highest grossing film hitherto released in the country. The producers were now sufficiently confident of their franchise that the end credits of *From Russia With Love* could declare: 'The End ... Not Quite the End. James Bond will return in the next Ian Fleming thriller, *Goldfinger*.' Thus began the tradition of naming the next film at the end of the current one – and, moreover, the process whereby Broccoli and Saltzman began planning for the long-term future of the Bond series.

The critics lined up much as they had for *Dr No*. The trade and popular press were ecstatic, and their enthusiasm was again shared by several of the more middle-brow critics. John Coleman of the *New Statesman* liked the cinematic Bond because he thought it downplayed the violence of the books and added a sense of humour:

> *From Russia With Love* is the new James Bond instalment and hilariously maintains the disinfecting [*sic*], larky tone of its predecessor. Two gypsy girls scrap (rather tamely), poisoned knives sprout from the toes of villains' boots, and a gun is ominously aimed at Bond's privates by Robert Shaw's assassin – 'homicidal maniac, splendid material', as the principal of a murder college points out. These screen doings-over of the Fleming books certainly have their small hints of real nastiness. But the interesting thing is that what has forcibly to become explicit on the screen is a hundred times milder than the horrible imaginings stimulated by Mr Fleming's elliptic pages: better yet it tends to come out funny. Terence Young and his screenwriter, Richard Maibaum, give Bond some nice laconic cracks to round off the surreal events of his working day. A bad man crawls out between Ekberg's lips on a giant hoarding and is picked off through telescopic sights. 'She should have kept her mouth shut,' drawls Bond. Mr Young's direction is still hazy when it comes to simple exposition, and Lotte Lenya's impersonation of evil old Rosa Klebb disappoints, but a genuine filmic sense animates the fantasy – from a blinding pre-credit sequence in the grounds of that school for murder on to the final, literal flare-up. There's even a death-dealing helicopter – and thank you, Hitchcock, Losey, and all who flew in her before.[53]

Coleman, therefore, acknowledged the debt which the film owed to others, while emphasising its filmic and visual qualities and recognising it for the 'fantasy' it was.

Other critics again questioned the morality of Bond. 'We tend to get the movie heroes we deserve, and I suppose nowadays that means James Bond,' said Thomas Wiseman. 'He is very much a figment of our times, the arch exponent of pop fascism ("licensed to kill"), the patriot-libertine, always ready to seduce a pretty spy for his country.'[54] And Nina Hibbin thought the film was 'sick', again detecting unpleasant undertones in that 'although the film appears to be sending up the cloak-and-dagger tradition, in reality (along with its predecessor *Dr No*) it is building up a tradition that is far more vicious'.[55]

The American release of *From Russia With Love* again followed on some six months after it had been shown in Britain. North American rentals of $9.9 million were an improvement on its predecessor, helped by a slightly wider release, though they were still only half the $19.5 million of foreign rentals (as a rule of thumb most movies make roughly the same amount of money in the North American market as in the rest of the world). Interestingly, the American critics were divided over the balance between the straight thriller and comic elements of the film. The *Esquire* critic was disappointed: 'A comedown after *Dr No*, whose brisk parody here slackens into a queasy compromise with the real thing that tries to have it both ways and so fails to have it either way.'[56] But Hollis Alpert in the *Saturday Review* suggested that 'Terence Young ... has now learned how to balance the thriller and the spoof qualities about equally, and the blend results in a superior kind of entertainment'.[57]

Whether audiences accepted it as a straight thriller or regarded it as a comedy is impossible to say, but what is certain is that *From Russia With Love* was sufficiently successful in the international market for United Artists to put up a budget for the next film which exceeded the combined cost of the previous two. It seems reasonable to suggest that, just as the choice of *From Russia With Love* as the second film had probably been made to consolidate Bond's popularity in Europe, so the choice of *Goldfinger* for the third film represented a strategy whereby the producers hoped to establish Bond in the American market. The setting of *Goldfinger* is predominantly American, and the conspiracy is directed against America.

Goldfinger was the seventh Bond novel, coming after *Dr No*, and maintains that book's trend towards fantastic and highly improbable plots. Like *Dr No*, what at first appears to be a relatively trivial matter turns out to be a grandiose criminal conspiracy. Bond first encounters Auric Goldfinger by chance in Miami, where he stops over while returning from an assignment in Mexico, and exposes him for cheating at cards. Back in London, Bond is assigned by M to investigate Goldfinger, a gold broker by trade, whom the Bank of England suspects of smuggling gold bullion, and whom M suspects of being the 'foreign banker' of SMERSH. It transpires that Goldfinger's ambitions extend far beyond smuggling: backed by the Russians, he plans to rob the US gold bullion depository at Fort Knox, having disabled the military defences by poisoning the local water supply. Bond is captured by

Goldfinger but manages to leak details of the plan to the authorities, who ambush Goldfinger's train when it arrives at Fort Knox. It is one of the most implausible of Fleming's plots – literal-minded critics pointed out that the sheer weight of gold bullion involved would make the plan impossible from the start – but this is partly mediated by the detailed description of small details and incidents, particularly the celebrated high-stakes round of golf during which Bond successfully out-cheats Goldfinger.

Richard Maibaum was once again employed to write the screenplay, though this time he had a different collaborator. Paul Dehn was the film critic of the *News Chronicle* who also worked occasionally as a screenwriter, his credits including the Boulting Brothers' *Seven Days to Noon* (1950) – for which he jointly won an Academy Award – and, later, two film adaptations of John le Carré novels, *The Spy Who Came in from the Cold* (1965) and *The Deadly Affair* (1966). According to Maibaum: 'On *Goldfinger* I did a first draft. Harry Saltzman didn't like it, and he brought in Paul Dehn, a good writer, to revise. Then Sean Connery didn't like the revisions, and I came back to do the final screenplay. That was the first time that happened: where I was followed by someone and then called back to finish up.'[58]

There was also to be a different director. Terence Young, who started pre-production work, decided instead to direct *The Amorous Adventures of Moll Flanders* (1965), a bawdy costume romp in the mould of *Tom Jones*. Guy Hamilton, who had originally been offered *Dr No*, took the director's chair. 'I'd enjoyed the previous two films, but felt there was a real danger of Bond becoming Superman; consequently there would be no suspense in whatever predicaments were dreamt up for him,' Hamilton said later. 'So we concentrated on the villains; Bond is only as good as his villains.'[59]

For many aficionados, *Goldfinger* is the best of the Bond films. John Brosnan, for example, writes:

> *Goldfinger* represents the peak of the series. It is the most perfectly realized of all the films ... It moves at a fast and furious pace, but the plot holds together logically enough (more logically than the book) and is a perfect blend of the real and the fantastic. It is full of sly humor but the humor doesn't detract from the excitement as it does in the more recent Bonds. It is also the most visually attractive of the films; the central theme of gold seems

to pervade every scene, giving it a distinctive motif that the other films have lacked.[60]

Goldfinger again illustrates that the generic development of the Bond series was not a linear process. It is closer to *Dr No* than *From Russia With Love* in that it foregrounds the science-fiction and technological trappings of the plot and marks a return to a grand conspiracy which Bond foils at the last possible moment. It is, however, slicker and more polished than *Dr No* – made possible by a larger budget, not to mention the increasing confidence of the film-makers with their formula – and also contains more humour.

As with the two preceding films, *Goldfinger* follows the basic storyline of the novel but makes some significant changes in the detail. One of these can be read as a direct response to some of the criticisms made of the novel. Bond, having overheard Goldfinger (Gert Frobe) briefing the American gangsters whom he has lured into collaborating with him, and who believe that his intention is to 'knock off' Fort Knox, makes the same point that several critics had of the novel. 'I've worked out a few statistics of my own,' Bond remarks. 'Fifteen billion dollars in gold bullion weighs ten thousand five hundred tons. Sixty men would take twelve days to load it onto two hundred trucks.' However, it is then revealed that Goldfinger's plan is not to rob Fort Knox, but rather to explode an 'atomic device' inside it in order to contaminate the bullion supply of the United States. The film therefore not only addressed the criticisms made of Fleming's original story, but it also allowed a more exciting finale in which Bond has to race against time to defuse the bomb. A similar plot device had been used in *Seven Days to Noon*, in which a mad scientist threatens to blow up London.

Another significant change is that whereas in the novel Goldfinger was a member of SMERSH, in the film his 'Operation Grand Slam' is backed by Communist China. The character of Mr Ling (Burt Kwouk) is explicitly referred to as a 'Red Chinese agent', and it is his government which has provided Goldfinger with the atomic bomb. The detonation of the bomb inside Fort Knox therefore has a dual purpose. As Bond observes: 'They get what they want – economic chaos in the West – and the value of your gold increases many times.' The substitution of Red China for the Soviet Union as the 'enemy' behind Goldfinger is intriguing. On one level, it continues the narrative strategy of detaching the Bond films from the context of the Cold War (defined in this sense as the political and diplomatic conflict between the Western powers and the Soviet bloc, not the People's Republic of China). On another level, it reflects growing fears in the West over the growth of Chinese military strength. It was entirely coincidental that in October 1964, a month after *Goldfinger*'s British release and shortly before its American release, China exploded its first atomic bomb; but it is reasonable to assume that the nuclear threat posed in *Goldfinger* would have a certain topicality, particularly in America, whose security and economic stability was threatened.

What is most remarkable about *Goldfinger* is that, for a Bond film at least, there is relatively little conventional action in it. There is the pre-title sequence, in which Bond blows up a semi-military installation somewhere in Latin America and has a punch-up with a heavy in his hotel room which culminates in the assailant being electrocuted in a bath ('Shocking, positively shocking,' Bond observes wryly). There is a car chase around Goldfinger's Swiss factory; a brief struggle between Bond and one of Goldfinger's Korean guards as Bond escapes (temp-orarily) from his imprisonment at Goldfinger's Kentucky stud farm; and a light-hearted tussle between Bond and Goldfinger's accomplice Pussy Galore (Honor Blackman), which really constitutes the foreplay to Bond's seduction of her. Other than that, it is not until the raid on Fort Knox, and Bond's fight with Goldfinger's manservant Oddjob (Harold Sakata), that the film sustains an extended action sequence of the sort which had proliferated in *From Russia With Love*.

However, the relative dearth of action is compensated for by greater visual excess. Hamilton's direction is less abrupt than Young's, and the camera moves around more freely. There are more extravagant touches, and a tendency towards bizarre visual jokes: in the first shot a seagull bobbing on the water turns out to be a disguise fixed to Bond's head, while shortly afterwards he removes his wetsuit to reveal an impossibly dry, immaculate white tuxedo underneath, nonchalantly placing a red carnation in the buttonhole. As Brosnan observes, the visual style of the film emphasises the colour gold. The main titles (again designed by Robert Brownjohn) are presented around the body of a golden girl, on which images from the film are projected as the title song is belted out, with customary gusto, by Shirley Bassey. This anticipates a scene shortly later in the film where Bond, having seduced Goldfinger's assistant Jill Masterson, is knocked unconscious and awakes to find her laying face down on the bed, dead, covered in gold paint. The scene is celebrated

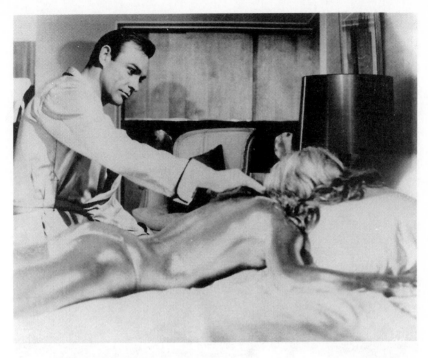

13. *Goldfinger*: Bond discovers the body of Jill Masterson (Shirley Eaton).
'The girl's dead ... And she's covered in paint. Gold paint.'

within the Bond fan culture as one which ensured actress Shirley Eaton
her moment of screen immortality, but it has disturbing undertones of
necrophilia: Bond, and the spectator, are invited to gaze at the near-
naked and very dead body of the girl, which nevertheless is presented
as a sort of erotic spectacle through the fetishistic covering of gold
paint. It is a scene which stands out in what, otherwise, is a more light-
hearted and humorous film than its two predecessors.[61]

Goldfinger foregrounds technology and gadgetry to a greater extent
than even *Dr No*, indicating the direction which the series was to take
thereafter. The publicity discourse emphasised the technological modernity of the film. An official press release made much of the industrial
laser which Goldfinger employs, first to threaten Bond and later to
effect his entry into Fort Knox, declaring that it was 'a scientific device
so new that only a minority of the general public have even heard of
it' and that its use in the film 'is sure to give the laser its greatest
international publicity as a scientific development of great power and
worth in the modern world'.[62] At one point Bond finds himself spread-

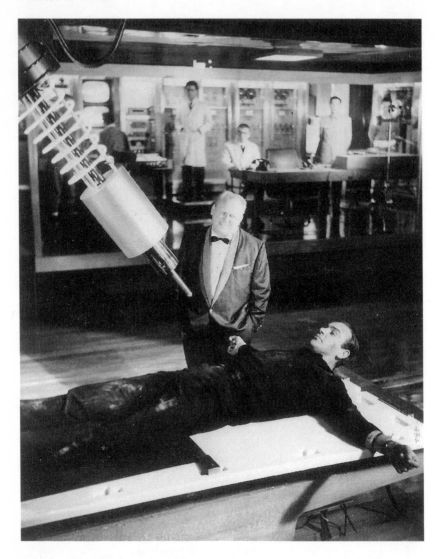

14. *Goldfinger*: 'Do you expect me to talk?' 'No, Mr Bond, I expect you to die!'
Goldfinger (Gert Frobe) advises Bond to choose his next witicism carefully –
'it may be your last'.

eagled beneath the laser which is burning its way through a table of
solid gold. The scene plays, obviously, on male castration anxiety as the
beam slowly creeps up between Bond's legs. But it also provides a
modern, up-to-date variation on an old cliché. In the novel Bond had
been threatened by a circular saw, a situation familiar from the old cliff-
hanger serial melodramas. Maibaum explained why this was changed for

the film: 'Vividly depicted on the screen, however, we were sure audiences would find the episode old-fashioned, hackneyed and ridiculous. What to do? We substituted an industrial laser beam, a development as fresh as tomorrow, for the antiquated circular saw.'[63] However, not all commentators approved of the change, which was seen by some as an unnecessary display of technology for its own sake rather than serving a logical narrative purpose. G. B. Zorzoli, for example, wrote that whereas the circular saw of the novel was 'sufficiently simple and efficacious within the grasp of everyone', in the film 'a laser is employed in an entirely gratuitous exhibition'.[64]

The other gadget that played an important role in *Goldfinger* was Bond's modified Aston Martin DB5. Unlike some of the later films, where gadgets are used for comic effect, in *Goldfinger* the car still serves a logical narrative purpose: Bond uses its radar to tail Goldfinger across Switzerland and employs its other devices during the chase around Goldfinger's factory. Suspense arises from the audience knowing the gadgets the car is equipped with and waiting for the moment when Bond will use them, particularly in the case of the ejector seat; there are several teasing shots of Bond's hand on the gear lever before he finally presses the button inside and ejects his unwanted passenger through the roof. The car, as Vittorio Bonicelli argued, represents a particular type of fantasy for the male spectator:

> The best invention of the film is the automobile: its destructive power belongs to the realm of dreams. The medium of the automobile, the metropolitan man who secretes at the wheel, hour by hour, his daily neurotic moods and then relieves himself in nightmares thronged with mechanical riches finds in *Goldfinger* the ideal instrument for his fantastic vendetta. This car wields, in fact, supreme power upon the road: the destruction at will of all other vehicles; the sadism (or the sado-masochism?) of exercising itself upon [the] bodywork and tyres of its enemies.[65]

The destructive power of the gadgets at Bond's disposal was to become an ever-more central aspect of the films, though in *Goldfinger* the car does not quite have the 'supreme power' which Bonicelli attributes to it, as the chase finishes with Bond crashing and being captured.

It was with *Goldfinger* that Ken Adam's designs for the films really came into their own. His interior of Fort Knox is a visual *tour de force*: rejecting any notion of authenticity (gold is so heavy that it can only be stored in small piles), Adam created a massive multi-storey set in which gold ingots are stacked forty feet high behind chrome bars. The gleaming, highly polished set exhibits the modernist aesthetic of the Bond visual style to perfection, emphasising once again the fantasy world of Bond's adventures. It also creates a marvellous arena for the fight between Bond and Oddjob. Unlike the Bond/Grant confrontation, which took place in a confined setting, the Bond/Oddjob fight utilises all the space available as the combatants circle around each other, and Bond is thrown across the smooth metal floor before electrocuting his opponent.

The representation of women in *Goldfinger* is again indicative of the ideological processes of popular cinema. Janet Thumim provides a useful summary of the very limited scope which the film allows for its female characters:

> In line with other films popular at the sixties box office there are relatively few women to be seen on the screen in *Goldfinger* (after the initial pan around the borders of the Miami swimming pool). Even fewer have any significant narrative function ... Tilly, Jill and Pussy follow each other as 'partners' to the central male character, James Bond. But what is interesting ... is the other narrative traits which these three women have in common. The actions of all three are motivated by a very limited view of self interest and are highly susceptible to male influence, and they are all suggested to be incompetent in at least one narratively crucial skill. Jill is working for Goldfinger because, as she tells Bond, 'he pays me' but is easily persuaded by Bond to change sides. Tilly is trying to avenge her sister's death but her incompetence with a gun leads to Bond's capture and her own death. Pussy is supposed to be a competent pilot and a trustworthy accomplice to Goldfinger, yet it is Bond who takes over at the end of the film when she panics as the punctured plane loses altitude.[66]

In fact, Tilly Masterson does not become a sexual partner for Bond, whereas both Jill Masterson and Pussy Galore do. This is explicable in terms of the ideological role which women play in the Bond narrative: Jill and Pussy both work for Goldfinger, and Bond needs to seduce them in order to 'reposition' them on the side of right, whereas in Tilly's case there is no need to do so as she has already sided against Goldfinger.

Thumim also suggests that with Pussy Galore's Flying Circus – the

15. *Goldfinger*: 'Isn't it customary to grant the condemned man his last request?' Bond tussles with Pussy Galore (Honor Blackman).

pulchritudinous female pilots who spray nerve gas over Fort Knox – 'the implication of lesbianism is thrown in for good measure'. 'It is curious,' she continues, 'that at a time when legal attitudes towards male homosexuality were finally being liberalised there should be this (admittedly minor) "backlash" against female homosexuality.' Yet the film is not so much of a 'backlash' against lesbianism as the novel, in which

Fleming's overt heterosexism had been writ large. Both Tilly and Pussy were lesbians in the novel; the former remained resistant to Bond and was killed, the latter succumbed to him and survived. For the film all references to Tilly's lesbianism have disappeared, and there is only the briefest hint of it with Pussy ('You can skip the charm,' she tells Bond. 'I'm immune'). As played by Honor Blackman, there is no denying that Pussy Galore has more to offer as a character than the bland personalities of the usual Bond starlets. Blackman's performance owes much to her already established persona as the leather-clad judo expert Cathy Gale in *The Avengers*, often claimed as the first 'feminist' heroine on television. Even so, Graham Rye's claim that 'Pussy Galore was a reflection of the more liberated and self-sufficient women of the Sixties' is rather over-stating the case.[67]

The release of *Goldfinger* in Britain was marked by an outbreak of 'Bondmania' on a massive scale. When it premiered at the Odeon, Leicester Square, on 17 September 1964, there was nearly a riot outside the cinema. One trade columnist who attended the premiere wrote: 'Never in 25 years of premiere-going have I experienced anything like it; rounds of applause, hoots of good-natured laughter.'[68] The film broke the house record for the Odeon, Leicester Square (previously set by *From Russia With Love*), taking £32,874 in its first fortnight, and went on to become the highest-grossing film released in Britain. Such was the public's appetite for Bond that a re-release of *Dr No* at the same time also proved hugely popular.

Critics responded to the enormous popularity of the Bond films in different ways. Nina Hibbin was still the most vociferous anti-Bond critic, and she launched a broadside against *Goldfinger* that was even more vitriolic than her reaction to the previous two:

> The cult of James Bondism is a vicious one, a symptomatic sick-ness of the age, and the latest in the film series is well in the mould of its predecessors, *Dr No* and *From Russia With Love*. Bondists are expected to shriek with laughter even before the first victim is kicked in the guts or battered against a wall. They must gurgle with relish whenever their nonchalant hero, created by the late Ian Fleming, rolls a girl he's hardly met and certainly hates into the nearest bed. Above all, they must be ready (as soon as they are given the magical wisecrack signal) to roll in the aisles as a man is electrocuted and disintegrates in a flame-coloured flash. ...

But this is all one vast, gigantic confidence trick to blind the audience to what is going on underneath. The constantly lurking viciousness, and the glamorisation of violence – they are real enough. So, too, are the carefully timed peaks of titillation and the skilfully contrived sensationalism – they're real, too. The racialism (inscrutably smiling villains of Oriental countenance), the cold-war implications of the plot – they are not in the film for a joke. All this is the underlying menace of the film which gives the laughter a dangerous and sinister ring. [69]

Hibbin's attack was directed as much against the fans who could laugh along with Bond as it was at the film itself, exhibiting a characteristic contempt for the audiences whom she believed had been taken in by the subterfuge of the film.

Hibbin's criticisms were rejected by Penelope Houston, the editor of *Sight and Sound*, who thought that *Goldfinger* 'perfects the formula' and 'assumes a mood of good-humoured complicity with the audience' that was the key to its popular appeal. Houston's response demonstrates how the critical establishment, as represented by the most prominent intellectual film journal of the time, was coming to realise that the enormous success of the Bond movies required that they should be taken, if not altogether seriously, then at least as significant and prominent artefacts of popular culture. Typically, for a serious critic used to a diet of European art cinema, Houston found it necessary to try to compare the Bond films, however tangentially, to other, preferred styles of film-making, and she found a parallel for their light-hearted playing with filmic conventions in the French *Nouvelle Vague*: 'There is an assumption – which you find, at quite the other end of the spectrum, in the Godard films – that we all know the clichés and can have a little fun with them.' The reason for the success of the Bond films, she argued, was that they so perfectly caught the mood of the times. For the same reason, she believed, the moment of the films would soon pass:

In a few years the films will seem dated by their assumptions as much as by the lines of their cars, or by Pussy Galore's extravagantly leathery wardrobe. At the moment, however, and for the moment, it's all sufficiently here: 'the brassy, swinging, ungallant taste of the Sixties', to quote Penelope Gilliat. Ian Fleming's Bond could still be considered – was in fact considered by Mr Bergonzi

— in terms of the ethics of Richard Hannay. The screen's Bond is at once the last of the clubland buccaneers and the first of the joke supermen. The transformation has earned the film-makers their place in the annals of popular taste. One must give the sociologists best and admit that *Goldfinger* really is rather a symbolic film.[70]

Houston's article marks one of the first serious attempts to place the Bond films in their social and cultural context, relating them to the attitudes and fashions of the early 1960s, though her belief that they would quickly become out of date was less prescient. As so often, sociological reasons are advanced for the success of popular entertainments, suggesting that the extraordinary degree of their success must be due to something more than just the films themselves, that it is somehow rooted in the *Zeitgeist*, the mood of the times which the films reflect. Whether this simply was the case, or whether, as has been argued, the impact of the early Bond movies was due in some measure to more long-term developments in the British film industry and film culture as a whole, there is no denying that by 1964 the phenomenon of 'Bondmania' had well and truly arrived.

3

Bondmania: *Thunderball,*
Casino Royale, You Only Live Twice,
On Her Majesty's Secret Service

The first three James Bond films introduced, developed and refined the generic formula of the series. If, as so many commentators have suggested, *Goldfinger* is the archetypal Bond film in terms of its narrative structure and balance of thriller, science-fiction and comedy elements, then the generic formula had already achieved its most perfect form. 'Between them, the first three movies had more or less covered all the variations that were possible,' observes John Brosnan; 'after *Goldfinger*, the producers were faced with the problem of what direction to take.'[1] The direction which the official series was to take was defined over the course of the next three films: *Thunderball* (dir. Terence Young, 1965), *You Only Live Twice* (dir. Lewis Gilbert, 1967) and *On Her Majesty's Secret Service* (dir. Peter Hunt, 1969). These three films belong together as a group in much the same way that *Dr No, From Russia With Love* and *Goldfinger* are a group. Collectively, they represent the trend towards longer running times, bigger budgets and ever more spectacular set pieces which have become a *sine qua non* of the Bond series. Whereas the first three films had been reasonably tight and well-structured narratives, the second three were longer, looser and more episodic. In production terms, while the first three films had been released at annual intervals, from *Thunderball* onwards the Bond series settled into a long-term release pattern whereby a new film would appear at roughly two-yearly intervals. At a time when imitations of the Bond films proliferated – and the mid-1960s were the heyday of gimmicky spy extravaganzas which sought, with varying degrees of success, to cash in on the popularity of 007, including a spoof version of *Casino Royale* in 1967 – the Bond producers sought to differentiate the genuine article by making it ever more spectacular and expensive, and by extending the time between each film, thus ensuring that the audience was ready and waiting each time a new Bond film was released.

The mid-1960s was the time when 'Bondmania' was at its height. On one level this is exemplified by the increasing box-office success of the films. *Goldfinger* far surpassed the box-office figures of the first two films, taking some $23 million in North America and $26.6 million in the rest of the world: its total worldwide rentals of over $49 million were almost as much as the combined rentals of *Dr No* and *From Russia With Love*. These figures were quickly surpassed, however, by *Thunderball*, which achieved domestic rentals of $28.6 million and foreign rentals of $27.8 million: its total worldwide rentals of over $56 million were the most for any Bond film until *The Spy Who Loved Me* in 1977. Given the effect of inflation and increased ticket prices since 1965, however, *Thunderball* is probably the most successful Bond film in real terms. Following the high point of *Thunderball*, the next two films showed evidence of a falling-off in Bond's box-office appeal. Even so, the $44 million worldwide rentals of *You Only Live Twice* were still extremely good at a time when more and more Hollywood movies were failing to recoup their production costs. It was not until *On Her Majesty's Secret Service* that a Bond movie could be said not to have lived up to box-office expectations: its worldwide rentals of $24 million were disappointingly low, less than *From Russia With Love* though still more than *Dr No*.[2]

It was the release of *Goldfinger* that marked the emergence of 'Bondmania' as a truly international phenomenon. Unlike the first two films, which had been released in smaller movie theatres and drive-ins across the United States, *Goldfinger* was chosen by United Artists as its major Christmas release. It opened on 22 December and premiered in prestigious locations, such as Grauman's Chinese Theatre in Hollywood, where, according to one commentator, 'lines of eager ticket buyers formed for blocks on opening day and afterward, this enthusiastic reception being duplicated all over the country'.[3] 'The success of *Gold-finger* was such', wrote another, 'that in one cinema in New York one showing followed another day and night, and the management imposed an interval only to sweep away from the auditorium the remains of popcorn which had reached a depth of several inches.'[4] *Goldfinger* was the film which firmly established Bond in America – and in other markets which had hitherto been resistant. In France, for example, where the Bond cult had not really taken off as it had elsewhere in Western Europe, it was *Goldfinger* which made the breakthrough. '*Goldfinger* has hit Paris like a thunderbolt,' the British press reported early in 1965. 'Only two weeks after this latest James Bond epic was launched here it is already creating cinematic history.'[5] The film broke box-office records at Parisian cinemas, and there were reports of thousands of cinema-goers queueing in the 'biting cold' and being prepared to sit in the aisles to see it. Nor was the Bond cult confined to North America and Europe. 'There seems to be no geographical limit to the appeal of sex, violence and snobbery with which Fleming endowed his British secret agent,' *Time* magazine declared in June 1965, reporting that in Tokyo 'the queue for *Goldfinger* stretches half a mile', while in Beirut 'even Goldfinger's hat-hurling bodyguard, Oddjob, has become a minor hero'.[6]

The spectacular box-office returns of the Bond films in the mid-1960s were made possible, to some degree, by the release strategy adopted by United Artists and Eon Productions. An unusually large number of prints were used worldwide – some 1,100 in the case of *Goldfinger*[7] – so that the film could be seen as widely and as quickly as possible. This practice is now commonplace for Hollywood blockbusters: the saturation of thousands of screens on the all-important opening weekend, which is regarded in the industry as the make-or-break time as to whether or not a movie is going to be a hit. This strategy means that a film maximises the effectiveness of pre-release publicity, benefits from word-of-mouth, and also reduces the interest payable on the money invested in the film by accelerating the rate of box-office returns. *Thunderball*, for example, earned back its production and distribution costs after only seven weeks in the North American market. It surpassed *Goldfinger*, which was 'withdrawn from domestic release to make way for *Thunderball*', despite being shown in fewer movie theatres. 'There are several reasons for the bigger, faster *Thunderball* grosses, the most obvious being that Agent 007's popularity has continued to build,' remarked Vincent Canby in the *New York Times*. 'Also, because of the success of the earlier films, the distributor has been able to get a larger share of the receipts and the theaters, in turn, have in many cases been charging higher admission prices.'[8]

However, the box-office success of the Bond films in the 1960s tells only part of the story. 'Bondmania' was not confined to the reception of the films themselves; it was a phenomenon which permeated into the wider realms of popular culture more generally. *Time* observed that 'James Bond has developed into the biggest mass-cult hero of the decade'.[9] In Italy, where Bond was known colloquially as 'Mr Kiss Kiss Bang Bang', the youth magazine *Ciao Amici* described him as 'the most popular personality of 1965'.[10] Bond's penetration of other areas of cultural production was evident at many levels: *Playboy* began running photo-spreads of Bond starlets; 'golden girl' Shirley Eaton appeared on the cover of *Life* magazine in September 1964; the title song of *Goldfinger* performed by Shirley Bassey reached number eight in the US singles charts, and the soundtrack LP went to number one; toy manufacturers produced James Bond toys; the Galeries Lafayette in Paris opened a 'James Bond Boutique' selling 007 cufflinks and shirts; and an Australian lingerie manufacturer even launched a range of women's underwear with the slogan 'Become fit for James Bond'. Furthermore, sales of the Bond novels reached their peak in the mid-1960s, as Pan produced paperback tie-ins with images from the films on the covers, though, as Bennett and Woollacott have shown, 'the effect of the films in this period was to revivify the market for the Bond novels *as a whole*. It was as an *integrated set*, rather than as individual titles, that the Bond novels sold over this period.'[11] In France, meanwhile, the publishers Plon sold 480,000 copies of the first four novels in French translation in three months during the summer of 1964, while *Dr No* was serialised in *France-Soir*.[12]

How is the phenomenon of 'Bondmania' to be explained? Various reasons have been advanced to account for the enormous popularity of the Bond films, and for the widespread currency of the figure of Bond as a popular cultural icon, at this time. Given the quite extraordinary success of the films, it seems rather too simplistic to suggest, as the trade press did, merely that they exhibited in full measure the sort of entertainment value that cinema-goers wanted. This may be true, but it is hardly adequate as an explanation. In order to account for the outbreak of 'Bondmania', it is necessary to consider the films, and particularly the character of Bond as he was portrayed therein, in the wider context of the society and culture of the 1960s. For, just as Ian Fleming's Bond was very much a product of the social and political conditions of Britain in the 1950s, so the cinematic Bond was a product of the social and political conditions of the 1960s.

On one level, the Bond films need to be seen within the context of the cultural regeneration which many commentators identified as taking place in Britain in the mid-1960s. This is most frequently expressed through the label of 'Swinging London', from the title of an article in *Time* in April 1966, though, as Arthur Marwick shows, similar views were also being expressed in a range of French and Italian magazines at the same time.[13] There was a perception that British society had suddenly thrown off its shackles and that, led by the newly emergent youth cultures, a more hedonistic, liberated, 'swinging' spirit had taken its place. Historians have since questioned whether this was the case – processes of change were gradual and on-going, while for many people the 1960s did not bring about the new freedoms they were popularly supposed to have done – but what is important in considering the impact of the Bond movies is the perception by contemporaries that Britain had become a more open, liberal, even permissive society. One sign of the 'new' Britain was the Labour government of Harold Wilson, elected in 1964 after a generation of Conservative rule, which gave the impression of being modern and meritocratic rather than old-fashioned and class-bound. But a more significant manifestation of different attitudes and behaviour was to be found in the new international prestige enjoyed by British popular culture. It was a popular culture led by pop music, and pre-eminently by The Beatles, but it also included new trends in fashion (especially the mini-skirt and the designs of Mary Quant), a new generation of attractive and sexy film stars with international appeal (Sean Connery, Michael Caine, Julie Christie, Terence Stamp), and films which featured hedonistic and sexually liberated characters such as *Tom Jones* (1963), *Darling* (1965) and, of course, James Bond. The Bond films need to be seen, therefore, as one component of a new British popular culture in the 1960s which emphasised youth, sex appeal and modernity. This line of argument is taken further by Bennett and Woollacott:

> More particularly, in the context of 'swinging Britain', Bond pro-
> vided a mythic encapsulation of the then prominent ideological
> themes of classlessness and modernity, a key cultural marker of
> the claim that Britain had escaped the blinkered, class-bound

perspectives of its traditional ruling elites and was in the process of being thoroughly modernised as a result of the implementation of a new, meritocratic style of cultural and political leadership, middle class and professional, rather than aristocratic and amateur.[14]

This is, of course, an interpretation which is based entirely on the Bond films, illustrating that the screen Bond had a different cultural meaning and significance to Ian Fleming's Bond.

In certain other respects, too, the Bond films reflected, mediated and even defined some of the distinguishing characteristics of the 'cultural revolution' of the 1960s.[15] In the first place, it was a decade in which technology and technological progress came to the fore. In America, Kennedy had used the metaphor of the 'new frontier' to describe any kind of technological innovation, particularly in respect of the expansion into space, while in Britain Wilson spoke of 'the white heat of science and technology'. The Bond films, from *Goldfinger* onwards, contributed to the obsession with technology by fetishising it. This aspect of the films was commented upon by numerous critics, including Richard Mallet of *Punch*, who pointed out how smoothly everything always worked on the screen:

> Watching the new James Bond film, *Goldfinger*, one can't help feel-ing that this time the gadgets have really taken over. Particularly in the second half of the film, there seems to be hardly a scene that does not involve the operation of some beautifully made, photogenic mechanical or electronic device. (Always, by the way, the *smooth* operation; a bit of grit in the works now and then would radically alter the course of the story).[16]

Mallet suggested that 'the gadgets, like everything else, are used above all to arouse laughter'. But in fact much of the technology displayed on the screen was authentic: the laser in *Goldfinger*, the Bell jet-pack and underwater camera in *Thunderball*, the autogiro and rocket-firing guns in *You Only Live Twice*, were all real technological innovations.

The 1960s is also perceived as the decade of 'permissiveness', which Marwick defines as 'a general sexual liberation, entailing striking changes in public and private morals and ... a new frankness, openness, and indeed honesty in personal relations and modes of expression'.[17] This openness and honesty concerning sexual relationships had been evident in Fleming's novels in the 1950s, and to some extent the films were actually rather more coy in their presentation of sex. There is, for example, no full nudity in the Bond movies. 'Nudity would destroy Bond's career,' Broccoli once observed. 'His image must be clean cut. We can't risk offending his massive family audience in any way.'[18] That having been said, Bond's various sexual encounters are illustrated in the films, albeit with due restraint, and on average he has more girlfriends per film than he did in the books. Bond is the perfect hero for the permissive society: hedonistic, sexually active, progressing from one girl to the next and treating them with the same casual indifference he shows towards the gadgets supplied to him by Q. The only occasion on which Bond has a more serious and romantic relationship is in *On Her Majesty's Secret Service*, wherein he marries the heroine – thus proving that even the most committed bachelor would make an exception for Diana Rigg.

The representation of women in the Bond films has been the subject of some debate. On the one hand, the films have been criticised for being overtly sexist, for presenting women as little more than disposable playthings for the dominant male hero. Certainly in the films of the 1960s it is hard to disagree with this charge. Most of the women's roles are fairly two-dimensional, with the Bond girls generally having a less active role in the narrative, and less interesting character traits, than they had in Fleming's original stories. Women are commodities, to be consumed by Bond and then discarded, often meeting grisly ends. As for the Bond starlets themselves, acting ability was an optional extra. With the exceptions of Honor Blackman and Diana Rigg, who both had established acting careers outside the Bond series, none of the Bond girls of the 1960s had much to offer beyond their obviously pulchritudinous charms, and, other than Ursula Andress, none of them achieved lasting stardom after their stint in 'Bondage'. The Bond starlets represented a *Playboy* male-fantasy image of female sexuality: well-scrubbed, big-breasted, long-haired and sexually available. The criteria for casting them would appear to have been their physical attributes: a story persists that Julie Christie was turned down for the role of Domino in *Thunderball* because the producers thought her breasts were too small.

On the other hand, the publicity discourse around the Bond girls suggested they were modern, liberated, independent women. Claudine Auger, a former Miss France who was preferred to Julie Christie for Domino in *Thunderball*, considered that her character was 'the ultimate in modern, emancipated woman'. Of the Bond girls, she said: 'They can live without a man doing everything for them because they are in-dependent. They like to decide their future destinies for themselves. They are highly sexual – but only with men worth their loving. They are free, you see, completely free. I may be married, but I feel I am like this. I am free. I always have been. I always will be.'[19]

Terence Young put forward a similar view: 'They are women of the nuclear age, freer and able to make love when they want to without worrying about it.'[20] Clearly this is a rather limited view of what con-stitutes freedom for women. It can be argued, indeed, that it represents a very male-oriented view of female behaviour in so far as women are free only in the sense of being able to have sex without having to get married or make a long-term commitment, which is presumably what many men wanted of them anyway. In this sense, the Bond films of the 1960s reflect the greater sexual freedom experienced by women during the decade but also embody an inherent contradiction of that freedom. As Marwick asks, 'was this sexual liberation for women, or simply enhanced liberation for men, a grand occasion for the even more ruthless sexual exploitation of women?'[21] Given that most of the Bond starlets would perform the obligatory photo-shoot for *Playboy* to coincide with the release of the films (and, indeed, were often contractually required to do so), it may be that they had rather less freedom than Claudine Auger believed.

To some extent, therefore, the impact of the Bond movies can be related to the various ways in which they reflected certain aspects of the 'cultural revolution' of the 1960s. A rather different explanation for their success, especially in America, has been advanced in a speculative essay by an American writer, Drew Moniot. 'Bond's success was probably due to the formula aspects of his series and the culturally relevant messages conveyed by the formula,' Moniot writes, '007 actually had a great deal in common with the American moviegoer of the Sixties.'[22] Moniot draws on Charles Reich's 1970 book *The Greening of America*, which had suggested that in the 1960s the American Dream had been destroyed by the rise of the 'corporate state', which created a social climate controlled by a hierarchical, mechanical, dehumanised, supremely powerful organisation that was indifferent to the rights and interests of the individual. Moniot draws a parallel between the notion of the corporate state and Bond's principal enemy in the films of the 1960s, the international crime syndicate SPECTRE. If, as Reich argued, the general mood of America in the 1960s was one of growing disenchantment with the corporate state, then the Bond films, Moniot suggests, struck a chord because they offered the possibility of the individual turning against the organisation: 'Thus the 007 fan, vaguely sensing a loss of identity and worth in the age of the corporate state, could vicariously experience a certain sense of triumph and relief when Bond struck a blow against SPECTRE.'[23] It is an intriguing argument, but ultimately unconvincing. Moniot admits that Bond himself is very much an organisation man, and that the secret service for which he works might itself be seen as another manifestation of the corporate state. The theme of the individual against a machine-like organisation was hardly a new idea in the 1960s, evidenced by Chaplin's *Modern Times* (1936). And the argument does not take account of the fact that, while the Bond films were popular in America, on a purely fiscal level they were that much more successful in markets outside America.

It was a sign of the success of the Bond series, and of the extent of 'Bondmania', that the mid-1960s witnessed a sudden upsurge in gimmicky secret agent movies which tried to copy the Bond formula. The film industry had initially proved slow to respond to the success of the Bond films and there had been relatively few other spy thrillers, and none in the style of the Bonds, between *Dr No* and *Goldfinger*. Indeed, the only film during this time which might be said to imitate the Bonds in any way was *Carry On Spying* (1964), an entry in the long-running British comedy series which spoofed the espionage film in general and the Bond movies in particular. However, it was in the wake of *Goldfinger*, and more particularly of *Thunderball*, that the floodgates opened and cinema screens were inundated with a glut of Bond spoofs and imitations. Hollywood made several attempts to get its own rival secret agent series off the ground, with mixed results. James Coburn starred as super-cool, super-stud, super-spy Derek Flint in the enjoyable *Our Man Flint* (1965) and its sequel *In Like Flint* (1967). The advertising for *Our Man Flint* emphasised Flint's Americanness, presenting him explicitly as an American alternative to James Bond.[24] Broccoli's former partner Irving Allen produced a series of four reasonably amusing spoofs adapted from Donald Hamilton's Matt Helm books, starring Dean Martin as the lazy, droopy-eyed, girl-chasing secret agent: *The Silencers* (1966), *Murderer's Row* (1966), *The Ambushers* (1967) and *The Wrecking Crew* (1969). In addition, there were no fewer than eight feature films derived from episodes of the television series *The Man From U.N.C.L.E.* which were released theatrically outside the United States.[25] In Britain, meanwhile, Bulldog Drummond was resurrected and updated to the 1960s by the producer–director team of Betty Box and Ralph Thomas. Richard Johnson, who had been one of those considered for the role of Bond, played Drummond in *Deadlier Than the Male* (1966) and *Some Girls Do* (1969). The mid-1960s were the high-point of the spy craze in British cinema: *The Liquidator* (1965), *Where the Spies Are* (1965), *The Quiller Memorandum* (1965), *Modesty Blaise* (1966), *Where the Bullets Fly* (1966), *Hammerhead* (1968) and *Assignment K* (1968) were among the many spy films made at this time. Harry Saltzman himself produced a trilogy based on the novels of Len Deighton – *The Ipcress File* (1965), *Funeral in Berlin* (1966) and *Billion Dollar Brain* (1967) – starring Michael Caine as Cockney spy Harry Palmer (the character had been nameless in the books) who was very different from James Bond. Along with *The Spy Who Came in from the Cold* (1965), based on the John le Carré novel, the Deighton trilogy represented a more realistic trend within the spy thriller which probed the seedier side and the moral uncertainties of espionage, eschewing the glamour and sophistication of the Bond movies for a shadowy world in which no one is to be trusted and treachery and deceit are everywhere.

British and American spy movies, however, were far outnumbered by the proliferation of derivative, low-budget European efforts to cash in on the success of the Bond franchise. From France, Spain and especially Italy there was a wave of 'spaghetti' spy movies which, like European westerns, became ever-more gimmicky and bizarre in their attempts to outdo the genuine article.[26] A coup of sorts was accomplished with *Operation Kid Brother* (1967), a dire spoof starring Sean Connery's brother Neil as the younger brother of agent 'zero zero', with a supporting cast familiar from the authentic Bonds (Bernard Lee, Lois Maxwell, Daniela Bianchi, Adolfo Celi, Anthony Dawson). So many Italian films used the '007' label that United Artists issued the following warning: 'Only James Bond, the character from the novels by Ian Fleming, can be agent 007 … Warning is given to all Italian companies which, exploiting the success achieved by agent 007, have distinguished the leading figures in their films by the same numerals.'[27]

The official Bond series, meanwhile, differentiated itself from its rivals and imitators by becoming more expansive and more expensive. The snowballing success of the films, particularly *Goldfinger* and *Thunderball*, was such that United Artists could provide Eon with much larger budgets than most other producers enjoyed. Thus, the negative cost of

Thunderball was $5.5 million, rising to $9.5 million for *You Only Live Twice*. The $6 million budget of *On Her Majesty's Secret Service* was as much as the negative costs of the first three films combined. Taken together, these films are an intriguing if ultimately slightly unsatisfying trilogy which collectively represent a trend towards longer and more episodic narratives.

The novels on which these three films were based form a trilogy in which Bond, like Bulldog Drummond before him, fights several 'rounds' against his arch enemy Ernst Stavro Blofeld. The order of the stories was different, however, in that *Thunderball* was published in 1961, *On Her Majesty's Secret Service* in 1963 and *You Only Live Twice* in 1964. (Another novel, *The Spy Who Loved Me*, had been published in 1962, though this was a minor story which did not really have anything to do with the 'Blofeld trilogy'.) The different order in which they were filmed, with *You Only Live Twice* preceding *On Her Majesty's Secret Service*, had significant implications for the continuity of the films.

Thunderball concerns a SPECTRE plot to blackmail Britain and America by hijacking two nuclear bombs and threatening to destroy a major city unless a huge ransom is paid. Although Blofeld is the mastermind behind the conspiracy, it is his second-in-command Emilio Largo who is in charge of the operation. As so often, Bond happens upon the conspiracy by chance after a run-in with Count Lippe at a private health farm, where he has been sent by M following his latest medical report. Lippe turns out to be a SPECTRE operative charged with posting the ransom demands to the prime minister and the American president; he tries to kill Bond but is himself liquidated by a SPECTRE assassin. As the worldwide hunt for the stolen bombs gets under way, Bond is assigned to the Bahamas, where he investigates Largo and seduces Largo's mistress, Domino, whose brother has been bribed by Largo to hijack the aircraft carrying the bombs. Bond is assisted by Felix Leiter and by the US Navy, who intercept the team of SPECTRE frogmen in the process of transporting one of the bombs. A fierce underwater battle ensues, in which Bond saves Leiter's life and is then saved himself by Domino, who shoots Largo with a harpoon-gun.

On Her Majesty's Secret Service begins a year later with Bond having been assigned to track down Blofeld, who it is revealed had escaped capture at the end of *Thunderball*. Bond has found no trace of his quarry and is tired of the assignment, which he considers routine police work, to such an extent that he is contemplating resignation. Driving through France he meets the Comtesse Teresa di Vincenzo, otherwise known as Tracy, a girl who seems hell-bent on killing herself, and with whom he makes love after bailing her out in a game of baccarat. The next day Bond is abducted by two gunmen who take him to see Marc-Ange Draco, head of the Union Corse (the Corsican Mafia), who turns out to be Tracy's father. In return for what Bond has done for his daughter, Draco provides him with information that Blofeld is in Switzerland. Blofeld is pressing his claim to the aristocratic title of Comte de Bleuville in order to buy himself a new identity. Bond, posing as Sir Hilary Bray from the College of Arms, travels to Blofeld's isolated mountain-top retreat in Switzerland, ostensibly an allergy clinic where the 'count' is engaged in medical research using twelve girls as guinea-pigs. When Bond's identity is discovered he is forced to make his escape on skis, and is rescued by Tracy who had been told by her father where to find him. Blofeld is planning biological warfare, using the twelve girls as unwitting germ carriers, but Bond and Draco's men return and destroy his headquarters before the plan can come to fruition. Bond, meanwhile, has fallen in love with Tracy, and the two of them marry, but driving away from the wedding their car is machine-gunned by Blofeld and Tracy is killed.

You Only Live Twice begins with Bond, grief-stricken after Tracy's death, on the verge of a nervous breakdown. Sir James Molony, neurologist to the British Secret Service, recommends that Bond should be given a near-impossible mission that will involve a supreme call upon his talents in order to jolt him out of his despair. M sends Bond on a semi-diplomatic mission to Japan to try to persuade the Japanese to make some intelligence secrets available to the British. Bond meets Tiger Tanaka, Head of the Japanese Secret Service, who agrees to make the material available if Bond in return will perform a 'favour' by assassin-ating one Dr Shatterhand, a foreigner who lives in a medieval castle on the southern island of Kyushu. Shatterhand has a 'garden of death', with the castle grounds full of poisonous plants and animals which attracts many Japanese to commit suicide there. When Bond sees a photograph of Shatterhand he recognises Blofeld, but keeps the in-formation to himself. Bond trains as a ninja and lives in a Japanese fishing village while preparing for the mission. One night Bond swims out to the castle and enters it, but is captured. He is savagely beaten, but finally kills Blofeld in vicious hand-to-hand combat before escaping from the castle on a helium balloon and falling into the sea. Back in

Britain Bond is presumed dead, and his obituary is published in *The Times*, but it turns out that he is alive, though suffering from amnesia, and is being cared for by Kissy Suzuki, a Japanese girl who is in love with him. One of Fleming's most accomplished novels, *You Only Live Twice* is really an allegorical story of Good and Evil told on an epic scale.[28]

Thunderball, of course, had been the subject of an on-going legal dispute between Fleming and Kevin McClory. The court case was resolved at the end of 1963. It was accepted that Fleming had acted in good faith in writing *Thunderball*, but that in future editions of the book an additional credit would be added to the effect that the novel was 'based on an original screen treatment by Kevin McClory, Jack Whittingham and Ian Fleming'. McClory disclaimed any further interest in the novel, but was awarded the screen rights to the story. McClory lost no time in announcing 'plans to make a film featuring the character of James Bond at an early date'.[29]

In the event, McClory did not produce his own rival Bond film, but instead came to an agreement with Broccoli and Saltzman that they would produce *Thunderball* together. Accordingly, McClory is credited as the producer of the film, with Broccoli and Saltzman as executive producers. To all intents and purposes, however, *Thunderball* fits into the Eon production ideology and bears the unmistakable stamp of the series' producers. McClory's own contribution would seem to have been minimal, though according to Steven Jay Rubin 'he had rewritten his script a dozen times and had covered every foot of the Bahamas, searching for possible locations'.[30] The screenplay for *Thunderball* was written by Richard Maibaum and John Hopkins, and Terence Young returned to direct.

Thunderball defined the direction which the Bond series was to take thereafter. 'Here Comes the Biggest Bond of All!', declared the posters. The official publicity discourse emphasised the size and scale, describing it as 'the most ambitious and lavishly-mounted of all the Bond films'.[31] It was the first of the series to be made in the widescreen process Panavision, and the first with a running time in excess of two hours. However, the scale and length of the film works against the narrative structure, so that rather than being a relatively tightly constructed thriller along the lines of the first three movies, *Thunderball* is an episodic narrative with a long middle section in which one action sequence follows another without significantly advancing the plot. Furthermore, much of the action takes place underwater, which in Young's view slowed down the tempo of the film. It was to be the last Bond that Young directed, and he did not rate it as highly as his other two:

> I really honestly don't know why I did *Thunderball*. I don't particularly like it. ... It was very successful, but to my mind all that underwater stuff was anti-James Bond, because it was slow motion. People swim slowly and you couldn't have them going very fast; we undercranked some of the shots and they looked ridiculous – the water was wobbling around so much it suddenly became stupid. On the whole, I would say it's not my favourite picture by a long way. It's a very efficient picture, but already the hardware was creeping into the stories.[32]

There are also more continuity errors in *Thunderball* than most Bond movies, particularly noticeable in the underwater battle when Bond's diving mask changes colour.

The narrative ideology of *Thunderball* exemplifies perfectly Bennett and Woollacott's notion of Bond as a hero of the NATO alliance. This is inscribed in the text itself, in so far as SPECTRE's threat is explicitly directed against NATO: Blofeld describes it as 'our NATO project', while Largo (Adolfo Celi) states that 'Our intention is to demand a ransom from the North Atlantic Treaty powers of two hundred and eighty million dollars, a hundred million pounds.' The nuclear bombs are stolen from a NATO training flight (albeit that it is a British Vulcan bomber which is hijacked) and the search for them is conducted jointly by the chief NATO allies, Britain and America. Like *Dr No* and *Goldfinger*, America is threatened – the target is Miami – and Bond works with his CIA colleague Felix Leiter. But, as in *Dr No*, the location (the Bahamas) is in the British Commonwealth, and Leiter functions as little more than a 'yes' man. Unlike *Dr No*, however, where the overtones of British colonialism were very apparent, *Thunderball* does not feature any of the apparatus of colonial government (other than a passing reference to the islands' governor, whose authority is required when Bond wants a power cut at Largo's residence, Palmyra). The climax symbolises Anglo-American collaboration: the frogmen who intercept the SPECTRE squad belong to the US Navy, while it is the Royal Navy which pursues and destroys Largo's yacht.

On another level, *Thunderball* offers an interesting commentary on the notion that one of the assumptions underlying the Bond narrative is

16. *Thunderball*: 'That's the first time I've tasted women – they're rather good.'
Bond sucks sea-egg spines out of Domino's (Claudine Auger) foot.

that Bond must seduce the heroine in order to 'reposition' her ideologically. In so far as the main girl, Domino, is Largo's mistress, then this
process can be seen to be enacted in Bond's pursuit and seduction of
her. However, it is made clear that Domino herself is aware of what is
happening. In one scene Bond and Domino meet at a secluded beach
and make love. Afterwards, Bond reveals to Domino that her brother
is dead, and that he has been killed by Largo, in order to enlist her help
in finding the bombs. 'So that is why you make love to me,' Domino
remarks. Therefore she realises that Bond has deliberately set out to
seduce her in order to further his mission, though, having thus been
repositioned, Domino becomes a willing accomplice, to the extent, as
in the novel, of killing Largo herself. A more direct challenge to Bond's
ability to convert women to his side through the sheer force of sexual
magnetism is provided by the character of SPECTRE assassin Fiona
Volpe (Luciana Paluzzi). Bond has sex with Fiona in the knowledge that
she is an enemy agent, but immediately afterwards finds himself captured
by her heavies. When taunted by Fiona about his vanity ('Vanity, Mr

Bond? Something you know so much about'), Bond reveals that he knew who she was all along and that sex was merely part of his job ('My dear girl, don't flatter yourself. What I did this evening was for king and country. You don't think it gave me any pleasure, do you?'). Fiona's reply challenges the very notion of ideological repositioning: 'But of course, I forgot your ego, Mr Bond. James Bond, who only has to make love to a woman and she starts to hear heavenly choirs singing. She repents and then immediately returns to the side of right and virtue. But not this one!' Fiona thus refuses to be repositioned – the first instance in the Bond films of a woman whose allegiance proves stronger than Bond's sex appeal. Bond shrugs and quips 'Well, you can't win them all' – thus showing that he too is aware of what is entailed in the seduction/ repositioning process. But if Fiona's refusal to be repositioned seems, on the face of it, a more progressive and independent character trait for a Bond girl, the film reasserts its sexist code by quickly killing her off. In the ideology of the films, any woman who resists Bond is problematic and needs to be disposed of: Fiona, pursuing the wounded Bond to the 'Kiss Kiss Club', is shot in the back by a bullet intended for him.

The form and style of *Thunderball* build on the innovations of the earlier films. The cinematography is bright and colourful, the set design extravagant and detailed. There are the usual topical references, such as the revelation that SPECTRE was paid a 'consultation fee' for the British Great Train Robbery. Snobbery and violence again go together. Thus, in the pre-title sequence, Bond realises that the 'widow' at a funeral he has just attended is really a man in disguise ('My dear Colonel Boivoit, I don't think you should have opened that car door by yourself') and there follows a furious fight in which Bond and his opponent manage to demolish most of the furnishings in the drawing room of an elegant French chateau. Opinions differ over this fight sequence. Pfeiffer and Lisa describe it as 'ferociously staged, and well choreographed and edited', whereas Barnes and Hearn consider it 'overcranked' (whatever that means).[33] Some of the action seems to have been slightly undercranked (meaning that the camera is slowed down so that when projected at normal speed the action is faster). Peter Hunt's editing makes the fight more stylised: several cuts do not match precisely on the action, so that the combatants change position or are suddenly back on their feet after being knocked down. Rather than being 'mistakes', this style of action editing should be seen as a stylistic innovation on Hunt's part that was to find its fullest expression in the only Bond film he directed, *On Her*

17. *Thunderball*: Bond combats Largo (Adolfo Celi) in a runaway hydrofoil.

Majesty's Secret Service. The jumpy, discontinuous, disorienting editing style accelerates the tempo of the fight sequence and accentuates the sensation of violence, particularly when accompanied by loud sound effects and strident music. This technique is also employed in the fight between Bond and Largo's men in the speeding hydrofoil at the end of the film, where the fast editing emphasises the impact of fists and bodies, the 'shock' of the slight discontinuities in the cutting making the violence seem more real than it actually is. While these two protracted punch-ups effectively 'bookend' the film, the most visually impressive action sequence in *Thunderball* is the underwater battle between SPECTRE and US Navy frogmen which has an aesthetic quality all of its own. Despite Young's reservations about underwater filming, the sequence manages to be fast and exciting, and is choreographed with the precision of an Esther Williams underwater ballet. With the combatants identified by the colour of their wetsuits (the US frogmen in bright orange, the SPECTRE team inevitably in black), the battle becomes a montage of writhing bodies, harpoons and oxygen bubbles, with the fast cutting overcoming the relative slowness of the underwater movement. It is also quite remarkably violent: some thirty men are killed within the space of seven minutes, and there are numerous shots of harpoons having pierced masks and bodies (though there is no blood – a reminder of the non-realistic, cartoonish style of violence in the Bond movies).

Thunderball was released in both Britain and America at the end of 1965. While the popular and trade press were as enthusiastic as ever, there were signs in Britain that some of the more middle-brow critics were beginning to tire of the formula aspects of the series, and their response was not as wholeheartedly enthusiastic as it had been for *Goldfinger*. The film critic of *The Times* wrote:

> *Thunderball* does show alarming signs that the series is going to seed. The plot, which after all is what keeps most of us watching between the set-pieces, has been thinned out at times almost to vanishing point, and the sexiness of the sexy scenes and the violence of the violent scenes correspondingly stepped up. But here this film's makers run into the law of diminishing returns: each time Bond ends up in bed with another glamorous young woman, or someone else is transfixed with a harpoon, strangled with a telephone cord, or drowned by having his airpipe cut, the effect becomes less surprising, titillating, or exciting.[34]

Nina Hibbin, oddly enough, thought that *Thunderball* 'isn't quite so vicious as the others'. 'It hasn't, thank goodness, any racialist overtones,' she wrote. 'Life and women are still as cheap as ever, but its deaths aren't so grisly, its sex is less in earnest, and its sadistic joke lines are more subdued.'[35]

Some American critics were rather more enthusiastic than their British counterparts. Bosley Crowther included it among his ten best films of the year. 'Here is the ultimate achievement of scenic excitements and melodramatic spoof in the series of James Bond movies,' he wrote. 'It combines a delightful hyperbole with the serio-comic twists of science-fiction, some amusing adumbrations on sex and always a cinematic satire of the contemporary culture of the hero comic strips.' Crowther considered, furthermore, that Bond had 'a much better sense of humor than he has shown in his previous films' and that accordingly *Thunderball* was 'the best of the lot'.[36]

It had originally been intended to make *On Her Majesty's Secret Service* the next film in the series, following the order of the books, and Saltzman had been scouting locations in Switzerland in the summer of

1965 while *Thunderball* was still in production.[37] In the event, production logistics worked against that and it was decided to make *You Only Live Twice* instead. In the meantime, however, a potential problem had emerged in the form of a rival Bond film which was in production at the same time as *You Only Live Twice*.

The screen rights for *Casino Royale*, which Fleming had sold to producer Gregory Ratoff in 1955, had been acquired from Ratoff's widow by Charles K. Feldman, a former showbusiness lawyer and talent agent who had become a producer with films including *The Seven Year Itch* (1954) and *What's New Pussycat?* (1965). Feldman had apparently intended to make a 'straight' film version of the novel, but having been unable to secure the services of Sean Connery, and sensibly realising that the public would be unlikely to accept anyone else in the role of Bond, he decided instead to make *Casino Royale* the spy spoof to end all spy spoofs. Backed by Columbia Pictures and filmed in conditions of great secrecy at no less than three British studios (Shepperton, Pinewood and Borehamwood), *Casino Royale* was far from being another cheapskate imitation in the manner of the Italian '007' movies. The range of talents involved was impressive. The stellar cast comprised Peter Sellers, Ursula Andress, David Niven, Orson Welles, Joanna Pettet and Woody Allen, supported by a host of international 'guest stars' including Deborah Kerr, William Holden, John Huston, Charles Boyer, George Raft and Jean-Paul Belmondo. Five directors were credited (John Huston, Kenneth Hughes, Val Guest, Robert Parrish and Joseph McGrath) and three writers (Wolf Mankowitz, John Law and Michael Sayers), and there were uncredited contributions from many others, including Billy Wilder, Ben Hecht and Joseph Heller, the author of *Catch 22*. However, the production was hampered by constant rewrites and by the erratic behaviour of Sellers, and ended up going months over schedule and way over budget. The final negative cost was $12 million, more than any of the official Bond films had cost. *Casino Royale* was finally released in April 1967, two months before *You Only Live Twice*.

'It's too much for one James Bond,' declared the posters. The main joke of *Casino Royale* – such as it is – is that nearly everyone in the film is known as 'James Bond 007'. The beginning of the film at least has the germ of an interesting idea. With the secret services of Britain, America, Russia and France having been decimated by an unknown enemy, their chiefs unite to persuade Sir James Bond (Niven), 'the greatest spy in history', to come out of retirement to meet the crisis.

'The true, one and only, original James Bond', is how M (Huston) describes him, and he is played by the actor who had been Fleming's preferred choice for the role. The film posits the notion that Bond is the embodiment of the noble spy of yesteryear, clean-living and appalled by the decadence of his modern-day namesake. 'In my day spying was an alternative to war,' he remarks, 'and the spy was a member of a select and immaculate priesthood, vocationally devoted, sublimely dis- interested – hardly a description of that sexual acrobat who leaves a trail of beautiful dead women like blown roses behind him.' This other James Bond – by implication Sean Connery's – was given the name and number after the real Bond retired because, as M tells him, 'it was essential that your legend be maintained – without a James Bond, oh- oh-seven, no-one would respect us'. Sir James is contemptuous of the new generation of 'joke-shop spies' with their gadgets and hidden weapons – another veiled reference to the official Bond series – and rejects the materialism of the modern world, 'including an Aston Martin complete with lethal accessories'. This Bond, like Fleming's, drives a vintage Bentley.

The rest of the film, however, does not develop this interesting premise. The actual plot of *Casino Royale* defies description; it is really more a series of separate incidents than a coherent narrative. Sir James does indeed come out of retirement when M is killed in a freak accident, and discovers a conspiracy by an organisation called SMERSH – a collective of beautiful women – to besmirch his reputation. Bond resists the advances of SMERSH agent Lady Mimi (Kerr), posing as M's widow, and avoids being killed by exploding flying ducks and a booby-trapped milkfloat. Taking over as head of the secret service, Bond decides to confuse the enemy by designating all remaining agents 'James Bond 007'. He seeks out Mata Bond (Pettet), his daughter by Mata Hari, and sends her on a mission to Berlin to infiltrate SMERSH headquarters. Meanwhile, cardsharp Evelyn Tremble is also recruited by fashion designer and occasional spy Vesper Lynd (Andress) to challenge Le Chiffre (Welles) at baccarat. The various plot strands come together at Casino Royale, where it turns out that the evil mastermind behind SMERSH, Dr Noah, is really none other than Bond's nephew Jimmy Bond (Allen), who suffers from an acute inferiority complex in the presence of his uncle, and whose plan is to remove all men over four feet six tall, thus making himself the tallest man alive in a world populated by beautiful women.

Critical judgements are irrelevant with a film like *Casino Royale*. Robert Murphy considers it one of those films 'which ought to be shipped to a desert island and screened continuously to those responsible for them'.[38] For Clive Hirschhorn, it is 'a self-indulgent mess – an inferior Monty Python sketch stretched way beyond its limits'.[39] There are, to be fair, one or two good visual jokes, mainly in the cinematography of Jack Hildyard, with additional photography by future director Nicolas Roeg. In Berlin, for example, the 'red side' literally is red, while Mata Bond's journey through SMERSH headquarters, all sloping walls and uneven staircases, is an amusing spoof of the visual style of German Expressionism. The psychedelic dream sequence in which Le Chiffre tortures Tremble with columns of bagpipe-playing Scots Guards is the most surreal moment in a surreal film. The climax – which somehow includes cowboys and Indians, Frankenstein's Monster, the French Foreign Legion and the Keystone Kops, not to mention George Raft accidentally shooting himself with a backward-firing gun – is a mad parody of generic clichés which anticipates the free-for-all ending of Mel Brooks's *Blazing Saddles*. But these are isolated moments in a film that is an overlong, confusing, disjointed, messy extravaganza, cinematic proof of the maxim that too many cooks spoil the broth. It is very far from being an authentic Bond movie, and as a spoof it is nowhere near as funny as the much less ambitious *Carry On Spying*. 'While Sean Connery and the original James Bond associates will not lose much sleep over this joshing of their goldmine pictures, *Casino Royale* may easily find a profitable audience among those who see in it the ultimate in hectic screen spy gimmickry,' predicted *Variety*.[40] And, astonishingly, it was quite successful at the box-office, with rentals of $17 million, suggesting either that audiences liked this kind of crazy comedy, or that it rode the wave of 'Bondmania' in anticipation of the real article.

You Only Live Twice opened with posters declaring 'Sean Connery IS James Bond', just so there could be no confusion with Feldman's spoof extravaganza. Some of the British critics had wondered how the filmmakers would adapt this particular novel given that it featured a grieving Bond on a personal vendetta against Blofeld; the solution was simply to discard Fleming's story entirely, keeping just the location and the character names. With Maibaum unavailable on this occasion, Roald Dahl was employed to write the screenplay. Dahl – a British writer of Norwegian parentage, famous for his children's stories – was a curious choice, as he had no previous experience as a screenwriter and admitted to having seen only one of the Bond films, 'the one with the crazy motorcar'. He had, however, known Ian Fleming, and was to be employed by Broccoli to adapt Fleming's *Chitty Chitty Bang Bang* (1968), presumably on the strength of his own children's fiction. In an amusing interview for *Playboy*, Dahl recounted how Broccoli and Saltzman had told him that 'You can come up with anything you like so far as the story goes', but that he was under strict instructions not to alter either the character of Bond or 'the girl formula':

> 'So you put in three girls. No more and no less. Girl number one is pro-Bond. She stays around roughly through the first reel of the picture. Then she is bumped off by the enemy, preferably in Bond's arms.'
>
> 'In bed or not in bed?' I asked.
>
> 'Wherever you like, so long as it's in good taste. Girl number two is anti-Bond. She works for the enemy and stays around throughout the middle third of the picture. She must capture Bond, and Bond must save himself by bowling her over with sheer sexual magnetism. This girl should also be bumped off, preferably in an original fashion.'
>
> 'There aren't many of those left,' I said.
>
> 'We'll find one,' they answered. 'Girl number three is violently pro-Bond. She occupies the final third of the picture and she must on no account be killed. Nor must she permit Bond to take any lecherous liberties with her until the very end of the story. We keep that for the fade-out.'[41]

While this was not strictly the formula followed in the previous four films, Dahl was to adhere to it very closely in his screenplay for *You Only Live Twice*.

Very little of the novel was retained for the film. The title, of course, refers to Bond's apparent death, but whereas in the novel he is assumed dead after the completion of his mission, the film begins with him apparently being shot dead in Hong Kong. Bond is buried at sea, but the shrouded body is collected by frogmen who take it on board a Royal Navy submarine where it turns out that Bond is not dead after all: his 'death' has been a ruse to put his enemies off the track. While Fleming's plot was discarded, however, Dahl's screenplay reworked numerous narrative elements from preceding Bond films. The basic premise is that SPECTRE is trying to start World War Three by intercepting both

American and Russian space capsules in orbit. The interference with the space programme, directed from a secret headquarters (SPECTRE's interceptor rocket which 'swallows' the capsules is launched from inside a volcano), reworks the science-fiction theme of *Dr No*. The policy of deliberately exacerbating Cold War tensions recalls *From Russia With Love*. When the American capsule is intercepted, the Americans naturally suspect the Russians: 'My government sees this as nothing less than a blatant attempt to gain complete and absolute control of space itself,' says the American representative at a secret summit meeting, warning that any future interference will be regarded as an 'act of war'. The British, for their part, are not convinced that the Russians are behind it all, though their suggestion that the interceptor vehicle may have come down somewhere in Japan is dismissed by the Americans. As in *Goldfinger*, it is implied that Red China is secretly behind the conspiracy; although not named, as in the earlier film, the official representatives seen negotiating with Blofeld, and who have provided SPECTRE with the space equipment, are of oriental appearance, and the dialogue makes clear that their government is paying SPECTRE to trigger a war between the Superpowers. 'In a matter of hours, when America and Russia have destroyed each other, we shall see a new power dominating the world,' Blofeld (Donald Pleasence) remarks towards the end of the film. In suggesting, however obliquely, that Red China was behind the conspiracy, *You Only Live Twice* can be placed within a trend in films of the late 1960s which identified China rather than the Soviet Union as the main Communist threat to the West. For example, the science-fiction film *Battle Beneath the Earth* (1967) had the Chinese using a giant laser to tunnel underneath America, while the spy thriller *The Most Dangerous Man in the World* (1969) had Gregory Peck as a scientist sent on a mission to China with a bomb implanted in his skull. The demonification of China at this time was almost certainly a reaction to the so-called 'Cultural Revolution' of Chairman Mao Tse-tung, as well as, in the longer term, a reflection of aggressive Chinese foreign policy in Tibet and on the Indian border.

Dahl's screenplay not only departs from the novel; it actually offers a complete ideological reordering of it. Thus, whereas the novel betrays some markedly anti-Japanese sentiments and seems morbidly concerned with the Japanese obsession with suicide, the film by contrast emphasises the modernity of Japan, especially its technological expertise. Made at a time when Japanese corporations were at the forefront of technological

18. *You Only Live Twice*: 'I've got you now.' 'Well, enjoy yourself.' Helga Brandt (Karin Dor) clearly has more than just killing Bond on her mind.

innovation, particularly in the manufacture of electronic consumer goods, the film foregrounds a plethora of ingenious gadgets, from miniature television monitors to rocket-guns. 'How's that for Japanese efficiency?' Tiger Tanaka (Tetsuro Tamba) asks after a car pursuing Bond has been lifted off the road by a helicopter equipped with a huge magnet and dropped into the sea. 'Just a drop in the ocean,' Bond replies, impressed.

As well as the very different representation of Japan, the film also mocks the ideology of national identity which characterised the novel. Fleming's original is an explicitly patriotic story in which Bond represents Britain on a symbolic level: in undertaking a special mission, Bond proves that Britain is not the second-rate power that the Japanese believe she has become and thus reaffirms her world power status. The screen Bond, however, parodies the values which the literary Bond stood for, mocking his notions of patriotism and duty. 'The things I do for England!', Bond remarks at one moment, but rather than being engaged on a deadly mission to prove that his country is still a great nation, he is at the time cutting away the dress straps of villainess Helga Brandt (Karin Dor). It is a highly ironic comment: the arduous task which Bond undertakes for his country is making love to a beautiful woman.[42] Indeed, the film seems to be implying that the patriotic code underlying the novels is redundant, an illustration of how the films modernised the image of Bond in a manner more suited to the irreverent popular attitudes of the 1960s.

For all these interesting points, however, *You Only Live Twice* is a poorly constructed, episodic, meandering film in which one incident follows on from another without much sense of narrative development. At times the film seems to resemble a travelogue of Japan – it is very attractively photographed by Freddie Young, the Oscar-winning cinematographer of David Lean's *Lawrence of Arabia* and *Doctor Zhivago* – in which the story has been written to suit the locations. Ken Adam's set design is as impressive as ever, particularly in the huge SPECTRE base, and the climactic battle in which Japanese ninjas attack it is exceptionally well staged by director Lewis Gilbert. And John Barry's score is one of his finest efforts, a sweeping melody with full orchestra which perfectly captures the atmosphere of the oriental locations. However, as Bosley Crowther observed, the film 'is evidently pegged to the notion that nothing succeeds like excess. And because it is shamelessly excessive, it is about a half-hour too long.'[43] As in *Thunderball*, gadgets and technology are foregrounded at the expense of characterisation. Bond's autogiro 'Little Nellie' is an amusing touch which makes for a visually impressive aerial dogfight, but, unlike the car chase in *Goldfinger*, there is little suspense as Bond mechanically uses its various weapons to destroy the four helicopters which attack it. Connery gives the impression of going through the motions, which in a sense he was, as he had already announced his intention of giving up playing James Bond.

19. *You Only Live Twice*: Bond comes face to face with his arch enemy
Ernst Stavro Blofeld (Donald Pleasence, with white cat).

When it became apparent that Connery was serious about not con-
tinuing, the producers faced the problem of finding another actor to fill
his shoes. A much-publicised worldwide search for a new James Bond
finally settled on George Lazenby, a thirty-year-old Australian model
whose acting experience was limited to carrying crates of chocolate in
television commercials as 'Big Fry'. Lazenby won the part because of
his tall, athletic physique and his ability to stage realistic fight sequences
– he broke stuntman Yuri Borienko's nose during his screen test – while
Peter Hunt, who was to direct *On Her Majesty's Secret Service*, was confident
that he could counter Lazenby's lack of experience in the cutting room.
Hunt had long harboured ambitions to direct. He was keen to put his
own stamp on the film, particularly in downplaying the gadgets that had
featured so prominently in the previous three. Upon the film's release,
Hunt elaborated his idea of the 'new' Bond:

> The James Bond films set the trend for tongue-in-cheek spy spoof
> movies and, as we know, they were fantastically successful. But

there have been so many imitators – not all of them very good by any means – that we were in danger of imitating our imitators.

We could have stuck to exactly the same formula, but we preferred to progress. Besides, *On Her Majesty's Secret Service* is better without the gadgetry and paraphernalia. It is a marvellous adventure story, with Bond surviving by his own physical skill and ingenuity, and at the same time it is a genuine love story, with 007 falling in love and marrying for the very first time. ...

I am more convinced than ever, now that the picture has been completed, that the choice of George Lazenby as Bond was right. With Lazenby, we revert to the concept of Bond implicit in Ian Fleming's books. The essence of Bond is a young man who has an inherent sexual assurance – which was the predominant thought in my mind during the search for the new 007.[44]

However, the relationship between Lazenby and the film-makers was strained and *Secret Service* was to be his one and only appearance as Bond.[45]

In all sorts of other respects, too, *On Her Majesty's Secret Service* is the odd-one-out in the Bond series. Like *From Russia With Love*, it does not fit into the overall direction the series was taking, illustrating once again that the evolution of the generic formula of the Bond films was not a linear process. Ever since *Goldfinger* the series had been moving further and further into the realms of technological fantasy, but *Secret Service* bucks this trend by downplaying the gadgets and hardware to focus on story and characterisation. Whereas *You Only Live Twice* had completely discarded Fleming's plot, *Secret Service* is the closest of all the films to its original source. 'As a novel I think it's the best of them and the one we had to do the least with to make a good motion picture script,' said Richard Maibaum, who received a solo credit for the screenplay. 'It was a solid novel, more of a serious effort than most of his books, which are really one hundred pages of brilliant exposition and then some good, swift action.'[46] Again, however, this fidelity to the original is out of step with the direction of the series as a whole in so far as the films which followed during the 1970s were to become completely removed from Fleming. The fidelity of *Secret Service* even extends to the downbeat ending, in which Bond marries Tracy only to see her killed by Blofeld (actually, in the film it is Blofeld's accomplice and mistress Irma Bunt who fires the fatal shots). This makes *Secret Service* unique as the only

Bond film with an unhappy ending, which probably accounts as much as any other factor for its relatively less successful performance at the box-office. As Molly Haskell said in *Village Voice*: 'If you like your Bonds with happy endings, don't go.'[47]

The film follows the novel very closely indeed. There are some changes, of course, but they actually improve the narrative structure of the film rather than detracting from it, as had been the case in the two previous efforts. Whereas in the novel Bond had contemplated resignation because he thought hunting Blofeld was routine police work, in the film he threatens resignation when M takes him off the case ('But sir, Blofeld's something of a must with me'). Bond's courtship of Tracy (Diana Rigg) is more protracted than in the book, conducted through a romantic montage sequence. There is a new sequence in Bern in which Bond breaks into the office of a Swiss lawyer to find proof of a link with Blofeld, who is claiming his aristocratic title ('Bleauchamp' rather than 'Bleuville'), during which Bond uses his only gadget of the film, a combined safecracker and photocopier that is lifted up to the office window by crane. Bond's masquerade as Sir Hilary Bray proceeds much as it does in the book, though his meeting with Blofeld (Telly Savalas) does not make strict narrative sense due to the films having been made in a different order (in the novel it is the first time Bond and Blofeld come face to face, but on screen they had already met in *You Only Live Twice*). Blofeld discovers Bond's masquerade and informs him of his plan, which is the distribution of 'virus omega', a sterility drug. Unless his demands are met, he will proceed with 'the systematic destruction of all species of cereals and livestock throughout the world'. Bond's escape from Piz Gloria is more protracted in the film, with a succession of chase and fight sequences. As in the book Bond is rescued by Tracy, but in the film she is captured by Blofeld and taken back to Piz Gloria, which provides a more logical motivation for Draco (Gabriele Ferzetti) to lead a helicopter attack on Blofeld's base.

The main problem confronting the film-makers was how to introduce the new James Bond to the audience. An idea that Bond would have plastic surgery to alter his appearance and thus disguise him from his enemies was quickly discarded.[48] Instead, *On Her Majesty's Secret Service* adopts a quite innovative narrative strategy for introducing Lazenby, through a series of textual references which playfully acknowledge the presence of the new lead actor while at the same time maintaining continuity with previous films. Thus, at the end of the pre-title sequence

20. *On Her Majesty's Secret Service*: George Lazenby made only one film as
James Bond, but it was one of the best; he won the role largely due to his
athleticism and ability to stage realistic fight sequences.

in which Bond has prevented Tracy from drowning herself and has had
a vicious fight with two heavies on the beach, only for Tracy to run off
and leave him holding her shoes, Lazenby remarks 'This never happened
to the other fellow' – a line which makes the audience complicit in the
changeover of leading man, therefore potentially disarming those who
would be unwilling to accept anyone other than Connery in the role.
But while the film itself acknowledges that Lazenby is *not* Connery, it
is at great pains to show that Lazenby *is* James Bond. Thus, when he
pinches Miss Moneypenny's bottom, her response is 'Same old James –
only more so!' The opening titles establish continuity within the Bond
series by including images of heroines and villains from the five previous
films; this continuity is later reinforced in a scene where Bond empties
his desk and takes out props from earlier films (Honey's knife-belt from
Dr No, Grant's watch-garotte from *From Russia With Love*, the miniature
underwater breather from *Thunderball*), while on the soundtrack there is
a brief reprise of the theme music from those films. Lazenby's intro-

duction, therefore, was carried out in a manner which maintained continuity with the earlier films, suggesting that while the actor may change, James Bond himself remains constant.

As for Lazenby himself, opinions are divided on his performance. Alexander Walker points out that casting a complete unknown did not help, but that in any case Lazenby was faced with an almost impossible act to follow: 'Another actor who had "paid his dues" in the same sort of adventure genre as the Bonds might – just *might* – have graduated to the prime role: but the public resented being asked to accept someone who had neither earned his right to be a contender, nor possessed enough distinctiveness of his own to dim the memory of his predecessor.'[49] But Lazenby's performance is actually quite assured for someone with no previous acting experience. Physically he looks the part, his on-screen movement combines athleticism with an arrogant swagger, and he manages to convey the snobbery of the character (for example in identifying Beluga caviar 'from the *north* Caspian'). Although his lack of experience is evident in some of the lengthy dialogue scenes, it also, paradoxically, has the effect of making his Bond a more believable character. Whereas Connery's Bond had become a heroic superman, Lazenby's Bond comes across as vulnerable and consequently more human. This is especially evident in the scene at the skating rink, where an exhausted Bond (he has just skied down a mountain and fought off two of Blofeld's men in a highly physical brawl) hides from his pursuers and appears to have reached the end of his tether – whereupon Tracy appears to rescue him.

For all the reservations about Lazenby, however, *On Her Majesty's Secret Service* is one of the richest and most interesting Bond films. It is, for example, the most explicitly patriotic film of the series. Whereas *You Only Live Twice* had mocked Bond's duty to his country ('The things I do for England!'), *Secret Service* emphatically reasserts the patriotic code of the literary Bond. Partly this is due to the special resonances of the title, and partly it is due to the film's fidelity to the book. Bond's patriotism and sense of duty are constantly asserted by references to 'Her Majesty's Secret Service', and just to reinforce the point a framed picture of Queen Elizabeth II is displayed prominently on the wall of his office. The setting of the College of Arms, and the role which heraldry plays in the story, further emphasises history and tradition.

The themes of patriotism and monarchy also operate on a visual level. The title sequence features silhouettes of women, one of whom bears the trident and shield of Britannia, against a Union Jack which is squeezed through an hour-glass. The figure of Britannia is a visual representation of the ideology of national identity constructed by the film (in which the Queen is symbolically at the head of things), while the motif of the hour-glass suggests that time is running out for Britain. Only Bond can save Britain, which he does by turning back the clock – literally, in so far as the titles show the silhouette of Bond hanging on to the hands of a giant clock which are turning anti-clockwise. (The image could also be read as illustrating Bond's desire to turn the clock back in order to save Tracy's life.) The picture of the Queen on Bond's office wall also serves a symbolic function in the narrative by figuring prominently in the *mise-en-scène* at two key moments. After he has dictated his resignation to Moneypenny, there is a shot of Bond's face reflected in the glass of the picture as he raises a hip flask and says, 'Sorry, ma'am', before taking a swig. Later, when Bond is telephoning Draco to arrange the unsanctioned raid on Blofeld's headquarters, he turns his head and looks over his shoulder at the picture. At moments which question Bond's relationship to the secret service, therefore, the image of monarchy reminds him of his duty.

On Her Majesty's Secret Service is unique in that for the first and only time in the series Bond experiences a conflict of interests between love and duty. The relationship between Bond and the girl is mapped on to the relationship between Bond and his country. Bond's love affair with Tracy performs an ideological role very different from his sexual conquests in any of the other films: rather than the girl being repositioned, it is Bond who finds his allegiance being called into question. At first, Bond sees his courtship of Tracy as a way of furthering his mission in that he wants to extract information from her father concerning Blofeld's whereabouts. This is information which Draco is prepared to give only on a personal basis ('I wouldn't tell Her Majesty's Secret Service, but I might tell my future son-in-law'). But when Bond realises that he has fallen in love with Tracy, and proposes to her, love and duty no longer go together. Unlike in the novel, where Bond intends to stay in the secret service, in the film he accepts, apparently quite willingly, that he will have to 'find something else to do'. When Tracy is captured by Blofeld, Bond's personal interests conflict with his job. M informs him that the United Nations has agreed to meet Blofeld's demands – an amnesty for all past crimes and official recognition of his title 'when he retires into private life' – and that no action is to be taken. M refuses to sanction a rescue mission for Tracy

21. *On Her Majesty's Secret Service*: 'We have all the time in the world.' Bond
marries Tracy (Diana Rigg), but the honeymoon will be cut tragically short.

despite Bond's protests ('This department is not concerned with your
private problems'). Bond therefore turns to Draco, head of a criminal
organisation, to mount the raid on Piz Gloria. When Bond marries Tracy,
and thus accepts a new life outside the secret service, narrative logic
demands that Tracy will have to be killed in order that Bond can return
to the service for the next film.

On Her Majesty's Secret Service therefore provides a rather more important role for the girl than any of the other films. Although introduced in a typically voyeuristic manner – Bond observes her through a telescopic lens as she walks along a beach – Tracy is no mere 'object of to-be-looked-at-ness'; she performs an active role in the narrative, rescuing Bond when he is cornered at the skating rink, and actually causing Bond to rethink his profession. Tracy's greater narrative importance necessitated a break from tradition for the film-makers in selecting an established actress to play her, which would also help to counterbalance the inexperience of Lazenby. The casting of Diana Rigg was propitious in that, like Honor Blackman before her, she was an established action heroine, having succeeded Blackman as John Steed's female partner in *The Avengers*. Rigg's popular image from her role as Emma Peel was that of a sophisticated, intelligent young woman who was capable of looking after herself in a fight – an image which *Secret Service* refers to when she fights and kills Grunther (Yuri Borienko) at the film's climax. While the role of Tracy challenged the traditional role assigned to the girl in the Bond films, the more usual characterisation of Bond girls as passive playthings is also represented by the 'patients' at Blofeld's 'clinic'; inevitably, Bond seduces two of them during his masquerade as Sir Hilary Bray.

It is not only in its narrative ideologies that *On Her Majesty's Secret Service* is so unique within the Bond series. It is the most attractively photographed of the films, with more attention seeming to have been given to visual composition than usual; this is particularly evident in the pre-title sequence on a Portuguese beach at sunrise and in the panoramic Swiss snowscapes where lines of skiers suddenly appear silhouetted against the white mountains in a manner that recalls Anthony Mann's *The Heroes of Telemark* (*Secret Service* was the only Bond assignment for cinematographer Michael Reed). The dramatic use of landscape is matched by the soaring heights of John Barry's score, which ranges from an insistent, minimal, instrumental title track to a gentle romantic ballad, 'We Have All The Time In The World', movingly performed by Louis Armstrong. The use of this song, which complements the romantic montage illustrating Bond's courtship of Tracy, is comparable to the use of 'Raindrops Keep Falling On My Head' in the same year's *Butch Cassidy and the Sundance Kid* (Hal David wrote the lyrics for both). The editing style of the film is also noticeably different. As Alexander Walker observes:

Above all, the direction of Peter Hunt – an editor on earlier Bond films – brought a cutting-room crispness to every set-up, though even he was not able to truncate a film that feels as if it is ending four times before it actually does so. John Glen, not only this film's editor, but its second-unit director (and later a Bond director in his own right) gave *O.H.M.S.S.* a completely different feeling from any earlier Bonds. Using the discontinuity of a cartoon strip (what would soon be called a 'video clip'), he made fist-fights look like the splitting of the atom, had blows boomeranging in from off-screen and bodies flying apart as if released from a spring-clip.[50]

The editing style of *Secret Service* marks the fullest extent of the techniques which Hunt had been developing in the earlier films. The fight sequences are stylised, kinetic and extremely physical, employing jump cuts and other disorienting devices to jar the spectator, and loud, exaggerated sound effects to accentuate the sensation of violence. And the chases, particularly the protracted ski–car–ski sequence in which Bond escapes from Blofeld's men, are most impressively staged and filmed. Unlike some of the later films, where a chase would be introduced gratuitously, often for comic effect, in *Secret Service* they serve a narrative purpose – the urgency of Bond's escape so that he can contact London and inform them of Blofeld's plan – and Bond has to rely on his strength and wits rather than gadgets.

How did the critics react to the 'different' James Bond film? Although it is generally assumed that *On Her Majesty's Secret Service* was not as well received as the Connery films had been, and that Lazenby was universally panned for his performance, in fact this was not the case. Reactions to the film and to Lazenby himself were mixed, though no more so than they had been for Connery and *Dr No*. Derek Malcolm considered that 'it's quite a jolly frolic in the familiar money-spinning fashion – not a penny spared on production values, smart direction from Peter Hunt, and a shrewd eye kept throughout on the well-worn mixture of sex, violence, thrills and laughs'. But he was less charitable towards Lazenby, whom he thought 'looks like a Willerby Brothers clothes peg and acts as if he's just come out of Burtons short on credit'.[51] David Austen in *Films and Filming*, by contrast, was less harsh on Lazenby – 'It's true that he doesn't have quite the right voice, nor does he parade the trappings of pseudo-sophistication with quite the same ease as his predecessor, but he does tackle the unenviable task with commendable vigour and apparent good humour' – and more critical of the film which, despite the impressive stunts and pyrotechnics, was showing signs that the formula was becoming rather worn:

> Peter Hunt directs the whole thing with an appropriately simplified comic-strip style, the wildly exaggerated fight sound effects being the film's equivalent for POW, ZOCK and ARGHHH. And there's been no penny-pinching on the stunt work. The set pieces – a ski chase gun-battle, a stock car race on ice, an avalanche, a fight on a runaway bobsled, and the explosive climax on a mountaintop – are all crowded into the second half; but while being agreeably spectacular they generate little real tension, since, like Fleming's books, all this action follows so predictable a pattern. But now, as with *Carry On* films, you're bound to know whether you like these things or not; if you do, you'll be pleased to learn that the end credits promise, yet again, that Bond will return.[52]

Austen's reference to the 'Carry On' films, scorned by the critical establishment, is a sure sign of his estimation of the place of the Bond movies in film culture.

One significant difference in the reception from the earlier films, however, was that the trade press, which hitherto had been enthusiastic about the series, was rather less keen on the new Bond. 'The appearance of a new Bond coincides, maladroitly, with a story less gloriously fantastic than its predecessors,' opined Marjorie Bilbow of *Today's Cinema*. 'Without the way-out weapons and weirdly designed vehicles the plot is exposed as a run-of-the-mill adventure in which any adequately athletic performer could take the leading role. This critic, for one, did not approve of the decision to do away with the gadgets and gimmicks.' While Bilbow thought that 'George Lazenby makes a tough, hard-hitting hero with plenty of man appeal', she added that he 'gives no hint of the tiger beneath the man about town skin that was the key to Bond Mark I's fascination for the female section of the audience'. For all her reservations, however, she still observed that 'the action of the last hour or so is superlatively exciting and as a result the film should do excellent business'.[53]

The American critics were also divided about Lazenby, though most of them were impressed by the production values and visual excitement of the film. Pauline Kael found the new Bond 'quite a dull fellow' and added that 'the script isn't much either', but thought that Hunt was 'a wizard at action sequences, particularly an ethereal ski chase that you know is a classic while you're goggling at it, and a mean, fast bobsled that is shot and edited like nothing I've ever seen before'. 'I know that on one level it's not worth doing,' she added, 'but it sure has been done brilliantly.'[54] Kael, therefore, was one of those critics who found the Bond movies essentially trivial, but nevertheless fun. Of the trade papers, *Variety* opined that the film-makers 'have packed so much break-neck physical excitement and stunning visual attractions into *On Her Majesty's Secret Service* that the initial disappointment of George Lazenby replacing Sean Connery as James Bond is almost forgotten by the film's climax'.[55] The *Hollywood Reporter* was the most fulsome in its praise for the new Bond, declaring that the series was 'revitalized' by the presence of Lazenby, who 'brings new youth and humor to a role which had begun to look and act tired'.[56]

However, the North American rentals of *On Her Majesty's Secret Service* were a disappointing $9.1 million, substantially less than the previous three films. It may have been that audiences were put off by the unhappy ending, or simply that they did not want to see anyone other than Sean Connery as James Bond. Some commentators, however, advanced deeper sociological reasons for the apparent decline in Bond's popularity. 'Bondmania', it seemed, had run its course. An article by one such critic in the *New York Times* in February 1970 suggested that the Bond films had suddenly become relics of the past. What had seemed fresh and exciting earlier in the 1960s had become outmoded by the end of the decade: the Bond films had failed to keep pace with the great social and cultural upheavals of the late 1960s, particularly the emergence of the various counter-cultures to whom James Bond now seemed a square and old-fashioned figure. The writer A. Marks admitted to being 'disturbed by the lavish violence which had previously amused so much', especially in the aftermath of the civil disorders of 1968–69, the assassinations of Martin Luther King and Robert Kennedy, and 'the useless obscenity of death in Vietnam'. The spectre of the Vietnam War blurred straightforward distinctions between good guys and bad guys. Complaining that Bond was 'intellectually fraudulent', the writer implied a parallel between Bond and the American military on the one hand, and SPECTRE and the Vietcong on the other:

> Spectre – that diabolical world organization of sin and corruption
> – seems less corrupt than Bond himself, not to mention his heart-

less superiors who license 007 to kill. Meanwhile, the enemy is an enigma. We aren't told why we must hate the enemy, but only that we must at all costs HATE the enemy. But it doesn't work. We are enlightened young men and women who have learned the importance of *knowing* the enemy – and we have learned to know him well in real life. In fact, we are downright intellectual about the enemy. And we aren't buying any hate propaganda; so the evil that lurks behind the guillotine shadows of childhood doesn't frighten the activist-oriented kids of the seventies. We don't get our jollies from sitting in dark theaters and hating prescribed enemies.[57]

But this polemic against the Bond movies provides a less than convincing argument for the relative failure of *Secret Service*. In the first place, straightforward escapist movies with 'prescribed enemies' continued to be popular: *Where Eagles Dare* (1969), a *Boy's Own*-style comic-book war adventure which owed much to the Bond movies in its kinetic action sequences and foregrounding of stunts and pyrotechnics, was one of the biggest box-office winners of the year. And, furthermore, the argument that the violence of the Bond movies was too disturbing for audiences who had witnessed the real thing is very unconvincing given the popularity in the late 1960s of American films such as *Bonnie and Clyde* (1967), *The Dirty Dozen* (1967) and *The Wild Bunch* (1969), all of which surpassed the Bonds in their graphic depiction of violence.

And, in fairness, it has to be said that *On Her Majesty's Secret Service* was not the outright failure that has generally been assumed. While its worldwide rentals of $24 million were just over half those of *You Only Live Twice*, this was a disappointment only in comparison to the other Bond movies, for it was still among the most successful films of the year. Its perceived failure, however, along with the fact that Lazenby made no more Bond movies, has led to the film being unfairly neglected and under-valued. For obvious reasons the producers were not interested in promoting Lazenby, and the film itself came to be treated as something of a poor relation to the rest of the series. Unlike the other films, which were continually and successfully reissued, *Secret Service* was not shown very frequently in revival houses. When it was first shown on American television in 1976 it was screened in a truncated version in two parts as a filler before the soap opera *Rich Man, Poor Man*. And when the Bond films were successfully released on home video, the

Sean Connery and Roger Moore films were privileged whereas a full version of *Secret Service* was only belatedly made available. In retrospect, however, the reputation of *Secret Service* has grown, particularly within the Bond fan culture, to the extent that many aficionados – the present writer included – number it among their favourite Bond films.[58]

4

Bond in Transition: *Diamonds Are Forever, Live and Let Die, The Man With the Golden Gun*

The perceived failure of *On Her Majesty's Secret Service* was to have highly significant consequences for the future direction of the Bond series. The films which followed during the 1970s were to be very different in style. The three Bond movies of the early 1970s – *Diamonds Are Forever* (dir. Guy Hamilton, 1971), *Live and Let Die* (dir. Guy Hamilton, 1973) and *The Man With the Golden Gun* (dir. Guy Hamilton, 1974) – mark a transitional phase in the development of the series. Most obviously, they facilitated the transition from one star to another: Sean Connery, who was lured back to the series for *Diamonds Are Forever*, then gave way to Roger Moore for *Live and Let Die*. Unlike Lazenby, Moore proved to be a successful replacement, to such an extent, indeed, that he carried the series on throughout the 1970s and into the mid-1980s, making a total of seven Bond films. On another level, the films of the early 1970s are transitional in that they offered various strategies by which the Bond series attempted to reinvent itself and keep apace of changing popular tastes at a time when many critics were saying loudly that in style and outlook it belonged to the 1960s. Taken together, these films mark a decisive shift away from the more character-driven and less gadget-oriented story of *On Her Majesty's Secret Service*, turning once again in the direction of gimmicky plot devices, technological fantasy and comedy. Finally, they also mark the point at which the series abandoned any fidelity to the Ian Fleming originals, opting instead for screen stories which used only Fleming's titles and character names.

The change from one star to another inevitably affected the style of the Bond films, particularly at the level of performance. Roger Moore was an established television star from the adventure series *The Saint* and *The Persuaders!*, in both of which his persona had been that of the charming, debonair, international playboy. Moore lacked Connery's brawn and physicality, and did not have the same grace of movement on screen, but what he brought to the role was greater polish and sophistication. Moore was two years older than Connery, but looked younger. 'Roger Moore is 45. I predict he could now be playing James Bond into his fifties,' one critic remarked, presciently, after the actor's series debut.[1] Alexander Walker provides a useful, if somewhat impressionistic, comparison of Connery and Moore:

> The contrast between the two stars was piquant – it was the substitution of the head prefect for the school bully. Moore looked such an essentially *nice* lad; Connery had brought with him a hint of macho relish. The retiring Bond had learnt to wear his wardrobe as if he had grown into it; the new man at first carried *his* with the slight self-consciousness of someone in uniform. Connery was a hairy man, though the growth was mainly on his chest; Moore was a smooth man, and his growth appeared at first glance to be mainly on his scalp. Both men, in their different ways, were virile specimens – and patriots. Roger would have gone all out to win the race for the school; so would Sean, but probably by nobbling his competitor in the locker room.[2]

The main difference, however, was that Moore's forte was light comedy and that his style of performance was more geared towards innuendo and self-mockery than Connery's had been. Both could deliver the Bond one-liners with aplomb, but whereas Connery's had a sardonic wit, Moore's humour was broader and delivered with an even greater wink at the audience. Whereas Connery's one-liners had been used to mitigate violent situations by making a joke about them – such as the occasion in *Thunderball* where he shoots a villain with a spear-gun (what in reality would be a very nasty death) and remarks 'I think he got the point' – Moore's one-liners were delivered in such a way as to suggest that the violence was all a joke to begin with. Thus, in *Live and Let Die*, he disposes of the villain Tee-Hee, who has a metal claw for his right arm, by throwing him out of a moving train in such a way that the arm itself is left behind. 'Just being disarming, darling,' Moore tells his female companion, effectively 'disarming' the violence by suggesting that it is all unreal anyway.

It is fashionable to regard Moore as a 'bad' actor: the former Bryl-creem boy who became the king of eyebrow-acting. This is a tendency reinforced by his own self-mocking attitude towards his profession, though in fact, as with stars such as Cary Grant, his performance style is such that the technique is completely hidden. Official publicity suggested that Moore was closer to Fleming's conception of Bond than Connery had been – though as the same claim was also made for both George Lazenby and Timothy Dalton it should perhaps not be taken too seriously. Certainly there are some traits of Moore's Bond – his preference for safari suits and flared trousers, the Cuban cigars which he smokes in his first two films – which reflect the actor rather than the role. His interpretation of Bond was not to the taste of all Bond fans, or even all members of the production team, including Richard Maibaum:

> In a strange way, some people like Roger better than Sean. I certainly don't. I think Roger does very well. He's suave, witty, and so forth, but as far as I'm concerned, he has a dimension of disbelief. He does what I consider unforgivable: he spoofs himself and he spoofs the part. When you start doing that, the audience stops laughing. *Just play the part.*
>
> The most important thing in the Bond pictures is a pretence of seriousness. If your leading man doesn't really appear to believe in what he is doing as either an actor or a character, that will count against the performance's effectiveness.[3]

Maibaum also complained that because Moore did not look as tough as Connery, the scripts had to be tailored accordingly to toughen up his image: 'We knew Roger was not a rough, tough guy like Sean. So, we deliberately gave him things to do that would make him tougher.'

For all that it was not to everyone's liking, however, Moore's performance style was perfectly in tune with the direction the series was taking at the time. Although some commentators have criticised the Moore films for overplaying the humour, this is to ignore a trend which was already becoming apparent before he joined the series. It was not the arrival of Moore which turned the Bond films in the direction of comedy, but rather the perceived failure of *On Her Majesty's Secret Service*, which had played the action straight and featured a serious love interest. Following *OHMSS*, and until the return to a slightly more serious style in the 1980s, the Bond series became ever more tongue-in-cheek, with elaborate stunts and set pieces usually being concluded with a joke. Action sequences were often played for laughs: all the three films under consideration in this chapter featured chases which invariably ended up with pursuing police cars being involved in multiple pile-ups. Gimmicks and visual jokes became more pronounced, but at the expense of narrative logic and characterisation. The Bond films of the 1970s became more outlandish: visual spectacle, fantastic technology, and increasingly bizarre narrative situations were the order of the day.

The direction which the films took also resulted in them moving further away from Ian Fleming. When *Diamonds Are Forever* was under development in 1970, one United Artists executive is reported to have remarked that 'for its annual one hundred thousand dollar fee, the Fleming estate was giving us a few nice characters, ten per cent of a usable plot and a great Fleming title'.[4] The trend towards screenplays which bore little or no resemblance to the Fleming originals might be seen, again, as a reaction to the lukewarm reception of *On Her Majesty's Secret Service*, which had been the closest of all the films to its literary source. Some commentators lamented that the essence of Fleming's Bond had now been lost. George Melly regretted that 'all links with Fleming's cunning exploitation of male fantasy in the fifties and sixties, the realism of technical detail masking the absurd omnipotence of the central figure, have long gone', though he qualified it in so far as 'on the credit side it means that Fleming's dubious morality – the sex, sadism and snobbery as Paul Johnson once categorised it – have vanished too, and good riddance'.[5] It was not only the social context that had changed since the 1950s, moreover, but also that the films' insistence upon technological fantasy meant that they inevitably left Fleming further behind. 'A few Fleming fans will no doubt regret that the films now have to be played strictly for the gags and special effects: but at this distance from the books it is the least incongruous approach,' remarked Christopher Hudson in the *Spectator*.[6]

In other respects, too, the early 1970s was a key transitional moment for the Bond series. The wave of 'Bondmania' had passed; Bond was no longer the cultural phenomenon of the day, but rather, as Bennett and Woollacott have argued, an 'institutionalised ritual'. The Bond films continued to be popular, but the image and character of Bond no longer permeated into the wider realms of popular culture as it had done during the 1960s. Sales of the novels decreased from their mid-1960s peak, and, whereas at the height of 'Bondmania' all the novels had sold well, in the 1970s it was more usually the case that the appearance of a new film would stimulate sales of that particular title (despite the fact that the films themselves now bore so little relation to the originals). Bennett and Woollacott suggest, furthermore, that 'the ideological and cultural concerns to which the figure of Bond resonated had become somewhat less vital, assessed in relation to the changing configuration of British popular culture as a whole'.[7] During the 1960s the Bond films had been one of the elements in the renaissance of British popular culture, but by the 1970s they represented almost the last remnant of that cultural renaissance. The Beatles had broken up, 'Swinging London' had ceased to swing, and there was a sense of what Christopher Booker described as an 'unwelcome explosion into reality'.[8]

For the British film industry, this explosion into reality took the form of facing up to the withdrawal of American finance, following Holly-wood's economic crisis at the end of the 1960s. After profligate expenditure on costly extravaganzas which failed to recoup their costs – including not only British-made films such as *Half A Sixpence*, *Goodbye Mr Chips*, *Battle of Britain* and *Cromwell*, but also Hollywood's own self-made disasters like *Doctor Dolittle*, *Star!*, *Hello Dolly* and *Darling Lili* – there was a period of fiscal retrenchment. The Bond series, indeed, was the only major exception, as United Artists continued to provide financial backing for Eon Productions at a time when it, along with the other Hollywood majors, was curtailing its operations in Britain. For British cinema, as for British society as a whole, the 1970s is often regarded as a moribund period in which there was precious little in the way of either cultural innovation or economic success. Whereas the 1960s had given rise to a new, vibrant, youth-oriented film culture which had produced films which succeeded in both artistic and commercial terms, the 1970s has generally been characterised as a time of stagnation. Alexander Walker wrote that British cinema 'looked like the country itself: it had a residual energy, but in the main was feeling dull, drained, debilitated, infected by a run-down feeling becoming characteristic of British life'.[9] There were precious few of the international successes on the scale of *Tom Jones*, *Alfie* or *Darling* which had brought such prestige to British cinema in the 1960s. In contrast, the most prolific British movies of the early 1970s were low-budget, low-brow comedies made solely for the domestic market: adaptations of television sitcoms, the ailing 'Carry On' series, and blue sex comedies.

The Bond films, which a decade earlier had symbolised the youthful, hedonistic, liberated spirit of the 'swinging sixties', now came to be regarded as a comfortingly old-fashioned ritual. Some critics, indeed, believed that the ideology of the Bond films remained rooted in the 1960s. 'As long as they keep on making James Bond films, the 1960s will never die,' John Russell Taylor remarked in 1973.[10] Vincent Canby thought that *Diamonds Are Forever* was 'a nostalgic journey down memory lane' which 'recalls the moods and manners of the sixties (which, being over, now seem safely comprehensible)'.[11] That such opinions should be expressed about both Moore's and Connery's films (Taylor's comment was made in his review of *Live and Let Die*) is significant in that it suggests the differences between the two stars were less important than the overall style of the films.

And what of the place of the Bond movies in film culture? Here, too, there is evidence of significant changes in the ways in which the Bond movies were perceived, and how they perceived themselves in relation to the rest of popular cinema. In the first place, the hostility with which some critics had greeted the early Bond films had entirely disappeared. Critical opprobrium was now reserved for films like Sam Peckinpah's *Straw Dogs* (1970) and Stanley Kubrick's *A Clockwork Orange* (1971), in comparison to which the violence of the Bond movies seemed very tame and unrealistic indeed.[12] A decade earlier some critics had complained about the sex and violence of the early Bond movies, but now they were widely regarded as family entertainment. As George Melly said of *Live and Let Die*: 'With the school hols in the offing, at least 121 minutes can be filled without any effort at all.'[13]

The Bond series found itself having to negotiate the changing nature of popular cinema in the early 1970s. Bennett and Woollacott suggest that the Bond series 'reorganised its cultural associations by referring it to more influential genres within the contemporary cinema'.[14] From Hollywood, for example, there came a new wave of tough law-and-order thrillers with violent heroes who operated both within and outside the law. Foremost among these was Clint Eastwood's rogue cop Harry Callaghan in *Dirty Harry* (1971) and its sequels *Magnum Force* (1973) and *The Enforcer* (1976); the vigilante alternative was personified by Charles

Bronson in *Death Wish* (1974). Films such as these typically featured lone heroes engaged in an urban war against low-life villains, and their content was extremely violent – far more so than the Bond movies. While the Bond series, made for the mainstream family audience, did not set out to compete directly with 'R'-rated (in Britain 'X'-certificate) films like *Dirty Harry* and *Death Wish*, it did have to take the new-style action thrillers into account. Bennett and Woollacott identify a 'law and order' inflection in *Diamonds Are Forever* and *Live and Let Die*: in both films Bond works in America alongside the CIA. (In reality the CIA was forbidden by law from operating inside the United States, though here the Bond films unwittingly reflected Nixon's improper domestic use of the Agency.) A more direct influence can be identified at the climax of *Live and Let Die* when Bond discards his usual Walther PPK in favour of a Smith and Wesson .44 Magnum, a massive long-barrelled handgun which was the weapon of choice of Eastwood's 'Dirty Harry'. It might be argued that this was one of the ways in which the films attempted to 'toughen up' Roger Moore's image through the gun's association with male machismo.

Although a relatively minor point in itself, the fact that Bond on one occasion adopted the weapon associated with another screen hero was indicative of how the Bond series had been overtaken by other trends in popular cinema. Whereas in the 1960s the Bond films had started trends – exemplified by the vogue for gimmicky spy movies in the middle of the decade – by the 1970s they seemed to be following trends which had been started elsewhere. So, for example, *Live and Let Die* may be seen as an attempt to cash in on the so-called 'blaxploitation' cycle of the early 1970s, while *The Man With the Golden Gun* features a martial-arts sequence which recalls the kung-fu craze of the time. As one critic remarked: 'It was only a matter of time before kung fu caught up with James Bond. And vice versa.'[15]

In the case of *Diamonds Are Forever*, the inspiration which the film-makers sought came not so much from other areas of popular cinema as from the successful pattern established by earlier films in the Bond series itself. Fleming's fourth novel had featured Bond investigating a case of diamond smuggling in which he followed the pipeline to America, travelling from New York to Las Vegas and coming up against a group of American gangsters known as the Spangled Mob. The film of *Diamonds Are Forever*, however, owes more to *Goldfinger* than it does to the original novel. *Goldfinger* was the film which had firmly established the Bond formula and which had marked the series' breakthrough in the

American market. *Goldfinger*'s Guy Hamilton returned to the director's chair, while the locations for *Diamonds Are Forever* were again predominantly American. The desire to rework the earlier film even extended as far as bringing back the same villain. Maibaum said that in his first treatment for *Diamonds Are Forever*, Bond was going to come up against Goldfinger's twin brother, a shipping magnate who is blackmailing the world with a giant laser mounted on a supertanker. 'This fellow is supposed to say to Bond at one point, "Oh, my brother Auric – mother always said he was a bit retarded." We were going to cast Gert Frobe again, but it didn't work out.'[16] The diamond-smuggling plot of the original novel was to be maintained in so far as Maibaum had discovered that the first laser beam was generated through a diamond, and Goldfinger would be stockpiling them to build his super-laser. But Maibaum's first treatment was rejected and the producers brought in Tom Mankiewicz, son of screenwriter Joseph L. Mankiewicz and nephew of Herman Mankiewicz (Orson Welles's co-writer on *Citizen Kane*) to revise it. The shooting script of *Diamonds Are Forever* bears Mankiewicz's name only, though on the film's titles the screenplay is credited jointly to Maibaum and Mankiewicz.[17] Goldfinger is gone, and Bond's enemy is once again Blofeld. The plot device of stockpiling diamonds to manufacture a powerful laser is maintained, but instead of it being mounted on a supertanker it is launched into space (the idea of a supertanker was to return in *The Spy Who Loved Me*). Blofeld has taken over the identity of a reclusive billionaire whom no one has seen for three years – widely said to have been based on Howard Hughes – and is using his business and industrial empire for cover. Blofeld has also undergone plastic surgery, and has several doubles of himself in order to throw Bond off the scent – thus reworking an idea that Maibaum had considered using for *On Her Majesty's Secret Service* to explain Bond's new appearance.

Bond might have had another new appearance in *Diamonds Are Forever*, for with George Lazenby out of the picture the producers had been obliged to look again for another leading man. American actor John Gavin, whose best-known film roles had been as Janet Leigh's boyfriend in Hitchcock's *Psycho* and as the young Julius Caesar in Stanley Kubrick's *Spartacus*, was actually signed to a holding contract. But United Artists were worried about introducing a new leading man after the disappointment of *OHMSS*, and decided that Connery must be brought back, whatever the cost. United Artists president David Picker personally

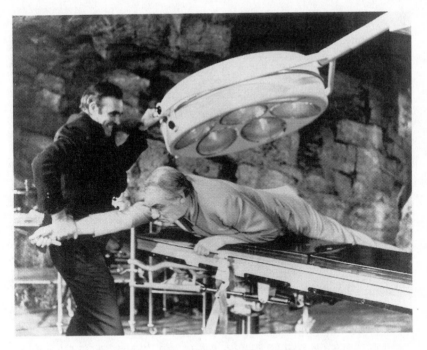

22. *Diamonds Are Forever*: Sean Connery back in action – though little does Bond know that this Blofeld (Charles Gray) is a double.

negotiated the one-picture contract that earned Connery a place in the *Guinness Book of Records* as the (then) highest paid actor in the world: a straight fee of $1.2 million (which Connery donated to his Scottish International Educational Trust charity), 10 per cent of the gross receipts, and an undertaking from United Artists to back two films of the actor's choice. In the event only one film was made as a result of this agreement: *The Offence* (1972), directed by Sidney Lumet, in which Connery played a police sergeant who beats up a suspected child molester and has a nervous breakdown after the man dies in custody. It is one of Connery's best performances, as far removed from his Bond image as could be imagined.

'*Diamonds Are Forever* revealed a Connery who was now packing flab as well as a Walther PPK,' writes Alexander Walker. 'His style resembled an elder statesman of espionage with an implanted pace-maker.'[18] Returning to the role at the age of forty-one, Connery was heavier in build and greying at the temples, but his relaxed, droll performance drew much praise from critics who responded enthusiastically following the disappointment of Lazenby. 'Connery's thickened figure is all to the good, contributing solidity to his imposture [sic], as well as a slight weariness which is usefully evident when two young women give him a savage drubbing at bare-handed combat,' remarked Esquire's Thomas Belger.[19] Connery's performance is very much in tune with the style of the film, which emphasises bizarre narrative situations and foregrounds the comic elements: Bond almost being cremated at a funeral parlour, Bond using a piton-gun to climb around outside his hotel whilst clad immaculately in a black dinner jacket, and Bond being knocked around by two athletic women called Bambi and Thumper. The film even sends up the myth of Bond as superman. When Bond kills one heavy and switches his own wallet for the dead man's, Tiffany Case (Jill St John) is incredulous: 'You've just killed James Bond!' she exclaims. 'Is that who it was? Well, it just goes to show nobody's indestructible,' Connery replies with comic irony. Indeed, Connery's performance in this film prefigures Roger Moore's interpretation of Bond in that he is sending up both the role and himself. The emphasis on comedy, however, is rather at odds with the ending of the previous film.

In narrative, as well as style, *Diamonds Are Forever* marks a complete change from *On Her Majesty's Secret Service*. There are no references to the death of Bond's wife (such references would, however, feature in some of the Roger Moore films), and no obvious burning desire for revenge on Bond's part in his confrontations with Blofeld (Charles Gray). In the pre-title sequence Bond tracks down Blofeld and (apparently) kills him in a pit of burning sulphur, but even when Bond says, 'Welcome to hell, Blofeld', it is done with a self-satisfied smirk rather than vengeful relish. M reminds Bond curtly that Blofeld is dead and tells him 'the least we can expect from you now is a little plain, solid work'. It is almost as if *Diamonds Are Forever* sets out to erase the memory of Lazenby and *OHMSS*, taking up the Bond story from the time when Connery left the series. Thus, when Sir Donald Munger (Laurence Naismith) asks, 'You've been on holiday, I understand. Relaxing, I hope?', and Connery replies, 'Oh, hardly relaxing, but most satisfying', the film is referring to his 'holiday' from the series and, by implication, to the four non-Bond films – *Shalako*, *The Molly Maguires*, *The Red Tent* and *The Anderson Tapes* – that he made in the interim.

Diamonds Are Forever also represents a significant departure from the ideology of national identity that had been constructed in *OHMSS*. Whereas the previous film had emphatically restored the patriotic code of the novels and had been nothing if not explicit in its foregrounding of the motifs of monarchy and country, *Diamonds Are Forever* suggests that such ideologies are redundant. 'Surely you haven't come to negotiate, Mr Bond? Your pitiful little island hasn't even been threatened,' taunts Blofeld – a remark which clearly suggests that Britain is a country of little significance in world affairs. As in *Goldfinger*, the threat is directed against America – Blofeld intends to destroy Washington, DC – and Bond's role is to act virtually as a surrogate American hero, with the American military lending support in the climactic destruction of Blofeld's headquarters.

Diamonds Are Forever is by far the most camp of the Bond films. 'Camp' itself is virtually impossible to define: originally a term used to describe any form of excessively affected, theatrical or ostentatious behaviour, it is now more often used to refer explicitly to stereotyped homosexual behaviour and mannerisms. All the Bond films are camp in the broader sense of the word, but *Diamonds Are Forever* is camp in a more specific sense. 'Camp,' according to Jack Babuscio, 'is a way of poking fun at the whole cosmology of restrictive sex roles and sexual identifications which our society uses to oppress its women and repress its men.'[20] Charles Gray's performance as Blofeld, with his affected voice and mannerisms which almost amount to an impersonation of Noël Coward, even down to the cigarette holder, is very camp indeed – especially in a scene where Blofeld appears in drag. The most obviously camp aspect of the film, however, is the characterisation of Blofeld's homosexual assassins Mr Wint and Mr Kidd (Bruce Glover and Putter Smith). In the novel Wint and Kidd had been a pair of unpleasant, vicious killers, but the nastiness of their characters is downplayed in the film to the extent that they function as comic relief rather than representing any real physical threat. Their homosexuality is displayed openly when they are shown holding hands and in Wint's jealous glance when Kidd remarks that 'Miss Case is very attractive – for a lady'; the campness is most evident in Wint's exaggerated mannerisms and his habit of spraying himself with perfume.

In other respects, too, *Diamonds Are Forever* foregrounds ostentation and excess. Hamilton's direction emphasises the glitzy colours and gaudy decor of the Las Vegas location, highlighting the excesses of the central character: Bond, in his white tuxedo, cuts a distinctive figure in the midst of the casually dressed clientele of the Whyte House casino. In an ironic reflection of the artificiality of Las Vegas, so many things in

23. *Diamonds Are Forever*: Tiffany Case (Jill St John) wants to know where the diamonds are; Bond is thinking of other matters.

the film turn out to be fake: Blofeld's doubles, the diamonds which Bond smuggles in for the villains, the circus sideshow in which a girl supposedly turns into a gorilla, the cat which Bond kicks to determine which is the real Blofeld ('Right idea Mr Bond'; 'But wrong pussy'); even what appears to be the landscape of the moon turns out to be a mock-up at a space research centre. Narrative development takes second place to visual spectacle, and there is an emphasis on the gratuitous destruction of property and vehicles. This is most pronounced in the car chase sequence – itself derivative of the squeal-and-slither chases of *Bullitt* (1968) and *The French Connection* (1971) – in which half a dozen police cars crash into each other as they pursue Bond's red Mustang around a parking lot and through the streets of Las Vegas. Indeed, other than a violent punch-up in a lift which recalls the train fight of *From Russia With Love* in its use of a confined space, most of the action sequences in *Diamonds Are Forever* are played for laughs, none more so than when Bond makes his escape from the Whyte Laboratories instal-lation in the Nevada desert in a cumbersome moon buggy.

How was *Diamonds Are Forever* received? The critics universally welcomed Connery back into the fold, and most found it an improvement on its immediate predecessor. The *Monthly Film Bulletin* thought it the most enjoyable in the series since *Goldfinger.*

> Although – or perhaps because – its plot is an unashamedly thin excuse for a colourful assortment of suspenseful set-pieces (an acrobatic car chase, Bond's near death in a crematorium, his cliff-hanging ascent of a Las Vegas skyscraper), the latest Bond film impresses as probably the most efficient and enjoyable since *Goldfinger.* The style has become genuinely distinctive, shaped partly by Connery's idiosyncratic hero with his impeccable grooming and throwaway innuendoes, partly by Ken Adam's highly inventive set designs. Connery proves again that he is irreplaceable as Bond, handling the script's most worn *double entendres* like a master ('There's something I want you to get off your chest', he purrs to a bikini-clad girl on a beach); while Adam's surrealistic designs for Blofeld's sumptuous penthouse apartment and Bond's hotel suite (a sunken bath whose walls encase a miniature aquarium) lift the film into a Langian world of high-class espionage. *Diamonds Are Forever* shares some of its predecessors' faults – the women, for all their exotic names, are so many *Playboy* mannequins, Guy Hamilton's direction is energetic but somewhat lacking in style, and the fascist elements of the Bond image still seem obnoxious (especially since Blofeld's rather appealing aim in holding Washington to ransom is to secure world disarmament). But the action set-pieces remain as watchable as ever, and the whole tone of the film improves, as in *Goldfinger,* with the makers' confidently tongue-in-cheek approach.[21]

The review, by Nigel Andrews, exemplifies one of the narrative ambiguities of *Diamonds Are Forever* in that it is never spelled out precisely what Blofeld's demands are. Although he tells Dr Metz (Joseph Furst) that their mutual aim is disarmament, it would seem that this is the story he has spun to enlist Metz's assistance (he is an expert in laser refraction). Willard Whyte (Jimmy Dean) tells Bond that Blofeld intends to hold 'an international auction – with nuclear supremacy going to the highest bidder'.

Diamonds Are Forever marked a return to the box-office heights of the Bond films of the mid-1960s. Its worldwide rentals were $45.7 million, of which $19.7 million came from the North American market – over twice as much as *On Her Majesty's Secret Service*.[22] While most critics attributed this to the return of Connery, some advanced more sociological reasons to explain the film's success. Only two years earlier the *New York Times* had suggested that Bond was out of date at the end of the 1960s, but another journalist in the same newspaper now argued that the Bond films provided just the sort of nostalgia that the weary and disillusioned America of the early 1970s was crying out for:

> *Diamonds Are Forever* stands to make about a zillion dollars, and nostalgia of an especially piercing sort will have a lot to do with it. Simply, the Bond brand of escapist fantasy – to a world where the two eternal verities are money and power and the two foregone conclusions are violence and sex – scratches an itch, and it's an itch that nothing else in the emotionally torpid Nixon era can reach as directly. Bond is as authentic an article of the sixties as Fred Astaire was of the thirties, and the issue of 'quality' hardly seems germane. I don't imagine many of the thousands of people who rushed to see *Diamonds Are Forever* when it opened paused en route to check the reviews. They just rushed.[23]

While some critics thought the film provided escapism from the problems of the present – Vietnam and Cambodia abroad, and violent incidents at home such as the Kent State University shootings and the Attica prison revolt – others argued that *Diamonds Are Forever* had caught the mood of American cinema-goers not because it offered a nostalgic escape into the past but because it offered a commentary on contemporary issues and concerns. Andrew Sarris, the influential film critic of *Village Voice*, suggested that the film successfully brought the Bond series up to date 'because it demonstrates how to enrich an established genre by digging deeper into the sociological subconscious of its audience'. He continued:

> Actually, the major positive virtues of the movie seem to originate from the cockily contemporaneous screenplay ... which manages to relate to recent headlines without being oppressively relevant to the in-depth continuations on the back pages. This process can be described as having your cake and throwing it like a custard pie. Thus, we get tantalizing glimpses of the Howard Hughes empire with its invisible emperor, the ecological nightmare of oil

rigs off the California coast, spoofs of moon men and their dune buggies, Russian nuclear subs and Red Chinese nuclear missiles, a Los Angeles mortuary out of 'The Loved One', jokes about the dullness of Kansas as nuclear target and about the deterioration of Great Britain into a third-rate power.[24]

Sarris added that 'the writers haven't missed a topical beat, even with the villains, one pair representing the gays, and another representing the man-hating branch of women's lib'. It is an interesting socio-political reading of the film by a critic more renowned for his advocacy of the *auteur* theory, though intriguingly Sarris said that his favourite Bond movie was *On Her Majesty's Secret Service*. What the review indicates, however, is that some critics recognised how the film-makers were deliberately trying to keep the Bond series up to date through topical references and plot devices which had some contemporary relevance, even if they were hardly used in a serious way.

The argument that *Diamonds Are Forever* was successful because it reflected certain contemporary concerns is rather more convincing than the view that it succeeded simply because it provided a nostalgic return to the heyday of the 1960s before the impact of Vietnam and social unrest had been felt. Throughout the 1960s, indeed, the most successful Bond films had enjoyed topical relevance, whether intentional or un-intentional: the relative failure of *On Her Majesty's Secret Service* might be explained in part by the fact that it had less obvious contemporary relevance than some of the others. The strategy of topicality can certainly be seen in the choice of *Live and Let Die* as the next film in the series, which was in response to a particular cultural and industrial phenomenon of Hollywood at the time – the hugely successful but short-lived cycle of black exploitation films of the early 1970s.

Approximately one-quarter of regular American film-goers in the late 1960s and early 1970s were black.[25] The size and importance of the black audience was illustrated by the box-office success of a cycle of cheaply made genre movies featuring relatively unknown black actors which proliferated between 1970 and 1973. Unlike earlier films with black stars which had explored the issue of racism in a well-intentioned and thoughtful way, and which were made for a general audience, such as *In the Heat of the Night* (1967) and *Guess Who's Coming to Dinner* (1967), the 'blaxploitation' movies were made primarily for the black, urban audience, and downplayed racial issues in favour of action-based narratives with heavy doses of sex and violence. The film which is often taken to represent the start of the cycle is *Cotton Comes to Harlem* (1970), based on the novel by black crime writer Chester Himes, and the most successful of the blaxploitation films which followed were private-eye and crime thrillers: *Shaft* (1971), *Shaft's Big Score* (1972), *Superfly* (1972), *Slaughter* (1972), *Black Gunn* (1972) and *Shaft in Africa* (1973) were among the more commercially successful of a glut of similar and inevitably derivative films. Richard Roundtree and Jim Brown were the foremost stars who came to prominence as a result of blaxploitation, though the distaff side was represented by Tamara Dobson in *Cleopatra Jones* (1973) and *Cleopatra Jones and the Casino of Gold* (1975) and by Pam Grier as *Foxy Brown* (1974).

Live and Let Die was the obvious choice for the Bond film-makers if they wanted to exploit the success of the blaxploitation cycle in that it was the book which most readily lent itself to a black theme. Fleming's second novel had Bond assigned to investigate the smuggling of seventeenth-century gold coins between the Caribbean and America – treasure which had been seized by the pirate Bloody Morgan and thought lost. The smuggling is traced to Mr Big, a black American gangster who is a member of SMERSH and who is using the treasure to finance Soviet operations in the United States. Mr Big, who was born in Haiti, uses voodoo to ensure the loyalty of his henchmen. Bond travels to New York and, along with Felix Leiter, goes to the Harlem nightclub where Mr Big's headquarters are. Bond meets Mr Big, who is accompanied by Solitaire, a beautiful young white woman who 'can divine the truth in people' and whom he dominates through fear. Bond kills several of Mr Big's men and escapes. He is contacted by Solitaire, who wants him to free her from Mr Big, and the two of them travel to Florida on the Silver Meteor. In Florida, Solitaire is recaptured and Leiter is seriously injured when he is thrown into a shark tank by one of Mr Big's henchmen, The Robber, whom Bond subsequently kills. Bond then follows Mr Big to Jamaica and swims out to the Isle of Surprise where Mr Big's yacht is moored. Bond is captured and, together with Solitaire, is dragged over a coral reef by Mr Big, but Mr Big is killed when his yacht is blown up by a limpet mine previously attached to its hull by Bond.

Although the novel was freely adapted by Mankiewicz, slightly more of Fleming's original plot remained than in *Diamonds Are Forever*. When three British agents are killed – one at the United Nations in New York,

24. *Live and Let Die*: An eyebrow too far as Roger Moore assumes
007's licence to kill and Bond takes on black American gangsters (witness
unconscious heavy) who have strayed into the series from the world of
'blaxploitation' cinema.

one in New Orleans, and one on San Monique, a small island in the
Caribbean – Bond is assigned to investigate. The villain is now one Dr
Kananga (Yaphet Kotto), the prime minister of San Monique, who is
manufacturing heroin for distribution in the United States. At first it
seems that Kananga is in league with Mr Big, but it turns out that the
two are one and the same. Kananga's plan is to create a nation of drug
addicts by flooding the United States with free heroin and thus putting
all his rivals out of business, after which he will have a monopoly in its
supply. The film maintains most of the locations of the novel (New
York and the Caribbean, though it substitutes Louisiana for Florida),
but most of the narrative incidents and action sequences have been
invented for the film. Richard Maibaum, who was not involved this
time, did not approve of the storyline. 'It was about nothing, a lousy
cooking-some-dope-somewhere-in-the-jungle movie,' he said. 'That's not
Bond at all. To process drugs in the middle of a jungle is not a Bond
caper.'[26]

To what extent can *Live and Let Die* be placed within the context of blaxploitation? In the first instance, the film is not in itself a blaxploitation picture, given that its hero is a white male and that it is set only partly in a black *milieu*. The producers probably hoped that by making some nods to the cycle of black action movies they would attract some of the audience for those films, but a Bond movie still needed to have broad-based audience appeal. Commercial imperatives, therefore, dictated that the film could not stray too far into blaxploitation territory for fear of alienating the mainstream, predominantly white audience. For example, Mankiewicz's original idea that Solitaire should be played by a black actress was vetoed.

By the time *Live and Let Die* was released in the summer of 1973, the blaxploitation cycle had almost run its course anyway. What the film does is to borrow and renegotiate some of the themes and motifs of blaxploitation within the narrative formula of the Bond series. The result, however, is a rather uneasy tension within the film between the use of these themes and motifs on the one hand and the stereotyped representation of black characters as villains on the other. The sequence where Bond goes to Harlem, for example, places him in the *milieu* of blaxploitation as he is captured by flamboyantly dressed gangsters with a nice line in irreverent dialogue ('Names is for tombstones baby. You all take this honky outside and waste him'). Bond's excursion into Harlem makes him look foolhardy, even foolish: he is easily spotted and tailed ('Can't miss him – it's like following a cue ball'), and is chided by black CIA agent Strutter (Lon Satton) for 'that clever disguise you're wearing – white face in Harlem. Good thinking, Bond.' In contrast to the colourful and flamboyant gangsters, Bond comes across as square and old-fashioned – a white man out of place at a time when the coolest and hippest screen hero was Richard Roundtree's John Shaft. But while Bond may seem out of place in Harlem, he does still best the villains at every opportunity, thus reasserting the supremacy of the white hero.

The script itself makes only scant reference to the fact that the villains are black, but at a deeper level the narrative ideology of the film does betray its racist undertones. This is especially evident in the relationship between Bond, Solitaire and Kananga. On one level, of course, Bond's seduction of Solitaire (Jane Seymour), who is in the power of the villain, represents the process of ideological repositioning that had been enacted so often before. But it also represents a different sort of repositioning in that, for the first time in the series, it is made

25. *Live and Let Die*: Solitaire (Jane Seymour) may look worried, but Bond's raised eyebrow suggests he has already thought of a way out of this one.

explicit that the heroine is a virgin. Solitaire has the power to predict the future, but knows that she will lose it once she has known 'earthly love'. Kananga, who relies on Solitaire's mystical power, informs her that she will lose it only when he decides, and, moreover, that he will be the one to take it away. Bond effectively tricks her into sleeping with him: knowing that she believes in Tarot cards, he uses a deck stacked with cards representing 'The Lovers' to persuade her they are destined to become lovers themselves. After the act, Bond misinterprets Solitaire's mood as disappointment at her first sexual experience ('Cheer up, darling, there has to be a first time for everyone'), but she is actually more concerned that she has lost her power and that Kananga will kill her because she is no longer of any use to him. Later, when Kananga learns that she has lost her virginity to Bond, he strikes her in fury and shouts hysterically that 'I myself would have given you love – you knew that!' In ideological terms, therefore, there is a racial dimension overlaid on the repositioning of Solitaire in that she is 'saved' from losing her virginity to the black villain by losing it first to the white hero. The film thus embodies one of the oldest themes of white culture: the resistance to miscegenation between black men and white women, which is invariably presented in terms of the black male representing a violent sexual threat to the white woman. In its attitude towards miscegenation, however, the film contrives to have its cake and eat it: while sex between a black man and a white girl is beyond the pale, Bond is allowed a sexual encounter with a black woman, Rosie Carver (Gloria Hendry), albeit that she turns out to be working for Kananga and is quickly killed off. In this sense, there is an undeniable racist subtext to the film, and it was to be noted by a number of critics.

In other respects, *Live and Let Die* develops many of the themes and characteristics of *Diamonds Are Forever*, particularly in its virtual Americanisation of Bond: much of the film is again set in America, the threat is directed against America, and Bond is assisted by Leiter and the CIA. It also resembles its predecessor in its comical action sequences and its evident delight in gratuitous displays of destruction. In *Live and Let Die* there are no fewer than four chase sequences which involve some form of vehicular destruction: Bond at the wheel of an out-of-control car on a busy New York freeway; Bond escaping from the San Monique police in an old double-decker bus, during which he slices the top off driving under a low bridge; Bond escaping from Mr Big's heavies at an aerodrome, during which he slices the wings off an aeroplane; and a lengthy speed boat chase through the Louisiana bayous which results in numerous boats and several police cars being written off. 'Personally, I can't get too much of machines smashing each other to smithereens,' declared John Coleman, suggesting that some critics, at least, enjoyed the aesthetic of destruction which had now come to characterise the Bond films.[27] This element of the films might be seen to prefigure the successful *Smokey and the Bandit* (1977), a chase comedy starring Burt Reynolds in which narrative complexity is reduced to the level of one spectacular car crash after another. *Smokey and the Bandit* also borrowed from *Live and Let Die* the characterisation of a dim-witted redneck southern lawman. Sheriff J. W. Pepper (Clifton James) proved so popular with audiences and critics that he was to be brought back in *The Man With the Golden Gun*.

At the level of visual style, however, *Live and Let Die* differs from *Diamonds Are Forever*. Both of Moore's first two films reverted to the standard aspect ratio, which had not been used since *Goldfinger*, rather than using Panavision – an odd decision given that the appeal of the Bond films was based so much on their visual spectacle, which was undoubtedly enhanced by the widescreen process. Like *From Russia With Love*, *Live and Let Die* does not have the 'epic' feel of other Bond films, due largely to the absence of any lavish interiors in the Ken Adam style: production designer Syd Cain favours real exteriors above studio sets. It was also the first Bond film for which John Barry did not write the music, though the score by former Beatles producer George Martin, and the title song written and performed by Paul McCartney and Wings, are both among the best of the series, using a mixture of rock and reggae motifs in place of Barry's more familiar orchestral compositions, effectively matching the music to the locations (Harlem, New Orleans, the Caribbean).

Live and Let Die is very much a transitional film in the Bond series, its main purpose, of course, being to introduce the new star. But the film does, intriguingly, explore other narrative possibilities, particularly through the introduction of a supernatural theme. 'Somewhere at the back of the script is an ingenious idea about fates and furies, the Tarot cards being intended to guide Bond's actions more closely than he'd care to admit,' observed Philip Strick; 'while the curious encounters with Baron Samedi suggest a chunk of plot that nobody finally cared to face up to.'[28] Tarot cards are used as a linking motif through the first half of the film. Each of the main characters is linked to one of the cards: Solitaire is 'The High Priestess', Rosie is 'The Queen of Cups' (a treacherous, deceitful woman), and Bond is 'The Fool' – a highly significant motif in that critics were coming increasingly to regard the films as comedies. The voodoo theme is maintained from the novel, particularly through the character of Baron Samedi (Geoffrey Holder) who appears both as one of Kananga's henchmen and as a performer in a dance routine. Although Samedi is killed when Bond knocks him into a coffin full of poisonous snakes, he reappears just before the end credits perched on front of the train on which Bond and Solitaire are travelling to New York. Inexplicable in narrative terms, this is the only explicitly supernatural moment in the Bond series which elsewhere, for all its implausibility, is insistent on rationality.

The critical reception of *Live and Let Die* was mixed. Most reviewers made the point that the Bond films had now become action comedies rather than action thrillers, a tendency reinforced by the performance of the new star. 'Roger Moore has none of the gravitas of Sean

Connery,' said Christopher Hudson, '... but he does fit slickly into the director's presentation of Bond as a lethal comedian let loose in a world of thuggish buffoons who are a little slower on the punch-lines'. 'As a matter of fact,' Hudson added, 'Guy Hamilton, after two mediocre films, has brought the Ian Fleming sequence back into top gear with as fast-paced and snappily entertaining piece of claptrap as we have a right to expect.'[29] But other critics felt that the film's attempt to reflect cultural trends had fallen flat. 'And if *Live and Let Die* does break new ground – perhaps it hopes topicality by having all its villains black – the advantages in terms of newsworthiness are nuanced by characterisation nearer to *Porgy and Bess* than to *Shaft*,' opined John Russell Taylor. 'Will James Bond live on in the 1970s? Not much further, if this episode is anything to go by.'[30]

It was the racial elements of the film which drew most comment, and which proved most controversial. In America the film was attacked for its alleged racial bias, with Richard Schickel of *Time* magazine sarcastically labelling Bond 'the Great White Hope' and describing the film itself as 'the most vulgar addition to a series that has long since outlived its brief historical moment – if not, alas, its profitability'. He went on:

> As for Bond's new character as a racist pig, there is a dubious rationale for it. Through the years he has kicked and chopped his way through most of the other races of man, so it could be argued that it is just a matter of equal rights to let blacks have their chance to play masochists to his pseudo-suave sadist. Not surprisingly, this strained justification fails to relieve the queasiness *Live and Let Die* induces. Why are all the blacks either stupid brutes or primitives deep into the occult and voodooism? Why is miscegenation so often used as a turn-on? Why do such questions even arise in what is supposed to be pure entertainment?[31]

However, charges of racism were rejected by Dilys Powell, who thought that 'the blacks are the true heroes of the latest fantasy on an Ian Fleming theme' and who offered a reading of the film which was precisely the opposite of Schickel's:

> Racist? Nonsense, unless you mean anti-white racialism, for it is true that the film is slanted against the incompetence of the whites, who let the blacks run rings around them and so far as I can see

would founder without trace if it were not for our old friend James Bond. As you were – our new friend: this time we have Roger Moore in the role.

It is the blacks, though, whom one watches most eagerly. I know they are generally designated as the enemy in the film (not always: Bond is glad of a hand from a black CIA man in New York, and he would never have got to the sinister Caribbean island without his faithful black boatman). But such charming enemies, so well-mannered, sometimes so pretty (don't you find the black decoy played by Gloria Hendry more appealing than the statuesque Tarot-card dealer played by Jane Seymour?). Clever too: such ingenious methods of disposing of a body (look out for the coffin in New Orleans), so startling a variety of man-traps, such perfection of communication: if they tail James Bond they tail him not with taxis (taxis are old hat) but with telephone calls to every street corner.[32]

Opinions differed, therefore, over the representation of the black villains. What is most intriguing about these reviews is that American and British critics could put forward such different, indeed diametrically opposed, interpretations of the same film – which says rather less about the film itself than it does about the prevailing racial attitudes of the two countries at the time.

In hindsight, however, *Live and Let Die* seems less offensively racist than it does merely dated. The colourful costumes and slang dialogue of the gangsters, redolent as it is of the blaxploitation cycle, dates the film at a precise historical moment in the early 1970s. The style and idiom of black cinema has since changed dramatically from that represented by blaxploitation, evidenced by the films of directors such as Spike Lee and Robert Townsend. And, while it is hard not to agree with Schickel's observations about the stupidity of the black villains in *Live and Let Die* – Powell's review reads more like an apologia – this is perfectly in line with the characterisation of villains in other Bond movies, and indeed in popular action cinema generally. In other words, they are stupid because they are villains, not because they are black.

The racist undertones which some critics detected in *Live and Let Die* did not damage its performance at the box-office. With worldwide rentals of $48.7 million it actually made slightly more than *Diamonds Are Forever*, though when the figures are broken down it took less in North America ($15.9 million) and more overseas ($32.8 million). This represented the biggest ratio difference between domestic and foreign earnings for any film in the series since *Dr No*. But the overall success of the film suggested that audience acceptance of Moore was great enough to sustain the series. In order to consolidate him in the role, Moore's second Bond film was produced quickly and released at the end of 1974, the first time that Bond films had been released in successive calendar years since the mid-1960s.

The Man With the Golden Gun had been Fleming's last full novel, and was not one of his best. The book begins with a bizarre oedipal situation in which Bond, presumed dead at the end of *You Only Live Twice*, returns to London and immediately tries to assassinate M in his office. It turns out that Bond, suffering from memory loss, had travelled from Japan to Russia, where he had been recognised by the Russians and brainwashed. After Bond's memory has been restored, M gives him the opportunity to redeem himself by terminating the career of Francisco Scaramanga, a Cuban-based gunman who has been responsible for the death of several British agents. Scaramanga is known as 'the Man with the Golden Gun' because he uses a gold-plated Colt .45 revolver with gold bullets. Bond travels to Jamaica, where he traces Scaramanga to a brothel where he is staying with a group of other gangsters. Bond insinuates himself into Scaramanga's entourage – it is implied that Scaramanga, who is thought to be homosexual, finds him attractive – and learns that Scaramanga is involved in sabotaging the Jamaican economy and smuggling drugs into the United States. When Bond's real identity is discovered there is a gunfight on a speeding train, which is derailed by an explosion. Bond follows Scaramanga into a swamp and kills him.

Given that Caribbean locations had been used in *Live and Let Die*, the film version of *The Man With the Golden Gun* changed the location to the Far East: Macao, Hong Kong and Thailand. In certain ways the film is an improvement on the novel, with the character of Scaramanga upgraded from a fairly run-of-the-mill hoodlum to the world's foremost assassin, whose price is $1 million per hit. Mankiewicz originally envisaged the relationship between Bond and Scaramanga as a reworking of that between hero and villain in the classic western *Shane* (1953), and veteran heavy Jack Palance, who had played the sadistic Wilson to Alan Ladd's morally righteous Shane, was considered to play Scaramanga, though in the event the role went to Christoper Lee. In hindsight it is hard to imagine Palance as Scaramanga: his brand of screen villainy was roughly sinister, whereas Lee's was smoothly sinister and much more in keeping with the character of a highly paid, sophisticated killer who, like Bond, enjoys the best things in life. However, the screenplay was revised by Maibaum after Mankiewicz pulled out following a disagreement with director Hamilton, and for some reason it was deemed necessary to introduce an extra layer of plot in which Scaramanga has stolen a device capable of harnessing the sun's energy and is planning on cornering the world market in solar power. This was a topical theme at the time due to the world oil crisis brought about when the Arab nations of OPEC (Organisation of Petroleum Exporting Countries) put an embargo on oil export due to the Yom Kippur War. Britain was particularly hard hit, as the oil crisis came at a time when there was also a growing shortage of coal but before the North Sea oil and gas fields had come on line. There was a massive cut in energy supplies, the price of oil increased fourfold and consequently there was huge inflationary pressure on the economy and the worst balance-of-payments deficit (some £1.5 billion in 1973) hitherto recorded. The result, in the words of historian Kenneth Morgan, was an 'intensified feeling of national weakness, even impotence, prevalent throughout the nation in the wake of the oil crisis and the inflationary explosion as never before'.[33]

Grafting the solar-energy plot on to the duel between Bond and Scaramanga does not work entirely successfully in *The Man With the Golden Gun*, which, despite many outstanding individual moments and a splendid villain, is overall one of the less satisfying Bond films. It is fundamentally structurally flawed in that it contains two lines of narrative which are only tangentially and coincidentally linked. On one level there is the topical solar energy theme, or what might be termed the public plot. Bond has been assigned to track down a missing solar energy expert who has perfected the 'solex agitator', which offers a way of solving the energy crisis. The solex is the 'McGuffin' of the film, much of which features the device passing from one person to another. On another level there is the private plot concerning the relationship between Bond and Scaramanga, which is far more interesting ideologically. The main threat is a personal one directed against Bond in that Scaramanga wants to fight him in a duel to the death ('You see, Mr Bond, like every great artist I want to create an indisputable masterpiece once in my lifetime – the death of double-oh seven, *mano a mano*, face to face'). Scaramanga admires Bond to the extent that he has a wax effigy of him in the bizarre shooting gallery where he tests his skills against his prey. There is none of the implied homosexuality of the novel; rather,

26. *The Man With the Golden Gun*: Guns in the afternoon as Scaramanga
(Christopher Lee) challenges Bond to 'a duel between titans'.

Scaramanga sees himself and Bond as professional equals. One scene,
where Scaramanga entertains Bond to lunch before their duel, perfectly
encapsulates one of the key ideological themes of the Bond series: the
notion of Bond as a servant of the Crown. Scaramanga taunts Bond by
mocking his allegiance to Queen and country ('You work for peanuts –
a hearty well-done from Her Majesty the Queen and a pittance of a
pension. Apart from that, we are the same'). Thus the monarchical
authority underlying Bond's profession is alluded to once again. Bond's
reply asserts the official and moral legitimation for his own actions
which differentiate him from Scaramanga ('When I kill it's on the specific
orders of my government, and those I kill are themselves killers').
Following this interesting rehearsal of ideologies, however, the duel
between Bond and Scaramanga is quite a tame affair, with Bond eventually killing his foe by posing as his own effigy – a moment which gave
critics of Moore's acting an obvious source of amusement. Moreover,
the flawed structure of the film is such that the duel, which should have
been the climax, is followed by a boring and redundant sequence in

which Bond has to retrieve the solex device from Scaramanga's solar energy plant before it blows up.

The flaws in the narrative structure of *The Man With the Golden Gun* are exacerbated by a constant tension between the serious and comic elements in the film. It does not seem sure whether it is intended as a straight action thriller or as a comedy thriller, resulting in an uneasy combination of the two. There are some thematically interesting ideas which are not fully developed. The film invokes the association of the gun with the phallus, an idea which has become widespread due to the popularisation of Freudian psychoanalytical theory. This is evident not only in the blatant lyrics of the title song ('He has a powerful weapon, he charges a million a shot'), but also in the scene where Scaramanga, after killing a victim, caresses the face and lips of his mistress Andrea (Maud Adams) with the barrel of his recently discharged golden gun. But, like the supernatural theme of *Live and Let Die*, the phallic symbolism and fetishism of *The Man With the Golden Gun* is not explored any further. On a political level, the film once again alludes to Britain's decline – secret service headquarters in Hong Kong are located, rather symbolically, on the submerged wreckage of the liner *Queen Elizabeth* – and again suggests that Red China is a threat lurking in the background: Scaramanga's island is in Chinese territorial waters, where he lives rent free in return for doing his landlords 'the occasional favour'. But elsewhere, the psychoanalytical and political aspects of the film are diffused by its insistence on broad comedy. The chase sequences verge on slapstick; heroine Mary Goodnight (Britt Ekland) is characterised as a scatter-brained bimbo in a bikini; the character of J. W. Pepper makes an irrelevant return as a loud-mouthed American tourist in Thailand; and there are some excruciating puns on oriental names which might be considered racist (character names like Hai Fat and Chu Mee, not to mention a wine called Phu Yuck). The tradition of physically bizarre villains in the Bond series, moreover, is spoofed by the character of Scaramanga's manservant Nick Nack (Hervé Villechaize): the name may recall Oddjob, but as he is a midget he presents no credible physical threat to Bond with the result that, like Wint and Kidd in *Diamonds Are Forever*, he functions mainly as comic relief. In comparison to the characterisation of Nick Nack, Scaramanga's own physical peculiarity of having three nipples – the source of some fairly obvious humour ('A fascinating anatomical titbit'; 'I think he found me quite titillating') – seems positively tasteful.

The Man With the Golden Gun is also highly derivative of other films. As visually impressive as Peter Murton's design for Scaramanga's hall of mirrors is, the sequences in the shooting gallery are strongly reminiscent of the famous climax of Orson Welles's *The Lady from Shanghai* (1948), though they are rather less suspenseful. And, just as *Live and Let Die* had been influenced to some extent by blaxploitation, so too *The Man With the Golden Gun* imitates another popular phenomenon of the early 1970s, namely the kung-fu craze. Martial-arts films emerged in Hong Kong and Taiwanese popular cinema in the late 1960s, though their international breakthrough came in the early 1970s with the emergence of the superbly athletic Bruce Lee as the kung-fu hero *par excellence* in films like *The Big Boss* (1971), *Fist of Fury* (1972) and *Game of Death* (1973). The kung-fu films, which bore some resemblance to Japanese *samurai* films, reduced narrative to a virtually non-existent level while foregrounding action as spectacle, their fight sequences choreographed with the precision of a complex dance routine and having an almost balletic quality of their own. The most successful, internationally, was the Hollywood-backed *Enter the Dragon* (1973), starring Bruce Lee, John Saxon and Jim Brown as secret agents on a mission to break up a gang of white slavers and drug dealers operating from a fortress on a Chinese island; the frenetic climax is among the most spectacular exhibitions of martial-arts fighting ever put on the screen. With Bond travelling to the Far East in *The Man With the Golden Gun*, it was inevitable that, given the success of kung-fu cinema at the time, the film would incorporate a martial-arts sequence. At one point Bond finds himself a prisoner in a karate school where he is forced to fight the star pupil, which he does reasonably capably, but once again an action sequence ends up being played for comedy. Thus, in a spoof of one of the conventions of kung-fu cinema in which the high-kicking heroes would take on dozens of opponents at the same time, Bond is saved from the entire assembly of the karate school by two teenage schoolgirls who chop and kick their way through the opposition.

The narrative and structural flaws of *The Man With the Golden Gun* go a long way towards explaining its rather lukewarm reception. It was the least successful film in the series since *On Her Majesty's Secret Service*: its worldwide rentals amounted to $37.2 million, but only $9.4 million of that came from the North American market. The overwhelming critical response was that the Bond formula was looking tired, despite the usual high production values. 'Guy Hamilton, the most experienced Bond director of them all, goes through his paces once again with admirable stoicism and occasional flair,' said Derek Malcolm. 'But he can't disguise the fact that the script is just about the limpest of the lot and that Roger Moore as 007 is the last man on earth to make it sound better than it actually is.'[34] Tom Milne found it 'sadly lacking in wit or imagination' and observed that it had resorted to imitations of other films: 'This series, which has been scraping the barrel for some time, is now through the bottom and tarting up a silly story about a stolen energy device with depressing borrowings from Hong Kong kung-fu movies, not to mention more depressing echoes of "Carry On" smut.'[35] Some critics even suggested that the Bond series had run its course, or at least that it should be given a rest. According to Jay Cocks in *Time*:

> Although the final screen credits promise that Bond will return in *The Spy Who Loved Me*, it is time to retire him. He should be packed off to a sanitarium, where he can give his liver a rest and wait in leisure for his moment to come again. Right now, Bond has been around too long to be fresh, but not long enough to qualify as a genuine antique.[36]

Clearly there was a feeling that the series had run out of steam, that it had become predictable and derivative. But, although there would be a slightly longer than usual gap until the release of the next film, Bond was not to be retired, and indeed would return in the late 1970s with all his popular appeal restored.

5

Keeping the British End Up:
The Spy Who Loved Me, Moonraker

The *Spy Who Loved Me* (dir. Lewis Gilbert, 1977) and *Moonraker* (dir. Lewis Gilbert, 1979) marked the return of the Bond series to the popular acclaim which it had enjoyed during the 1960s. *The Spy Who Loved Me*, which was the first Bond movie to be produced by Broccoli alone following his split with Saltzman in 1975, earned total worldwide rentals of $80 million, over twice as much as *The Man With the Golden Gun*, of which some $24 million came from North America. These figures were surpassed by *Moonraker*, which earned total worldwide rentals of $87.7 million, of which $33 million came from North America.[1] When converted to estimated wordwide grosses, these figures approximate to $186 million for *The Spy Who Loved Me* and $203 million for *Moonraker*.[2] While these increased figures were due in no small measure to the effect of inflation, they still represent a significant upturn in Bond's box-office fortunes following the relatively disappointing performance of *The Man With the Golden Gun*. Taking inflation into account, *Moonraker* was probably not quite as successful as *Thunderball* had been, but its total grosses were the biggest for any of the Bond films until *GoldenEye* in 1995.

For all the popular success of these films, however, it was not a stable time for the film industry or for the Bond franchise itself. Alexander Walker considers that the mid-1970s marked 'the lowest point in British film-making' and 'the lowest, most shameful nadir of film

industry fortunes'.[3] Cinema attendances continued to decline, while the
number of British feature films produced per year fell dramatically from
an average of between seventy and eighty during the 1960s, and between
eighty and ninety in the early 1970s, to sixty-four in 1976, forty-two in
1977, and fifty-one in 1978.[4] Most British productions were low-budget
comedies and 'sexploitation' films made for the domestic market –
Confessions of a Window Cleaner (1974), for example, was the most successful British film of its year – though there were still a handful of
big-budget films aimed at the international market such as *Murder on the
Orient Express* (1974), *The Eagle Has Landed* (1976), *Shout at the Devil*
(1976) and *The Wild Geese* (1978). At a time when there were numerous
expensive flops, most notoriously the spectacular failure of Lord Lew
Grade's $34 million production *Raise the Titanic!* (1980), the continuing
international success of the Bond series came as welcome relief for the
British film industry.

The production base of the Bond series in Britain had substantial
economic benefits for both the series' producers and the film industry.
In 1974 it was estimated that the Bond films had drawn over £3 million
from the Eady Levy.[5] Given that the Eady money was distributed among
eligible producers on the basis of box-office takings, it amounted, in
effect, to a subsidy for commercial success. At the same time, however,
the Bond films were big-budget productions which invested in British
personnel and facilities. At a time when British studios were faced with
serious under-employment and loss of revenue due to the sudden decline
in production – Elstree, for example, halved its workforce in 1975 – the
presence of the Bond series had become increasingly important to
Pinewood. As *Screen International* reported in August 1976: '*The Spy Who
Loved Me* has taken somewhat longer than the average Bond film to get
to the production stage – as many people in the film industry will have
noticed, not least the management of Pinewood Studios, which rather
depends on the Bond pictures these days to absorb some of the studio's
own costs.'[6] Pinewood had even greater reason to be thankful, for in
1976 Eon Productions invested some £400,000 in the construction of
a new silent stage, then the biggest in the world, when it was realised
that existing stages would be too small to accommodate the massive
sets planned for *The Spy Who Loved Me*. Opened by former Prime Minister
Sir Harold Wilson on 5 December 1976, the '007 Stage' was a permanent
stage (unlike the volcano set built for *You Only Live Twice*) which could
be rented out to other producers.

However, the future of the Bond series at this time was not as stable as the investment in the '007 Stage' would seem to suggest. For all the popular success which the films enjoyed, there were a number of problems. For one thing, there was a dramatic increase in production costs in the late 1970s. Whereas the previous three films had all cost around $7 million, the negative cost of *The Spy Who Loved Me* was $13 million. This was due mostly to inflation, though it also reflected the series' return to the scale of visual spectacle and level of production values which had characterised the mid-1960s films, following the relatively low-key style of Roger Moore's first two films. Broccoli hinted to the trade press that *The Spy Who Loved Me* might be a make-or-break film for the series: 'Hopefully, we'll reach that if the picture is successful. If it isn't, we've had it, that's all – you roll the dice and that's it.'[7] But while *The Spy Who Loved Me* was almost twice as expensive as each of the three films before it, *Moonraker* was over two-and-a-half times as expensive as *The Spy Who Loved Me*, with a negative cost of $34 million.

Moonraker was also the first Bond movie not to be based at Pinewood Studios. Although *Screen International* had suggested in 1976 that Broccoli 'feels it would be sacrilege to take Bond elsewhere', by early 1977 (before the completion of *The Spy Who Loved Me*) it was being rumoured that future Bond films might be lost to Britain.[8] Early in 1978 it was announced that *Moonraker* would be made in France. Broccoli was highly critical of the circumstances which had forced him to abandon, albeit as it happened only temporarily, the British production base, complaining, with much justification, that he had been making films in Britain since the early 1950s. 'I made pictures, stayed during the industry's trials and tribulations and invested a great deal of money,' he said. 'But now "they" are turning people out.'[9] 'They' were the Callaghan government, which had increased tax to such an extent that it not only affected Broccoli personally, who moved back to California after living for twenty-five years in Britain, but also made the production of a film on the scale of *Moonraker* prohibitively expensive. In the event, *Moonraker* was filmed at three major French studio complexes – Epinay, Billancourt and Boulogne – with only the special effects work carried out at Pinewood.

The rising costs of production were not the only problem which the Bond series faced in the late 1970s. There had been difficulties over the screen adaptation of *The Spy Who Loved Me*, the rights for which had been granted on the condition that only the title could be used, and not the story. The novel of *The Spy Who Loved Me* had been an experiment in which Fleming varied the usual Bond formula. It was written as if from the point of view of a woman, Vivienne Michel, who once had a liaison with James Bond. Vivienne leaves England after two disappointing love affairs and, after a series of travels, ends up at a motel in New York State where she is offered a job running it. However, it turns out that the owner is involved in an insurance scam, and two gangsters, Horror and Sluggsy, arrive with the intention of burning the motel down. They are about to assault Vivienne when James Bond arrives, entirely by chance (it is later explained that the episode occurs after *Thunderball* when Bond is engaged in tracking down the fugitive Blofeld). Bond kills the two gangsters, spends the night with Vivienne and leaves in the morning.

'It is true that Fleming forbade the film adaptation of *The Spy Who Loved Me*, but that was no excuse for attaching the title to a very unflemingian hotchpotch,' remarked Anthony Burgess.[10] Intriguingly, Burgess himself had at one stage been commissioned to write a screenplay for *The Spy Who Loved Me*, which was to feature the relationship between Bond and a female Russian spy, though his treatment was rejected. Other writers involved at one stage or another included John Landis and Stirling Silliphant, while Guy Hamilton was once again slated to direct until he withdrew and was replaced by Lewis Gilbert.[11] Richard Maibaum wrote a screenplay reintroducing SPECTRE, which had been absent from the most recent films, and which began with a new, radical group of terrorists 'comprised of everyone from the Red Brigade to the Weathermen' taking over SPECTRE headquarters:

> They level the place, kick Blofeld out, and take over ... They're a bunch of young idealists. In the end, Bond comes in and asks, 'All right, you're going to blow up the world. What do you want?' They reply, 'We don't want *anything*. We just want to start over – the world is lousy. We want to wipe it away and begin again. So, there's no way we can be bribed.'
>
> I never had Stromberg – or whomever the hell it was in that movie – or that interminable thing that went on in the tanker.[12]

This treatment was turned down, according to Maibaum, because 'Cubby thought it was too political. So many young people in the world support those people that we would have scrambled sympathies in the picture.'

A rather more plausible explanation for doing away with Maibaum's plot, however, was that at the time of pre-production on *The Spy Who*

Loved Me Broccoli was involved in a legal dispute with Kevin McClory. McClory, who was planning to produce his own rival Bond film in the mid-1970s, based on the treatments he had developed with Fleming in 1959, now claimed that the organisation SPECTRE had been his brain-child and that Eon Productions were not entitled to use it at all. In order to avoid protracted legal problems which might further delay production of the film, Eon decided to remove all references to SPECTRE from *The Spy Who Loved Me*. The final shooting script was by Christopher Wood, hitherto best known as writer of the 'Confessions' films; on the film itself Maibaum and Wood share the writing credit.[13]

'It's the Biggest. It's the Best. It's Bond – and B-E-Y-O-N-D', declared trailers and posters for *The Spy Who Loved Me*. It is a film in which size and spectacle are everything. The series returned to the widescreen Panavision process and to the massive Ken Adam sets that had been absent since *Diamonds Are Forever*. The villain has not one but two headquarters: an ocean research laboratory called Atlantis, which rises from beneath the sea on spider-like legs, and an ocean-going supertanker. The cinematography of Claude Renoir (nephew of the great French director Jean Renoir) emphasises the 'epic' (in the sense of size) canvas against which the action takes place by constantly showing human beings who are dwarfed by the physical environment around them. This is evident not only in the studio sets, but in the real locations, which obviously were chosen for the visual possibilities they offered: the Pyramids, the Temple of Karnak and the Valley of Kings. The film juxtaposes the ancient and the modern: the dusty, crumbling edifices of Ancient Egypt are contrasted with the smooth, metallic modernity of Atlantis. In plot terms, *The Spy Who Loved Me* returns to the countdown-to-doomsday theme that had been absent from Roger Moore's first two Bond outings. There is also an emphasis on ever more elaborate and visually exciting technological gadgetry, ranging from Bond's rocket-firing ski-stick to his sleek Lotus Esprit sports car which transforms into a submersible.

The foregrounding of visual spectacle is established from the begin-ning of the film with the justly celebrated pre-title sequence in which Bond, pursued by a KGB hit squad, skis off the side of a vast precipice and free falls into space, whereupon a parachute (inevitably decorated with a Union Jack) opens above his head. Widely regarded as one of the most spectacular stunts in cinema history, it was to have a pronounced effect on the future development of the series in that whereas the pre-title sequences of previous films had generally featured punch-ups (*Goldfinger*, *Thunderball*) or atmospheric scene-setting (*From Russia With Love*, *The Man With the Golden Gun*), the trend hereafter was to use the pre-title sequence as an excuse to display a stunt of an ever more spectacular and excessive nature. Following the sheer audacity of the parachute stunt, the theme song 'Nobody Does It Better', performed over the main titles by Carly Simon, reaffirms Bond's status as the premier movie action hero. (It might also be read, of course, as a statement of Broccoli's ability to produce the series alone following his break with Saltzman.)

Its sheer size and spectacle make *The Spy Who Loved Me* the perfect illustration of the 'Bondian' production ideology in which everything has to be the 'biggest' and the 'best'. The film was not only expensive, it was deliberately intended to look expensive as well; it follows in exemplary measure the old adage of putting the budget on the screen. There are other ways, too, in which it can be seen, rather like *Goldfinger*, as one of the definitive Bond movies in which all the required ingredients are in place. As a genre film, it is a compendium of the narrative formulae and conventions of the entire series. The source for the film is not Fleming, but rather all the previous Bond movies themselves. '*The Spy Who Loved Me* is basically an anthology of all the Bond films that have gone before,' writes John Brosnan. 'It's as if Broccoli and his team deliberately set out to take a number of the more memorable set-pieces and remake them, even bigger and more spectacular.'[14] Brosnan identifies ingredients such as a ski chase (*On Her Majesty's Secret Service*), a train fight (*From Russia With Love*, *Live and Let Die*), Bond's modified sports car (*Goldfinger*), and an underwater battle (*Thunderball*), as reworking tried and trusted elements from other films in the series. At the level of plot, the closest resemblance is to *You Only Live Twice*, significantly also directed by Lewis Gilbert, in that it revolves around a criminal megalomaniac with his own private army who intends to destroy the world by causing the United States and the Soviet Union to destroy each other in a nuclear war. Stromberg (Curt Jurgens), a shipping magnate and 'one of the richest men in the world', has perfected a submarine tracking system which he uses to hijack British and Russian ballistic missile submarines. With Stromberg's own crews in place, the submarines are then sent out to fire missiles at Moscow and New York and thus trigger mutual nuclear annihilation. The climax again recalls *You Only Live Twice* in that Bond releases the imprisoned submarine crews who battle against

Stromberg's men for control of the tanker, and Bond must break into the fortified control room before the submarines can launch their missiles.[15]

However, there is another film which invites comparison to *The Spy Who Loved Me*, and which reaffirms the generic links between the Bond series and the British imperialist spy thriller. There are some intriguing plot similarities between the tenth Bond spectacular and the relatively less well-known *Q-Planes* (1939), directed by American Tim Whelan. This was one of the eve-of-war cycle of spy thrillers which the British cinema produced in 1939 (others included *The Four Just Men*, *Traitor Spy*, *Spies of the Air* and *The Spy in Black*) and which were seen, both at the time and in hindsight, as reflecting the increased international tensions of the time. A polished and entertaining thriller which, like the Bond films, combines both action and comedy, *Q-Planes* also anticipates several of the specific plot devices of *The Spy Who Loved Me*. Thus, while *The Spy Who Loved Me* revolves round the mysterious disappearance of nuclear submarines, which transpire to have been hijacked by a super-tanker equipped with a tracking system, *Q-Planes* revolves around the mysterious disappearance of secret prototype bomber planes, which transpire to have been hijacked by a salvage ship equipped with a radio-beam which cuts out the engines and radios of the aeroplanes. The planes are picked up by crane and concealed in the hold of the ship, called the *Viking*, just as in *The Spy Who Loved Me* the tanker *Liparus* opens its bows to capture the submarines which are then concealed inside. The *Viking* belongs to a 'foreign power' which is unnamed but which, given the political situation at the time, is surely meant to be Germany. There are two hero-figures in *Q-Planes*: test pilot Tony McVane (Laurence Olivier) and secret service agent Major Hammond (Ralph Richardson). Hammond, an eccentric character who wears a homburg and always carries a rolled umbrella (seen by some commentators as a satiric allusion to Neville Chamberlain), was said by Patrick Macnee to have been the inspiration for his performance as John Steed in *The Avengers*. Although he is the most memorable of the characters, it is the more conventional hero-figure McVane who is involved in the action at the film's climax. His plane is intercepted by the enemy ship but, in another anticipation of *The Spy Who Loved Me*, McVane frees the imprisoned crews of the other planes who take over the ship after an exciting battle. The similarities between the two films may be co-incidental, but they are sufficient to show that *The Spy Who Loved Me* should be seen not merely as a compendium of all the other Bond movies, but also as part of a generic lineage of the British spy film which extends back to the 1930s.

In identifying the similarities between *The Spy Who Loved Me* and other films, both Bond and non-Bond, however, that is not to say that *The Spy* itself has nothing new to offer. Indeed, the film rings some changes on the underlying ideologies of the Bond films which makes it particularly important in the overall development of the series. Tony Bennett's reading of the narrative, while seeing it essentially as a re-working of the 'SPECTRE genre', also suggests that it has a particular meaning and relevance in the political context of the late 1970s when fears about nuclear proliferation threatened to undermine the fragile détente in the Cold War:

> Indeed, bearing no relation to the novel from which it derives its title, the film is in a sense the perfection of the SPECTRE genre, although SPECTRE is never mentioned, inasmuch as Stromberg's ransom plan is applied indiscriminately to East and West, playing upon the tensions which subsist beneath detente, Stromberg himself being presented to us as a personification of the irrational forces which permanently threaten the delicate balance of peaceful coexistence. In this sense, particularly at this precise moment in history, Bond's adventures take on a new significance inasmuch as it is through his endeavours that the ever impending world crisis which threatens the world with calamity is averted. The world is led to the brink of nuclear holocaust, and back again. It is thus by effecting a purely imaginary resolution of real social contradictions, which are themselves misrepresented in the form of the fantastic and the grotesque, that the Bond films attain their ideological effect.[16]

Bennett's reading is useful, though flawed in so far as it overlooks the modifications which *The Spy Who Loved Me* makes of the 'SPECTRE genre'. While *The Spy* may have started out as a SPECTRE film, there is a significant difference between it and, say, *Thunderball* or *You Only Live Twice*. The purpose of SPECTRE's acts of terrorism and threats of nuclear destruction had always been extortion and blackmail. In *The Spy Who Loved Me*, however, Stromberg's ambition is to destroy the world so that he can create a new social order. He is not, as Bennett suggests, holding the world to ransom, a point made explicit when he scoffs at

Bond's notion to name his price for not firing the missiles: 'You are deluded, Mr Bond. I am not interested in extortion. I intend to change the face of history. ... Today civilisation as we know it is corrupt, decadent. Inevitably it will destroy itself. I am merely hastening the process.' In this sense, the character of Stromberg maintains some links to Maibaum's idea of a group of idealists who want to destroy the world and start all over again. The grotesque element which Bennett identifies is to be found in the fact that Stromberg has webbed hands, thus maintaining the Fleming tradition of physical deformity in the Bond villains.

There are other ways, too, in which *The Spy Who Loved Me* modifies the ideological structures of the Bond series. While previous films had mostly detached themselves from the Cold War by focusing instead on supra-national villains, with the occasional hint of Red China lurking in the background, *The Spy* actually moves the Bond series for the first time towards a positive ideology of détente. It is not merely suggesting that the threat to civilisation does not come from the Eastern bloc; it actively promotes the idea that East and West should work together to combat the threat which Stromberg poses to both sides. Thus, after a few initial skirmishes, Bond teams up with his Russian opposite number, Agent Triple X, to investigate the disappearance of their submarines. 'We have entered a new era of Anglo-Soviet co-operation,' declares General Gogol (Walter Gotell), head of the KGB. As so often, the Bond films were slightly ahead of their time in prefiguring warmer Anglo-Soviet relations during the mid-1980s when Prime Minister Margaret Thatcher famously said of Soviet Premier Mikhail Gorbachev that 'I think we can do business together'.

The role accorded to Britain in this new world of détente is a central one. *The Spy Who Loved Me* once again reverses the trend of preceding films (particularly *Diamonds Are Forever*) by placing Britain at the forefront of the world stage. The film presents Britain as a power of equal status with America and the Soviet Union. It could be argued, indeed, that *The Spy* is an allegory of the international alliance of the Second World War in which the 'Big Three' (Britain, Russia and America) combine to defeat the common threat presented by an enemy which is hostile to all their ways of life. In this reading Stromberg represents Hitler: a power-crazed megalomaniac with his own private army (Stromberg's men have uniforms and insignia not unlike the SS) who is intent upon genocide on a massive scale. The allegory extends further: Britain is the first power to become involved (the first submarine to be hijacked is British); it enters into an uneasy alliance with Russia just before the halfway point; and the Americans are the last to join in. Indeed, it is not until the last third of the film that there is an American presence, in the form of a submarine with the highly symbolic name of USS *Wayne* – a reminder of the iconic All-American who virtually single-handedly won Hollywood's Second World War. The big battle on board the *Liparus* has British, American and Russian crews fighting side by side under Bond's leadership – the 'Big Three' united through the efforts of the British. If Stromberg represents Hitler in this reading, then Bond must surely represent Churchill. It is a fanciful reading, perhaps, though an irresistible one given that the film constructs its own version of the wartime Grand Alliance.

In all, the patriotic code of the Bond series is at its most strongly evident since *On Her Majesty's Secret Service*. When Bond is called away from a romantic liaison with a blonde in the pre-title sequence, he responds to her plea, 'But James, I need you!', with the line 'So does England!' (delivered in this instance without any discernible irony). The Union Jack parachute which saves Bond following his ski jump is a reminder of British pluck and ingenuity, and the motif of the flag is carried through into the title sequence where it figures prominently, as it had in *OHMSS*. The most obvious explanation for this renewed degree of patriotic display in *The Spy* is that it was released in the year of Elizabeth II's Silver Jubilee, a focus for pageantry and expressions of national pride at a time of increased economic problems and rising unemployment. On another level, the naval motifs of *The Spy* – Bond is seen for only the second time in his Royal Navy uniform, while the end credits are presented over shots of naval vessels and helicopters – is a reaffirmation of British maritime power at a time when it had recently been involved in a so-called 'cod war' with Iceland.

Perhaps the most significant modification in the narrative ideologies of *The Spy Who Loved Me*, however, is that it marks the point at which the centre of narrative interest in the Bond films switches from the relationship between Bond and the villain to the relationship between Bond and the girl. The difference in this respect to the immediately preceding film is quite pronounced: whereas in *The Man With the Golden Gun* it was Scaramanga who had been Bond's professional equal, in *The Spy* it is the heroine Major Anya Amasova who is his opposite number in the KGB. In a broader sense, it would probably be fair to say that

©1977 DANJAQ S.A.

27. *The Spy Who Loved Me*: Bond's train journey is rudely interrupted
when Jaws (Richard Kiel) drops in for a bite.

in most of the earlier films the most memorable characters had always
been the villains (Dr No, Rosa Klebb, Grant, Goldfinger, Oddjob, Largo,
Blofeld) whereas most of the heroines had been little more than eye-
catching adornments. From *The Spy* onwards, however, the villains were
to become ever more bland and colourless, whereas slightly more
interesting roles would be written for the heroines. Generally supposed
to have been a response to the criticisms levelled at the Bond films for
their sexism, *The Spy* provided the most prominent role for a heroine
since *OHMSS*. According to actress Barbara Bach, Anya was 'really not
one of Bond's girls so to speak. She's in the film doing her own bit ...
Most of the girls in the Bond films have just been merely beautiful girls
that you know have small parts and come in and go out. Anya stays
from the beginning to the end.'[17] Certainly Anya is more cool-headed
and capable than the feather-brained heroines of early 1970s films such
as Tiffany Case or Mary Goodnight. Her introduction is a neat reversal
of audience expectations: when a call goes out for Agent Triple X, it
is not the handsome, hairy-chested Bond-like man who answers but

rather the woman in bed with him. However, it would be stretching the point to suggest that Anya is in any serious way a 'liberated' or even 'feminist' heroine. Bach was still cast for her physical charms rather than her acting ability, and ultimately her character is subordinated to Bond, both professionally and sexually: feminism may have been on the upsurge in the 1970s, but it met its match with James Bond.

What is important, however, is not so much the characterisation of the Bond girl as the symbolic role she plays in the narrative. The relationship between Bond and Anya represents on a personal level the ideology of détente which underlies the narrative strategy of *The Spy Who Loved Me*. As Stromberg remarks when Bond arrives at Atlantis to rescue Anya: 'Well, well, well, a British agent in love with a Russian agent – détente indeed.' The thawing of the Cold War – already alluded to in the title sequence in which a line of bare-breasted goose-stepping Russian female soldiers fall like dominoes when pushed over by Bond – is played out through the love scenes between Bond and Anya in which they make repeated references to 'shared bodily warmth'. There is also a more personal dimension to the relationship: half way through the film Anya discovers that it was Bond who killed her previous lover and vows to kill Bond herself when the mission is over. Thus the personal and public lines of narrative are much more successfully integrated than they had been in *The Man With the Golden Gun*. In the end love (or sex) overcomes ideology: Anya inevitably relents and the film ends in the conventional fashion.

The ending of *The Spy Who Loved Me* is symbolic on several levels. Bond and Anya have escaped from the sinking Atlantis in an escape capsule which is picked up by a Royal Navy vessel. Their superiors – M, Gogol and the British Minister of Defence (Geoffrey Keen) – peer in through the window of the capsule and interrupt their moment of passion. When the minister demands, 'Bond, what do you think you're doing?', Bond's reply (the last line of the film) is 'Keeping the British end up, sir'. The comment may be interpreted in several ways. Most obviously, it is a sexual innuendo in that Bond is keeping his own end up (maintaining an erection) with Anya. In another way, it is reasserting Britain's position in world affairs in that Bond, as ever, is on top of the situation. And on a different level again, it could be read as a comment on the role which the Bond films themselves were playing in keeping the British end up in the international film market at a time when very few British films were being made, let alone proving successful at the box-office.

28. *The Spy Who Loved Me*: The massive visual spectacle of the Bond films is perfectly exemplified in Ken Adam's set for Stromberg's submarine pen, so large that the '007 Stage' was built at Pinewood Studios to accommodate it.

In various ways, therefore, *The Spy Who Loved Me* redefines the narrative ideologies of the Bond series. In other ways, too, it develops what had gone before, particularly through a slightly different style of humour. Inter-textuality – which may be defined as the ways in which a text resembles and explicitly borrows from others – had been a feature of the Bond series almost from the beginning, but it became more pronounced with *The Spy*, which makes numerous, obviously deliberate references to other films. For some reason there are several references to the epic films of David Lean: Anya's music-box-cum-radio plays the love theme from *Doctor Zhivago* (the Boris Pasternak novel was banned in the Soviet Union at the time), and later Bond and Anya set off walking across the desert to the music from *Lawrence of Arabia*, and spot a boat on the Nile in a scene which recalls a moment in the Lean film. The most obvious filmic reference, however, is the heavy called Jaws (Richard Kiel), a seven feet two inches man-mountain with steel teeth, which refers explicitly to Steven Spielberg's record-breaking 1975 film. The humorous strategy of *The Spy* thus acknowledges the success of other popular movies, while at the same time distancing itself by poking gentle fun at them: the terror of a shark attack so effectively captured in *Jaws* is mocked in *The Spy* when Jaws, having been dumped by Bond in Stromberg's shark tank, bites the shark himself.

The critical reception of *The Spy Who Loved Me* was divided between the popular and trade press on the one hand, which for the most part regarded it as a return to form for the series, and the more serious critics on the other, who were rather less impressed with what they saw as heavily formulaic and derivative entertainment. The veteran trade reviewer Marjorie Bilbow thought it was the best entry in the series for some time, and made some interesting observations on the director's role in making a Bond movie:

> How exhilarating it is to find an old friend in such splendid form, simply bursting with youthful health and vigour. Lewis Gilbert modestly praises everybody but himself when speaking of the team effort that went into making the latest Bond extravaganza such an imaginative variation of the familiar, but it takes the right director to encourage and co-ordinate wayward talents and skills. Without diminishing the excitement-value of the fast-moving action, the comedy is used to particularly good effect … It's all been done before, of course, but the glory of it is that the old tricks are performed with such cheeky panache that the saucy title of the theme song sums it all up. 'Nobody does it better' than all those who were involved in rejuvenating 007.[18]

The reaction of the more middle-brow critics, however, indicates that, for all it was supposed to be the 'biggest' and the 'best', *The Spy* was widely regarded as being much the same as before. Tim Pulleine in the *Monthly Film Bulletin* was clearly tired of the innuendoes and thought the latest film was little more than a rehash of highlights from the others:

> 'Tell Bond to pull out', says 'M'; cut to 007 in coitus with (anonymous) damsel in a mountain chalet. Responding to the call of duty, Bond polishes off sundry (anonymous) attackers before soaring over a cliff on skis, a Union Jack parachute blossoming over his head. In the ensuing two hours, seaside-postcard smut and comic-strip feats of derring-do continue unabated, suggesting that the makers are being driven to desperate extremes to keep the formula going (having roped in the author of the *Confessions* series for the purpose). Sometimes, however, it is difficult to be certain how deliberate the absurdities are, particularly with a lacklustre, clock-

work villain like Stromberg, incarnated by all-purpose international guest star Curt Jurgens. The strip-cartoon aspect of the film extends beyond such running gags as the presence of a superhuman, steel-toothed heavy called 'Jaws', who emerges unscathed from one lethal hardship after another and drops huge boulders on his toes in careless moments, and permeates the structure itself. Narrative coherence has been disregarded (the takeover of Stromberg's HQ, for instance, looks too easy by half) in favour of a succession of self-contained set pieces. This might not matter if these were more precisely organised or less derivative of earlier movies in the series – a train sequence out of *From Russia With Love*, for instance, and a death-dealing car straight out of *Goldfinger*. Indeed, where Ian Fleming's novel offered an attempt to ring some changes in terms of scale and viewpoint, the film – bearing no relation to its nominal source – seems to do nothing more than anthologise its forerunners, and comes out looking, for all the expensive hardware and location shooting, like a Saturday serial risen grandiloquently above its station.[19]

The popular reception of the film, however, was extremely favourable, as it became the second biggest-grossing film of the year behind the record-breaking space opera *Star Wars*. In Britain, and other territories where *Star Wars* was not released until 1978, *The Spy Who Loved Me* was the top box-office attraction of 1977. What was most significant, however, was that it was successful in America, which had not proved so receptive to Moore's previous two Bond outings. In an article in the *New York Times*, film critic Frank Rich echoed the views of the trade press in arguing that the Bond films succeeded because they provided the sort of entertainment value which audiences wanted. 'The continued appeal of the Bond movies is a real phenomenon – particularly when you consider what a dated cultural artefact James Bond is,' he observed. The appeal of the Bond movies, Rich suggested, was one of nostalgia, 'a throwback to a vanished past – a Hollywood past'. 'This movie,' he wrote, 'takes us back to the time when craftsmanship and good humor were standard fixtures in light film entertainments; it's a movie that actually fulfils the conventional expectations that an audience brings to it.' At a time when many contemporary film-makers had lost the ability to tell uncomplicated stories which did not wallow in sordid realism, or so Rich believed, the Bond movies were guaranteed crowd-pleasers:

What we really want from big-budget summer films like *The Spy Who Loved Me* are the simple things: a little romance, some visceral thrills, a hell of a ride. These are the goods that the Bond pictures fairly consistently deliver, and if the 007 movies are not as inspired as such blockbuster entertainments as *Star Wars* or *Jaws*, they're more dependable than all the rest. Maybe we no longer need James Bond to defend the honor of the free world, but how lucky we are that he's survived to defend the increasingly endangered traditions of the well-made commercial film.[20]

The comparison to *Jaws* and *Star Wars* is a highly pertinent one, as between them these two films had redefined the expectations of the blockbuster movie and of the audience that existed for it. In 1975 *Jaws* became the first film to return over $100 million rentals in the North American market, while *Star Wars*, released two years later, had staggering domestic rentals of $193 million. Both *Jaws* and *Star Wars* were special-effects-driven movies which foregrounded spectacle over narrative complexity and characterisation, and were accorded nationwide saturation release accompanied by high-profile advertising campaigns.[21] In this sense they exemplified the sort of popular cinema which the Bond series had represented for the last fifteen years. But the difference now was that the films of the new generation of American 'movie brats' personified by Spielberg and Lucas were that much more successful than the Bonds. As successful as *The Spy Who Loved Me* was, it was not on the same box-office plateau as *Jaws* or *Star Wars*.

The success of *Star Wars* in particular had a pronounced effect on the Bond series. In 1977 Broccoli had announced that the next Bond title would be *Octopussy*, and said that the budget 'will return to the seven and a half to eight million dollar range', suggesting, perhaps, that the scale of the film would be smaller than *The Spy Who Loved Me*.[22] The title of the next film had been changed by the time *The Spy* was released: the end credits declared that 'James Bond will return in *For Your Eyes Only*'. Shortly after, however, this was changed again to *Moonraker*. There were two, related reasons for this decision. One was that the success of *Star Wars* brought about a science-fiction boom in the cinema, illustrated by films such as *Superman* (1978), *Alien* (1979), *The Black Hole* (1979) and *Star Trek: The Motion Picture* (1979), which the Bond producers decided to join in by using the only remaining Fleming title which suggested a science-fiction theme. The other reason was that the American space shuttle programme was approaching a stage where the first flights would soon be taking place – in the event the first shuttle launch was in April 1981 – and which thus offered topical possibilities in that space flight had once again caught the public imagination. In Broccoli's words: 'Putting James Bond in orbit brought Ian Fleming into the space age.'[23]

There was, however, very little of Fleming in the film version of *Moonraker*. The third Bond novel, which unusually was set entirely in England, had Bond investigating the millionaire industrialist Sir Hugo Drax. Ostensibly an English patriot, Drax has pledged millions of pounds to build a nuclear rocket, the 'Moonraker', for the defence of Britain, which he has built to his own specifications at his plant in Kent. However, he arouses M's suspicions when, as a member of Blades, he is unmasked as a card cheat. As so often in the books, a relatively trivial incident leads to the unravelling of a great conspiracy. Bond is sent to investigate a death at Drax's plant and discovers that Drax is really a German who harbours an intense hatred of the British and who, backed by the Russians, plans to target the 'Moonraker' at London. For the film, Drax (Michael Lonsdale) became a multi-billionaire who is funding the 'Moonraker' space shuttle programme. When a shuttle on loan to the British government is hijacked, Bond is sent to investigate. It turns out that Drax stole his own shuttle because he needed to use it in his conspiracy, which is to kill off the world's entire population with a deadly nerve gas, launched in capsules from an orbiting space station, while a handful of specially selected astronauts breed a physically perfect new order.

Once again, *Moonraker* illustrates how the Bond films constantly updated and modified their ostensible source material. 'But naturally, the plot had to be up-dated,' the publicity material said. 'For who now in the realms of imaginative fiction would be satisfied with such an unambitious piece of villainy as a nuclear rocket hitting London?'[24] Whereas in the book the threat was directed against England and was motivated by Drax's intense hatred of the English, in the film it is directed against the entire world and is motivated by Drax's obsession with racial purity. Even more so than Stromberg before him, Drax is to all intents and purposes a Hitlerite villain. His astronauts have been chosen according to his own physical criteria (most of them are tall, blonde and Aryan-looking), and, just to make the point explicit, Bond refers to Drax's ambition of creating a 'new master race'. The substitution of a conspiracy with Nazi overtones for the Communist-backed threat of the book demonstrates the ideological flexibility of the Bond films: the forces which threaten the world with destruction do not represent a particular political ideology, but rather an irrational and anarchic threat to civilisation as we know it which may derive equally from left or right.

Moonraker also develops one of the themes of *The Spy Who Loved Me* in providing a narratively more significant role for the Bond girl. If the relationship between Bond and Anya had represented Anglo-Soviet détente, then that between Bond and Holly Goodhead (Lois Chiles) represents the 'special relationship' between Britain and America, with CIA agent Holly as a female equivalent of Felix Leiter. The film mocks Bond's male chauvinism: he is surprised to find that Dr Goodhead is 'a woman' ('Your powers of observation do you credit, Mr Bond,' she replies sarcastically). For the first time in the Bond series, the girl possesses a narratively important skill which Bond does not: she is able to pilot the space shuttle that is necessary for them to reach Drax's space station, and, later, to track and destroy the nerve gas globes. Within the admittedly limited scope of the Bond films, Holly is perhaps the most 'progressive' heroine of the series to date. Having said that, of course, the ending of the film reassigns her to the more traditional female role as sexual partner for Bond. Although it is Holly who pilots the shuttle, her last line is to ask Bond to 'take me around the world one more time', thus reassigning Bond to the dominant role.

Whereas the publicity discourse surrounding *The Spy Who Loved Me* had made much of the 'new' type of Bond girl, for *Moonraker* it was not the characterisation of the heroine that was emphasised but rather the technological hardware. The producers were keen to emphasise that the space technology shown in the film was based on the real thing, and official publicity constantly asserted that *Moonraker* was 'science fact, not science fiction'. This even extended so far as commissioning an article on the making of the film from Eric Burgess, author of many books on space technology and rocket propulsion, who had been a founder of the British Interplanetary Society in the 1930s and was now a contracted author for America's National Aeronautics and Space Administration (NASA). Burgess argued that *Moonraker* should be differentiated from the recent 'spate of fantasies which ignored physical laws but appealed to popular imagination' (he cited *Close Encounters of the Third Kind*, *Star Wars* and *Battlestar Galactica*), and should instead be considered as one of the rare 'attempts at serious technology forecasting

29. *Moonraker*: Bond joins the space race to save the world with Dr Holly
Goodhead (Lois Chiles).

... into the immediate future based on current technology while keeping
within accepted physical laws' (a tradition which he traced back to Fritz
Lang's *Die Frau im Mond* of 1929 and George Pal's *Destination Moon* of
1950):

> The Bond series of motion pictures evolved as a natural medium
> for looking at practical aspects of spaceflight. Over the years these
> films developed as motion pictures which aimed at a level of
> credibility even though pushing the imagination beyond what is
> actually being done today (satellites to control Earth, cities beneath
> the seas, mountain top eyries of super scientists, and the like) and
> they thrust toward spaceflight applications in the clandestine satel-
> lites of *Diamonds Are Forever* and *You Only Live Twice*.[25]

Burgess was at pains to point out how 'the producer and director of
Moonraker attempted to achieve space reality'. Thus they used space
suits modelled on those used by real astronauts, and personal propulsion
units of a sort which had already been tested in the space station Skylab;

the space shuttles in the film were based closely on the real thing; and Drax's space station was designed along the sort of lines which scientists at the time were planning, albeit that it also had to be 'aesthetically pleasing, functional, and visually suitable for various camera angles and viewpoints'. Burgess described the special effects and model work in great detail, pointing out that they 'had to reach new heights of realism'. Indeed, there is a contradiction running throughout his essay between the emphasis on how realistic the space hardware was supposed to be on the one hand, and the artifice that went into creating the impression of realism on the other. For example, real laser beams were found not to be bright enough for filming, so they were created by special effects instead: 'It was much easier to simulate the lasers, and then they seemed "more realistic".' A better example of how the Bond films resist categorisation in terms of conventional notions of realism could hardly be imagined. For all that it might be based on 'science fact' or 'space reality', *Moonraker* is still essentially a fantasy film.

Moonraker follows the direction of *The Spy Who Loved Me* in foregrounding visual spectacle above all else. The narrative is reduced virtually to a travelogue of highly photogenic locations (California, Venice, Rio de Janeiro) which serve as backdrops for improbable action sequences. Again there is a juxtaposition between the ancient and the futuristic: Drax's secret shuttle launch silo is hidden in the ruins of an ancient city deep in the Amazonian jungle. With the cost of the film having been offset partly by deals with companies and manufacturers anxious to have their products associated with James Bond, *Moonraker* also exhibits what might be described as an aesthetic of product placement: Christian Dior perfume, Bollinger champagne and Canon cameras are featured prominently. In one sequence, as Bond fights with an assailant in the back of an ambulance driving up a hillside outside Rio, the struggle is intercut with narratively irrelevant shots of the vehicle passing advertising billboards for 7 Up, Seiko watches and Marlboro cigarettes, while the villain ends up careering on a runaway stretcher into the mouth of a stewardess on a giant British Airways advertisement ('We'll take more care of you'). The special effects and model work are very impressive, and the climactic battle in space between Drax's army and US Space Marines, with its criss-crossing laser beams and bodies cartwheeling into space, is at least the equal of any of the other science-fiction blockbusters of the late 1970s. However, the outer space storyline and reliance on visual effects were not to the liking of most critics, who complained that the Bond films were imitating the science-fiction boom with disappointing results. Marjorie Bilbow, who had been so effusive about *The Spy Who Loved Me*, remarked that 'we have been so deluged with films about space flights that journeys and chases in shuttles have not [*sic*] built-in excitement and call for great stretches of directing and screenwriting imagination to be more than run of the mill'. Although she predicted that the film 'will be enjoyed by millions', Bilbow added that, for her own part, 'I shall be glad to see Bond return to terra firma and stay there'.[26]

Other critics simply found *Moonraker* tedious and derivative. 'If the preceding Bond opus, *The Spy Who Loved Me*, rather resembled a con-glomerate remake of the series to date, the latest instalment looks like nothing so much as a remake of *The Spy Who Loved Me*,' observed Tim Pulleine. 'In fact, the kind of double vision which has increasingly fogged the Bond pictures, as they have sought to parody an already parodic model, here becomes virtually complete.'[27] At the level of narrative structure, certainly, *Moonraker* is simply a reworking of *The Spy*. Many of the specific incidents are the same: it begins with a hijacking, the pre-title sequence has Bond making a death-defying escape when an attempt is made to kill him (pushed out of an aeroplane, Bond wrests a parachute from one of his assailants after a mid-air tussle), and it ends with Bond and the heroine being caught *in flagrante delicto* by their embarrassed superiors ('I think he's attempting re-entry, sir,' says Q, while the shuttle's onboard camera shows Bond and Holly in a zero-gravity clinch). In between are the usual succession of stunts and set pieces, though most of them lapse into broad comedy. Thus, after escaping from pursuers in his motorised gondola, which then turns into a hovercraft, Bond performs a lap of honour around St Marks Square while tourists stare in astonishment and a pigeon performs a double take. The inter-textual references which had characterised *The Spy* are again in evidence: the entry-code to a secret laboratory is the same tune used to communicate with the aliens in *Close Encounters of the Third Kind*, and Bond, wearing a poncho and sombrero, rides a horse to the strains of Elmer Bernstein's theme from *The Magnificent Seven*. The comic strategy of the film is reinforced by the return of Jaws, who had proved such a popular character in *The Spy*, and whose attempts to kill Bond are so remarkably incompetent that he becomes the comic relief rather than a believable threat. Indeed, the character is softened to such an extent that he is even given a small, short-sighted girlfriend called Dolly. Dilys Powell, for one, found this distasteful: 'I doubt whether the surrender of Jaws (himself, of course, a reference-joke) to the diminutive blonde would have seemed as funny if one didn't remember Frankenstein's Monster encountering the innocent child.' Powell, who had been one of the Bond series' biggest admirers among British critics, found *Moonraker* too disjointed to be thoroughly enjoyable: 'Its two hours could be divided into independent episodes: Bond at the pigeon-shoot, Bond in the velocity-test, Bond attacked from a canal-hearse, or acrobatic in a cable-car, or resourceful with a tropical reptile.' 'In fact,' she added, '*Moonraker* is a serial: it would gratify the desire, common in the silent days, to see all the episodes in one go.'[28]

It is ironic that *Moonraker*, which is generally regarded as one of the most derivative of the Bond series and which critically was among the least well received, actually became the biggest-grossing Bond to date at the box-office. There is no clearer indication of the difference between critical and popular tastes. If judged solely on the basis of popular reception, then *Moonraker* has to be considered a triumph. Like *The Spy Who Loved Me*, it was that rarity in British cinema of the late 1970s, an international box-office hit, proving that the Bond films were indeed 'keeping the British end up' in the international film market. However, the sheer size and scale of *Moonraker* were such that it represented the fullest lengths to which visual spectacle could be taken in the Bond movies. Having sent Bond into outer space, the only direction he could take thereafter was to come back down to earth.

6

Cold Warrior Reborn: *For Your Eyes Only, Octopussy, Never Say Never Again, A View To A Kill*

The direction of the Bond series during the first half of the 1980s once again demonstrates that the generic formula of the Bond films is not permanently fixed, but adapts and modifies itself according to various industrial, political and cultural determinants. The official series continued with three films which belong together as a group in much the same way as *The Spy Who Loved Me* and *Moonraker* belong together as a pair: *For Your Eyes Only* (dir. John Glen, 1981), *Octopussy* (dir. John Glen, 1983) and *A View To A Kill* (dir. John Glen, 1985). The narrative ideologies of these films marked a change of direction after the détente-themed narrative of *The Spy Who Loved Me* in that they relocated Bond, partially at least, within the political and ideological co-ordinates of the Cold War. At the level of visual spectacle, while they maintained the exotic and colourful locations, they downplayed the massive sets of the two preceding films in favour of a slightly less fantastic look in which authentic locations took precedence over futuristic technology. 'It may be that by then we had overworked the sophisticated hardware in our pictures,' Broccoli admitted of *Moonraker*, and that with *For Your Eyes Only* a decision was taken 'to focus more upon character and story than the familiar set-piece fireworks'.[1] And in terms of characterisation, Roger Moore's Bond came increasingly to represent an old-fashioned construction of Englishness, a National Heritage hero whose ageing masculinity is tested by a succession of more assertive and challenging women, culminating with the appearance of Grace Jones in *A View To A Kill*. Another challenge to Moore's Bond came in the form of Sean Connery's return to the role in *Never Say Never Again* (dir. Irvin Kershner, 1983), a one-off production made outside the Eon series which revived debates about who was the 'best' James Bond.

In comparison to the spiralling production costs of the late 1970s, the early 1980s was a period of relative stability in which the negative costs of the Bond films averaged $28–30 million. The Bond films continued to be among the most successful at the box-office, if not in the same league as the phenomenally successful Spielberg–Lucas spectaculars, including the two *Star Wars* sequels *The Empire Strikes Back* (1980) and *Return of the Jedi* (1983), the Indiana Jones films *Raiders of the Lost Ark* (1981) and *Indiana Jones and the Temple of Doom* (1984), and Spielberg's record-breaking *E.T.: The Extra-Terrestrial* (1982). The total worldwide grosses of the Bond films at this time were $196 million for *For Your Eyes Only*, $188 million for *Octopussy* and $153 million for *A View To A Kill*, figures which look impressive enough on their own but which are put into perspective by the fact that *E.T.* took over $200 million *rentals* in North America alone (the North American rentals of the three Bond films were, respectively, $26.5 million, $34 million and $25.3 million). Yet for a series that was now twenty years old, the fact that the Bond films were still consistently successful at the box-office was a considerable achievement in its own right. It was in markets outside North America that the Bond films performed best, with their international grosses generally being between two to three times their North American figures.[2]

The British film industry during the early 1980s was undergoing one of its periodic revivals following the doldrums of the 1970s. The critical and commercial success of *Chariots of Fire* (1981), a dramatisation of the real-life stories of British athletes Harold Abrahams and Eric Liddell who won gold medals at the 1924 Paris Olympics, won the Oscar for Best Picture in 1982 and prompted screenwriter Colin Welland to declare optimistically 'The British are coming!' What *Chariots of Fire* also heralded was a cycle of period costume pictures which have subsequently been labelled 'heritage' films. The film-makers most associated with this cycle of films are the producer-director team of Ismail Merchant and James Ivory, responsible for films such as *Heat and Dust* (1983), *A Room with a View* (1986), *Maurice* (1987), *Howard's End* (1992) and *The Remains of the Day* (1993). These films, and those like them by other hands, represent the critically respectable 'quality' end of British cinema and need to be seen in terms of a long tradition of literary adaptation encompassing films such as David Lean's *Great Expectations* (1946) and *Oliver Twist* (1948) and even Cecil Hepworth's *Comin' Thro' the Rye* (1923). They are characterised by their adaptation of classic literature (particularly E. M. Forster), by their highly pictorialist visual style which foregrounds sites of national heritage (Oxbridge, country houses), and by their narrative concern with the upper classes. The heritage films were popular with 'art house' audiences in Britain and America, and as such they exported a traditionalist and Anglocentric construction of national identity to overseas audiences.

While the Bond series was not itself part of the heritage cycle, it was at this moment that the films began to draw upon the sort of visual motifs which asserted their Englishness more explicitly than ever before. In *Dr No* Fleming had evoked the picture-postcard image of London, though the films had hitherto steered away from using such imagery. Indeed, there are remarkably few indicators of the London location of secret service headquarters before the 1980s: the most subtle is the first shot of *On Her Majesty's Secret Service* (missing from some prints) in which Big Ben can be seen reflected in the brass wall-plate of 'Universal Exports (London) Ltd.', the cover-name for the secret service.[3] In the early 1980s, however, the sequence of Bond's briefing with M would be preceded by an exterior shot of the building in which a visual signifier of location features prominently: a red double-decker bus in *Octopussy*, a mounted horse guard in *A View To A Kill*. The purpose of these images is to say to audiences 'this is London': snapshots which could have been lifted straight from a postcard. It is yet another indication of how the Bond series had changed since the 1960s: once seen as an embodiment of progressive modernisation, they had now come to represent a heritage industry construction of British culture.

'With the retreat of the Cold War,' writes Sarah Street, 'the English-ness of Bond betrays a concern to insert a comforting national stereotype (particularly with Roger Moore's Bond) into a world which is increasingly governed by international forces and threatened by an unidentified enemy.'[4] But while in the films of the early 1980s the ageing Moore does indeed represent a 'comforting national stereotype', the Cold War was far from being in retreat at this time. Indeed, Cold War tensions assumed a greater narrative significance in the Bond films of the early 1980s than at any other moment in the series' history. Even in *From Russia With Love* the Russians had been secondary villains and latent Cold War antagonisms were exacerbated by an even more sinister, initially unknown enemy. However, *For Your Eyes Only* is based around a contest between Bond and a Soviet-backed villain for possession of the 'McGuffin', thus resurrecting Bond as a cold warrior and reassigning him to an ideological role he had not performed since the novels of the 1950s. Dissident and renegade Russian villains also featured in both *Octopussy* and *A View To A Kill*, in which the peaceful co-existence of East and West is shown to be under threat from extremists on the Soviet side.

How is the renewed foregrounding of Cold War tensions in the Bond series at this time to be explained? While it is difficult to make straightforward causal links, it seems reasonable to relate the modified ideological structures of the films to changes in the international political climate. Although the Cold War had never really gone away, tensions had not been especially acute since the Russian invasion of Czecho-slovakia in 1968. Indeed, the 1970s had seen a mild thaw, which the Bond films reflected through the détente-themed narrative of *The Spy Who Loved Me*. But dormant tensions came to the surface again through events such as the Russian invasion of Afghanistan in 1979, the American boycott of the 1980 Moscow Olympics (and the tit-for-tat Russian boycott of the 1984 Los Angeles Games), and the suppression of the Solidarity trade union in Poland in the early 1980s. The proliferation of medium-range nuclear missiles in Europe (American Cruise and Pershing missiles were stationed in Britain and West Germany from 1983) further increased East–West tensions. This period coincided with the election of strongly right-wing governments in Britain and the United States, under Margaret Thatcher and Ronald Reagan respectively. Aggressive anti-Communist rhetoric was part of the ideological platform of both Thatcherite and Reaganite foreign policy: Reagan famously referred to the Soviet Union as an 'evil empire'. This hawkish climate was reflected in a spate of aggressively nationalistic Hollywood films, including the hysterically paranoid *Red Dawn* (1984) in which a Soviet-Cuban invasion of the USA was defeated by a group of American teenagers, and the brutal *Rambo: First Blood, Part II* (1985) in which Sylvester Stallone's musclebound killing machine returned to Vietnam to rescue forgotten American prisoners and single-handedly decimated the North Viet-namese and Russian armies.

While there were no Red-bashing films as such in British cinema, there was much evidence of a more hawkish and nationalistic mood. Even before the Falklands War of 1982, this was exemplified by events such as the terrorist siege of the Iranian Embassy in London, which was ended in dramatic fashion by the SAS (Special Air Service). Margaret Thatcher wrote in her memoirs: 'Wherever I went over the next few days, I sensed a great wave of pride at the outcome ... we had sent a signal to terrorists everywhere that they could expect no deals and would extort no favours from Britain.'[5] This bullish mood was perfectly captured in the blatantly exploitative action film *Who Dares Wins* (1982), which dramatised a terrorist take-over of the American Embassy in London and its storming by the SAS. With its unequivocal anti-terrorist message and its celebration of ruthless, clinical military force, *Who Dares Wins* is surely one of the most ideologically right-wing tracts ever produced by the British cinema. While the Bond films did not resort to the jingoistic extremes of *Who Dares Wins* or to the nihilistic aggression of Rocky or Rambo, they did nevertheless reflect the mood of the times in that they exhibited a tendency towards the foreign policy agendas of Thatcherism and Reaganism.

The new direction of the Bond series in the 1980s was indicated by *For Your Eyes Only*, in which the production team made a conscious decision to steer away from the technological futurism and massive visual spectacle of *Moonraker*. 'That kind of production design isn't really in the nature of this story, and I don't think there would be any point in building super-grand sets just so people can walk around in front of them,' director John Glen said, distancing himself from the preceding Lewis Gilbert films. Interestingly, the film which Glen compared it to was the one generally supposed to have been a failure: 'I think the best way of describing it is as more of a straight thriller; the one closest to it might be *On Her Majesty's Secret Service*. It's a bit of a throwback in the sense that the emphasis is back on people rather than gadgets.'[6] The Bond film which *For Your Eyes Only* most closely resembles, however, is *From Russia With Love*, in that it is a straight espionage thriller set entirely in Europe in which the Cold War provides the political background to the plot. It is also the closest of the latter-day Bond films to Ian Fleming, drawing on characters and incidents from two short stories, 'For Your Eyes Only' and 'Risico'. The character of the heroine Melina (Carole Bouquet), whom Bond meets when she sets out to track down and kill the men who murdered her parents, is derived

30. *For Your Eyes Only*: Bond comes back down to earth in a taut espionage thriller intended to return to the style of the early Bond movies.

from 'For Your Eyes Only', while the characters of rival smugglers Kristatos (Julian Glover) and Columbo (Topol) are taken straight from 'Risico'. Although the original Fleming stories were over twenty years old, and the most recent films had increasingly distanced themselves from their ostensible source materials, several films in the 1980s (*For Your Eyes Only, Octopussy, The Living Daylights*) were to return to specific incidents in Fleming as their starting point, while expanding them into broader and more contemporary narratives.

The main line of narrative in *For Your Eyes Only* is located squarely within the geo-political co-ordinates of the Cold War in that the struggle for possession of the 'McGuffin' takes place in Europe between Bond and a Soviet-backed villain. A British spy ship equipped with a device known as ATAC (Automatic Targeting Attack Computer), which can be used to transmit coded orders to Polaris missile submarines, is sunk accidentally off the Albanian coast. The British government fear the Russians getting their hands on the device because in the event of war they could use it to order British nuclear submarines to launch their missiles against British cities. For the first time in the Bond series the principal villain is working for the Soviet Union: Kristatos is a freelance operative who is sympathetic to the Russians – General Gogol refers to him as 'our usual friend in Greece' – while one of his associates, an East German biathlon champion called Kriegler, is a KGB assassin. The détente theme of *The Spy Who Loved Me* is reversed in so far as Gogol, an uneasy ally in *The Spy*, now assumes the role of Cold War enemy. The fragility of détente is underlined at the end when Bond, facing Gogol and a Russian gunman, throws the ATAC off a cliff where it is smashed to pieces. 'That's détente, comrade,' Bond remarks. 'You don't have it – I don't have it.' Gogol departs with a wry chuckle and a gesture which suggests that, while this may be the end of one incident, the larger war goes on.

The presence of Gogol is an example of how the Bond films at this time maintained continuity with their predecessors (Walter Gotell as the KGB chief was a recurring character in every film from *The Spy Who Loved Me* to *The Living Daylights*). *For Your Eyes Only* also refers back explicitly to other films, particularly *On Her Majesty's Secret Service*. In doing so it establishes a link between the past and the present of the Bond series which has significant implications for the interpretation of the Bond character. Up to this point in the series Bond had remained basically the same age, generally assumed to be permanently in his late thirties. *For Your Eyes Only*, however, is suggestive of an older hero. The textual evidence for this is to be found in the opening shots, where Bond is seen laying flowers in an English country graveyard where the headstone reads 'Teresa Bond. 1943–1969. Beloved wife of James Bond. We have all the time in the world'. The scene was written, apparently, when the producers thought Roger Moore might not make the film, and was devised to introduce a new lead actor by providing a point of identification with the series' past. What is unusual, however, is not that the film refers back to Bond's wife (this had already happened once in *The Spy Who Loved Me* and would occur again in *Licence To Kill*), but that it should do so in such a temporally precise way. The dates on the gravestone place the Bond of *For Your Eyes Only* as being twelve years older than the Bond of *OHMSS*. Assuming that Bond is usually taken to be in his late thirties, then the Bond of *For Your Eyes Only* would therefore be approaching fifty. In this sense, the film brings Bond roughly in line with Roger Moore's own age (he was fifty-three when the film was released) and works better for Moore than it would likely have done for a younger, incoming actor.

Another link to the past is provided by the ensuing pre-title sequence, unrelated to the main narrative, in which Bond's helicopter is hijacked and flown by remote control by an old enemy who intends to crash it in order to kill him. Although not referred to by name, this man is clearly meant to be Blofeld: he is a bald man in a neck brace and a wheelchair who strokes the white cat which the films had introduced as a prop for the character of Blofeld from his first appearance in *From Russia With Love*. A line from the script which is not in the finished film – 'Good afternoon, Mr Bond. I thought we should celebrate the tenth anniversary of our last meeting' – makes it even more obvious that the man is meant to be Blofeld, who had last appeared in *Diamonds Are Forever* in 1971.[7]

Yet at the same time as establishing these links with the series' past, *For Your Eyes Only* also stresses its contemporaneity. The film locates itself explicitly in Thatcher's Britain through a number of topical references which, unusually for the Bond films, refer specifically to the government of the day. Occasionally in previous films there had been references to 'the prime minister', but always in anonymous terms which did not specify any particular person. In *For Your Eyes Only*, however, there are several direct references to Mrs Thatcher herself. In a film which on the whole eschews the excessive parody of some of the 1970s Bonds, Thatcher is the subject of several in-jokes which play upon the novelty of Britain's first woman prime minister, and particularly on her famous reputation as the 'Iron Lady'. Thatcher's legendary ability to intimidate her male Cabinet colleagues is illustrated when the Minister of Defence is shown to be afraid of her ('She'll have our guts for garters'). And Thatcher herself appears in the fade-out joke, which is rich in ideological and gendered meanings. The prime minister has been put through to Bond on a phone-link from the kitchen at 10 Downing Street, in order to congratulate him personally on the successful completion of his mission. Even when placed in a traditionally domestic feminine role (she is preparing a meal), Mrs Thatcher is shown to exercise authority over men (she slaps the wrist of husband Denis when he tries to steal from the salad bowl). Her message of congratulation asserts in the strongest terms notions of patriotism and duty ('Your courage and resourcefulness are a credit to the nation'). However, she is unaware that she is speaking not to Bond, who has gone swimming with Melina, but rather to Melina's parrot Max. When the parrot squawks 'Give us a kiss', Mrs Thatcher pats her hair and, clearly flattered, says 'Really, Mr Bond!' Even the fearful Iron Lady, therefore, resorts to feminine gestures when propositioned (or so she thinks) by Bond. A further, culturally specific reference is that Mrs Thatcher and Denis are portrayed by impressionist Janet Brown and comedian John Wells, who were well-known in Britain for their impersonations of the Thatchers.

While Mrs Thatcher becomes the butt of a typically Bondian sexual joke, in other respects the film follows the trend of its immediate predecessors in again providing a more prominent role for the Bond girl. The public and personal lines of narrative are neatly interwoven: Bond's mission to retrieve the ATAC and Melina's desire to avenge the death of her parents bring them together in the common objective of destroying Kristatos. Melina is not a professional secret agent, like the heroines of the two previous films, but she is no mere damsel in distress. She is shown to be competent and resourceful, dispatching sundry villains by means of a crossbow. The film's allusion to classical mythology ('Greek women, like Electra, always avenge their loved ones') places her within a tradition of determined and vengeful women which has a long cultural history. Indeed, the narrative importance accorded to Melina's desire for revenge is such that it takes precedence over the romance between Bond and herself. Co-writer Richard Maibaum was not happy with the way the relationship was handled, suggesting that the underlying idea was missed: 'The whole idea was that the great lover James Bond can't get to first base with this woman because she's so obsessed with avenging her parents' death. Nothing was ever done with it. It was as if the director didn't feel there was a love story there at all.'[8] Marjorie Bilbow, however, thought Bond's relationship with Melina made a welcome change from the usual sexual shenanigans. 'I perceived, with relief,

31. *For Your Eyes Only*: Melina (Carole Bouquet) looks suitably grave at the prospect of being hauled over a coral reef; perhaps Bond's scowl is because he has not slept with her yet.

that his use 'em and dump 'em treatment of his women has been whittled down to a much more likeable selectivity and some caring,' she said. 'In fact, the film as a whole is nothing like as old-hat sexist as the image put over in the graffiti-attracting posters.'[9] The posters for the film, which featured a shapely pair of woman's legs shown from behind with the smaller figure of Bond between them, attracted much criticism from militant feminist groups, and it is part of Bond folklore that they were censored on some American university campuses.

Most critics responded favourably to this back-to-basics Bond after the overblown extravagance of *Moonraker*. *Variety* offered a particularly favourable review, opining that it was 'one of the most thoroughly enjoyable of the 12 Bond pix despite the fact that many of the usual ingredients in the successful 007 formula are missing this time out'. The review continued that 'all the action has been staged with an expertise and excitement unusual even for this exceptionally well produced series' and considered that '[the] entire film is probably the best-directed since *On Her Majesty's Secret Service*, as John Glen, moving into the director's chair after long service as second unit director and editor, displays a fine eye and as often as not keeps more than one thing happening in his shots'. For once, a Bond film 'benefits from [the] presence of a truly sympathetic heroine, fetchingly played by Carole Bouquet, who exhibits a humanity and emotionalism not frequently found in this sort of pop adventure and who takes a long time (the entire film in fact) to warm up to Bond sufficiently to jump into the sack with him'. What the reviewer found most praiseworthy, however, was the way in which the film-makers had kept the Bond franchise fresh by offering some variations on the usual formula:

> After all these years, producer Albert R. Broccoli and his writing cohorts, Richard Maibaum and Michael G. Wilson, are certainly entitled to play around with their standard formula a bit if they feel like it, and some of the variations here seem like deliberate attempts to counter what one has come to expect from these efforts.
>
> After a smashing helicopter prolog, next action set piece is a super car chase. This time, however, Bond isn't driving his super-charged sports car, but Bouquet's tin can 2CV Citroen thereby proving his own value rather than that of his vehicle.
>
> M is gone, due to Bernard Lee's death; Bond doesn't make his first feminine conquest until halfway through the picture; there's no technology introduced by Q which saves the hero in the end; no looming supervillain dominates the drama; Bond's bon mots are surprisingly sparse, and the fate of the whole world isn't even hanging in the balance at the climax. But the fact that these omissions don't matter much just proves the durability of the basic

premise and leading character, and absence of some of them even proves somewhat refreshing, for a change.

Ultimately, the more basic prosaic nature of the weapons and villainy here brings Bond closer to the 'real world', if such a thing was ever on view in this series, than any of the pix since *From Russia With Love*, which remains the Bond film par excellence for most devotees. It's a terrific, nonstop romp, and only those exclusively into Bondian hardware should be disappointed.

To boot, [a] final throwaway scene featuring Margaret Thatcher lookalike Janet Brown will have Britons, particularly, rolling in the aisles.[10]

What this review proves more than anything else is that critics identified subtle changes and modifications in the generic formula of the Bond series and, in this particular case, approved. Furthermore, the favour with which *For Your Eyes Only* was greeted, following the lukewarm critical reaction to *Moonraker*, suggests that the producers were more receptive to critics' views than perhaps they would care to admit. Their decision to bring Bond back down to earth won critical plaudits, at least from the trade and popular press.

Octopussy reworks the themes and narrative ideologies of *For Your Eyes Only*. It is even more directly rooted in Cold War conflicts and equally topical in its references; once again narrative interest focuses on the relationship between Bond and the heroine rather than Bond and the villains; and it is again suggestive of an older Bond. Furthermore, as in *For Your Eyes Only*, incidents from two Fleming short stories ('Octopussy' and 'The Property of a Lady') are worked into the plot. The film has Bond travelling to India to investigate a jewellery smuggling operation run by Kamal Khan (Louis Jourdan), an exiled Afghan prince, and Octopussy (Maud Adams), a fabulously wealthy woman who lives on an island populated exclusively by beautiful girls. Bond discovers that, unbeknown to Octopussy, Kamal is in league with a senior Russian military commander, General Orlov (Steven Berkoff), who plans to use the Octopussy Circus (front for the smuggling pipeline) to smuggle an atomic bomb across the border from East to West Germany and explode it on an American air force base.

In terms of structure, *Octopussy* falls somewhere between the taut espionage narrative of *For Your Eyes Only* and the expansive travelogue of *Moonraker*. Much of the film is set in India, a location which was

32. *Octopussy*: In his Indian workshop Q (Desmond Llewelyn) demonstrates
his latest gadget to Bond, while unlikely secret service colleague Vijay
Amritraj looks on.

chosen not merely for the visual possibilities which it offers. *Octopussy*
also needs to be seen in the context of a cycle of British films and
television series of the early 1980s which showed a fascination with
India. ITV's *The Jewel in the Crown* (a dramatisation of Paul Scott's 'Raj
Quartet'), Channel 4's *The Far Pavilions* (made by Goldcrest Films and
based on M. M. Kaye's novel), and films such as Merchant-Ivory's *Heat
and Dust*, Richard Attenborough's *Gandhi* (1982) and David Lean's *A
Passage to India* (1984) can be placed within the heritage genre in so far
as they were all narratives of Britain's imperial past. But whereas they
all adopt a critical perspective towards British rule in India, *Octopussy* is
set in a present where Anglo-Indian relations are uncomplicated by
racial or political problems. The film presents a tourist's view of India
in which there is no indication of the poverty and social distress
experienced by millions of the sub-continent's inhabitants. Instead, the
India of *Octopussy* is one of colourful bazaars, luxurious hotels and
sumptuous palaces. The casino, where Kamal plays a retired English
major at backgammon while turbaned waiters attend the predominantly
white European clientele, is a throwback to the culture of the Raj.
Bond, to all intents and purposes, travels around India like a tourist: at

one point he even escapes from Kamal's men, who have been hunting him through the jungle, by clambering aboard a river boat full of camera-clicking American tourists. Bond's reply to the query 'Are you with our group?' – 'No, ma'am, I'm with the economy tour' – might be read as an ironic comment on the relative poverty of British resources (Q has already complained of having no proper facilities in his Indian workshop) in comparison to the wealthy Americans.

For all that the greater part of the film is set in India, however, the conspiracy plot in *Octopussy* is, like *For Your Eyes Only*, rooted in the geo-political situation in Europe. It is here that a structural flaw in the film becomes very evident: while Kamal Khan is the most prominent of the villains, it is General Orlov who fulfils the more important ideological role. Early in the film, Orlov opposes disarmament talks between the Warsaw Pact and NATO, reminding his colleagues of the Eastern bloc's overwhelming superiority in conventional forces which he forecasts could over-run Western Europe in five days. He asserts that NATO would not dare resort to using nuclear weapons in retaliation ('The West is decadent and divided. It has no stomach to risk our atomic reprisals. Throughout Europe, daily, demonstrations demand unilateral nuclear disarmament'). The film reflects the military and political circum-stances of the time. It was military reality that the Warsaw Pact had such overwhelming superiority in conventional forces that the NATO forces stationed in West Germany would probably not have been able to hold a full-scale invasion. And there were loud calls for unilateral disarmament in the West. In Britain, for example, the Campaign for Nuclear Disarmament (CND), which had waned in influence since its heyday in the early 1960s, received a fresh stimulus from the stationing of American nuclear missiles in Britain. In 1981 both the Labour Party and the Trades Union Congress passed motions in favour of unilateral nuclear disarmament at their annual conferences, while one of the most notable protest movements of the early 1980s was the series of demon-strations by women at Greenham Common air base in Berkshire, where Cruise missiles were to be based.

Although the film makes clear that Orlov is a renegade whose war-mongering ambitions are not shared by the Politburo – the chairman, who with his huge bushy eyebrows resembles the recently deceased Soviet leader Leonid Brezhnev, declares that 'World Socialism will be achieved by peaceful means' and states that 'our military role is purely defensive' – all the same it reinforces the notion that the Soviet Union

represents a threat to the West. The ideological impetus behind Orlov
is underlined by the giant portrait of Lenin which dominates the wall
of the conference chamber where he makes his blustering speech. The
film suggests a difference of opinion between politicians and the military,
the latter rejecting diplomacy in favour of armed force (Orlov refers
contemptuously to 'a handful of old men in Moscow [who] bargain
away our advantage in disarmament talks'). Orlov's motivation would
seem to be a combination of ideology and his desire for personal glory
– even as he dies he believes he will be seen as 'a hero of the Soviet
Union' – and as portrayed by a manically twitching Berkoff, who played
a similar part in *Rambo*, he can be seen in the same tradition of hard-
line military lunatics in the cinema as Sterling Hayden's General Jack D.
Ripper in Stanley Kubrick's *Dr Strangelove* (1963).

Although topicality was always one of the features of the Bond
series, *Octopussy* is slightly unusual in that it tackles such a controversial
political issue as nuclear disarmament. The film is nothing if not
Thatcherite in its unequivocal assertion that the nuclear deterrent, and
especially the presence of American missiles in Europe, is essential to
the defence of the West. Orlov's plan is to detonate an atomic bomb
on a US air force base, which will look like an accident as early warning
radar would rule out the possibility of a Russian attack. The catastrophe
of a nuclear accident would lead to loud demands for nuclear disarmament that politicians in the West would be unable to resist. The
consequences of this are spelled out by Bond, who realises it would
leave Europe defenceless against the Red Army ('Europe will insist on
unilateral disarmament, leaving every border undefended for you to
walk across at will'). It is not an entirely fanciful scenario, and is certainly
more plausible than the doomsday plots of *The Spy Who Loved Me* and
Moonraker. Indeed, a similar plot featured in *The Fourth Protocol* (1987),
based on a novel by Frederick Forsyth, in which a Soviet agent (played
by future James Bond star Pierce Brosnan) is sent to detonate an atomic
bomb at a US air force base in Britain.

While the face of the enemy has changed in the films of the early
1980s, however, the professional code of ethics which Bond stands for
remains the same. The meeting between Bond and Octopussy serves an
important narrative role, for two reasons. First, it ingeniously incorporates Fleming's original tale into the film as a backstory for the title
character. In 'Octopussy' Bond had gone to Jamaica to investigate Major
Dexter-Smythe, an army officer who had disappeared after the Second

World War with a cache of Nazi gold. Bond listens to Dexter-Smythe's confession, then leaves to write his report; Dexter-Smythe swims out to see his pet octopus, and commits suicide by allowing himself to be stung by a scorpion fish. In the film, Octopussy reveals that Dexter-Smythe was her father (the details of the story are altered slightly to Chinese gold and the Korean War, with Bond tracking him down to Sri Lanka). 'I had hoped that fate would bring us together,' Octopussy tells Bond, but not for revenge, as he assumes, but rather to thank him for giving her father the 'honourable alternative' of suicide. The backstory is again suggestive of an older Bond: given that Octopussy was only a young girl when her father died and, according to the script is now a woman in her early thirties, then this would place Bond as being around fifty.[11]

The second reason why the Bond/Octopussy confrontation is significant is that it again rehearses the ideologies of patriotism and duty. Their exchange recalls similar moments in earlier films, particularly *The Man With the Golden Gun*. Octopussy believes that she and Bond are 'two of a kind', just as Scaramanga had declared 'We are the best'. However, Bond declines Octopussy's invitation to join her organisation ('I'm not for hire'). She scoffs angrily at his sense of duty ('A man of principle … naturally you do it for Queen and country!') and sets herself apart from him ('I have no country, I have no price on my head. I don't have to apologise to you, a paid assassin, for what I am!'). The crucial difference between *Octopussy* and *The Man With the Golden Gun*, however, is that now Bond's ethic of duty is being mapped on to his relationship with the heroine rather than his relationship with the villain. It is another example of how, by this time in the series, greater narrative importance was being attached to women in the Bond films than to the male villains. However, the ideological potency of the Bond/Octopussy relationship is never really developed; immediately after they argue, Bond kisses her forcefully and she relents. As ever, Bond's irresistible charm is sufficient to convert even a supposedly powerful and intelligent woman like Octopussy into a simpering sex kitten who begs him to 'come back to bed'.

In other respects, *Octopussy* displays some of the parodic humour that had been absent from *For Your Eyes Only*. Thus, in-jokes are back: at one point Bond imitates celebrity animal trainer Barbara Woodhouse in telling a tiger to 'Sit!', and shortly later swings on a vine while letting out a Tarzan-yell. There are some excruciatingly racist jokes ('That'll keep you in curries for a while,' Bond quips as he hands some of his backgammon winnings to his Indian colleague). In an example of the policy of territorial casting that became particularly important in the later Bond films, Bond's amiable assistant Vijay is portrayed by Indian tennis star Vijay Amritraj, the cue for some fairly predictable jokes about backhands. One sequence recalls the gondola in *Moonraker*: pursued by Kamal's men in a three-wheeler taxi, Vijay uses his tennis racket as a weapon, while the watching crowds turn their heads from side to side as if watching a match on centre court.

Critical reaction to *Octopussy* was muted. Nick Roddick, writing in the *Monthly Film Bulletin*, noted 'the usual flurry of lavish sets, ingenious gadgets and inventive stunt work', but felt that the plot was too complicated and overloaded with details. 'The problems start when we get down to the plot, which is more intrusive – and more difficult to follow – than in previous films,' he wrote. '*Octopussy* frequently tends to bog down in explanations, and the impressive array of touristy Indian locations and the string of rather old-fashioned action sequences have a little difficulty in keeping up the pace.'[12]

It may have been that some critics were lukewarm about *Octopussy* because they were awaiting the return of the cinema's original James Bond. Sean Connery had returned to the role after twelve years in the ironically entitled *Never Say Never Again*, a rival Bond film produced outside the official series which for a while looked set to go head-to-head with *Octopussy* at the box-office but which in the event was delayed until later in the year due to post-production problems. *Never Say Never Again* was another instalment in Kevin McClory's persistent efforts to launch his own Bond franchise. After producing *Thunderball* in association with Eon in 1965, McClory, who retained the screen rights to the story, had agreed not to make another film based on the same story for a period of ten years. In the mid-1970s McClory began working on a new Bond film, entitled *Warhead*, with Len Deighton and Sean Connery, who had expressed an interest in the project if he could be involved in the writing and production. However, the storyline – which involved a SPECTRE base in the Bermuda Triangle, an underwater flotilla attacking New York and a climactic battle on the Statue of Liberty – soon ran into litigation when Eon alleged that it went beyond McClory's rights, which were limited to a remake of *Thunderball*. In the face of these legal obstacles, McClory was unable to raise the financial backing to make the film, and, although a film entitled *James Bond of the Secret Service* was occasionally reported to be in development during the late 1970s, it was not until 1981 that the project took on a more definite shape. McClory made an agreement with Jack Schwartzman, a former executive at the television company Lorimar who had left to become an independent producer, whereby Schwartzman bought McClory's rights to the *Thunderball* story. Schwartzman's background as a showbusiness lawyer enabled him to sort through the tangled legal minefield surrounding the project. He rejected the *Warhead* script and hired screenwriter Lorenzo Semple Jr, who had written the tongue-in-cheek remakes of *King Kong* (1976) and *Flash Gordon* (1980), to develop a new screenplay which updated the *Thunderball* story. For all that the new film had to follow the plot of the original to avoid further legal entanglements, Schwartzman denied it was simply a remake:

> The key point for us is that this film has no reference to any other film. And by that I mean that if no other Bond film had been made, this film would not be any different. It has its own story and approach. ... We're happy with the basic plot, which, with its nuclear overtones, holds up very well. But obviously it's not a remake of a film that has already been done.
>
> I think the best way we can compare it is to say was *Heaven Can Wait* a remake of *Here Comes Mr Jordan*? On one level yes, but it existed in its own right as a new film.[13]

Schwartzman also suggested that *Never Say Never Again* was going to be a more 'realistic' type of Bond film:

> The best way to describe how our film will look is rich, grand, even magnificent, but totally realistic. It has a definite 1980s feel, and if Bond were being written about in the Secret Service of now, we reckon that this is roughly how he would behave. He is getting on a bit, and to some extent he's a maverick in that he relies mainly on his wits in a computer age. I think Sean is rather enjoying that side of it. It's funny and a little cynical, but totally believable.[14]

Never Say Never Again survived a last-ditch attempt to block its release, brought at the High Court in London by Fleming's trustees in the spring of 1983, and was released in the autumn.

Although made outside the official series, *Never Say Never Again* deserves to be seen as a genuine Bond film in a way that the spoof

33. *Never Say Never Again*: The hair may be thinner and greyer, but cinema's original 007 is back again as Sean Connery returns for some gratuitous sex and violence in a film produced outside the official series.

Casino Royale was not. It contains essentially the same ingredients as the Eon films: an improbable plot, exotic locations, technological hardware and visual excess. The plot is a reworking of *Thunderball* rather than a straight remake. SPECTRE's conspiracy – masterminded by Blofeld (Max Von Sydow, complete with white cat – a motif borrowed from the

Eon films) and carried out by Maximilian Largo (Klaus Maria Brandauer) – acquires an added topicality in that it revolves round the hijacking of two American Cruise missiles from Britain, which will be detonated unless each of the member countries of NATO pays a ransom equivalent to 25 per cent of their annual oil purchases. The locations extend beyond those of *Thunderball*, moving from the Bahamas to the South of France and North Africa. There are some novel touches, including a black Felix Leiter (Bernie Casey), though he still functions as nothing more than a 'yes' man, while comic relief is provided by British comedian Rowan Atkinson as our man in the Bahamas. The set design eschews the modernism of Ken Adam; the ancient underground temple where Largo conceals one of the warheads is more reminiscent of *Raiders of the Lost Ark*. However, Schwartzman's assertion that it was 'totally realistic' should certainly not be taken at face value. Indeed, the film itself foregrounds its own improbability: 'Let's think of a more logical explanation,' says M (Edward Fox) when Bond suggests (correctly as it turns out) that the presidential authority required to substitute dummy warheads for real ones may have been accomplished by using a false eye (the authorisation procedure involves a retinal scan).

The most significant difference between *Never Say Never Again* and *Thunderball* is that Bond is now older and semi-retired. The film begins with him clad in military fatigues apparently on a mission to rescue a girl hostage kidnapped by South American terrorists, but it turns out to be a training exercise – and one which Bond fails when the hostage stabs him (the exercise scenario had her brainwashed by her captors). Bond now spends most of his time teaching, and the new, younger M believes he is a relic of the past ('I'll make you no secret I hold your methods in far less regard than my illustrious predecessor did'). But when the missiles are hijacked, M is ordered by the Foreign Secretary to reactivate the Double-O Section. Connery's return to the role is alluded to in one scene which recalls a similar moment in *Diamonds Are Forever* in which Connery/Bond is welcomed back into the fold after time away. 'Good to see you, Mr Bond,' says the new Q (Alec McCowen). 'Things have been awfully dull around here. ... Now you're on this, I hope we're going to have some gratuitous sex and violence.'

The narrative ideology of *Never Say Never Again* replays that of *Thunderball* in so far as Bond functions principally as a hero of the NATO alliance. It differs from the official films of the same period in that it makes only tangential reference to the Cold War, opting instead

34. *Never Say Never Again*: Bond's tango lessons come in useful as he dances with the delectable Domino (Kim Basinger).

to base its ideological operations on the Anglo-American relationship. However, the power relationship between Britain and America has shifted since *Thunderball*; it is American military force alone which provides the back-up necessary to defeat Largo's men. There are numerous references to the British Secret Service being financially depleted: M complains of his 'meagre budget', while Q works in a freezing workshop, complains about the lack of spare parts, and is generally gloomy about the austerity regime he has to endure ('If the CIA made me an offer, I'd be off like a shot. Unlimited resources, air conditioning, twenty-eight flavours of ice cream in the restaurant'). But Bond is still able to strike a blow for Britain when he informs an American submarine captain that he knows about the US Navy's latest top-secret gadget 'from a Russian translation of one of your service manuals'.

Never Say Never Again also provides one of the most ordered and thoroughgoing sets of structural oppositions between characters in all the Bond films. The contest between Bond and Largo takes place on two levels: public and private. The public contest is for power, symbolically represented when they play a game known as 'Domination' in which they battle for control of the world – the Bond narrative encapsulated in a computer game. The personal contest is for Domino (Kim Basinger), whom Largo treats as a possession but Bond treats as a woman, the scene of their tango together performing an elaborate sort of seduction ritual. Largo's belief that money buys love is illustrated in his belief that he could not lose Domino to 'an underpaid British agent'; when he discovers this has happened, his reaction is to sell Domino to the highest bidder from among a group of filthy and lascivious Arabs. The opposition between the demure, blonde, blue-eyed, Nordic Domino and the sensual, dark-haired Latin villainess Fatima Blush (Barbara Carrera) is the sort of visual contrast familiar from countless films. Fatima is once again the woman who refuses to be 'repositioned' by Bond, though in contrast to the coolly calculating Fiona Volpe of *Thunderball* she is characterised as psychologically un-stable. Holding Bond at gunpoint, she demands that he issue a public statement that she had provided him with 'the greatest rapture' of his life. Any woman who presents such a challenge as Fatima to Bond's masculinity (to underline the point she aims her revolver at his groin) naturally has to meet a grisly end: she is dispatched spectacularly, blown to smithereens by Bond's exploding Union Jack fountain pen.

Critics welcomed Connery's return to the role he had made his own some twenty years earlier, but were more equivocal about the film itself. Inevitably, comparisons were made to the Eon series, which was the yardstick against which any other Bond film would be judged. Philip Strick in the *Monthly Film Bulletin* considered that Connery 'now in-carnates more 007 in one raised eyebrow than subsequent claimants have come anywhere near emulating'. The film itself he thought provided just the right mixture of the old and the new:

> Ingeniously reconstructing *Thunderball* ... *Never Say Never Again* has a usefully engaging familiarity which it embroiders and extends: this time, the sharks are electronically motivated, the duel with Largo is on a holographic computer game, it's Bond himself on the rocket-assisted motorbike, and the dance-floor embrace that led to the death of Fatima (previously Fiona) has been replaced by an eradication so thorough that only her smouldering shoes are left.[15]

Variety, however, found the storyline too familiar, remarking that 'a heavy sense of deja vu hangs over the picture, with few surprises now being possible within the standard format. Given the familiarity of the mission,' the review went on, 'pic's success depends entirely upon the moment-to-moment pleasure it can provide and results here are moderately good, but hardly enthralling'. It complained, furthermore, that '[the] pace is extremely relaxed and [a] running time of 137 minutes proves excessive given pic's lack of anything new to offer'. It suffered in comparison to the Eon films 'from lack of the accustomed accoutrements of the series, such as the Maurice Binder credits and familiar musical theme'. But *Variety* did approve of the casting, considering that 'Klaus Maria Brandauer ... makes one of the best Bond opponents since very early in the series', while reserving most of its praise for Connery himself: 'In fine form and still very much looking the part, he gets knocked around more than Bond is accustomed to and has cut down a bit on both his vices and his quips, but the actor has brought Bond very gracefully, and pleasurably, into middle-age.'[16]

A View To A Kill was to be the swansong for another middle-aged Bond. Roger Moore's seventh film, the fourteenth of the official series, is not highly regarded by aficionados. For Nicholas Anez, it is 'one of the most derivative films in the series with only superficial changes in the story and characterizations. The threadbare script includes the requisite villain, henchman, good girl, bad girl, chase scenes, visual stunts and other familiar elements.' [17] But while *A View To A Kill* is undoubtedly a very flawed film, it is not without its points of interest. It is not as entirely derivative as Anez suggests, and although the narrative construction of the film as a whole is unsatisfying, it does offer some intriguing variations on the usual formula.

Unlike the preceding films, *A View To A Kill* bears no relation to the Fleming story from which it derives its title. 'From A View To A Kill' had Bond investigating the death of a dispatch rider near SHAPE headquarters outside Paris. He discovers an underground Soviet hideout, which is destroyed. The film had Bond investigating the activities of millionaire industrialist Max Zorin (Christopher Walken), who arouses M's suspicions when a Soviet-made microchip, recovered from 002's body in Siberia, turns out to be identical to a new British chip (capable of withstanding electro-magnetic pulse radiation) manufactured by a company recently taken over by Zorin Industries. Zorin — who, it turns out, is the result of a genetic engineering experiment carried out by a Nazi doctor during the Second World War — is now planning to corner the world market in microchips by destroying Silicon Valley, where 80 per cent of the world's microchips are manufactured.

While the action set pieces of *A View To A Kill* are familiar – a pre-title ski sequence (*The Spy Who Loved Me*), Bond's pursuit of an assassin through Paris (recalling the gondola sequence of *Moonraker*), Bond in a stolen fire truck pursued by the San Francisco police (replaying the gratuitous demolition of police cars from *Diamonds Are Forever* and *Live and Let Die*) – the plot itself offers some alternative narrative possibilities which are not, however, developed to their fullest extent. Bennett and Woollacott argue that *A View To A Kill* 'shows signs of considerable effort having been made to adjust and renovate the Bond formula in order to accommodate new cultural and ideological concerns'. In this case, however, the adjustments do not work, so that 'the film is caught between a traditional formula which it does not entirely jettison and a new one which it does not fully develop'.[18] The narrative ideologies of *A View To A Kill* are rather more confused than in previous films, offering an uneasy compromise between the Cold War themes of *For Your Eyes Only* and *Octopussy* and the détente narrative of *The Spy Who Loved Me*. On the one hand there are Cold War overtones in the fear that the Soviet Union may catch up technologically with the West. The idea of a microchip that is resistant to electro-magnetic pulse radiation (of the sort that would follow the detonation of a nuclear bomb) associates the film with the technologically advanced 'Star Wars' defence programme initiated in the United States by President Reagan as a counter to the threat of a Soviet missile attack. On the other hand, Zorin's conspiracy is distanced from the ideologies of the Cold War. While his business empire was initially a cover for his activities as a Soviet agent, Zorin now distances himself from his superiors, who disapprove of his unauthorised commercial activities. 'I admit no association – I no longer consider myself a KGB agent,' he informs General Gogol. It is made clear that Zorin's plot to destroy Silicon Valley is his own freelance venture and is not supported by the Soviet Union. Indeed, the KGB are just as keen as the British to find out what Zorin is up to, as Bond discovers when he comes across Pola Ivanova (Fiona Fullerton), a KGB agent and former lover on the same case as himself. There are echoes of *The Spy Who Loved Me* as Bond enjoys an amorous interlude with Pola ('Détente can be beautiful', she murmurs as they share a spa bath). But here Bond's relationship with a female Russian spy plays only a subsidiary role in the narrative. The main Bond girl is an American geologist,

35. *A View To A Kill*: A day at the races for Miss Moneypenny (Lois Maxwell), Bond, Q (Desmond Llewelyn), Sir Godfrey Tibbett (Patrick Macnee) and M (Robert Brown).

Stacey Sutton (Tanya Roberts), whose father had been one of Zorin's financial victims. In this sense *A View To A Kill*, like *Moonraker*, reaffirms the Anglo-American special relationship as the one most likely to succeed (reflecting perhaps the political and personal friendship between Thatcher and Reagan) rather than opening up the alternative of an Anglo-Soviet alliance as in *The Spy*. Nevertheless, the film ends with a unique gesture towards détente: Gogol offers the Order of Lenin for 'Comrade Bond'. 'I'd have expected the KGB to celebrate if Silicon Valley had been destroyed,' remarks M. 'On the contrary, admiral' Gogol replies. 'Where would Russian research be without it?' The result, in Bennett and Woollacott's view, is that 'the plot becomes confused and its ideological articulations fuzzy as it zig-zags between the discourse of Cold War and that of detente and, ultimately, distances itself from both of them'.[19]

There is much substance in Bennett and Woollacott's discussion of the confusions and contradictions within the narrative ideologies of *A View To A Kill*, but their argument is less convincing when they come to analyse the nature of the conspiracy plot itself. Their reading is worth quoting at length as an example of how over-theorisation can lead up a blind alley of interpretation:

It is, however, the nature of Zorin's conspiracy which most unhinges the traditional Bond formula. Having manufactured and
accumulated a massive stockpile of micro-chips, Zorin's ambition
is to head a syndicate that will dominate the world's micro-
electronics market by eliminating its main rival: California's Silicone
[*sic*] Valley which Zorin plans to flood by means of an explosion
strategically placed to activate the region's major geological fault-
lines. While this conspiracy incorporates aspects of the SPECTRE
formula, two crucial ingredients are lacking. The first concerns the
motivation of the conspiracy. Although there are exceptions –
Stromberg in *The Spy Who Loved Me*, for example – the villain is
usually motivated by a compound of avarice and a utopian altruism. ... Zorin's motivation, by contrast, is entirely devoid of any
ethical rationalisation, no matter how warped or perverted. As a
power-hungry industrialist and a psychotic, Zorin has only two
ends in view. To express these in terms of the somewhat laboured
play that is made with the film's title, his conspiracy is motivated
with a view to making a financial killing and 'with a view to a kill'
– that is, to the pleasure of witnessing the infliction of pain,
suffering and death by observing the destruction of Silicone Valley
from an airship. Secondly, the conspiracy is localised in its import.
Far from threatening a global catastrophe, it portends merely the
end of America's dominance of the high-tech economy and, as a
consequence, lacks the broader political and ideological articulations of either the SMERSH or the SPECTRE formulae.[20]

However, this reading fundamentally misinterprets the nature of Bond
villainy. In the first place, it is simply untrue to say that the villain is
'usually motivated by a compound of avarice and a utopian altruism'.
It is either one or the other: the grand conspiracy of extortion (particularly the SPECTRE films) or the desire to create a new social order
(Stromberg and Drax). Furthermore, in arguing that Zorin's conspiracy
'unhinges the traditional Bond formula', Bennett and Woollacott completely miss the point that *A View To A Kill* is essentially a reworking
of *Goldfinger*, a film widely regarded as the archetypal Bond narrative.
Goldfinger had wanted to destroy Fort Knox so that the value of his
own gold would increase; Zorin wants to destroy Silicon Valley so that
he can corner the world market in microchips. Goldfinger's 'Operation
Grand Slam', like Zorin's 'Project Main Strike', threatens to destroy the

36. *A View To A Kill*: The psychotic Zorin (Christopher Walken) explains his gift for 'intuitive improvisation' while his sidekick May Day (Grace Jones) menaces; Bond and Stacey (Tanya Roberts) are unimpressed.

American economy (which, far from being localised, would in both cases have catastrophic consequences for the rest of the world). Goldfinger was no less psychotic than Zorin: he had planned to use nerve gas to kill off the local population. The narrative similarities between *A View To A Kill* and *Goldfinger* work on other levels too: both films follow a trajectory from Europe to the United States; both feature Bond working in America alongside the CIA; and both have a shadowy Communist presence lurking in the background (Goldfinger was backed by Red China, Zorin is ex-KGB).

One aspect of *A View To A Kill* which does offer something new, however, is the prominence accorded to its female villainess, Zorin's sidekick/lover May Day. As played by the bizarre pop-singer-turned-actress Grace Jones, May Day is physically strong and expert at martial arts, coming across as a sort of female Oddjob in thigh boots and a black leotard. She was privileged in the advertising campaign for the film: posters featured Bond and May Day standing back-to-back with the question 'Has James Bond finally met his match?' Jones's appearance emphasises the physicality and sexuality of May Day: her lithe body and animalistic gestures (she snarls and snaps her jaws at Zorin as he pins her down following their karate work-out) suggest the grace and aggression of a black panther. Yet May Day is a highly problematic character within the terms of the Bond series: as a dominant woman (and, moreover, a dominant black woman) she represents a challenge to Bond's masculinity which is never properly resolved. When May Day finds Bond in her bed she climbs in with him, but when he leans over to her she roughly turns him over so that she is on top, thus assuming the dominant position and placing Bond in an unaccustomed submissive role. Given that May Day has killed two of Bond's colleagues, the film seems to be moving towards a showdown between her and Bond, which, given May Day's strength and martial arts ability, he would be hard pressed to win. But having offered up this tantalising possibility, the film does not fulfil the expectation it has created. Like Jaws in *Moonraker*, May Day turns 'good' at the end. Just at the moment when it seems that Bond and May Day are about to come to blows, Zorin lets off the explosive charges which cause the mine to flood, oblivious to the fact that May Day and his men are still inside. Thus feeling betrayed by Zorin ('And I thought that creep loved me!'), May Day helps Bond remove the bomb that will blow up the geological lock and flood Silicon Valley. So while May Day may have changed sides, it is not due to the force of Bond's sexual charisma, as had been the case with Pussy Galore in *Goldfinger*, but rather due to her own feelings of betrayal and desire for vengeance against Zorin. In terms of the sexist code of the Bond films, May Day is simply too problematic to be allowed to live. And the more problematic the woman, the more emphatic her death has to be: like Fatima Blush in *Never Say Never Again*, May Day is not merely killed but is blown to pieces by the bomb which she is transporting clear of the mine. But in killing off May Day in this way, the film denies Bond the opportunity of proving his masculinity against her in a straight fight – and, moreover, denies the audience the confrontation which it had seemed to offer. Yet despite this deeply unsatisfactory resolution, May Day remains a far more memorable character than the main Bond girl who, as played by Tanya Roberts, represents a throwback to the worst excesses of 1970s bimboism.

In contrast to the flamboyant and colourful villains, the Bond of *A View To A Kill* comes across as little more than a caricature. Bond's Englishness is foregrounded even more than usual, but it verges on parody: the identities which he adopts – a rich racehorse owner called James St John Smythe, a *Financial Times* reporter called James Stock –

are stereotypes straight from the drawer marked 'English types' and redolent of the sort of class distinctions that had been absent from Sean Connery's Bond. Indeed, Roger Moore's performance in this film, to a greater extent than any of his previous outings, relocates the character of Bond in the tradition of the English gentleman hero, thus differentiating himself even further from Connery's rugged Celtic machismo. The stage Englishness of the film is reinforced by Patrick Macnee's cameo as Sir Godfrey Tibbett, the horse-fancier who facilitates Bond's entry to Zorin's stables. Macnee brings to any part the inter-textual association of his role as John Steed, the dandified English gentleman hero of *The Avengers*, and the combination of Moore and Macnee works as a nostalgic reminder of a kind of screen heroism now eclipsed by the likes of Stallone's Rocky and Rambo, Mel Gibson's Mad Max and Arnold Schwarzenegger's Conan the Barbarian. But to add insult to injury, the former John Steed is all too easily killed off by May Day, as if to suggest that his style of heroism is now outdated. Even Bond's legendary status as Britain's foremost secret agent is mocked: when Bond reveals his name to a San Francisco police captain in the time-honoured fashion ('The name is Bond. James Bond'), the reply is: 'And I'm Dick Tracy, and you're still under arrest.' (Although the ensuing chase, to be fair, does restore some of Bond's mythic potency, evidenced by the police chief's memorable line: 'To all units. Intercept murder suspect in stolen fire truck. He may be armed – and he sure is dangerous.')

It was Moore's performance – and, more particularly, the fact that even he was now starting to show his age – that most reviews focused on. As they had done at various moments in the series' past, critics asserted that the formula was looking stale and that an injection of new ideas, and new blood, was becoming necessary if the series was to continue. This view was expressed, for example, by Richard Buskin in *Films and Filming*:

> Although an improbable plot line has always been part and parcel of the Bond films, and one of the key factors behind their continuing success, this time the story fails to convince on any level – the filmmakers evidently having spent less time patching up the holes in the plot than in applying layers of mascara and eye-liner to Roger Moore's face. For the most part, Moore looks tired, and so are many of the corny double entendre jokes (seemingly cribbed from a *Carry On* film script), whilst Tanya Roberts as the

damsel in distress provides much glamour but little else. Grace Jones, meanwhile, plays Grace Jones, as she did in *Conan the Destroyer*.

The stunt work, as usual, is absolutely outstanding, but director John Glen has failed to instil the film with the atmosphere reminiscent of the earlier Bond movies. However, the fact that for the first time the closing credits simply promise that Bond will return – without naming a title – hopefully means that the producers are giving much thought to casting a new 007 as well as infusing some much-needed fresh ideas.[21]

Variety's prediction that *A View To A Kill* would not be as successful as recent films and that audience interest would wane – 'Trading on the Bond name, outlook is good for initial business, but momentum is likely to falter, just as the production does'[22] – proved to be accurate in that its box-office was down noticeably from the previous four Roger Moore films. There was a widespread feeling that Moore's tenure had come to an end, which was confirmed shortly after the release of the film when the actor announced that it would be his last Bond movie. Within the space of a little over a year and a half, therefore, both Connery and Moore – who between them had starred in no fewer than fourteen Bond films – had made their last bows in the role. And, according to some critics, it was not before time. 'I think it's time to say farewell to old friends,' said one reviewer at the time of *Never Say Never Again*. 'The earlier movies look increasingly dated, the new ones merely out-dated.'[23] Once again, the Bond series was faced with the task of reinventing itself if it was to continue.

7

Continuity and Change:
The Living Daylights, Licence To Kill

The phrase 'continuity and change' has become one of the clichés of historical scholarship, but it perfectly describes the nature of the Bond series which constantly strives to maintain a balance between familiarity and tradition on the one hand and variation and innovation on the other. The phrase is especially pertinent to the last two Bond films of the 1980s: *The Living Daylights* (dir. John Glen, 1987) and *Licence To Kill* (dir. John Glen, 1989). These two films exhibit processes of continuity and change at several levels. At the level of production they maintain continuity with the films of the early 1980s through the maintenance of the same core personnel (director Glen, screenwriters Maibaum and Wilson), while at the same time marking an important moment of change through the introduction of a new lead actor (Timothy Dalton). And at the level of narrative ideology, *The Living Daylights* exhibits continuity with the three preceding films through its replaying of Cold War themes, whereas *Licence To Kill* represents a complete change of direction in that it dispenses with the Cold War background entirely and provides a new ideological role for Bond by relocating him in the war against the international drugs trade. Indeed, *Licence To Kill* marks the furthest deviation from the generic formula of the Bond series by any of the official films. Its relatively less successful reception might be attributed, in part at least, to the equation between continuity and change being overbalanced in favour of change, to the extent that too many of the expected conventions of the Bond narrative were absent on this occasion.

The casting of a new, younger James Bond naturally impacted on the style of the films. Timothy Dalton had been approached about the role on several previous occasions when Roger Moore had been threatening to leave the series, though he had turned down Broccoli's overtures on the grounds that he thought he was too young to play Bond. When he accepted the role Dalton was forty, and thus the right sort of age to return Bond to his more accustomed permanent late thirties, following the slightly older character implicit in Moore's last three films. With serious acting credentials behind him for both his stage and film work, Dalton was a surprise choice for the role. He had often been compared to the young Laurence Olivier, on account of his chiselled, dark, brooding looks which were not unlike Olivier's in his 1930s matinée idol days. Official publicity once again suggested that the new actor was closer to Ian Fleming's conception of Bond, and there was a general view that Dalton would make a more serious, hard-edged Bond than his predecessor. John Glen elaborated on the differences between Dalton and Moore thus:

> Roger had done three or four films before I directed him and he knew his role backwards, his style ... Timothy Dalton was very different, much more sinister in the sense he's very real – you can believe he's going to kill someone. He's very much nearer Fleming's Bond. He's the hardest Bond we've ever had ... He's very agile, extremely fit and keen, and very professional.[1]

Dalton's style of performance, in fact, is different both from the eyebrow-acting of Moore and from the brawny physicality of Connery. His Bond is more intense, saturnine, byronic; he moves purposefully, and smiles only rarely. Dalton brought a brooding, dangerous quality to the character which differentiates his Bond from all the others. The film-makers emphasised this in their advertising strategy for his two Bond films, which used the slogans 'The new James Bond ... living on the edge' (*The Living Daylights*) and 'His bad side is a dangerous place to be' (*Licence To Kill*).

In many respects Dalton *is* closer to Fleming's Bond. Dalton, for example, is clearly less comfortable than either Connery or Moore with the witty asides and one-liners, which are downplayed in his films so that he becomes something closer to the Bond of the books, who rarely displays a sense of humour. Dalton's Bond also exhibits some of the self-doubts with which Fleming occasionally endowed his hero. One critic observed that 'Timothy Dalton promises to become the first James Bond with angst, a moody spy for the *fin de siècle*'.[2] Dalton himself evidently saw Bond as something more than just an action hero, as a character riddled with all sorts of moral ambiguities:

> One is constantly reminded by Fleming, both from Bond himself and through the mouths of other characters, that Bond really is as bad as the bad guys. He is a killer, but he does have a moral sense of what good is. That throws him into conflict because of his self-knowledge of who he is and what he does. I find that interesting because it does go back to the Hero; to what it is that makes a hero, to what it is that real people respond to in a hero. We know that good and evil are combined in an individual, and that good must triumph. But unless you have both, you don't have the conflict either within the individual or within the world. It's one of the curious fascinations that made the character interesting, believable.[3]

While this may sound like the voice of a serious actor trying to convince himself that he is not slumming it by starring in popular action movies, Dalton certainly brought a dimension to the role that has not been present in any of Bond's other screen incarnations. Nor was it entirely fanciful for him to speak as he did about the combination of good and evil in the character of the hero. In this respect Dalton's Bond can be seen in the same context as the revisionist tendencies in the characterisation of other mythical hero figures at this time. The hugely successful *Batman* (1989), to take the most prominent example, explored, albeit in a neutered sort of way, the psychosis of its hero figure, a dark avenger far removed from the campy excess of the 1960s television series. The casting of comic actor Michael Keaton as Bruce Wayne/Batman was downright quirky, but no more so than the casting of a classically trained Shakespearean actor as James Bond.

The moral ambiguities of Bond's profession had been foregrounded in the short story from which Dalton's first Bond film took its title. In 'The Living Daylights', Bond had been sent to Berlin to cover the escape of a British agent across the no-man's land between the Russian and British sectors. His job is to kill a KGB sniper who has been detailed to shoot the agent. Bond watches for three nights, and takes a fancy to a girl who plays the cello in an orchestra which practises nearby. On the third night, as the agent makes his escape, Bond sights the enemy sniper, who turns out to be the girl cellist. At the last moment Bond alters his aim and wounds the girl rather than killing her outright, as he had been ordered to do.

The Living Daylights follows *For Your Eyes Only* and *Octopussy* in that it uses Fleming's story as a starting point and works out from there into a much more expansive narrative. After a pre-title sequence in which an unknown killer disrupts a Double-O training exercise in Gibraltar, Bond is assigned to cover the defection of General Koskov (Jeroen Krabbé) and, as in the original story, changes his aim when the apparent sniper turns out to be a beautiful girl. Koskov says he is defecting because his superior, General Pushkin (John Rhys-Davies), Gogol's successor as head of the KGB, has initiated an operation called *Smiert Spionam* ('Death to Spies') to kill off British agents. When Koskov is snatched back from a safe house, Bond reluctantly accepts his assignment to kill Pushkin. Bond discovers that the sniper was in fact Koskov's girlfriend Kara Milovy (Maryam d'Abo) and that her rifle was loaded with blanks. Realising that Koskov's defection had been an elaborate ruse, Bond poses as Koskov's friend in order to discover from Kara what he is up to. Koskov is in league with an American arms dealer, Brad Whitaker (Joe Don Baker), in a convoluted drugs-and-arms deal that will net them millions of dollars. The plot to kill British agents turns out to have been instigated by Koskov, and was intended to get the British to kill Pushkin, who had been about to have Koskov arrested before his 'defection'.

In its narrative structure and ideologies, *The Living Daylights* is a film split eloquently down the middle in several key respects. On one level, it straddles the boundary between the sensational and realist lineages of the spy thriller. While the narrative clearly belongs to the sensational thriller in that it revolves round the requisite action sequences, fights, chases and so on, the convoluted plot of a defection that is not really a defection at all is closer to the world of John le Carré, with its themes of treachery and deception, than to the more familiar world of the Bond films where the lines of opposition are usually clearly drawn. Moreover, *The Living Daylights* refers to one of the most celebrated British thrillers, Carol Reed's *The Third Man* (1949), a reference which may have been intentional in so far as John Glen had worked on that film as an assistant editor. *The Third Man,* with its Graham Greene script and its expressionist photography by Robert Krasker, had created its own world of moral ambiguity and uncertainty in post-war Vienna during the Allied occupation. The Viennese section of *The Living Daylights* presents, in every respect, an image of the city that is precisely the opposite of *The Third Man,* and does it so thoroughly that it seems deliberate. Thus, whereas the Vienna of *The Third Man* was a bleak black-and-white landscape of crumbling buildings and bomb sites, the Vienna of *The Living Daylights* is a colourful fairy-tale land of plush hotels, opera houses and Strauss waltzes. It presents the usual romanticised tourist's-eye view: Bond and Kara arrive at the Schonbrunn Palace in a horse-drawn carriage while brightly costumed dancers twirl around in the open air. When Bond and Kara go on the ferris wheel at the Wiener Prater, it is impossible not to recall the famous meeting between Joseph Cotten and Orson Welles at the same location. James Bond meets Harry Lime, and the sensational and realist lineages of the British spy film converge.

While, on one level, it is caught between different traditions of the thriller, on another level *The Living Daylights* is also, like *A View To A Kill,* caught between the discourses of Cold War and détente, with the result that the film performs an uncomfortable sort of ideological splits. Uniquely, *The Living Daylights* manages simultaneously both to enforce and to transgress the geo-political boundaries of the Cold War. The Cold War background is highly prominent, with much of the story taking place behind the Iron Curtain in Czechoslovakia (filmed in Vienna) and in Russian-occupied Afghanistan (filmed in Morocco). The film takes for granted the existence of the secret war between Soviet and Western intelligence services, a war in which Britain plays a prominent role. When Koskov is apparently snatched back by the KGB it comes as a severe blow to the British government, who are 'the laughing stock of the intelligence community' according to the minister of defence. When the action moves to Afghanistan, and Bond teams up with the Mujaheddin, who launch a full-scale attack on a Russian air base, the film is unequivocally taking the side of the Afghan resistance against the Red Army. In the sort of conceit which only the Bond films can pull off successfully, the Mujaheddin leader Kamran Shah (Art Malik) turns out to have been educated at Oxford. This is a not insignificant point: Kamran, alone among the Mujaheddin, does not burst into laughter when Bond reveals that he works for the British government. Only the foreigner who has lived in Britain understands what the British are really like; the old boy network is alive and well in the Khyber Pass.

Yet at the same time as taking a pronounced anti-Russian stance as far as the war in Afghanistan is concerned, *The Living Daylights* is also, paradoxically, concerned to distance itself from the political dimensions of the Cold War through its suggestion that Soviet Communism is not, as Raymond Durgnat puts it, 'enemy No. One'.[4] It borrows from *Octopussy* the idea of a renegade Russian general in league with a more conventional Bond villain and whose conspiracy does not have official sanction. However, there is no suggestion of any political or ideological rationale behind Koskov, who in this sense is more akin to Zorin of *A View To A Kill* in that he is motivated purely by greed. The complicated drugs-and-arms deal, in which Koskov deals not only with an American arms dealer but with the Afghan resistance fighters whom the weapons are destined to be used against, crosses both geographical and ideological boundaries. Durgnat, among others, identified certain topical references which suggested the films were moving in yet another direction:

> Although *The Living Daylights* involves heavier references to Second World oppression (not inappropriate in a Czechoslovakian setting), it eschews any further concessions to Cold War revival, *Rambo*-style, instead attributing trouble to collusion between deviationist ultras on both sides ... Here, Afghanistan, ambivalence and amorality call the tune. If the plot is rarely coherent, let alone plausible, its penultimate twists are quite fascinating. They happily mix, into a moral chiaroscuro worthy of Machiavelli himself, (a) a mercenary-capitalist dressed as a US general (virtually an incarnation of the 'contra' spirit), (b) a Russian equivalent of Irangate, and (c) freedom fighters who keep going by dealing dope.[5]

The 'Irangate' affair which Durgnat mentions – a complex scheme to free American hostages held by terrorists in Lebanon by selling arms illegally to Iran, and then secretly diverting the proceeds to provide financial support for the Contra guerrillas in Nicaragua – once again provided a Bond film with a degree of topicality which the film-makers may not have intended. Details of the Iran–Contra affair, which was to plague the last years of the Reagan administration, came to light in November 1986, when *The Living Daylights* was already in an advanced

37. *The Living Daylights*: Timothy Dalton takes over the reins as 007, while
Bond joins the Mujaheddin; 'They'll save you for the harem,' he tells
the worried Kara (Maryam d'Abo).

stage of production. While it would therefore be misleading to suggest
that the plot was based directly on 'Irangate', there are nevertheless
some intriguing similarities. It is certainly tempting to see the character
of Whitaker, a zealous right-wing extremist who has a 'personal pan-
theon of great commanders' (Hitler, Napoleon, Julius Caesar, Genghis
Khan, Alexander the Great) modelled in his own image, as a thinly
veiled representation of Colonel Oliver North, the officer most closely
implicated in the Iran–Contra dealings.

If the conspiracy plot of *The Living Daylights* is somewhat confused,
however, that is not to say that the film is unsuccessful in terms of its
other ideological operations. Quite the contrary, in fact, for there are
various aspects of the film which nuance, often in a very subtle way,
some of the conventions of the Bond series. For a start, Bond's relationship to the secret service is problematised for the first time since he had
threatened resignation in *On Her Majesty's Secret Service*. Whereas the Roger
Moore films had asserted unequivocally Bond's sense of duty and loyalty
('I'm not for hire' he had told Octopussy), Dalton's Bond has an
altogether more ambiguous relationship towards the service and towards
his superiors. When a fellow agent admonishes him for not shooting to

kill when he first sighted Kara and says he will report to M that Bond deliberately disobeyed orders, Bond's reply hints at an underlying sense of bitterness which hitherto had been the preserve only of the literary Bond: 'Stuff my orders! I only kill professionals. That girl didn't know one end of a rifle from the other. Go ahead – tell him what you want. If he fires me I'll thank him for it.' Scenes like this would seem to have been written especially for Dalton – it is hard to imagine either Roger Moore or Pierce Brosnan, who had been widely tipped to take over from him, carrying it off as convincingly – and foreshadow *Licence To Kill* in which Bond actually repudiates the service and embarks on a personal vendetta.

It is Dalton's performance which, in large measure, is responsible for the success of *The Living Daylights*. Memorably introduced in the pre-title sequence – sight of his face is withheld until the moment when another Double-O man falls to his death from a cliff face, and there is a close-up of Dalton as he turns and reacts – his Bond clearly means business. The hard edge which he brought to the role is best displayed in the key confrontation scene between Bond and Pushkin, in which Bond holds the KGB chief at gunpoint in his hotel room. Dalton himself suggested that 'the movie had been written for Roger Moore, and originally they were just to sit across the table having a glass of champagne with each other'.[6] In the scene as played, however, Bond is tougher and more ruthless: he savagely clubs both Pushkin and his KGB minder with his gun, tears off the dress of Pushkin's mistress, and makes Pushkin kneel on the floor while holding his gun against Pushkin's forehead.

The greater seriousness of Dalton's Bond is also evident in his relationship with the heroine. *The Living Daylights* is unique among the Bond films in that there is only one love interest for the hero. Even in previous films where Bond's relationship with the girl had been conducted on a slightly more romantic basis, such as *On Her Majesty's Secret Service* and *For Your Eyes Only*, there had still been one or two incidental conquests along the way. The disavowal of casual liaisons in *The Living Daylights* was linked by some commentators to the new sexual climate which had supposedly emerged in the wake of the AIDS scares of the mid-1980s – Raymond Benson, for instance, believes that 'the AIDS epidemic was changing everyone's outlook on sex, and motion pictures and television were just beginning to reflect the new attitudes'[7] – but this seems an unlikely explanation given that the Bond character has never been a role model for notions of political correctness. A rather more likely reason for the existence of a sole Bond girl this time around is the decision by the film-makers to return to something more akin to Fleming's Bond, who was far from being the sort of Casanova that some critics alleged. 'Bond collects almost exactly one girl per excursion abroad, which total he exceeds only once, by one,' observes Kingsley Amis. 'This is surely not at all in advance of what any reasonably personable, reasonably well-off bachelor would reckon to acquire on a foreign holiday or a trip for his firm.'[8]

The release of *The Living Daylights* was something of a milestone in that it marked the twenty-fifth anniversary of the Bond series. The publicity and marketing strategy, like the film itself, was split down the middle. On the one hand there was an understandable urge to celebrate the silver anniversary of the series, which was illustrated in the congratulatory special editions of the trade papers *Variety* and the *Hollywood Reporter* which paid lavish tribute to the achievement of the Bond films in becoming far and away the most successful series of films in box-office history. But on the other hand there was the necessity of introducing the new James Bond, and of proving that while the series had been running for such a long time it was still fresh and vital. In the event *The Living Daylights* did well enough at the box-office, with worldwide grosses of $191 million (against a production cost of approximately $32 million). However, when broken down, these grosses represented a ratio of nearly three-to-one between overseas and North American revenues, thus once again highlighting the importance of non-US markets for the Bond films.[9]

Critical reaction to *The Living Daylights* followed the direction of the advertising in highlighting continuity and change – though there was some difference of opinion as to how much in the way of change there really was in the film. 'A new 007, Timothy Dalton, but generally the Bond mixture as before – relentless action, pretty girls, labyrinthine plot and comic-strip acting,' opined *Screen International*, complaining that 'the script seems feebler than usual and three baddies don't really compensate for one really colourful villain (as of yore)'. [10] *Films and Filming*, however, felt that 'within the limitations of that well-oiled formula, *The Living Daylights* could be termed a modest departure from the norm'. It approved, with some qualifications, of Dalton, who brought new vigour to the proceedings:

Under the lightweight influence of jolly Roger Moore, the Bond series had deteriorated into something of an arthritic joke heavily reliant on the expertise of the backroom team and death-defying stuntmen. The introduction of Timothy Dalton has afforded the makers an opportunity to return to the drawing board and take Bond back to basics. The Dalton Bond is a more flavourful character than of late; a rugged, romantic hero, anti-authoritarian, tinged with a streak of self-disgust and brusque to the point of rudeness. His one fault is perhaps a certain lack of humour, once handled with impeccably sardonic aplomb by Sean Connery, still the original and best inhabitant of the role.[11]

American critics also differed in their assessment of the degree of change evident in the film. 'Carry On, James' was the title of Janet Maslin's review for the *New York Times*. 'At this late date, the James Bond formula doesn't require much modification,' she wrote. 'Keeping it afloat, as *The Living Daylights* succeeds in doing, is achievement enough.'[12] But *Variety* thought it was 'a healthy cut above the series norm of super hero fantasy' which provided 'a human dimension for Bond not hitherto plumbed'. Showing one of its occasional flashes of socio-political insight, *Variety* detected 'a more mature story of its kind ... Early apprehensions of yet more ho-hum Cold War shenanigans become tempered. By the conclusion, there's even a strong hint of the new *glasnost* spirit – in both directions, with more than one Soviet honcho sporting a decidedly human face.'[13] *Variety* was not alone in reading into the ending of the film overtones of the policy of *glasnost* ('openness') initiated by new Soviet leader Mikhail Gorbachev. General Gogol, who has now moved from the KGB to the Russian foreign service, is seen alongside M and, quite bizarrely, Kamran's guerrillas, in attending Kara's cello recital, where it is revealed that he has arranged a special visa so that she can travel freely between East and West.

With Dalton's performance having attracted critical plaudits, especially from the hard core of the Bond fan culture, the next film was tailored specially for his more serious interpretation of Bond. *Licence To Kill* was the first Bond film not to use an original Fleming title – those that remained, such as 'Quantum of Solace' and 'The Hildebrand Rarity' hardly offered exciting possibilities – though the phrase itself is part of the lexicography of the Bond mythology and thus had the sort of resonance which would identify it as a 'Bondian' title. Originally the film was to have been called *Licence Revoked*, but this was dropped after audience research in the United States revealed that too many cinema-goers did not understand what it meant.[14] Plans to set the film in China fell through when political and logistical difficulties became insurmountable. The story idea was that Bond would be pitted against an evil oriental drugs lord. In the event the drugs theme was maintained but the action was relocated to the Florida Keys and to a fictional Latin American country called Isthmus. The production base for the film was moved to Churubusco Studios in Mexico City, as the exchange rate made filming the $35 million production there more economical.

Licence To Kill represents a complete change of direction for the Bond series on several different levels. The Cold War background of the previous four films disappears entirely. Instead, the enemy is a drug cartel headed by Franz Sanchez (Robert Davi), who operates from a power base in Isthmus City where he has killed or bribed all the politicians and controls the military. Julian Petley was among the commentators who read this as a reflection of the late 1980s *Zeitgeist* which had seen a marked thawing in the Cold War following the new openness evident in the Soviet Union:

> The fact that the villains on this occasion are tied up with extreme right-wing forces, however, does show that the Bond myth is fairly flexible in an ideological sense. On the whole, the films have served as a rather good barometer of East–West relations, and it would be difficult to imagine an anti-Soviet Bond in this era of *glasnost*. Instead, the universally reviled figure of the drug baron provides a much more effective target, and the film abounds with scenes in which dealers get their just deserts.[15]

If Whitaker of *The Living Daylights* had been a spiritual cousin of Colonel Oliver North, then Sanchez bears comparison to General Manuel Noriega of Nicaragua, whom the Americans were shortly later to 'snatch' and put on trial for conspiring to distribute drugs in the United States. The film begins with Sanchez being captured by the American DEA (Drug Enforcement Agency) when he makes a lightning visit to the Bahamas to reclaim his mistress who has run off with another man. Sanchez subsequently escapes and threatens to shoot down an American airliner with Stinger missiles unless the DEA leaves him alone. In taking on Sanchez, Bond is effectively relocated from the secret war against the Soviet Union to America's war against the para-military drug cartels in its own back yard.

However, a major difference between *Licence To Kill* and previous films in which Bond had adopted the role of a surrogate American hero (*Diamonds Are Forever*, *Live and Let Die*) is that his pursuit of Sanchez amounts to a personal vendetta rather than an officially sanctioned mission. In an incident borrowed from Fleming's *Live and Let Die*, Felix Leiter (David Hedison, who had also played Leiter in the film of *Live and Let Die*) — now working for the DEA — is captured by Sanchez's men and thrown into a shark tank. He survives, though loses his leg; his newlywed bride, however, is murdered (and by implication raped) by Sanchez's men.[16] Upon discovering what has happened, Bond vows revenge and sets out to kill Sanchez and destroy his operation. This course of action puts him at odds with the DEA, who are restricted by legal procedures ('It just so happens we have laws in this country, commander,' says Leiter's colleague after Bond has killed several heavies; 'Do you have a law against what they did to Leiter?' Bond replies bitterly). Even more significantly, Bond disobeys the order given to him by M to leave the whole thing to the Americans ('This personal vendetta of yours could easily compromise Her Majesty's Government'). The key confrontation between Bond and M, in which Bond proffers his resignation and M informs him that his licence to kill is revoked, represents a fundamental shift in the underlying ideology of the Bond mythology. Fleming's Bond had always been fiercely loyal towards M, if occasionally resentful; the filmic Bond, particularly in the Connery films, had been rather more ironic and slightly rebellious towards his superior, though there had never been any question about his loyalty. Petley points out just how far *Licence To Kill* reconfigures, even violates, the relationship between Bond and M: 'The scene in which Bond is disciplined by M and ends up assaulting both his boss and his fellow agents will be as outrageous to Fleming purists as Marlowe's shooting of Terry Lennox in Robert Altman's *The Long Goodbye* was to Chandler disciples.'[17] If M represents Bond's symbolic father-figure, as has often been suggested (by Eco and Bennett among others), then this scene is acting out an oedipal scenario otherwise absent from the Bond films (though present in the novels). In fact, Bond does not physically assault M (that would be going too far), though he does punch and kick M's minders. For the rest of the film Bond is a rogue agent, operating outside the secret service and thus cut off from official resources, though the venerable Q does take leave to equip and assist him in the field. However, in assigning Bond to a personal vendetta rather than an official mission,

38. *Licence To Kill*: 'His bad side is a dangerous place to be.' Bond sets out on a personal vendetta in the film that most breaks with the generic formula of the series.

the film repudiates the professional code of ethics that Bond himself had so often asserted in the past ('When I kill it's on the specific orders of my government,' as he had told Scaramanga in *The Man With the Golden Gun*).

It is not only in its narrative ideology that *Licence To Kill* breaks with the usual codes of the Bond series. It significantly remodels the generic conventions of the Bond narrative so that many of the expected incidents and situations are missing from the film. For example, there is no scene in which M briefs Bond with details of his mission, and no opportunity for the playful flirtation between Bond and Miss Moneypenny that had been one of the hallmarks of the series ever since *Dr No*. While this may be seen as an attempt to ring the changes on the Bond formula, it can be argued that the changes made are so drastic that *Licence To Kill* loses the distinctive generic identity of a Bond film and instead comes to resemble something more like *Dirty Harry* or *Lethal Weapon*. In his relentless pursuit of Sanchez, Bond crosses the boundary from secret agent with a 'licence to kill' to vengeance-driven cop or vigilante – a familiar figure from Hollywood action movies, but far removed from the cool, sophisticated hero audiences are accustomed to in the Bond films.

Licence To Kill also differs stylistically from other Bond movies. The visual style is less glossy than usual: the cinematography is more low-key, the colour definition less pronounced. The Florida locations and designer clothes are more *Miami Vice* than James Bond. The restrained elegance of Bond's usual tailored suits gives way to Dalton's more casual, dressed-down look. The music, too, is less distinctive than usual. Composed by Michael Kamen, the score for *Licence To Kill* – with the exception of the title song performed *à la* Bassey by Gladys Knight – is bland and undistinguished, too similar to his scores for *Lethal Weapon* (1987) and *Die Hard* (1988) and lacking the lush orchestrations that John Barry had brought to most previous Bond films. The result is that *Licence To Kill* lacks the distinctive 'feel' of a Bond film, again seeming more like a run-of-the-mill action movie.

In various ways, therefore, *Licence To Kill* does not 'fit' into the generic pattern of the Bond series; it is a break from what has gone before, not a natural evolution. However, this is not to say that it entirely lacks 'Bondian' characteristics. While not being the usual madman bent on world domination, Sanchez is one of the most charismatic and physically threatening villains in the series' recent history. Like Bond, he has his own code of ethics ('Loyalty is more important to me than money'), though he is also vicious and, it is suggested, a sexual sadist, whipping his treacherous girlfriend Lupe (Talisa Soto) with the hide of a stingray. This incident was taken from Fleming's story 'The Hildebrand Rarity', in which a boorish American called Milton Krest uses a similar instrument to beat his wife; in the film Krest (Anthony Zerbe) becomes one of Sanchez's associates. The Fleming villain whom Sanchez most closely resembles is Scaramanga of *The Man With the Golden Gun*: a Latin American gangster involved in narcotics who takes Bond on as one of his men for no obvious reason, though in both cases it might be inferred that the villain finds Bond sexually attractive. There is certainly a suggestion of homo-eroticism in the relationship between Sanchez and Dario (Benicio del Toro), a baby-faced young killer.

After the monogamous Bond of *The Living Daylights*, *Licence To Kill* again provides him with more sexual interest, though Latin temptress Lupe Lamora is little competition for main Bond girl Pam Bouvier (Carey Lowell). The character of Pam is an illustration of how far the Bond series has gone towards incorporating discourses of feminism into its representation of women while still maintaining the sexist code that is essential to the make-up of the Bond character. On their first meeting Pam is completely indifferent to Bond; on their second meeting she is shown to be capable of taking care of herself in a bar-room brawl and handles a pump-action shotgun with ease. But as well as being the possessor of a mighty phallic weapon (she tut-tuts when Bond reveals he is armed only with his trusty Walther PPK), Pam is also possessed of dainty feminine guile, keeping a small Beretta .25 (the pistol so contemptuously referred to as a 'lady's gun' by Major Boothroyd in *Dr No*) concealed in her garter. When Bond's speedboat runs out of fuel, Pam's ironic 'I haven't heard that one in a long time' recalls, whether intentionally or not, the ending of *Dr No* in which Bond and Honey had found themselves similarly stranded. A former army pilot, Pam flies Bond into Isthmus City and stays around to help him. She resents having to masquerade as Bond's 'executive secretary', but is firmly put in her place by Bond, who reasserts the sexist code ('We're south of the border – it's a man's world'). An assertive woman at the beginning, by the end of the film Pam adopts a more conventional nice-girl-next-door role when, seeing Lupe kissing Bond, she runs away and cries. Whereas earlier in the film Pam had taken the initiative, at the end she waits for Bond to kiss her first; their dialogue from the boat ('Why don't you wait until you're asked?' 'Then why don't you ask me?') is reversed.

Critical reaction to *Licence To Kill* was sharply divided. Indeed, of all the latter-day Bond films it was the one which most polarised critical opinion, with some responding favourably to its harder-edged style but others thinking that it had strayed too far away from traditional 'Bondian' territory. Even the American trade press, which generally tends to speak with much the same voice, was divided over its merits. *Variety* was enthusiastic. 'The James Bond production team has found its second wind with *Licence To Kill*, a cocktail of high-octane action, spectacle and drama,' it declared. 'It's a sure-fire click worldwide for the 16th in the United Artists 007 series and one that will rate among the best.'[18] But a rather more negative note was sounded by the *Hollywood Reporter*, which felt it lacked the usual panache of the Bond series and was rather more violent than usual:

> It's neither shaken nor stirred, but rather blasted, this latest James Bond. If this movie were compared to the peripatetic secret agent's favored vodka martini, it would be of the airport bar variety – formulaic, pre-measured and dispensed through a hose. A harsh refreshment that the discerning Mr Bond would send straight back to its maker. ... Although there are dollops of drollery throughout, *Licence* has little of the champagne-comic sparkle of vintage James Bond; instead, under John Glen's heavy-artillery direction, it has gory carnage and murder death scenes of such explicit gruesomeness that the series' armchair aficionados are likely to find their stomachs soured and their sensibilities nettled.[19]

This criticism was not without some justification. *Licence To Kill* is the most violent of the Bond movies. Several scenes – including Sanchez whipping Lupe, Leiter's descent into the shark tank, Krest's gory death in a depressurisation chamber, and Sanchez's final fiery demise – attracted the attention of censors in both the United States and Britain. In America it was given a 'PG-13' rating ('special parental guidance recommended for those younger than 13'), while in Britain it was given a more restrictive '15' certificate which denied it the usual family audience that the Bond films traditionally attracted. Some commentators wondered whether the more violent than usual content was a deliberate strategy to compete with Hollywood action movies. 'While this must clearly restrict the box office potential in the UK – where 11–14 year olds have been a huge and loyal audience for years – the reasoning may be that a "realistic" storyline about drugs allied to some graphic violence will more than help to compensate in other markets, notably the US where Bond has never [*sic*] been a giant drawing card,' *Screen International* suggested.[20] However, Broccoli was highly critical of the BBFC's category decision: 'What I also found hard to take was the harsh reaction of the British censor in restricting the age group for our picture while giving *Batman* a clean bill of health.'[21] In fact, *Batman* was only slightly less restricted than *Licence To Kill* in that it caused the BBFC to introduce a new '12' certificate.

Licence To Kill performed less well at the box-office than *The Living Daylights*. Its total worldwide grosses were $157 million, approximately the same as *A View To A Kill*, but only $36 million of that (roughly equal to the film's negative cost) came from North America – a disappointing return in an age when a big-budget film needs to earn back three times its production cost to be in the black. Its relatively disappointing showing at the box-office can be attributed partly to the fact that it was released during Hollywood's blockbuster summer of 1989 when *Indiana Jones and the Last Crusade*, *Batman* and *Lethal Weapon 2* all provided stiff competition. *Batman* grossed more on its opening weekend ($40.5 million) than *Licence To Kill* did throughout its entire run in US cinemas. It is unlikely that the more restrictive certificates given to *Licence To Kill* made any significant difference, as *Lethal Weapon 2* was 'R-rated' in the USA and classified '18' in Britain. The *Lethal Weapon* series, which starred Mel Gibson as a maverick Los Angeles cop, was representative of a new style of violent action movie that had emerged in Hollywood, which also included the *Die Hard* films with Bruce Willis and the films of Arnold Schwarzenegger, such as *Commando* (1985), *Raw Deal* (1986) and *Red Heat* (1988). All these films copied from the Bond series the one-liners which the hero makes after dispatching the latest heavy, the difference being that the deaths were that much more violent and gory: the violence of *Licence To Kill* seems mild in comparison to the bloody, bullet-riddled bodies of *Lethal Weapon* and *Die Hard*.

Some commentators again expressed their doubts about the future of the Bond films. *Screen International* observed that 'a question mark seems to hang over the whole future of the series as the jury remains out on this new-look "adult" Bond'.[22] Broccoli conceded that *Licence To Kill* had deviated too far from the usual formula of the Bond series, that 'in making Bond an altogether tougher character, we had lost some of the original sophistication and wry humour', though he remained adamant that Dalton was the right man for the role.[23] However, there was to be a six-year hiatus between *Licence To Kill* and the next Bond film. The lukewarm reception of *Licence To Kill* caused the production team to rethink the Bond formula, and it was even reported (inaccurately as it turned out) that Broccoli was considering selling the Bond franchise.[24] The main reason for Bond's absence from the screen for the first half of the 1990s, however, was that Broccoli's company Danjaq, which holds copyright in the Bond films, entered into a protracted legal dispute with MGM/UA Communications – itself the subject of an abortive take-over by Giancarlo Parretti's Pathé Communications – which, it was alleged, had sold video and television rights for the Bond films at a cut-price rate. The dispute was resolved in 1993, at which time Dalton was still set to star in the forthcoming 'Bond 17'. However, the production was delayed further by script re-writes, and Dalton dropped out of the running. When Bond returned to the screen in *GoldenEye* in 1995, it was to be in the more lightweight persona of Pierce Brosnan.

8

For England: *GoldenEye,*
Tomorrow Never Dies

With the successful *GoldenEye* (dir. Martin Campbell, 1995) and *Tomorrow Never Dies* (dir. Roger Spottiswoode, 1997) the Bond series was once again revivified following a six-year hiatus in which there had been no new Bond film and constant speculation about the future of the series. As was the case with the Dalton films, Pierce Brosnan's first two outings as James Bond exemplified the twin processes of continuity and change which have been the key to the longevity of the series. Following the generic deviation of *Licence To Kill*, in which Bond had been detached from his usual official status, the films of the late 1990s restored him to the more familiar role of defender of western civilisation in general and England in particular. In both *GoldenEye* and *Tomorrow Never Dies* the threat is once again directed at England, unlike the trend in mid- and late 1980s films where Bond had been occupied in saving Silicon Valley or taking on a Latin American drug cartel. The patriotic code of the Bond films is restored, and Bond himself reassumes his role as the foremost champion of Britannia. In terms of style, *GoldenEye* and *Tomorrow Never Dies* successfully repackage the Bond formula, updating the technology and keeping apace of rival action series through their spectacular stunts and set pieces, while at the same time maintaining the distinctive generic identity of the Bond formula that had been lost in *Licence To Kill*. 'Old wine in new bottles' might be the most apt phrase to describe the 1990s Bond films, as the content remains essentially the same but the packaging is newer, slicker and more expensive than before. That this strategy has been successful in restoring Bond to the forefront of popular cinema is illustrated by the box-office success of these films, against the predictions of some critics and industry insiders. With worldwide grosses of $357 million, *GoldenEye* took more at the box-office than both *The Living Daylights* and *Licence To Kill* combined – and that is before the ancillary markets of home video, satellite and cable television, which in the 1990s have become even more significant than the theatrical market, are taken into account.[1] When the CBS network paid a record $20 million for the terrestrial broadcast rights for *Tomorrow Never Dies* before the film was even released to cinemas, it was a sure sign that Bond was once again a viable commercial property.[2] *Tomorrow Never Dies* itself was also the first Bond film to be made after the death (in 1996) of Cubby Broccoli, the producer whose commercial instincts had turned the Bond series into such a successful franchise.

The popular success of the 1990s Bond films is all the more remarkable given that the thirty-five-year-old series faced stiffer than ever competition in the action movie market. The early 1990s had seen a wave of rival action thrillers which threatened to displace the Bond films from their position as the premier action movie series. The *Lethal Weapon* and *Die Hard* series, which combined explosive and violent action with the sort of tongue-in-cheek humour pioneered by the Bond movies back in the 1960s, had both run to three films before the release of *GoldenEye*. The success of the Cold War thriller *The Hunt for Red October* (1990), starring Sean Connery as a Russian nuclear submarine commander playing cat-and-mouse with the Soviet and American navies as he attempts to defect, led to a further two film adaptations of Tom Clancy's high-tech novels, *Patriot Games* (1992) and *Clear and Present Danger* (1994), in which Harrison Ford took over the role of CIA agent Jack Ryan, a suited hero described in the promotional discourse as a 'James Bond for the 90s'. Another 'James Bond for the 90s' was threatened when Arnold Schwarzenegger recovered from the flop of *The Last Action Hero* (1993) with the Bond-derivative *True Lies* (1994), a massively budgeted ($100 million-plus) action movie in which the Austrian *übermensch* played an American secret agent called Harry Tasker, the 'twist' being that his wife (Jamie Lee Curtis) believes him to be a boring computer salesman and is contemplating an affair with a used car salesman who pretends he is a secret agent. 'I thought this could be made into a James Bond kind of movie,' Schwarzenegger is quoted as saying. 'But instead of having Bond with a playboy bunny waiting at every port, he would have a more realistic [*sic*] situation with a wife and child.'[3] That the Bond movies were a point of reference for the film is evident from the outset, as Schwarzenegger emerges from the water and removes his wetsuit to reveal an immaculate dinner suit *à la* Connery in *Goldfinger*; imitation is the sincerest form of flattery. But for all its kinetic style and expensively staged pyrotechnics, *True Lies* lacks the unique generic identity of the Bond films, and Schwarzenegger himself can never be anything more than an *ersatz* Bond, despite his fetching deadpan way with heavily accented one-liners.

In relaunching the Bond series in the mid-1990s, the film-makers were at pains to differentiate Bond from the many competitors in the action movie market. Producer Michael G. Wilson described the Bonds as 'action-adventure' rather than simply 'action' films and emphasised the global scale of Bond's adventures. 'There are very few action-adventure films,' he states. 'Action films tend to be located in one particular city or one building, plane, boat or airport. So I never think of them as direct competition.'[4] This is certainly one of the differences between the Bond series and the *Lethal Weapon* and *Die Hard* films. Another difference, as *GoldenEye* director Martin Campbell put it, is that Bond is a 'white collar hero' whereas the other action heroes are all 'blue collar'.[5] Campbell, who had directed the acclaimed BBC thriller serial *Edge of Darkness* (1987) and the futuristic action film *No Escape* (1994), nevertheless did not immediately jump at the chance to direct a Bond picture:

> I thought long and hard about it. I felt that Bond was getting very tired. I thought that the franchise had slightly passed its sell-by date and that the 17th film would need a shot in the arm. I questioned whether Bond was part of the '90s or an anachronism. It was a question of deciding whether he was relevant or not, whether he could still be as entertaining and successful as he had been in the past.[6]

The casting of Irish actor Pierce Brosnan as the new James Bond had a certain air of inevitability about it. Brosnan had been considered for the role in 1986, but was tied to a contract for the television series *Remington Steele*, even though it had been cancelled by the NBC network. In the absence of any other likely candidates for the role – though Mel

Gibson had been touted in the media – the choice of Brosnan was virtually a *fait accompli*. Now in his early forties, Brosnan was the right age for Bond, and with his old-fashioned, darkly handsome matinée idol looks he certainly had the right image for the part. Some critics alleged that he had little to offer beyond his looks. 'The choice of Brosnan is less a piece of casting and more a masterstroke of art direction: those Littlewood-catalogue looks; hair in all the right places … the man looks as though he was born to model jumpers,' wrote Tom Shone in the *Sunday Times*. [7] 'Pierce Brosnan, a classless Celt, has a superficial resemblance to Sean Connery but … the agency you'd associate him with is the one that supplies escorts, not spies,' observed Philip French.[8] Comparisons to his illustrious predecessors were inevitable. 'We know 007 is a tailor's dummy wired for wisecracks,' said Nigel Andrews. 'But Connery and Moore suggested wit and mischief in reserve. Brosnan seems to have signed on at the charm clinic and come away with a personality by-pass.'[9] 'With his chocolate-box good looks, Pierce Brosnan as Bond could break any female's diet, but with my savoury palate I was secretly pining for Sean Connery and felt that Brosnan was more of a Milk Tray man who failed to deliver,' was the verdict of Brigit Grant.[10]

Other critics, however, were more charitable to the new 007. Geoff Brown thought he was 'undoubtedly the best Bond since Sean Connery'.[11] Comparisons between Brosnan and his immediate predecessor tended to be in the new man's favour, as critics welcomed his lighter and more relaxed style of performance following the intensity and seriousness of Dalton's Bond. 'He [Brosnan] has the sexual mischief of the old James with a superman's derring-do and self-confidence in handling wit and weaponry,' said Alexander Walker. 'The last licence-holder, Timothy Dalton, pre-eminently a stage actor, seldom looked fully at ease in front of the camera.'[12] And Mariella Frostrup opined that the popular success of Brosnan's Bond 'is proof that the martini-swilling superhero has been successfully reinvented since the dire Dalton days'.[13] Such comments are indicative of a trend, particularly among the popular press, to disparage Dalton's Bond in hindsight, even though his performance had been well received by most critics at the time.

GoldenEye was the most expensive Bond film to date, though its $50 million cost was less than half that of *True Lies* and much of the budget was provided through the use of product placement (BMW cars, Omega watches, IBM computers, Perrier water). Although the Bond series came back to Britain, Pinewood Studios was full to capacity at the time of production and so Eon converted a disused Rolls-Royce factory at Leavesden Aerodrome, near Watford, into a makeshift studio facility. This logistical improvisation certainly had no adverse effect on the quality of the film itself, which is a more polished and sophisticated Bond thriller than *Licence To Kill*, and one which adheres closer to the generic conventions of the series. Even so, *GoldenEye* is not without its contradictions.

The fact that Brosnan had so nearly been Bond instead of Dalton some eight years earlier adds a particular *frisson* to the pre-title sequence of *GoldenEye*, which, unusually for a Bond film, is set in the past, some nine years before the main story. Assuming that the main narrative is contemporaneous with the film's release (1995), then the pre-title sequence takes place in 1986, the year in which Brosnan had lost the Bond role to Dalton when he was unable to free himself from his television contract. It is almost as if the film is turning the clock back to suggest that Brosnan should really have been Bond all along, that Dalton had been an aberration. In this sense it can be compared to *Diamonds Are Forever*, which had set out to erase the memory of George Lazenby by emphasising that Sean Connery was back as James Bond.

The main purpose of *GoldenEye*, however, was to find a place for Bond in the changing world of the 1990s. This was acknowledged in the publicity, exemplified by the following extract from a marketing document produced by the international distributors UIP:

It is six and a half years since the last Bond film (*Licence To Kill*) was released, and the 'classic' Bond films (as Nos. 1–16 are now referred) are a memory, a past associated with the pre-Glasnost era. The world has changed – the Berlin Wall has come down and those that were regarded as enemies are now our allies, and some who were friends cannot necessarily be regarded as so. 'Political correctness' is now taken for granted. Is there still a place in the modern world for a Secret Agent like 007?

The answer is emphatically *yes*. *GoldenEye* presents a Bond for the 90s. This is a *contemporary* action film clearly reflecting the world in which we live. There are many elements that position the story in today's world – from bungee-jumping and computer hacking to a female M, and a sports car that hasn't even been launched yet![14]

This sort of publicity material illustrates the way in which a film is intended to be received, and as such it represents an attempt to pre-determine critical interpretation from an 'official' point of view. What is interesting about *GoldenEye*, however, is that the film itself does not entirely conform to the intended meaning that is being overlaid on to it by the official publicity machine. While in some respects *GoldenEye* does present a 'Bond for the 90s', in other respects it offers the possibility for alternative readings which are ignored or marginalised by the official publicity discourse. Indeed, close analysis reveals a considerable tension between official pronouncements on the one hand and the film itself on the other.

On one level, certainly, *GoldenEye* does perform the role assigned to it by the official publicity discourse in locating Bond in the 1990s. Most obviously this takes the form of taking account of the end of the Cold War. Since the release of *Licence To Kill* in the summer of 1989, the geo-political map of Europe had been substantially redrawn: the Communist regimes in Eastern Europe had collapsed, the Berlin Wall had fallen, the two Germanys had been reunified, the Soviet Union had been dismantled and new democratic governments had been elected in most former Soviet bloc states. *GoldenEye* straddles the end of the Cold War by setting its pre-title sequence in the past. Thus, the film begins with Bond and his colleague 006, Alec Trevelyan (Sean Bean), penetrating a Soviet chemical weapon research centre near Archangel. Trevelyan is apparently killed by Colonel Ourumov (Gottfried John), but Bond manages to blow up the centre and escape. Nine years later, when a Russian satellite weapon known as 'Goldeneye', which uses an electro-magnetic pulse to knock out anything with an electronic circuit (shades of *A View To A Kill*), is hijacked by an unknown enemy, Bond is assigned to investigate. Travelling to St Petersburg, Bond discovers that Ourumov, now a general, is in league with the 'Janus' crime syndicate, and that the mysterious Janus himself is none other than Trevelyan, who it turns out was not killed after all, but who has been permanently scarred by the explosive charges which Bond set off. As the publicity material indicates, a degree of realignment between friend and foe has taken place: Bond's former colleague and friend is now his sworn enemy, while Bond turns for help to former KGB agent Valentin Zukovsky (Robbie Coltrane).

On closer inspection, however, the relocation of Bond to a post-Cold War context needs to be nuanced rather more subtly. For all that the old Communist regime has fallen, the threat still emanates from Russia. General Ourumov, a renegade military commander who plots

39. *GoldenEye*: Pierce Brosnan brings Bond into the 1990s
after a six-year hiatus.

his own personal conspiracy, recalls similar characters in *Octopussy* and *The Living Daylights*. And *glasnost* only extends so far: when the Russians claim the firing of Goldeneye was 'an accident during a routine training exercise', Bond detects a familiar cover-up ('Governments change, the lies stay the same'). In a sense, it could be argued that *GoldenEye* does not really modify the ideological structures of the Bond narrative to any great degree. It still belongs squarely in the generic lineage of the

British spy thriller in which Russia had always been represented as a mysterious and sinister enemy, even before the rise of Communism overlaid a more overt political dimension on to the genre. It could be argued, in fact, that for all its contemporary references to the powerful Russian Mafia which had emerged after the fall of Communism, *Golden-Eye* simply represents a continuation of the tradition of Russian villains which had been a staple of the British imperialist spy thriller since the days of William Le Queux and E. Phillips Oppenheim.

There is another respect, too, in which *GoldenEye* looks to the past. The reason why Trevelyan turns against Britain is rooted in a historic betrayal. It is revealed that his parents were Lienz Cossacks, Russians who fought for the Germans during the Second World War and surrendered to the British in 1945, but were handed back to Stalin, who executed them ('Not exactly our finest hour,' Bond observes ruefully). Trevelyan plans to use the Goldeneye weapon on London, after hacking into the computer of the Bank of England to transfer money to his own accounts, which he sees as his own revenge on the country that betrayed his parents ('England is about to learn the cost of betrayal – inflation-adjusted for 1945').

In *GoldenEye*, therefore, the conspiracy is once again directed against England, relocating Bond within the generic lineage of the imperialist spy thriller following his excursion into *Lethal Weapon* territory in *Licence To Kill*. *GoldenEye* recalls *On Her Majesty's Secret Service* in its foregrounding of the codes of patriotism and duty. As Bond and Trevelyan set out on their mission together in the pre-title sequence, Trevelyan asserts the patriotic code which they both share ('For England, James'). When they come face to face nine years later, however, Trevelyan scorns and rejects that code. The dialogue exchange between the two men rehearses some familiar ideologies:

BOND: Why?

TREVELYAN: Hilarious question, particularly coming from you. Did you ever ask why? Why we toppled all those dictators, undermined all those regimes? Only to come home, 'Well done, good job, but sorry, old boy, everything you risked your life and limb for has changed'.

BOND: It was the job we were chosen for.

TREVELYAN: Of course you'd say that. James Bond, Her Majesty's loyal terrier, defender of the so-called faith.

This confrontation between former friends, one of whom no longer holds the values they once shared and who now scorns the other for clinging to outmoded boy-scout beliefs, recalls the similar exchange between Holly Martins and Harry Lime in *The Third Man*, thereby again reinforcing *GoldenEye*'s generic links within the thriller genre. Just as Martins kills Lime at the end of *The Third Man*, the climax of *GoldenEye* has Bond taking a personal relish at his former friend's demise. 'For England, James?' Trevelyan says, ironically recalling his earlier words; 'No, for me,' Bond replies, letting Trevelyan fall to his death from a great height.

Another way in which the publicity discourse tried to suggest that *GoldenEye* had updated the Bond series to reflect the world of the 1990s was in its representation of women. 'What is different about this film is that gone are the bimbos!' declared the publicity material. 'Izabella Scorupco and Famke Janssen play the two female leads. Both play highly intelligent and highly independent characters who have their own opinions and course of action, which are integral to the storyline of the film.'[15] But this was far from being a new discourse, as similar statements had been made about the women in every Bond film since *The Spy Who Loved Me* in 1977. And, moreover, as had been the case with previous films, the supposed intelligence and independence attributed to the female characters needs to be qualified. Heroine Natalya Simonova (Scorupco) is a computer programmer who possesses certain skills that Bond does not, though her independence is expressed mainly through bossiness rather than intelligence. And villainess Xenia Onatopp (Janssen), who gets her kicks from asphyxiating men between her legs during sex – as her name implies, she likes to go on top – is simply the latest in a long tradition of beautiful but deadly females such as Fiona Volpe and Fatima Blush who live fast (she drives a Ferrari) and die spectacularly.

This is not to say, however, that *GoldenEye* makes no concessions to feminism at all. Its strategy for incorporating feminist discourses is not to alter Bond's attitude towards women, but rather to alter the attitudes of the women around him to Bond himself. Indeed, the film presents Bond as being beleaguered by women in positions of power and authority. These women are no longer confined solely to the realms of villainy, such as Onatopp, but are also to be found on Bond's own side. Thus, the main narrative begins with Bond being evaluated by secret service psychologist Caroline (Serena Gordon), though she quickly melts when he turns on the charm ('I have no problem with female authority,' Bond tells her as a prelude to seduction). Miss Moneypenny suggests that his flirtation could be construed as sexual harassment, though she is still clearly flattered by the attention. The most obvious challenge to Bond's male chauvinism, however, comes from the new M (Judi Dench). In making M a middle-aged career woman, the film drew obvious comparisons to the real-life appointment of mother-of-two Stella Rimington as Director-General of MI5. However, the casting of a female M should be seen not merely as another example of the Bond series' topical contemporary references, but also as a deliberate strategy for renegotiating the sexist code which remains essential to the make-up of the Bond character. In the most-quoted line of the film, M makes it clear to Bond that she regards him as an anachronism, telling him to his face that he is 'a sexist, misogynist dinosaur, a relic of the Cold War whose boyish charms, though wasted on me, obviously appealed to that young woman I sent out to evaluate you'. Thus the film diffuses the obvious criticisms that could be made of the Bond character (that his attitude towards women is out of date in the 1990s) by voicing them itself through the agency of a female authority-figure.

In its narrative ideologies, therefore, *GoldenEye* offers only a partial reworking of the Bond formula in a 1990s context. The tension between the film and the publicity discourses around it is evident at other levels too. For example, although the publicity material had claimed that the previous Bond films were now nothing more than a 'memory' – 'Pierce Brosnan *is* James Bond. Forget all who have preceded him'[16] – *GoldenEye* explicitly locates Brosnan in the Bond heritage by showing him, immediately following the title sequence, driving a silver-grey Aston Martin DB5, thus invoking the memory of Connery who had driven the same vehicle in *Goldfinger* and *Thunderball.*[17]

The visual style of *GoldenEye* also represents a mixture between new and traditional elements. It restores the deep visual texture of earlier Bond films, following the more low-key look of *Licence To Kill*. The main title sequence, designed by pop video and commercial director Daniel Kleinman, is a stunning *tour de force* which pays homage to the late Maurice Binder while surpassing his most recent title designs in its level of visual imagination. Kleinman uses the title sequence as a metaphor for the plot itself, something which Binder did only occasionally, providing a surrealistic illustration of the fall of Communism: giant hammers and sickles float against a red background, women smash them with sledgehammers, statues of Lenin are toppled. There is a Daliesque quality to some of the imagery, especially the floating guns and the giant 'golden eye' which serves as a linking motif. The titles also anticipate the key confrontation scene between Bond and Trevelyan, which takes place symbolically among the relics of Russia's Communist past in a 'statue park' in St Petersburg. Elsewhere in the film, Peter Lamont's production design recalls the heyday of Ken Adam, particularly in the multi-layered Goldeneye control centre which resembles Dr No's gantried laboratory, and in the hidden satellite dish which rises from beneath the surface of a lake rather like the volcano base in *You Only Live Twice*. The new M's office eschews the traditional wood panels and leather-backed furniture in favour of a clinical modernist functionalism, while the secret service operations room features walls of giant monitor screens which emphasise the technological sophistication of modern spying. In the midst of all this technological modernity, however, Bond himself has a comfortingly 'retro' appearance through the elegant sophistication of Brosnan's tailored suits, complete with tucked-in pocket handkerchief. Phil Meheux's cinematography, furthermore, recalls the bright, glossy, high-contrast style of Ted Moore's work on the 1960s Bonds. This might be seen as a form of product differentiation, as the tendency in most other action thrillers of the 1990s, including the *Lethal Weapon* and *Die Hard* films, had been towards a grainier, grittier look in which much of the action is under-lit.

In locating *GoldenEye* in the lineage of the Bond series, the films which it most closely resembles are those directed by Guy Hamilton and John Glen. Martin Campbell's direction recalls Hamilton's in its visual extravagance and foregrounding of signs of conspicuous consumption (*Goldfinger* in particular springs to mind) and Glen's in its highly efficient staging of protracted action sequences. The film strikes a nice balance between action as spectacle, exemplified in the chase through the streets of St Petersburg with Bond at the controls of an unusually manoeuvrable T-64 tank which demolishes everything in its path, and more intimate set pieces such as the bruising close-quarters fight between Bond and Trevelyan at the film's end which recalls the train compartment fight of *From Russia With Love* and the lift fight in *Diamonds Are Forever*. Where the film lacks the distinctive Bond style, however, is once again in its music: Eric Serra's synthesised score eschews John Barry's orchestral flourishes in favour of a more restrained electronic sound and makes only sparing use of the 'James Bond Theme'. 'The absence of the latter,' said one critic, 'is sure to throw some audience members into a two-hour Pavlovian twitch.'[18]

The reception of *GoldenEye* was mixed, with some critics welcoming Bond's return to the screen after his extended leave of absence while others lamented that the film was so formulaic it felt as if he had never really been away at all. Geoff Brown belonged to the former camp, opining that *GoldenEye* marked a return to the high camp style of the classic Bond films and was stylish enough to put the over-muscled action men of Hollywood back in their place. 'Other action heroes may have sprung up in the 1980s while the Bond series nosedived with dull Timothy Dalton and then disappeared into legal wrangles; but, as Bond gets to work in his tailored clothing, you feel Schwarzenegger and Stallone shrivelling,' he wrote. 'Camp fun has returned to action movies.'[19] But there were some voices in the trade who doubted that a Bond film could hold its own in the age of the modern action cinema. Mike Goodridge, the London critic of *Screen International*, thought *GoldenEye* was 'hampered by a feeble story, flabby pacing and too strict an adherence to the series' traditional formula. A 1995 Bond pic needs tighter plotting and more palpable suspense to seduce a generation groomed on the never-let-up tension of *Die Hard*, *Speed* and *True Lies*.' Goodridge felt that the film would appeal most to existing fans rather than the mainstream cinema audience: 'The marketing frenzy surrounding a new 007 picture – and a new 007 – will be enough to get ageing Bond fans into the cinema ... but beyond that, this dated package might drop off dramatically at the box office, missing the target with the cinema's core 16-to-24-year-old audience.'[20] This was hardly the sort of verdict the producers wanted to hear, as much of their marketing strategy had been designed to attract new audiences to Bond.

Variety, however, was much more enthusiastic about the film's box-office prospects, arguing that it not only successfully repackaged the Bond formula, but that it also worked as a first-rate action picture in its own right:

> James Bond definitely is back in business with *GoldenEye*. Among the better of the 17 Bonds and, perhaps more important for to-day's audience, a dynamic action entry in its own right, this first 007 adventure in six years breaths fresh creative and commercial life into the 33-year-old series. Pierce Brosnan makes a solid debut in the role he almost got eight years earlier, and Ian Fleming's very mid-century secret agent has been shrewdly repositioned in the '90s in ways that will amuse longtime fans and prove engaging

for viewers not born when Bond started saving the world. The very definition of escapist fare, this should restore Bond's golden touch at the international box office.[21]

Whereas *Variety*'s instincts had been wrong with *Licence To Kill*, this time the showbusiness bible was spot on, for *GoldenEye* became the biggest-grossing Bond film yet; taking inflation into account it was probably the most successful since the mid-1960s. It did well in the US market, where its grosses broke the $100 million threshold that is now regarded as the indication of a major box-office hit, though the bulk of its revenues still came from overseas markets, with the film doing particularly well in Western Europe, Scandinavia and Japan.

For all the doubts of some critics, the popular success of *GoldenEye* proved that the Bond series could prosper in the film culture of the 1990s. The eighteenth film, *Tomorrow Never Dies*, consolidated that success, though its production was anything but a trouble-free process. It was hampered by constant rewrites, by a hastily revised location when plans to film in Vietnam fell through at the last moment, and by friction on the set between director Roger Spottiswoode and writer Bruce Ferstein which was widely reported in the press. The start of principal photography was delayed until 1 April 1997 for a film due to be released at the end of the year, and the budget escalated to an estimated $80 million. Once again a makeshift studio was built to accommodate the production, this time in a former supermarket warehouse at Frogmore in Hertfordshire, though some work was done at Pinewood, while the underwater sequences were filmed at the massive tank built in Baja by 20th Century-Fox for James Cameron's *Titanic*. Considering the difficulties involved, the completion of the film to meet its December release date was an achievement in itself.[22]

Tomorrow Never Dies was originally to have revolved around the hand-over of Hong Kong from Britain to China, though that story was dropped because it was deemed too political. Instead the film features a megalomaniac multimedia baron, Elliot Carver (Jonathan Pryce), who attempts to start a war between Britain and China. The film presents the figure of the media mogul as the modern equivalent of the traditional Bond villain, a man whose control of the channels of communication allows him to manipulate the course of governments. The publicity discourse hinted that Carver was an exaggerated version of global media tycoons such as Ted Turner and Rupert Murdoch, though a more useful comparison would be to William Randolph Hearst; to make the point explicit, Carver quotes the famous dictum attributed to Hearst ('You provide the pictures, I'll provide the war,' he is supposed to have told one of his reporters). Carver uses a secret satellite encoder to send a British frigate off course into Chinese territorial waters and a Stealth boat that is invisible to radar to sink it, making it look as if the Chinese are responsible.

Like *GoldenEye*, therefore, *Tomorrow Never Dies* locates Britain at the centre of the conspiracy and assigns to it the status of a world power. While the story itself bears no relation to Ian Fleming, one of the narrative ideologies of the original stories is still evident through the playing out of the *Pax Britannica*. If Fleming's novels had provided an imaginary reversal of Britain's decline on the world stage following the Suez Crisis, the main point of reference for *Tomorrow Never Dies* is the Falklands War. The sinking of the frigate HMS *Devonshire* is a blow to national pride which recalls the very real shock felt when ships were lost in the Falklands. In the imaginary world of the Bond film, however, Britain sets out to take on not a tin-pot South American dictatorship, but the military might of Red China. 'We're sending the fleet to China,' Moneypenny tells Bond, in a gloriously anachronistic assertion of Britain's maritime power. Moreover, the film also recalls the jingoistic extremes of the British tabloid press during the Falklands Conflict: 'The Empire Will Strike Back' screams one headline in a manner reminiscent of the *Sun*'s notorious 'Gotcha!' and 'Stick It Up Your Junta' banners of 1982. America's role, meanwhile, is sidelined: 'Uncle Sam is completely neutral in this turkey shoot,' CIA agent Jake Wade (Joe Don Baker) tells Bond. 'We have no interest in World War Three, unless we start it'.

The politics of *Tomorrow Never Dies* are intriguing. Red China, which at various times in the past had been a shadowy threat lurking in the background of the Bond movies, here assumes a position of much greater prominence, the collapse of the Soviet Union leaving China as the world's leading Communist power. At a time when there had been friction between China and Taiwan, as the Chinese navy carried out belligerent manoeuvres off the Taiwanese coast, the Bond films were once again reflecting the international political situation through references to Chinese military strength. However, *Tomorrow Never Dies* replays the narrative strategies of *From Russia With Love* and *The Spy Who Loved Me* in that the conspiracy revolves around a third party trying to provoke conflict, and Bond teams up with a Chinese agent, Wai Lin (Michelle

Yeoh), to defeat the villain. Carver is in league with a renegade Chinese warlord, General Chang, but the possibilities of internal dissent within China are never fully explored. Indeed, although Chang is mentioned frequently he is glimpsed only fleetingly, and as a character serves no narrative function.

Tomorrow Never Dies is replete with topical references. There are some teasing in-jokes as to which media tycoon Carver might have been modelled on. 'The PM would have my head if he knew we were investigating *him*,' M remarks, a line which could be read as a veiled comment on new British Prime Minister Tony Blair's political friendship with Rupert Murdoch, whose News International Corporation owns *The Times* and *Sun* newspapers and whose support, after years of siding with the Conservative Party, was seen by some as a major factor in Labour's 1997 general election victory. When, at the end of the film, M covers up Carver's role in the crisis by issuing a press statement to the effect that he is missing after falling overboard from his yacht, the mysterious death of disgraced newspaper proprietor Robert Maxwell, owner of the Mirror Group, springs irresistibly to mind. One scene even suggests that Carver is blackmailing the (unnamed) US president with a 'video of him with the cheerleader in the Chicago motel room' – a not entirely fanciful scenario given President Bill Clinton's much-publicised sexual peccadilloes.

As well as providing a topical modern variation on the figure of the Bond villain, *Tomorrow Never Dies* also features the most progressive heroine of the series to date. The character of Wai Lin performs the same ideological role as Anya Amasova of *The Spy Who Loved Me* in that she represents the feminine face of Communism. However, as played by Michelle Yeoh, the foremost female star of Hong Kong action cinema, Wai Lin actually has less in common with previous Bond girls than she does with another tradition of popular cinema: the fighting woman. Yeoh is the latest in a lineage of martial-arts heroines in the cinema which includes Angela Mao Ying (the female Bruce Lee of the 1970s), Tamara Dobson, Pam Grier and Cynthia Rothrock. While these performers made their name in non-mainstream genres such as Hong Kong 'chop socky' and 'blaxploitation', the figure of the fighting woman crossed over into mainstream Hollywood movies during the 1980s and 1990s, the two foremost examples being Sigourney Weaver in the *Alien* films and Linda Hamilton in *Terminator 2*, women who adopt masculine characteristics through their assertiveness, physical courage and ability to handle big guns. *Tomorrow Never Dies* provides plenty of scope for Yeoh to display her martial-arts skills, even to the extent of borrowing one of the conventions of Hong Kong action cinema when she combats a whole gang of villains. Initially resistant to Bond both sexually and ideologically (she calls him 'the decadent agent of a corrupt western power'), it is only at the very end of the film, when the mission has been accomplished, that she succumbs to the inevitable.

Like so many of its predecessors, *Tomorrow Never Dies* foregrounds technology, particularly through its emphasis on systems of communication and military hardware. The pre-title sequence, in which Bond is transmitting camera pictures of a terrorist arms bazaar on the Russian–Afghan border back to the Ministry of Defence in London, establishes a motif of technological spying which is a key thematic concern of the film. Both the MOD and Carver's high-tech headquarters in Hamburg are dominated by a wall of giant video screens which transmit pictures from around the world, while Carver's associate Gupta (Ricky Jay) uses sophisticated eavesdropping equipment to listen in on a conversation between Bond and Carver's wife Paris (Teri Hatcher), who is one of Bond's old girlfriends. Modern military technology is represented in the form of the ship-launched Cruise missile which can unerringly find its target, with the film recalling the media coverage of the Gulf War in which 'smart' weapons had been portrayed as the most efficient and clinical means of hitting enemy targets. 'One strike and we take out half the world's terrorists,' remarks the belligerent Admiral Roebuck (Geoffrey Palmer), unwittingly anticipating the US Cruise missile strikes on terrorist training camps in Afghanistan in the summer of 1998. But, just as in reality 'smart' weapons are not as accurate as they are widely supposed to be, the film ends with the Royal Navy reverting to tried and trusted methods: when radar contact with the damaged Stealth boat is too weak for a missile lock, the British flagship destroys it 'the old-fashioned way' with its 4.5-inch gun.

While the narrative ideologies of *GoldenEye* and *Tomorrow Never Dies* have much in common through their reassertion of the patriotic code of the Bond series, the films are quite different in style. If *GoldenEye* is more polished and visually sumptuous, then *Tomorrow Never Dies* has a rawness and urgency that recalls the Bond films of Terence Young and Peter Hunt. The pace is extremely swift; Spottiswoode's direction creates a sense of constant movement, and his *mise-en-scène* is full of busy detail, especially in the first half of the film. For example, rather than the usual

40. *Tomorrow Never Dies*: Explosive action, but not a hair out of place, as
Bond disrupts a terrorist arms bazaar on the Afghan border.

sit-down office scene, Bond's briefing with M takes place on the move,
in the back of a limousine speeding to the airport surrounded by police
motorcycle outriders. It is as if the speed at which the film was made
is reflected in the urgency of the narration; it was the first Bond film
for over two decades with a running time under two hours (though only
just). If the film lacks the deep visual texture of other Bond films (the

one it most closely resembles in this sense is *Licence To Kill*), it compen-
sates by providing more action highlights than is common. The pre-title
sequence contains enough explosions and spectacular destruction to
provide the climax to most action movies, but here it serves as a prelude
to a succession of action sequences and extended chases which punctuate
the film at regular intervals. The highlight is a motorcycle chase through
the backstreets of Saigon (actually filmed in Thailand and on the studio
lot) which mirrors the tank chase in *GoldenEye*: it occurs about two-
thirds of the way through the film as Bond and the heroine are making
their escape from the villains, but this time on a vehicle which is
completely exposed and which depends on speed and manoeuvrability
rather than armour-plated bulk. In so far as Bond and Wai Lin are
handcuffed together throughout this sequence, the film borrows a motif
from Hitchcock's *The 39 Steps*, but whereas in Hitchcock's film the situation
had been used to generate sexual tension (the handcuffed couple, who
dislike each other, have to spend the night together), here it becomes
simply a logistical exercise (how to drive a bike while cuffed together).
It is only towards the end that the pace flags, with the climax on Carver's
Stealth boat resembling the *Lethal Weapon* and *Die Hard* films as Brosnan
struts around firing a submachine-gun with one hand in a manner too
reminiscent of Gibson and Willis. Finally, after the disappointing scores
of the two preceding films, *Tomorrow Never Dies* marks a return to the
distinctive sound of the Bond series through the music of David Arnold,
a worthy successor to John Barry, whose score mixes Barry-esque motifs
with the pop and rock music of the 1990s. The 'James Bond Theme'
is restored to prominence following its virtual absence in *GoldenEye*,
with Arnold's heavier bass arrangement comparable to the way in which
Lalo Schifrin's original music was rejigged for the Brian De Palma–Tom
Cruise film of *Mission: Impossible* (1996).

However, critical reaction was generally less favourable than for
GoldenEye. Alexander Walker, who had liked *GoldenEye*, declared that
'the new Bond is a shambles. Made in admitted haste and chaos, the
18th in the series looks that way, too.' He disliked the technological
modernity of the film and longed for the style of the Bond of yesteryear:
'Give me the old words, the old weapons. For all its new-fangled,
computerised, multiscreen razzmatazz, *Tomorrow Never Dies* can't match
the bold hokum of the cartoon-styled classic 007 adventures.'[23] In
contrast, José Arroyo in *Sight and Sound* felt that the film bore too much
of a resemblance to its predecessors and echoed the same journal's

review of *The Spy Who Loved Me* some two decades earlier: 'The film-makers' attempts at making this Bond film bigger and better seem to have taken the form of cannibalising the series' history.' Thus the crop-haired blonde German heavy Stamper (Götz Otto) recalls Robert Shaw's Grant in *From Russia With Love*, the Far Eastern archipelago where Bond and Wai Lin sail in search of the Stealth boat recalls the same location in *The Man With the Golden Gun*, and the main title sequence refers back to both the golden girl of *Goldfinger* and the diamond motif of *Diamonds Are Forever*. 'Even the set-pieces, although generally satisfactory, attempt to outdo those of earlier Bonds by evoking as many of their elements as possible,' Arroyo adds. '*Tomorrow* is like a photocopy of a collage of previous Bonds: there's more, but it looks second-generation.' [24] One of the critics who did like the film, however, was Richard Williams of the *Guardian*, who felt that the action sequences did offer some new variations on the familiar:

A concentration on the usual set-pieces – the parachute jump, the underwater sequence, the climactic destruction of the villain's high-tech lair – is predictable, but there is enough imagination to sustain interest, notably throughout a car chase in which Bond sends his 7-series BMW slaloming between the pillars of a multi-storey car park by remote control, treating it like a giant Scalextric toy.[25]

Williams felt that Spottiswoode's aim had been 'to match the non-stop energy of movies by such action specialists as John Woo and Wolfgang Petersen'.

Tom Shone in the *Sunday Times* was one of those who felt the Bond movies had passed their sell-by date, but his review is interesting in that for all his criticisms of the film itself he recognised that Bond still exerted a great hold over audiences:

GoldenEye was justly praised for getting audiences back into theatres, rooting for Bond, although it seemed to me that after the heady high of its opening stunt, the film followed Bond's example and nose-dived. *Tomorrow Never Dies* continues the slide, although the audience I saw it with kept a brave face on things, whooping and hollering their way through each successive disappointment – the stunts, the low-testosterone levels of Pryce's performance, and of Brosnan's – right through to the end, where they were left cheering – well, what, exactly? Their own patriotism, their communal decision to gather together in a cinema and cheer on a British hero. It's enough to single-handedly restore your faith in the British film industry, which, to judge by the lungs of the audience out there, is roaring and ready to go. It's the films I'm worried about. Not even the modern media trimmings of this movie can convince you that Bond is anything other than old news. Tomorrow may never die, but it would be nice if we could lay yesterday to rest.[26]

Shone's review thus indicates a difference between critical and popular reception, as, indeed, did Walker's, which observed that 'A Bond film represents such a keenly anticipated event, and such a valuable investment, that it is virtually critic-proof'.

The box-office success of *Tomorrow Never Dies*, which had grossed some $340 million worldwide by May 1998, proves that the Bond films are indeed critic-proof. While it may not have done quite as well as *GoldenEye*, Brosnan's second outing was not too far behind the grosses of his series debut. This is a not insignificant point, for the second film of any new James Bond star is at least as important as the first, if not more so. While the first will usually attract audiences through sheer curiosity (how will his performance compare with the others? will he be as good as Sean Connery?), it is the second which proves whether or not the new James Bond has been widely accepted. With both Roger Moore and Timothy Dalton, for example, there was a marked drop in box-office revenues for their second films in comparison to their first; whereas Moore had opportunity to recover, Dalton did not. The popular success of *Tomorrow Never Dies*, despite many critics' disparaging remarks about Brosnan's performance ('This is Brosnan's second outing as Bond and he still looks a little timorous in the role, sporting the nervous good looks of a man who fully expects to be called back at any moment and told to model sweaters for the rest of the day,' Shone wrote), suggests that audiences around the world have accepted him as a 'Bond for the 90s' and that the licence to kill is likely to remain his for as long as he wants to exercise it.

Postscript: A Licence
to Thrill

I have labelled this end section 'Postscript' rather than 'Conclusion'
because it would be academically disingenuous to do otherwise. It is
difficult to draw any conclusions about the place of the Bond movies
in cinema history and film culture while the series itself is still on-going
(*The World is Not Enough*, directed by Michael Apted, is scheduled for
release in late 1999). Only when the series ends, when the cycle is
complete, will it be possible to arrive at a conclusive assessment of its
overall historical and cultural significance. What I offer here, therefore,
are not definitive conclusions about the Bond series, but rather some
observations on its history so far. 'To be continued …', as the legend
goes.

It is surely no exaggeration to suggest that the Bond films have been
the most popular and enduring series in motion picture history. That
the Bond series is still on-going is perhaps the most extraordinary facet
of its extraordinary history. The very longevity of the series is quite
remarkable. For over thirty-five years, a time span which represents
roughly a third of the entire history of the cinema and half the period
since the introduction of talking pictures in the late 1920s, the Bond
films have been one of the constants of the film industry: ever present,
ever familiar, ever popular with audiences around the world. The con-
tinuing popular appeal of the films is enough to confound those critics
who assert that James Bond has had his day and should be pensioned

off to a retirement home for secret agents and super heroes. Ever since the early 1970s, when the Bond series was already ten years old, there has been a constant undercurrent of criticism to the effect that Bond himself is a complete anachronism, and that the longer the films continue the more derivative and depressingly formulaic they become. As an ideological and cultural construct, James Bond has long since outlived his historical moment. To quote, for example, one 1990s commentator:

> But then times have changed, and James Bond was of his time – a time when Britain (and British Intelligence) held a certain position in the world. A time when Johnny Foreigner knew his place. A time when beautiful women from other countries existed primarily to be seduced, and the phrase 'sex tourism' held no dark overtones. A time when an obsessive interest in guns and hardware seemed a logical outlet for an adult male brain.
>
> Read Ian Fleming's books today, and they seem terribly snobbish, silly and dated. The sun has set for good on Fleming's heyday, the era that produced James Bond. Now let it set on the old boy's films, too.[1]

Such a comment, however, merely highlights the gulf between the critical and popular reception of the films, for whereas many commentators are ready to consign Bond to the dustbin of history, his screen adventures continue to find a large and enthusiastic audience.

So why have the Bond films proved so popular? Various reasons have been advanced to explain their success. For the film industry's own discourse, exemplified by the trade press, the answer is simply that the Bond movies provide those qualities of 'entertainment' and 'escapism' that audiences want. While this is undoubtedly true, however, it explains little. Entertainment value is virtually impossible to define; most films possess it to some degree, so what is it about the entertainment provided by the Bond films that makes them stand out? According to Cubby Broccoli, the films' appeal has been due in large measure to their production values. 'The success of James Bond has always depended upon the values we put up there on the screen,' he said in his autobiography. 'People may argue about the relative merits of the Bond films, but few would deny that they reveal the highest production values and technical skill.'[2] For John Brosnan, it is the visual qualities of the films that stand out and explain their popularity with audiences around the world:

... the most obvious answer is that they are *pure* cinema in the sense that they are highly visual films depending on lots of fast-paced action and sheer spectacle. This assures them of a large international audience because they are able to bypass language and cultural barriers and appeal directly to people of various nationalities and age groups, in the same way as did the slapstick comedies of the silent era and the cartoon films of Disney (two film genres that the Bonds have grown increasingly to resemble of late).[3]

According to this argument, it is the style of the films which accounts for their success. Brosnan attributes to the Bond films a universal filmic language that transcends national and cultural boundaries. The Bond films, in this sense, represent the continued existence of a 'cinema of attractions' based on visual spectacle rather than narrative or characterisation. The 'cinema of attractions' – a term originally applied to the study of early cinema before the emergence of the narrative feature film – is exemplified, variously, in the 'trick' films of Georges Méliès, in the cliff-hanger serial melodramas of the silent era, in the Cinema-Scope and Cinerama epics of the 1950s, and, more recently, in the high-tech special-effects blockbusters of George Lucas, Steven Spielberg and others.

Simply attributing the success of the Bond films to their qualities of visual spectacle and 'pure cinema', however, does not explain why they have sustained their popularity over such a long period. Other popular films which foreground style and spectacle over narrative, such as the Superman and Indiana Jones series, have rarely been sustained beyond three or four instalments. The Bond films, however, have been consistently successful since the 1960s, winning the approval of several generations of audiences. Many of the cinema-goers who flocked to see *GoldenEye* and *Tomorrow Never Dies* in the late 1990s would not even have been born when *Dr No* and *From Russia With Love* were released in the early 1960s. That the Bond films should have sustained their popularity in this way suggests they have successfully negotiated changes in film culture over the period during which the series has been active. The impact of the first Bond movies, especially in Britain, was due largely to the way in which they offered a particular style and pattern of entertainment that was completely unlike anything else in popular cinema at the time, but the same can hardly be true of the more recent films which are part of a film culture in which the high-tech action thriller, which the Bond series itself in large measure spawned, is one of the most prolific genres.

The pivotal historical period of the Bond series was the 1960s. This was the period when the distinctive formula and style of the films were forged, and when the phenomenon of 'Bondmania' was at its height. The Bond films embodied certain aspects of the 'cultural revolution': the new vitality of British popular culture, the prominence of science and technology, and the increasing permissiveness in sexual attitudes and behaviour. As *Screen International* observed upon the thirty-fifth anniversary of the series: '*Dr No* instantly tapped the 60s' feel-good *zeitgeist*, parlaying a $1m. budget into a worldwide gross of $60m. and launching the most successful franchise in box-office history.'[4] This quotation illustrates, albeit probably unintentionally, one of the contradictions of the Bond series. On the one hand the success of the early films is attributed to the way in which they reflected the mood of the 1960s, whereas on the other hand the films have continued to be successful long beyond that particular historical moment. If the 1960s Bond films struck a chord because they seemed so modern and new, in subsequent decades the films have become institutionalised, a biennial ritual in which familiarity breeds the contempt of critics but the loyalty of audiences. For Bennett and Woollacott, writing in the mid-1980s, Bond 'is now, more than anything else, a trademark which, having established a certain degree of brand loyalty among certain sections of the cinema-going public, remains a viable investment in the film industry'.[5]

As genre films, the Bond movies have to find the right balance between repetition and variation, between continuity and change, so that they can simultaneously provide the sort of entertainment pattern which audiences expect while at the same time providing new thrills, new set pieces, new variations on old situations. On the one hand the narrative formula of the Bond series remains constant. Audiences have come to expect the familiar situations such as Bond's briefing by M, his visit to Q's workshop to collect his equipment, or alternatively Q equipping him in the field, the seduction of the girl, and the scene where the villain reveals his grand design to Bond before leaving him in a bizarre and elaborately improbable death-scenario, from which he escapes, and so on. It is surely no coincidence that those films which have deviated furthest from the usual narrative conventions, such as *On*

Her Majesty's Secret Service (unhappy ending) and *Licence To Kill* (non-secret service storyline), have been the least successful. But the Bond formula also extends beyond narrative conventions. Ingredients such as the opening gun barrel motif, the visually inventive title sequences and the 'James Bond Theme' have become institutionalised to such an extent that, without them, a Bond film would not feel like a Bond film at all.

On the other hand, however, the Bond series is in a process of constant renewal. The films have remained at the forefront of popular cinema because the producers have followed a strategy of continually modernising the formula. Thus the conflicts must be updated, the technology must remain on the cutting edge of what is scientifically feasible, and the jokes must be suitably topical to strike a chord with audiences. In this way the Bond films have responded to changes in the film industry, film culture, and society at large, keeping apace of changing tastes and popular attitudes. Their conspiracy plots have reflected changes in the international political situation, from Cold War to détente and back again, before relocating themselves in the 'new world' of the 1990s, while the slight modifications made in some of the later films of the relationship between Bond and the girl may be seen as a response (albeit a fairly limited one) to the greater prominence and confidence of women in society since the 1960s. The periodic changes of star, further-more, enable Bond to remain a contemporary hero whose age remains roughly the same even as the world around him changes.

The character of Bond remains the most constant element of the films. It is to the eternal credit of the film-makers that they have resisted the attempts of American studio executives to cast a big Hollywood star as James Bond and have instead remained loyal to a group of actors who, if not all British themselves (they include an Australian and an Irishman), have nevertheless been capable of playing Bond as British. The Britishness of Bond has been central to the ideology of national identity which the films project; it also serves as a means of dif-ferentiating Bond from the All-American action heroes incarnated by the likes of Mel Gibson, Bruce Willis and Sylvester Stallone.

In the view of film critic and Bond fan Giles Whittell, the Bond films have thrived for so long 'as realisations of wild adolescent fantasies about sex, gadgetry, invincibility and what it means to be British'.[6] According to this line of argument, the Bond films work in much the same way as the original Ian Fleming books, creating a fantasy world of beautiful women, easy sex and consumer affluence, and, moreover, one in which the decline of British power never took place. The sexist and patriotic values of the Bond films, therefore, rather than being criticised for their lack of political correctness, should be seen as the essential ingredients which make the Bond films so distinctive. Certainly the foregrounding of patriotic motifs – so brilliantly exemplified in the Union Jack parachute jump of *The Spy Who Loved Me* – has played an important role in the Bond series, though, as the analysis of individual films has shown, the patriotic code has not been asserted with equal stridency in all the films, some of which do allude to Britain's decline.

One recent commentator, however, has offered a reading of the films which detaches Bond completely from his British roots. In his book *American Dreamtime*, Lee Drummond reacts against those critics who have seen Bond as an essentially British ideological construct and claims him instead for American popular culture. 'The *story of Bond*, his *geste* or *saga*, has become fully incorporated into the larger, ongoing *story of America*, the Dreamtime chronicle of that rich, gimmicky and bizarre land that is less a place than a state of mind,' Drummond writes. The essence of his argument is that the Bond films were the first truly international media phenomenon of the modern age:

> If there were any question about assigning the story of Bond to an American Dreamtime, it would lie in the *universality* of Bond's appeal, and not in a parochial Britishness that ... others have insisted on ascribing to him. For Bond's career has paralleled, and impelled, the process of media saturation of the planet made possible by postwar technology and the booming sixties. When movie theatres went up and began showing Western films to the burgeoning urban populations of Manila, Jakarta, Lima, Rio de Janeiro, Mexico City, and points north, east, south, and west, James Bond became a star attraction, perhaps the very first truly global media sensation. Enormous differences in language, social background, and cultural values melted away in the cerebral furnace of the theatre showing a Bond movie, reduced in many instances to the lowest common denominator: Bond was the 'kiss, kiss, bang, bang' loved by Third World audiences and immortalized in Pauline Kael's book title. Luke Skywalker, Indiana Jones, E.T., Sue Ellen and J. R. Ewing, Rocky and Rambo – these and other international media sensations would follow Bond into those dingy Third World theatres, some with their wooden benches and dirty floors, and

into the sleepy towns with their public television sets. But it was
Bond who showed the way, and it is Bond who remains at or near
the pinnacle of world-wide popularity.[7]

Drummond's book, as this extract illustrates, is an impressionistic
discussion of the role of popular movies in American culture. While it
throws up occasional points of interest, it is, nevertheless, methodo-
logically flawed and intellectually shallow. Drummond marginalises the
motifs of Britishness which are drawn so explicitly in the films; nor
does he locate them in relation to the British generic and cultural
contexts from which the character of James Bond originally came. His
disavowal of the Britishness of the Bond films perhaps has something
to do with the fact that of all the popular cultural icons which he cites,
Bond is the only one which does not originate in America itself. The
twentieth century, after all, has been one dominated by America, not
only politically but also in the spread of mass culture. If the Britishness
of the Bond films were to be emphasised, it would prove an exception
to the rule of American cultural imperialism, the Coca-Colonisation of
global culture. For the American critic, it seems, James Bond is just too
successful to be considered as anything other than a product of American popular culture.

What the Bond films present is an image of Britishness carefully
packaged for the international market. Bond is a modern, virile, classless
character who combines the suave sophistication of the traditional
British gentleman-hero with the toughness and sexual magnetism of
the Hollywood leading man. He is also very much the Englishman
abroad, a professional tourist whose job (saving the world from diabolical
masterminds) takes him to exotic foreign locations which are presented
with all the glossy sophistication of an upmarket travel brochure. While
foregrounding the Britishness of the central character, therefore, the
globe-trotting travelogue narratives bring an international and cosmo-
politan dimension to the films. This is one of the major differences
between the Bond films and, say, the *Die Hard* or *Lethal Weapon* type of
films which are usually set in one city. The only other screen hero
whose adventures take him around the world is Indiana Jones, whose
films are set, of course, in a comic-book past of Nazi villains and
sword-wielding warriors rather than in the modern technological fantasy
world of the Bond movies.

The internationalism of the Bond movies is also evident in the nature of their conspiracy plots. A crucial difference between the films and the novels is that in the films the conspiracy is rarely directed against England alone. In some films America is the main target (*Goldfinger, Diamonds Are Forever, Live and Let Die, A View To A Kill*), while in others the entire world is threatened with destruction (*You Only Live Twice, The Spy Who Loved Me, Moonraker*). In this respect Bond is an international hero who just happens to be British. The most explicit statement of Bond's role as an international Mr Fix-It comes, ironically, from one of the films made outside the official series. As Nigel Small-Fawcett (Rowan Atkinson) tells him in *Never Say Never Again*: 'M says that without you in the service he fears for the security of the civilised world.'

A fully cognitive explanation of the success of the Bond films must take into account all the reasons advanced hitherto. Indeed, it is the combination of all these elements – the production values, the visual spectacle, the pattern of repetition and variation, the Britishness *and* the internationalism – which accounts for the distinctive style of the Bond films. The Bond series has its own unique generic identity, as there is no other example of popular cinema which includes all these elements in precisely the same combination. While it may represent a form of film-making by numbers, as so many critics have alleged, this should not obscure the fact that the Bond formula has proved remarkably durable and consistently successful over a very substantial period of the cinema's history. Moreover, there is every indication that, for the foreseeable future at least, the James Bond films are likely to go on being what they have always been, a unique and very special kind of popular cinema.

Notes

For the endnotes, books are cited by the place of publication and the date of the edition used. Full details of all books referred to are given in the Bibliography. Where film reviews or newspaper articles are cited without a page reference, the source is the British Film Institute's microfiche collection, which does not usually include page numbers. Reviews from *Variety* are taken from *Variety's Film Reviews* and *Variety's Television Reviews*; reviews and articles from the *New York Times* are taken from *The New York Times Film Reviews* and *The New York Times Encyclopedia of Film*.

Introduction: Taking James Bond Seriously

1. Ian Fleming, 'How To Write A Thriller', *Books and Bookmen*, May 1963, p. 14.

2. Quoted in John Pearson, *The Life of Ian Fleming* (London, 1966), p. 206.

3. Many extravagant claims have been made about Fleming's war. A made-for-television film, *Spymaker: The Secret Life of Ian Fleming* (1992), had Fleming undertaking a secret mission in Lisbon, where he kills a German agent, and included an entirely fictional sequence in which Fleming takes part in a commando raid on German secret service headquarters in Norway which owes more to *Where Eagles Dare* than the reality of Fleming's wartime service. In an intriguingly inter-textual piece of casting, Fleming was played by Jason Connery. An even more bizarre fiction is offered by ex-actor John Ainsworth-Davis, writing as Christopher Creighton, in his book *Op. JB: The Last Great Secret of the Second World War* (London, 1996), in which he claims that during the dying days of the war in 1945 Fleming masterminded and led a secret mission into Germany to kidnap Hitler's deputy, Martin Bormann. The reality, according to intelligence experts Norman Polmar and Thomas B. Allen in their definitive *Spy Book: The Encyclopedia of Espionage* (London, 1997) was rather less dramatic: 'Most of Fleming's espionage work was cerebral and deskbound, though he occasionally carried a commando knife and a fountain pen that he said contained tear gas' (p. 212).

4. Jack Fishman, ''007 and Me, by Ian Fleming', in Sheldon Lane (ed.), *For Bond Lovers Only* (London, 1965), pp. 10, 15.

5. Quoted in Andrew Lycett, *Ian Fleming* (London, 1995), pp. 289–90.

6. Paul Johnson, 'Sex, Snobbery and Sadism', *New Statesman*, 5 April 1958, p. 431.

7. Quoted in Laura Lilli, 'James Bond and Criticism', in Oreste Del Buono and Umberto Eco (eds), *The Bond Affair*, trans. R. A. Downie (London, 1966), p. 172.

8. Kingsley Amis, *The James Bond Dossier* (London, 1966), p. 9.

9. Ibid., p. 144.

10. Terry Eagleton, *Literary Theory: An Introduction* (Oxford, 1983), p. 96.

11. Umberto Eco, 'The Narrative Structure in Fleming', in Del Buono and Eco (eds), *The Bond Affair*, p. 58.

12. Anthony Burgess, 'The James Bond Novels: An Introduction', for the Hodder and Stoughton 1987 edition of the novels (unpaginated in the Coronet paperback editions of the same).

13. *Daily Worker*, 6 October 1962.

14. Quoted in the *Evening Standard*, 18 May 1965. The quotation is from an article entitled 'The James Bond Case' in the Vatican newspaper *Osservatore Romano*.

15. *Observer*, 7 October 1962.

16. *Saturday Review*, 1 June 1963 (Arthur Knight).

17. *Variety*, 17 October 1962 ('Rich').

18. *Monthly Film Bulletin*, 34/403, August 1967, p. 122.

19. Ronald Bergan, *The United Artists Story* (London, 1986), p. 305.

20. John Brosnan, *James Bond in the Cinema* (London, 1981), p. ix.

21. *Motion Picture Herald*, 5 January 1966, p. 433.

22. Robin Wood, *Hitchcock's Films* (London, 1977), p. 96. Noting that *Goldfinger* was awarded 'three stars' (out of a possible four) in *Sight and Sound*'s 'Guide to Current Films', which lists 'films of special interest to *Sight and Sound* readers', Wood was prompted to ask 'do *Sight and Sound* readers accept such blackening of their characters?'

23. Ibid., p. 38.

24. Roy Armes, *A Critical History of British Cinema* (London, 1978), pp. 254–7.

25. Sarah Street, *British National Cinema* (London, 1997), p. 87.

26. Burgess, 'The James Bond Novels', n.p.

27. Alan Barnes and Marcus Hearn, *Kiss Kiss Bang! Bang!: The Unofficial James Bond Film Companion* (London, 1997), p. 5.

28. 'Trails of the Unexpected', *Screen International*, 5 December 1997, p. 24.

29. Julian Petley, 'The Lost Continent', in Charles Barr (ed.), *All Our Yesterdays: 90 Years of British Cinema* (London, 1986), p. 98.

30. Julian Petley and Alan Burton, 'Introduction', *Journal of Popular British Cinema*, 1, 'Genre and British Cinema' (1998), pp. 2, 4.

31. Film critic David Robinson (*Financial Times*, 11 October 1963) was so impressed with the stylistic similarities between *From Russia With Love* and the Hammer horror films that he confused Bond director Terence Young with Hammer director Terence Fisher: 'Terence Fisher brings to the assignment a technical proficiency gained over a 30-year career in pictures ... and which was probably sharpened up on the run of horror films that he directed in the late 50s, *The Curse of Frankenstein*, *Dracula*, *The Hound of the Baskervilles*, and so on ... '

32. '007 Sights $2–Bil in Ducats Overall', declared *Variety* on 13 May 1987, p. 57. For those unfamiliar with *Variety*'s particular style of journalese, this meant that the Bond films, in their twenty-fifth year, were approaching total box-office earnings of $2 billion (i.e. $2,000,000,000). 'No other celluloid concept has come close to a similar giga-take: i.e. hitting 10-digit sales twice over', said trade journalist Roger Watkins. In 1997 it was estimated that the total box-office grosses of the first seventeen films (up to and

including 1995's *GoldenEye*) exceeded $2.5 billion (*Screen International*, 5 December 1997, p. 21).

33. Raymond Williams, *Keywords: A Vocabulary of Culture and Society* (London, 1983), p. 237.

34. Nick Roddick, '"If the United States spoke Spanish, we would have a film industry ..."', in Nick Roddick and Martyn Auty (eds), *British Cinema Now* (London, 1985), p. 4.

35. Tony Bennett and Janet Woollacott, *Bond and Beyond: The Political Career of a Popular Hero* (London, 1987), p. 1.

36. Ibid., pp. 5–6.

37. Ibid., p. 7.

38. Ibid., p. 24.

39. Ibid., p. 29.

40. Ibid., p. 38. The practice of showing a Bond film on Christmas Day – and, where possible, the television premiere of a particular Bond film – lasted for some fifteen years until it petered out in the 1990s, by which time the advent of home video, satellite broadcasting and cable television meant that all the films became more easily and frequently available to domestic audiences, and the television broadcast of a Bond film was no longer the 'event' that it had been in the 1970s and 1980s. Even so, television schedulers still tend to save Bond films for holiday periods. Along with *The Great Escape*, Bond has become a staple of Christmas, Easter and bank holiday television schedules.

1. Bond and Beyond: the James Bond Films and Genre

1. Barry Keith Grant, 'Introduction', in Grant (ed.), *Film Genre Reader II* (Austin, 1995), p. xv.

2. *Sight and Sound*, New Series, 6/1, January 1996, p. 40 (José Arroyo).

3. 'Four Just Men Rolled into One', *The Times*, 10 October 1963.

4. Raymond Durgnat, *A Mirror for England: British Movies from Austerity to Affluence* (London, 1970), p. 151.

5. Andrew Rissik, 'Indiana Jones and the 007 Myth', *Films and Filming*, 362, November 1984, p. 13.

6. Jim Harmon and Donald F. Glut, *The Great Movie Serials: Their Sound and Fury* (London, 1973), p. 368.

7. Larry Gross, 'Big and Loud', *Sight and Sound*, New Series, 5/8, August 1995, p. 8.

8. 'Bond of Gold', *Screen International*, 17 November 1995, p. 22.

9. Janet Woollacott, 'The James Bond Films: Conditions of Production', in James Curran and Vincent Porter (eds), *British Cinema History* (London, 1983), p. 210.

10. John A. Sutherland, *Fiction and the Fiction Industry* (London, 1978), p. 176.

11. Anthony Burgess, 'The James Bond Novels: An Introduction', n.p.

12. Kingsley Amis, *The James Bond Dossier* (London, 1966), p. 11.

13. Jerry Palmer, *Thrillers: Genesis and Structure of a Popular Genre* (London, 1978), p. 53.

14. Tom Ryall, *Alfred Hitchcock and the British Cinema* (London, 1986), p. 120.

15. Michael Denning, *Cover Stories: Narrative and Ideology in the British Spy Thriller* (London, 1987), pp. 1–2.

16. Ibid., p. 6.

17. Ibid., p. 34.

18. Colin Watson, *Snobbery With Violence: English Crime Stories and their Audience* (London, 1987), p. 234.

19. 'An Extremely Engaging Affair', *The Times Literary Supplement*, 17 April 1953, p. 249.

20. Richard Usborne, 'Introduction', to 'Sapper', *Bulldog Drummond* (London, 1983), p. vi. The novel itself was first published by Hodder and Stoughton in 1920.

21. Jack Fishman, '007 and Me, by Ian Fleming', in Sheldon Lane (ed.), *For Bond Lovers Only* (London, 1965), pp. 12–13.

22. John G. Cawelti, *Adventure, Mystery and Romance: Formula Stories as Art and Popular Culture* (Chicago, 1976), p. 31.

23. Amis, *The James Bond Dossier*, p. 87.

24. Ibid., p. 96.

25. The mythical imagery of the Bond novels is the subject of an interesting, if rather fanciful, monograph by Ann Boyd, *The Devil with James Bond!* (Westport, 1975). Approaching the novels from a Christian/moralist perspective, Boyd argues that Bond is 'one of the seven legendary champions of Christendom' (p. 25) and reads his adventures in terms of man's struggle against the seven deadly sins, particularly that of sloth, as represented by the villain. However, her reading is overdetermined by Fleming's own statements – including his series of essays on 'The Seven Deadly Sins' – and does not account sufficiently for contradictory evidence within the novels themselves. Given that the books would hardly seem to regard lust as a sin – indeed, there is much evidence to the contrary – then Boyd's attempt to overlay a Christian dimension on to them is problematic.

26. Andrew Lycett, *Ian Fleming* (London, 1995), p. 221.

27. Umberto Eco, 'The Narrative Structure in Fleming', in Oreste Del Buono and Umberto Eco (eds), *The Bond Affair* , trans. R. A. Downie (London, 1966), pp. 35–75.

28. Tony Bennett, 'James Bond as Popular Hero', *Politics, Ideology and Popular Culture 2* (Milton Keynes, 1982), p. 13.

29. David Cannadine, 'James Bond and the Decline of England', *Encounter*, 53/3, November 1979, p. 46.

30. Ibid., p. 55.

31. Arthur Marwick, *British Society Since 1945* (London, 1996), p. 110.

32. Christopher Booker, *The Neophiliacs: A Study in the Revolution in English Life in the Fifties and Sixties* (London, 1969), pp. 42–3.

33. Ian Fleming, 'How To Write A Thriller', *Books and Bookmen*, May 1963, p. 14.

34. Denning, *Cover Stories*, pp. 109–10.

35. Quoted in John Pearson, *The Life of Ian Fleming* (London, 1966), p. 304.

36. Andrew Bear, 'Intellectuals and 007: High Comedy and Total Stimulation', *Dissent*, Winter 1966, p. 24.

37. Bernard Bergonzi, 'The Case of Mr Fleming', *Twentieth Century*, March 1958, pp. 220–8.

38. Tony Bennett and Janet Woollacott, *Bond and Beyond: The Political Career of a Popular Hero* (London, 1987), p. 99.

39. Amis, *The James Bond Dossier*, p. 90.

40. Lycett, *Ian Fleming*, p. 264.

41. Several versions of the television *Casino Royale* have been released on home video. In the United Kingdom, it was issued by Retro Video in 1995 and by Visual Corporation Ltd in 1996. Both feature the same telerecording of the broadcast, in which the last minute (approximately) is missing. The most complete version of *Casino Royale* currently available is the 'Collector's Edition' released in the United States by Spy Guise and Cara Entertainment. This restores the ending, missing from other versions, in which the apparently dead Le Chiffre suddenly springs up again and threatens Vesper with a

razor blade held against her breasts before Bond shoots him dead; it also contains the original end credits. Although a story persists that during the live broadcast of *Casino Royale* Peter Lorre was seen getting to his feet and walking off to his dressing room after his 'death', this is not to be seen on any of the versions currently available.

42. Steven Jay Rubin, *The James Bond Films: A Behind the Scenes History* (London, 1981), p. 2; Alan Barnes and Marcus Hearn, *Kiss Kiss Bang! Bang!: The Unofficial James Bond Film Companion* (London, 1997), p. 3.

43. Peter Haining, *James Bond: A Celebration* (London, 1987), p. 88.

44. *Daily Variety*, 26 October 1954 ('Helm').

45. Quoted in Lycett, *Ian Fleming*, p. 250.

46. Ibid., p. 337. In his autobiography Cubby Broccoli quotes the same 'Editorial Notes', which Fleming apparently gave him while preparing the first Bond film. Albert R. Broccoli, with Donald Zec, *When the Snow Melts: The Autobiography of Cubby Broccoli* (London, 1998), pp. 159–60.

47. *Kinematograph Weekly*, 1 October 1959, p. 21.

48. Richard Schenkman, 'The Terence Young Interview', *Bondage*, 10, 1981, p. 3.

49. The eight Drummond films made by Paramount were: *Bulldog Drummond Escapes* (1937), starring Ray Milland, and *Bulldog Drummond Comes Back* (1937), *Bulldog Drummond's Revenge* (1937), *Bulldog Drummond's Peril* (1938), *Bulldog Drummond in Africa* (1938), *Arrest Bulldog Drummond* (1939), *Bulldog Drummond's Bride* (1939) and *Bulldog Drummond's Secret Police* (1939), all with John Howard.

50. The eight Saint films made by RKO were: *The Saint in New York* (1938), starring Louis Hayward, *The Saint Strikes Back* (1939), *The Saint in London* (1939), *The Saint's Double Trouble* (1940), *The Saint Takes Over* (1940) and *The Saint in Palm Springs* (1941), all starring George Sanders, *The Saint's Vacation* (1941) and *The Saint Meets the Tiger* (1941), both with Hugh Sinclair. Hayward also starred in *The Saint's Girl Friday* (1954), made in Britain by Hammer.

51. *Monthly Film Bulletin*, 15/1, April 1948, p. 46.

52. Kristin Thompson and David Bordwell, *Film History: An Introduction* (New York, 1994), p. 394.

53. James Naremore (ed.), *North by Northwest; Alfred Hitchcock, director* (New Brunswick, 1993), p. 6.

54. It has often been reported that Cary Grant was offered the Bond role. In his autobiography Broccoli says: 'I talked to Cary Grant, who liked the project. He had the style, the sophistication and, in fact, had been born in Britain. He also happened to be a Bond aficionado. But he said no. As a very important actor and a world-class star, he didn't feel he could lock himself into the Bond character. Anyway I felt strongly that we had to have an unknown actor, not a star'. *When the Snow Melts*, p. 164.

55. See, for example, John Brosnan, *James Bond in the Cinema* (London, 1981), pp. 1–9, and Alexander Walker, *Hollywood, England: The British Film Industry in the Sixties* (London, 1986), pp. 178–85. Broccoli's own account is given in *When the Snow Melts*, pp. 146–53.

56. Pat McGilligan (ed.), *Backstory: Interviews with Screenwriters of Hollywood's Golden Age* (Berkeley, 1986), p. 284.

57. Quoted in Walker, *Hollywood, England*, p. 185.

58. *Kinematograph Weekly*, 20 July 1961, p. 17.

59. *Motion Picture Herald*, 3 April 1963, p. 785.

60. 'The Gilt-Edged Bond', *Business Observer*, 16 January 1972.

61. Bennett and Woollacott, *Bond and Beyond*, pp. 26–7.

62. Quoted in Tony Bennett et al., *The Making of 'The Spy Who Loved Me'* (Milton Keynes, 1977), p. 23.

63. McGilligan (ed.), *Backstory*, p. 287.

64. Penelope Houston, '007', *Sight and Sound*, 34/1, Winter 1964–65, p. 15.

65. McGilligan (ed.), *Backstory*, p. 286.

66. Houston, '007', pp. 15–16.

67. Schenkman, 'The Terence Young Interview', p. 3.

68. Ibid., p. 4.

69. François Truffaut, with Helen G. Scott, *Hitchcock* (London, 1986), pp. 130–1.

70. Richard Maibaum, 'James Bond's 39 Bumps', *New York Times*, 13 December 1964.

71. 'Broccoli goes one bigger and better', *Screen International*, 23 June 1979, p. 17.

72. 'James Bond: 25 Years', *Variety*, 13 May 1987, p. 84.

73. Quoted in Walker, *Hollywood, England*, p. 195.

74. Quoted in Bennett et al., *The Making of 'The Spy Who Loved Me'*, p. 20.

75. Charles Barr, *Ealing Studios* (London, 1993), p. 39. Barr uncovers a quite remarkable statistic: some 60 per cent of all the films made at Ealing during Michael Balcon's reign as head of production, from 1938 to 1958, were directed by one of six men (Charles Crichton, Basil Dearden, Charles Frend, Robert Hamer, Alexander Mackendrick and Harry Watt).

76. Tony Bennett, 'Text and Social Process: the Case of James Bond', *Screen Education*, 41, Winter/Spring 1982, p. 11.

2. Snobbery With Violence: *Dr No, From Russia With Love, Goldfinger*

1. Quoted in Roy Armes, *A Critical History of British Cinema* (London, 1978), p. 231.

2. Linda Wood (ed.), *British Film Industry: BFI Information Guide No. 1* (London, 1980), p. A-1.

3. Robert Murphy, *Sixties British Cinema* (London, 1992), p. 164.

4. Quoted in ibid., p. 28.

5. 'The Gilt-Edged Bond', *Business Observer*, 16 January 1972.

6. John Francis Lane, 'Young Romantic', *Films and Filming*, 13/5, February 1967, p. 58.

7. Arthur Marwick, '*Room at the Top, Saturday Night and Sunday Morning*, and the "Cultural Revolution" in Britain', *Journal of Contemporary History*, 19/1, January 1984, p. 138; Jeffrey Richards, *Films and British National Identity: From Dickens to Dad's Army* (Manchester, 1997), p. 163.

8. Sarah Street, *British National Cinema* (London, 1997), p. 87.

9. Lane, 'Young Romantic', p. 58.

10. The annual assessments of box-office winners offered by *Kinematograph Weekly*, the British fan magazine *Picturegoer* and the American trade paper *Motion Picture Herald* are correlated and analysed in Janet Thumim, 'The "Popular", Cash and Culture in the postwar British Cinema Industry', *Screen*, 32/3, Autumn 1991, pp. 245–71.

11. 'Three British Films Head the General Releases', *Kinematograph Weekly*, 13 December 1962, p. 5.

12. Dalton was speaking on the television programme *30 Years of James Bond*, broadcast on the ITV network on 30 September 1992.

13. 'British Films Again Ahead on General Release', *Kinematograph Weekly*, 19 December 1963, p. 5.

14. Lane, 'Young Romantic', p. 58.

15. Andrew Lycett, *Ian Fleming* (London, 1995), p. 297.

16. Richard Schenkman, 'The Terence Young Interview', *Bondage*, 10, 1981, p. 7.

17. *Kinematograph Weekly*, 27 July 1961, pp. 13f.

18. Pat McGilligan (ed.), *Backstory: Interviews with Screenwriters of Hollywood's Golden Age* (Berkeley, 1986), p. 284. Aubrey Mather was in fact a British character actor.

19. Schenkman, 'The Terence Young Interview', p. 7.

20. BFI S6500: *Dr No. From the Novel by Ian Fleming*. Fourth Draft Screenplay, by Richard Maibaum and Wolf Mankowitz, 12 December 1961. This script contains some features which did not, fortunately, find their way into the finished film. For example, after assigning Bond to his mission, the script has M wishing him luck and shaking hands – a fundamental misunderstanding of the relationship between Bond and his boss. Honey has the tedious habit of referring to animals by their full Latin names. The script contains none of the famous Bond one-liners. Lines such as Connery's droll 'I think they were on their way to a funeral' after the hearse pursuing him has plunged over a cliff and exploded into flames were apparently devised on the set by Young and Connery himself.

21. Tony Bennett and Janet Woollacott, *Bond and Beyond: The Political Career of a Popular Hero* (London, 1987), p. 33.

22. Raymond Durgnat, *A Mirror for England: British Movies from Austerity to Affluence* (London, 1970), p. 151.

23. Andrew Rissik, *The James Bond Man: The Films of Sean Connery* (London, 1983), p. 50.

24. Schenkman, 'The Terence Young Interview', p. 4.

25. Ibid., p. 9.

26. Laura Mulvey, 'Visual Pleasure and Narrative Cinema', *Screen*, 16/3, Autumn 1975, pp. 6–18.

27. All the female voices in *Dr No*, except Miss Moneypenny (Lois Maxwell) and Miss Taro (Zena Marshall), were dubbed by actress Nikki Van Der Zyl, who also dubbed Shirley Eaton in *Goldfinger* and Claudine Auger in *Thunderball*. Daniela Bianchi in *From Russia With Love* was dubbed by British actress Barbara Jefford.

28. *Sunday Times*, 7 October 1962.

29. *Monthly Film Bulletin*, 29/345, October 1962, p. 136.

30. *Spectator*, 12 October 1962.

31. Derek Hill, 'The Infallible *Dr No*', *Scene*, 4, October 1962, p. 19.

32. *The Times*, 5 October 1962.

33. Thomas Wiseman, 'Is Mr Bond your idea of a hero?', *Sunday Express*, 7 October 1962.

34. *Daily Worker*, 6 October 1962.

35. *Films and Filming*, 9/2, November 1962, p. 36.

36. John Trevelyan, *What the Censor Saw* (London, 1973), p. 90.

37. There is some anecdotal evidence of censorship of *Dr No*. Broccoli told authors Lee Pfeiffer and Philip Lisa that in the scene where Bond shoots Professor Dent, originally he 'gives Dent six shots. They made us cut out three shots.' Quoted in Lee Pfeiffer and Philip Lisa, *The Incredible World of 007* (London, 1992), p. 192. Bond actually shoots Dent twice in the film.

There was some comment at the time over another scene which was excised from the finished film, which some attributed to censorial intervention. According to Isabel Quigley (*Spectator*, 12 October): 'In the book we are told that Honey ... is staked out to be eaten by land-crabs, and this episode was mentioned in one or two notices of the film. Only in the version I saw it was never stated at all. True, she was chained in a dungeon with the water rising through a sluice, but we were not told she was going to be eaten. This was either deleted by the censor or furnished by the critics. I should like to know which.' The scene was evidently filmed, as production stills showing the crabs crawling over Ursula Andress do exist, and it was mentioned in reviews by Alexander Walker (*Evening Standard*, 4 October 1962) and Leonard Mosley (*Daily Express*, 5 October 1962). According to Mosley: 'The beautiful blonde has been shackled to the ground and a couple of Oriental villains are grinning lasciviously as poison spiders [*sic*] crawl over her limbs.' Editor Peter Hunt later said that, rather than having anything to do with the censors, the scene was removed because it looked too silly.

38. 'No, No, A Thousand Times No', *Time*, 19 October 1962.

39. Michael Davie (ed.), *The Diaries of Evelyn Waugh* (London, 1976), p. 789.

40. According to Josh Billings (*Kinematograph Weekly*, 25 October 1962, p. 4): 'Every night of the week there are long queues waiting to get into the London Pavilion to see *Dr No*, although it's on show in the suburbs at nearly half the price. The Ian Fleming thriller is marvellous escapist fare and obviously just the medicine the cash customers need. What a box-office tonic!'

41. J. Hoberman, 'When Dr No Met Dr Strangelove', *Sight and Sound*, New Series, 3/12, December 1993, p. 18.

42. *New York Times*, 30 May 1963, p. 20.

43. 'Hairy Marshmallow', *Time*, 31 May 1963.

44. *Motion Picture Herald*, 3 April 1963, p. 785.

45. 'James Bond's 25th Anniversary', *Hollywood Reporter*, 14 July 1987, p. S-26.

46. Albert R. Broccoli, with Donald Zec, *When the Snow Melts: The Autobiography of Cubby Broccoli* (London, 1998), p. 177. According to the *Hollywood Reporter* (25 March 1963, p. 3), *Dr No* 'will premiere in the US with a massive 450-theater engagement in the midwest and southwest starting May 8'. It was not so much the number of cinemas where the film was shown that Broccoli objected to as it was their location in the sticks.

47. McGilligan (ed.), *Backstory*, p. 284.

48. BFI S6501: *Ian Fleming's From Russia With Love*. Final Draft Screenplay by Richard Maibaum, 18 March 1963.

49. Albert R. Broccoli, 'Introducing James Bond', in Jay McInnerney et al., *Dressed To Kill: James Bond, the Suited Hero* (Paris, 1996), p. 9.

50. Richard Roud (*Guardian*, 11 October 1963) wondered whether there was political pressure behind the plot changes: 'Those who have read the book will wonder at my calling the divine Klebb *former* head of the Russian secret service; I was surprised, too. For some reason (Foreign Office? post-test-ban-euphoria? distribution in the uncommitted countries?) the straight fight between us and the Russians has been changed in the film to a battle between us and "Spectre", the international crime syndicate which preys on Communists and capitalists alike.'

51. Penelope Gilliat, 'Laughing it off with Bond', *Observer*, 13 October 1963.

52. *Kinematograph Weekly*, 24 October 1963, p. 11.

53. *New Statesman*, 11 October 1963.

54. Thomas Wiseman, 'Such jolly fun – this latest Bond 007 epic', *Sunday Express*, 13 October 1963.

55. Nina Hibbin, 'No, James Bond is not "fun" – he's just sick', *Daily Worker*, 12 October 1963.

56. *Esquire*, September 1964.

57. *Saturday Review*, 18 April 1964.

58. McGilligan (ed.), *Backstory*, p. 285.

59. Brian McFarlane (ed.), *An Autobiography of British Cinema* (London, 1997), p. 275.

60. John Brosnan, *James Bond in the Cinema* (London, 1981), p. 75.

61. In the screenplay, Bond's hands are also painted gold, as if to suggest his responsibility for Jill's death. BFI S6508: *Ian Fleming's Goldfinger*. Final Draft Screenplay by Richard Maibaum and Paul Dehn, 26 February 1964.

62. BFI microfiche for *Goldfinger*: undated press release.

63. Richard Maibaum, 'James Bond's 39 Bumps', *New York Times*, 13 December 1964.

64. G. B. Zorzoli, 'Technology in the World of James Bond', in Oreste Del Buono and Umberto Eco (eds), *The Bond Affair*, trans. R.A. Downie (London, 1966), p. 127.

65. Quoted in Laura Lilli, 'James Bond and Criticism', in Del Buono and Eco (eds), *The Bond Affair*, pp. 161–2.

66. Janet Thumim, *Celluloid Sisters: Women and Popular Cinema* (London, 1992), p. 204.

67. Graham Rye, *The James Bond Girls* (London, 1989), p. 11.

68. *The Daily Cinema*, 21 September 1964, p. 2.

69. Nina Hibbin, 'Bond's Latest Film Repeats the Dose', *Daily Worker*, 16 September 1964.

70. Penelope Houston, '007', *Sight and Sound*, 34/1, Winter 1964–65, p. 16.

3. Bondmania: *Thunderball, Casino Royale, You Only Live Twice, On Her Majesty's Secret Service*

1. John Brosnan, *James Bond in the Cinema* (London, 1981), p. 99.

2. 'James Bond's 25th Anniversary', *Hollywood Reporter*, 14 July 1987, p. S-26.

3. Nicholas Anez, 'James Bond', *Films in Review*, 18/9–10, September/October 1992, p. 316.

4. Lietta Tornabuoni, 'A Popular Phenomenon', in Oreste Del Buono and Umberto Eco (eds), *The Bond Affair*, trans. R. A. Downie (London, 1966), p. 19.

5. *Daily Telegraph*, 1 March 1965.

6. 'Bondomania', *Time*, 11 June 1965, p. 59.

7. Alexander Walker, *Hollywood, England: The British Film Industry in the Sixties* (London, 1986), p. 198.

8. *New York Times*, 26 January 1966.

9. 'Bondomania', p. 59.

10. Quoted in Arthur Marwick, *The Sixties: Cultural Revolution in Britain, France, Italy, and the United States, c.1958–1974* (Oxford, 1998), p. 476.

11. Tony Bennett and Janet Woollacott, *Bond and Beyond: The Political Career of a Popular Hero* (London, 1987), p. 32.

12. Tornabuoni, 'A Popular Phenomenon', p. 19.

13. Marwick, *The Sixties*, p. 456.

14. Bennett and Woollacott, *Bond and Beyond*, pp. 34–5.

15. In my discussion of various aspects of the 'cultural revolution', I am drawing on the work of my Open University colleague Professor Arthur Marwick, to whose exhaustive researches this particular section of the book is heavily indebted.

16. *Punch*, 30 September 1964.

17. Marwick, *The Sixties*, p. 18.

18. *Sunday People*, 26 June 1977.

19. Quoted in Bennett and Woollacott, *Bond and Beyond*, p. 231.

20. 'Whatever happened to the Bond girls?', *Telegraph Sunday Magazine*, 17 September 1978.

21. Marwick, *The Sixties*, p. 680.

22. Drew Moniot, 'James Bond and America in the Sixties: An Investigation of the

Formula Film in Popular Culture', *Journal of the University Film Association*, 28/3, Summer 1976, p. 32.

23. Ibid., p. 30.

24. The cinema trailer for *Our Man Flint* had this voice-over: 'I know – you're tired of those British super secret agents. Now, here's your chance to buy American. Our Man Flint is here. ... He's the clean shaven, red-blooded, super-American secret agent everybody turns to when the world is really in trouble.' The film itself is replete with sideswipes at the Bond movies, such as an Agent 0008 and the assertion that the criminal syndicate GALAXY is 'bigger than SPECTRE'.

25. *The Man From U.N.C.L.E.* (an acronym of United Network Command for Law and Enforcement) ran on the American NBC television network from 1964 to 1968. Executive producer Norman Felton was a friend of Ian Fleming, who had been involved at the inception of the show and suggested the name of the hero Napoleon Solo (played in the series by Robert Vaughn). Eight movies, stitched together from double episodes of the TV series, were released theatrically outside America by MGM: *To Trap A Spy* (1965), *The Spy With My Face* (1965), *One of Our Spies is Missing* (1966), *One Spy Too Many* (1966), *The Spy in the Green Hat* (1966), *The Helicopter Spies* (1967), *The Karate Killers* (1967) and *How To Steal the World* (1968).

26. Some indication of the glut of 'spaghetti' spy movies is provided by the number of them listed in the *Monthly Film Bulletin* between 1965 and 1968 (referred to here by their English titles). Agent 077, the 'Italian James Bond', had his own series with *Mission Bloody Mary*, *From the Orient With Fury* and *Killers Are Challenged*, though *DA 077: Espionage in Lisbon* seems to have been about a different character entirely; Agent oSS 17, the 'French James Bond', featured in *Mission for a Killer* and *Terror in Tokyo*; two other secret agents, *Coplan – Agent 005* and *Secret Agent FX 18*, would somehow seem to have merged into one with *Coplan FX 18: The Exterminators*; the Italian heroes of *Agent OS 14: Operation Poker* and *Agent 3.S.3: Passport to Hell* seem only to have had one outing each, as did the West German *Agent 505*. However, these titles represent only those films that were released in Britain, and would therefore be the tip of an iceberg of films which never travelled beyond their own shores. Several Italian films used a variation on the 'Mr Kiss Kiss Bang Bang' tag attached to Bond, including *Kiss Kiss, Kill Kill* and *Kiss the Girls and Make Them Die*. Not all European spy films were necessarily derivative of Bond: *That Man in Rio* (1964), starring Jean-Paul Belmondo, and Claude Chabrol's *An Orchid for the Tiger* (1965) were quite favourably reviewed. Tornabuoni mentions a film called *002 Secret Agents and the Goldfinger Mission*, though I have been unable to verify the existence of this particular title.

27. Quoted in Tornabuoni, 'A Popular Phenomenon', p. 23.

28. I am using the word 'epic' in its proper sense, from the Latin *epos*, as referring to a type of narrative (such as epic poetry) which celebrates and eulogises the endeavours of a heroic character. The film version of *You Only Live Twice* is an epic in the sense in which the term is now more usually understood, particularly in respect of films, as a 'big' picture, with high production values, an expensive budget and a large canvas on which the story unfolds.

29. *Kinematograph Weekly*, 5 December 1963, p. 5.

30. Steven Jay Rubin, *The James Bond Films: A Behind the Scenes History* (London, 1981), p. 55.

31. BFI microfiche on *Thunderball*: 'Advance Production Story'.

32. Richard Schenkman, 'The Terence Young Interview', *Bondage*, 10, 1981, p. 6.

33. Lee Pfeiffer and Philip Lisa, *The Incredible World of 007* (London, 1992), p. 44; Alan Barnes and Marcus Hearn, *Kiss Kiss Bang! Bang!: The Unofficial James Bond Film Companion* (London, 1997), p. 47.

34. *The Times*, 29 December 1965.

35. *Daily Worker*, 1 January 1966.

36. *New York Times*, 26 December 1965, S2, p. 1; 22 December 1965, p. 23.

37. *Kinematograph Weekly*, 5 August 1965, p. 14.

38. Robert Murphy, *Sixties British Cinema* (London, 1992), p. 246.

39. Clive Hirschhorn, *The Columbia Story* (London, 1989), p. 266.

40. *Variety*, 19 April 1967 ('Rich').

41. '007's Oriental Eyefuls', *Playboy*, June 1967, p. 87.

42. This particular line features in the trailer for *Thunderball* – Connery says, 'The things I do for England!' as Fiona Volpe removes his shirt – but the scene was dropped from the finished film.

43. *New York Times*, 14 June 1967, p. 40.

44. Quoted in Herb A. Lightman, 'The "Cinemagic" of 007', *American Cinematographer*, 51/3, March 1970, pp. 204–5.

45. Lazenby did, however, make a cameo appearance in the 1983 television movie *The Return of the Man from U.N.C.L.E.*, as a character known as 'JB' whose rocket-firing Aston Martin helps Napoleon Solo out of a tight spot.

46. Pat McGilligan (ed.), *Backstory: Interviews with Screenwriters of Hollywood's Golden Age* (Berkeley, 1986), pp. 286–7.

47. *Village Voice*, 24 December 1969.

48. 'Richard Maibaum: 007's Puppetmaster', *Starlog*, 68, March 1983, p. 27.

49. Alexander Walker, *National Heroes: British Cinema in the Seventies and Eighties* (London, 1985), p. 56.

50. Ibid., p. 57.

51. Derek Malcolm, 'Off-the-peg Bond', *Guardian*, 16 December 1969.

52. *Films and Filming*, 16/4, February 1970, p. 38.

53. *Today's Cinema*, 19 December 1969, p. 5.

54. *New Yorker*, 27 December 1969.

55. *Variety*, 16 December 1969 ('Rick').

56. *Hollywood Reporter*, 17 December 1969.

57. *New York Times*, 1 February 1970, S2, p. 19 (A. Marks).

58. In programme notes for a screening of *OHMSS* at the National Film Theatre on 22 February 1992, Andrew Pilkington of the James Bond 007 International Film Club wrote: 'To most informed Bond fans it is considered possibly the best film in the entire series. The film features consistently in the top three of the Bond Fan Club's "running" poll, often in the Number One slot.' This is an example of how the Bond fan culture distinguishes itself from the general audience, identifying qualities in the film that others have missed. But it is not only the die-hard Bond fans who now rate the film so highly. American critic Danny Peary, for example, while preferring Connery's Bond and finding that 'it's impossible to ever fully adjust to Lazenby', nevertheless adds, 'I think that it might still be the best Bond film, as many Bond cultists claim. At the very least, it ranks with *Goldfinger*, Connery's best film ... and *The Spy Who Loved Me*, Roger Moore's one top-flight Bond film.' See his *Cult Movies 3* (New York, 1988), pp. 172–6. Nicholas Anez is even more certain, describing *OHMSS* as 'a perfect movie and the crowning achievement of the series'. See his 'James Bond (Part 2)', *Films in Review*, 18/11–12, November/December 1992, pp. 383–8. However, this view is still by no means widespread. Even Robert Murphy, so often the champion of under-valued movies, finds *OHMSS* 'a very dull film despite its ascension to cult status' (*Sixties British Cinema*, p. 317).

4. Bond in Transition: *Diamonds Are Forever, Live and Let Die, The Man With the Golden Gun*

1. *Sunday People*, 8 July 1973 (Kenneth Bailey).

2. Alexander Walker, *National Heroes: British Cinema in the Seventies and Eighties* (London, 1985), p. 58.

3. 'Richard Maibaum: 007's Puppetmaster', *Starlog*, 68, March 1983, p. 63.

4. Quoted in Steven Jay Rubin, *The James Bond Films: A Behind the Scenes History* (London, 1981), p. 112.

5. *Observer*, 8 July 1973.

6. *Spectator*, 14 July 1973.

7. Tony Bennett and Janet Woollacott, *Bond and Beyond: The Political Career of a Popular Hero* (London, 1987), p. 37.

8. Christopher Booker, *The Seventies: Portrait of a Decade* (London, 1980), p. 32.

9. Walker, *National Heroes*, p. 15.

10. *The Times*, 6 July 1973.

11. *New York Times*, 18 December 1971.

12. That is not to say that debates about the violence of the Bond films did not still exist; rather, the participants in the debate were no longer the film critics. A correspondence in *The Times* in March 1972 was concerned with the subject of children at Bond films. One correspondent complained that, in taking children to see *Diamonds Are Forever*, parents were 'irresponsibly encouraging infants to enjoy unsuitable entertainment. ... Mrs Whitehouse does have the courage to speak out with conviction and consistently'. Another correspondent, however, believed that the film 'was pure slapstick which made it impossible to identify with either the hero or the victims, and contained less sadism and reality than a Tom and Jerry cartoon'.

13. *Observer*, 8 July 1973.

14. Bennett and Woollacott, *Bond and Beyond*, p. 40.

15. Felix Barker, 'Is James Bond running out of steam?', *Evening News*, 19 December 1974.

16. 'Richard Maibaum: 007's Puppetmaster', p. 27.

17. BFI S6502 *Diamonds Are Forever*, Final Draft Screenplay, by Tom Mankiewicz. The script is undated, but several yellow revision pages are marked 14 April 1971.

18. Walker, *National Heroes*, p. 57.

19. *Esquire*, June 1972.

20. Quoted in Andy Medhurst, 'Batman, Deviance and Camp', in Roberta E. Pearson and William Uricchio (eds), *The Many Lives of the Batman: Critical Approaches to a Superhero and his Media* (London, 1991), p. 155.

21. *Monthly Film Bulletin*, 39/457, February 1972, p. 30.

22. 'James Bond's 25th Anniversary', *Hollywood Reporter*, 14 July 1987, p. S-26.

23. Peter Schjeldahl, 'Bond Is Back – and "Diamonds" Got Him', *New York Times*, 28 December 1971.

24. *Village Voice*, 16 December 1971.

25. John Belton, *American Cinema/American Culture* (New York, 1994), p. 291.

26. 'Richard Maibaum: 007's Puppetmaster', p. 63.

27. *New Statesman*, 6 July 1973.

28. *Monthly Film Bulletin*, 40/475, August 1973, p. 172.

29. *Spectator*, 14 July 1973.

30. *The Times*, 6 July 1973.

31. Richard Schickel, 'Dirty Trick', *Time*, 9 July 1973.

32. *Sunday Times*, 8 July 1974.

33. Kenneth O. Morgan, *The People's Peace: British History 1945–1990* (Oxford, 1990), p. 363.

34. *Guardian*, 19 December 1974.

35. *Observer*, 22 December 1974.

36. Jay Cocks, 'Water Pistols', *Time*, 13 January 1975.

5. Keeping the British End Up: *The Spy Who Loved Me, Moonraker*

1. 'James Bond's 25th Anniversary', *Hollywood Reporter*, 14 July 1987, p. S-26.

2. *Screen International*, 5 December 1997, p. 21.

3. Alexander Walker, *National Heroes: British Cinema in the Seventies and Eighties* (London, 1985), pp. 135–6.

4. Linda Wood (ed.), *British Film Industry: BFI Information Guide No. 1* (London, 1980), p. A-2.

5. Walker, *National Heroes*, p. 276.

6. 'Cubby counts the cost of keeping 007 in the manner ...', *Screen International*, 26 August 1976, p. 11.

7. Ibid.

8. 'No more Bond films to be made in Britain?', *Screen International*, 26 March 1977, p. 6.

9. 'Britain "turning people out" says Bond producer', *Screen International*, 9 September 1978, p. 4

10. Anthony Burgess, 'The James Bond Novels: An Introduction', n.p.

11. 'Midas Touch', *Screen International*, 17 November 1995, p. 28.

12. 'Richard Maibaum: 007's Puppetmaster', *Starlog*, 68, March 1983, p. 63.

13. BFI S4498: *The Spy Who Loved Me*. Revised Final Shooting Script, 23 August 1976. Although there are no references to SPECTRE in this script, some traces of the SPECTRE formula remain, such as Sandor referring to Stromberg as 'Number One', the designation used for Blofeld in the SPECTRE films.

14. John Brosnan, *James Bond in the Cinema* (London, 1981), p. 256.

15. One Bond fan listed no fewer than forty-six specific plot similarities between *You Only Live Twice* and *The Spy Who Loved Me*: Saul Fischer, 'The Spy Who Lived Twice', *Bondage*, 7 (no date).

16. Tony Bennett et al., *The Making of 'The Spy Who Loved Me'* (Milton Keynes, 1977), pp. 29–30.

17. Quoted in Janet Woollacott, 'The James Bond Films: Conditions of Production', in James Curran and Vincent Porter (eds), *British Cinema History* (London, 1983), p. 221.

18. *Screen International*, 16 July 1977, p. 16.

19. *Monthly Film Bulletin*, 44/523, August 1977, p. 176.

20. Frank Rich, 'Why James Bond Is Still A Crowd Pleaser', *New York Times*, 21 August 1977, S2, p. 11.

21. For an informed discussion of the significance of *Jaws* and *Star Wars* for the film industry, see Thomas Schatz, 'The New Hollywood', in Jim Collins et al., *Film Theory Goes to the Movies* (London, 1993), pp. 8–36.

22. 'No more Bond films to be made in Britain?', *Screen International*, 26 March 1977, p. 6.

23. Albert R. Broccoli, with Donald Zec, *When the Snow Melts: The Autobiography of Cubby Broccoli* (London, 1998), p. 254.

24. BFI microfiche on *Moonraker*: typed notes entitled 'The Book', undated.

25. Eric Burgess, 'The Making of *Moonraker*', *New Scientist*, 21 June 1979, p. 984.

26. *Screen International*, 7 July 1979, p. 17.

27. *Monthly Film Bulletin*, 46/547, August 1979, p. 180.

28. Dilys Powell, 'Inhuman Bondage', *Punch*, 4 July 1979.

6. Cold Warrior Reborn: *For Your Eyes Only, Octopussy, Never Say Never Again, A View To A Kill*

1. Albert R. Broccoli, with Donald Zec, *When the Snow Melts: The Autobiography of Cubby Broccoli* (London, 1998), p. 254.

2. *Screen International*, 5 December 1997, p. 21.

3. In Fleming's novels, secret service headquarters is in a 'gloomy building overlooking Regent's Park' (*Casino Royale*, p. 23).

4. Sarah Street, *British National Cinema* (London, 1997), p. 87.

5. Margaret Thatcher, *The Downing Street Years* (London, 1993), p. 90.

6. 'Bond is back with a new spy master', *Screen International*, 3 January 1981, p. 13.

7. BFI S17894: *For Your Eyes Only*. Screen Story and Screenplay by Richard Maibaum and Michael G. Wilson, 12 August 1980.

8. 'Richard Maibaum: 007's Puppetmaster', *Starlog*, 68, March 1983, p. 63.

9. *Screen International*, 11 June 1981, p. 15.

10. *Variety*, 19 June 1981 ('Cart').

11. BFI S18120: *Octopussy*. Screenplay by Richard Maibaum and Michael G. Wilson, based on a Draft Screenplay by George MacDonald Fraser, 10 June 1982.

12. *Monthly Film Bulletin*, 50/594, July 1983, p. 192.

13. 'Independent way for Mr Fixit', *Screen International*, 20 November 1982, p. 13.

14. Ibid.

15. *Monthly Film Bulletin*, 50/599, December 1983, pp. 334–5.

16. *Variety*, 1 October 1983 ('Cart').

17. Nicholas Anez, 'James Bond (Part 3)', *Films in Review*, 19/1–2, January/February 1993, p. 34.

18. Tony Bennett and Janet Woollacott, *Bond and Beyond: The Political Career of a Popular Hero* (London, 1987), p. 287.

19. Ibid., p. 288.

20. Ibid., pp. 289–90.

21. *Films and Filming*, 370, July 1985, p. 46.

22. *Variety*, 21 May 1985 ('Jagr').

23. *Films and Filming*, 351, December 1983, p. 41 (Brian Baxter).

7. Continuity and Change: *The Living Daylights, Licence To Kill*

1. 'James Bond Returns', *Starburst*, 107, July 1987, p. 12.

2. *New York Times*, 14 July 1989, p. C-8 (Caryn James).

3. Quoted in Richard Schenkman, 'Timothy Dalton Revisited', *Bondage*, 16, Winter 1989, pp. 22–3.

4. *Monthly Film Bulletin*, 54/643, August 1987, p. 244.

5. Ibid.

6. Schenkman, 'Timothy Dalton Revisited', p. 22.

7. Raymond Benson, *The James Bond Bedside Companion* (London, 1988), p. 258.

8. Kingsley Amis, *The James Bond Dossier* (London, 1966), p. 46.

9. *Screen International*, 5 December 1997, p. 21.

10. *Screen International*, 4 July 1987, p. 38.

11. *Films and Filming*, 395, August 1987, p. 35 (Allan Hunter).

12. *New York Times*, 31 July 1987, p. C-3.

13. *Variety*, 1 July 1987 ('Pit').

14. There were mischievous reports in the British press that the title was changed because most Americans did not understand the meaning of the word 'revoked', though this rather distorted the truth which was that American audiences associated the title *Licence Revoked* with having their driving licence recalled. There were further problems over the title in so far as 'licence' is spelled 'license' in American English. The shooting script for the film held by the British Film Institute (S18050) is entitled *License to Kill*, but for the finished film the Queen's English was restored.

15. *Monthly Film Bulletin*, 56/666, July 1989, p. 208.

16. Bizarrely, in John Gardner's novelisation of the screenplay, which maintains a semblance of continuity with the literary Bond, this is the *second* occasion on which Bond has found Leiter in this state. This time around the shark had managed to chew off Leiter's false arm and leg, which Sanchez and his men had not noticed!

17. *Monthly Film Bulletin*, 56/666, July 1989, p. 208.

18. *Variety*, 14 June 1989 ('Coop').

19. *Hollywood Reporter*, 30 June 1989, p. 4f.

20. *Screen International*, 17 June 1989, p. 22.

21. Albert R. Broccoli, with Donald Zec, *When the Snow Melts: The Autobiography of Cubby Broccoli* (London, 1998), p. 294.

22. *Screen International*, 17 June 1989, p. 22.

23. Broccoli, *When the Snow Melts*, p. 295.

24. This story was broken in *Variety* on 8 August 1990: 'Bond Bombshell: 007 Goes on the Block', p. 1. It was repeated, and slightly modified, in the British press, for example the *Sunday Times* on 12 August: 'Hollywood mogul puts $200m price on James Bond's head', S1, p. 3.

8. For England: *GoldenEye, Tomorrow Never Dies*

1. *Screen International*, 5 December 1997, p. 21.

2. *Screen International*, 19 December 1997, p. 4.

3. 'Big Bang Theory', *Time Out*, 3 August 1994, p. 16.

4. 'The Avatar of Espionage', *Screen International*, 5 December 1997, p. 21.

5. *In Search of James Bond ... with Jonathan Ross*, ITV network, 9 December 1995.

6. 'Bond of Gold', *Screen International*, 17 November 1995, p. 22.

7. Tom Shone, 'The gilt-edged Bond', *Sunday Times*, S10, 19 November 1995, p. 67.

8. Philip French, 'Oh, put it away, James', *Observer Review*, 14 December 1997, p. 12.

9. *Financial Times*, 23 November 1995, p. 21.

10. Brigit Grant, 'Deadly but dull', *Sunday Express Classic Magazine*, 26 November 1995, p. 49.

11. Geoff Brown, 'Bond comes in from the cold', *The Times*, 23 November 1995.

12. Alexander Walker, 'Bond rescues action man', *Evening Standard*, 23 November 1995, p. 13.

13. *News of the World*, 14 December 1997.

14. Quoted in *GoldenEye Film Education Study Guide 3* (London, 1997), p. 3.

15. Ibid.

16. Ibid.

17. Eagle-eyed Bond fans may have spotted that the number plates of the cars are different, however. The Aston Martin DB5 in *Goldfinger* and *Thunderball* had been BMT 216A, whereas the car Brosnan drives in *GoldenEye* is BMT 214A. The fascinating story of the various different cars which have featured in the Bond films is told in Dave Worrall's book *The Most Famous Car in the World: The Complete History of the James Bond Aston Martin DB5* (Christchurch, 1991 and subsequent editions).

18. *New York Times*, 17 November 1995, p. C-17 (Janet Maslin).

19. Geoff Brown, 'Bond comes in from the cold', *The Times*, 23 November 1995.

20. *Screen International*, 17 November 1995.

21. *Variety*, 20 November 1995 (Todd McCarthy).

22. Some indication of the trials and tribulations is provided by Garth Pearce, *The Making of Tomorrow Never Dies* (London, 1997), though even so the book was endorsed by Eon Productions and was clearly intended, in some measure, to downplay the on-set frictions. This was also strongly evident in the television interviews given by Pierce Brosnan to promote *Tomorrow Never Dies*.

23. Alexander Walker, 'Unshaken and totally unstirred', *Evening News*, 11 December 1997, p. 27.

24. *Sight and Sound*, New Series, 8/2, February 1998, p. 53.

25. Richard Williams, 'Premium Bond', *Guardian*, 12 December 1997, p. 10.

26. Tom Shone, 'The oldest swinger in town', *Sunday Times*, S10, 14 December 1997, p. 5.

Postscript: A Licence To Thrill

1. David Gritten, '00–Dear', *Daily Telegraph Weekend Magazine*, 12 August 1995, p. 33.

2. Albert R. Broccoli, with Donald Zec, *When the Snow Melts: The Autobiography of Cubby Broccoli* (London, 1998), p. 308.

3. John Brosnan, *James Bond in the Cinema* (London, 1981), p. 11.

4. 'The Avatar of Espionage', *Screen International*, 5 December 1997, p. 21.

5. Tony Bennett and Janet Woollacott, *Bond and Beyond: The Political Career of a Popular Hero* (London, 1987), p. 294.

6. Giles Whittell, 'Forever shaken not stirred', *The Times*, 3 November 1995, p. 16.

7. Lee Drummond, *American Dreamtime: A Cultural Analysis of Popular Movies and their Implications for a Science of Humanity* (Lanham, 1996), pp. 128–9.

Filmography

The filmography lists all the James Bond 'films' (including the television *Casino Royale*) in chronological order. Note that the films *Casino Royale* and *Never Say Never Again* were produced outside the 'official' James Bond series. The filmography is compiled from the credits of the films themselves and the information provided by the *Monthly Film Bulletin*; credits vary according to different terminology and industry conventions.

Casino Royale

Columbia Broadcasting System. 1954.

Climax! television series. *Hosted by:* William Lundigan. *Director:* William H. Brown. *Producer:* Bretaigne Windust. *Written for television by:* Antony Ellis and Charles Bennett. *Associate producer:* Elliott Lewis. *Art direction:* Robert Tyler Lee and James De Val. *Running time:* 50 minutes.

Cast: Barry Nelson (James Bond), Linda Christian (Valerie Mathis), Peter Lorre (Le Chiffre), Michael Pate (Clarence Leiter), Eugene Borden (Chef de Partie), Jean Del Val (Croupier), Gene Roth (Basil), Kurt Katch (Zoltan).

Dr No

United Artists/Eon Productions. 1962.

Director: Terence Young. *Producers:* Harry Saltzman and Albert R. Broccoli. *Screenplay:* Richard Maibaum, Johanna Harwood and Berkeley Mather. *Production manager:* L. C. Rudkin. *Editor:* Peter Hunt. *Director of photography:* Ted Moore. Technicolor. *Production designer:* Ken Adam. *Art director:* Syd Cain. *Costume designer:* Tessa Welborn. *Stunt arranger:* Bob Simmons. *Special effects:* Frank George. *Main titles:* Maurice Binder. *Music:* Monty Norman. *Orchestrated by:* Burt Rhodes. *Conducted by:* Eric Rodgers. 'The James Bond Theme' *played by:* The John Barry Orchestra. *Certificate:* A. *Running time:* 111 mins.

Cast: Sean Connery (James Bond), Ursula Andress (Honey Ryder), Joseph Wiseman (Dr No), Jack Lord (Felix Leiter), Bernard Lee (M), Anthony Dawson (Professor Dent), Zena Marshall (Miss Taro), John Kitzmiller (Quarrel), Eunice Gayson (Sylvia Trench), Lois Maxwell (Miss Moneypenny), Peter Burton (Major Boothroyd), Yvonne Shima (Sister Lily), Michele Mok (Sister Rose), Marguerite Lewars (Girl photographer), Lester Prendergast (Puss-Feller), William Foster-Davis (Superintendent), Louis Blaazer (Pleydell-Smith), Tim Moxon (Strangways), Dolores Keator (Mary), Reggie Carter (Jones), Colonel Burton (General Potter).

From Russia With Love

United Artists/Eon Productions. 1963.

Director: Terence Young. *Producers:* Harry Saltzman and Albert R. Broccoli. *Screenplay:* Richard Maibaum. *Adaptation:* Johanna Harwood. *Production manager:* Bill Hill. *Editor:* Peter Hunt. *Director of photography:* Ted Moore. Technicolor. *Art director:* Syd Cain. *Costume designer:* Jocelyn Rickards. *Stunt arranger:* Peter Perkins. *Special effects:* John Stears. *Assisted by:* Frank George. *Main titles:* Robert Brownjohn. *Assisted by:* Trevor Bond. *Music:* John Barry. *Title song performed by:* Matt Monro. *Lyrics:* Lionel Bart. *Certificate:* A. *Running time:* 116 mins.

Cast: Sean Connery (James Bond), Daniela Bianchi (Tatiana Romanova), Pedro Armendariz (Kerim Bey), Lotte Lenya (Rosa Klebb), Robert Shaw (Grant), Bernard Lee (M), Eunice Gayson (Sylvia), Walter Gotell (Morzeny), Vladek Sheybal (Kronsteen), Lois Maxwell (Miss Moneypenny), Francis de Wolff (Vavra), George Pastell (Orient Express conductor), Nadja Regin (Kerim's girl), Alizia Gur (Vida), Martine Beswick (Zora), Leila (Belly dancer), Fred Haggerty (Krilencu), Peter Bayliss (Benz), Desmond Llewelyn (Boothroyd – Q),* Neville

---

* Llewelyn took over the role of the Armourer, Major Boothroyd, when Peter Burton who had played him in *Dr No* was unavailable for *From Russia With Love*. Llewelyn has appeared in every subsequent Bond film except *Live and Let Die*, and holds the record for most appearances in the series. He was first billed as 'Q' in *Goldfinger* and generally has been known by that designation ever since, though in *The Spy Who Loved Me* Anya Amasova does say to him 'Good morning, Major Boothroyd'.

Jason (Kerim's chauffer), Nushet Ataer (Mehmet), Peter Brayham (Rhodes), Jan Williams (Masseuse), Peter Madden (McAdams).*

Goldfinger

United Artists/Eon Productions. 1964.

Director: Guy Hamilton. *Producers:* Harry Saltzman and Albert R. Broccoli. *Screenplay:* Richard Maibaum and Paul Dehn. *Production manager:* L. C. Rudkin. *Editor:* Peter Hunt. *Director of photography:* Ted Moore. Technicolor. *Production designer:* Ken Adam. *Art director:* Peter Murton. *Wardrobe supervisor:* Elsa Fennell. *Action sequences:* Bob Simmons. *Special effects:* John Stears. *Assisted by:* Frank George. *Main titles:* Robert Brownjohn. *Music:* John Barry. *Title song performed by:* Shirley Bassey. *Lyrics:* Leslie Bricusse, Anthony Newley. *Certificate:* A. *Running time:* 109 mins.

Cast: Sean Connery (James Bond), Honor Blackman (Pussy Galore), Gert Frobe (Goldfinger), Shirley Eaton (Jill Masterson), Tania Mallet (Tilly Masterson), Harold Sakata (Oddjob), Bernard Lee (M), Cec Linder (Felix Leiter), Martin Benson (Solo), Richard Vernon (Colonel Smithers), Lois Maxwell (Miss Moneypenny), Bill Nagy (Midnight), Hal Galili (Strap), Lenny Rabin (Henchman), Austin Willis (Simmons) Michael Mellinger (Kisch), Peter Cranwell (Johnny), Burt Kwouk (Mr Ling), Desmond Llewelyn (Q), Mai Ling (Mai Lei), Alf Joint (Capungo), Nadja Regin (Bonita), Margaret Nolan (Dink), Raymond Young (Sierra), Varley Thomas (Swiss gatekeeper).

Thunderball

United Artists/Eon Productions. 1965.

Director: Terence Young. *Producer:* Kevin McClory. *Executive producers:* Harry Saltzman and Albert R. Broccoli. *Screenplay:* Richard Maibaum and John Hopkins. From an original screenplay by Jack Whittingham. Based on an original story by Kevin McClory, Jack Whittingham and Ian Fleming. *Production supervisor:* David Middlemas. *Supervising editor:* Peter Hunt. *Director of photography:* Ted Moore. Panavision. Technicolor. *Underwater photography:* Ricou Browning. *Production designer:* Ken Adam. *Art director:* Peter Murton. *Costume designer:* Anthony Mendleson. *Action sequences:* Bob Simmons. *Special effects:* John Stears. *Main titles:* Maurice

---

* Ernst Stavro Blofeld, who made his first screen appearance in *From Russia With Love*, was billed on the end credits as a mysterious '?'; it seems that he was in fact played by Anthony Dawson, while Eric Pohlmann provided his voice.

Binder. *Music:* John Barry. *Title song performed by:* Tom Jones. *Lyrics:* Don Black. *Certificate:* A. *Running time:* 132 mins.

Cast: Sean Connery (James Bond), Claudine Auger (Domino), Adolfo Celi (Largo), Luciana Paluzzi (Fiona Volpe), Rik Van Nutter (Felix Leiter), Guy Doleman (Lippe), Molly Peters (Patricia Fearing), Martine Beswick (Paula), Bernard Lee (M), Desmond Llewelyn (Q), Lois Maxwell (Miss Moneypenny), Roland Culver (Home Secretary),* Earl Cameron (Pinder), Paul Stassino (Palazzi), Rose Alba ('Widow'), Mitsuoko (French liaison agent), Philip Locke (Vargas), George Pravda (Kutze), Michael Brennan (Janni), Leonard Sachs (Group Captain Prichard), Edward Underdown (Air Vice Marshal), Reginald Beckwith (Kenniston), Harold Sanderson (Hydrofoil captain).**

Casino Royale

Columbia Pictures/Charles K. Feldman. 1967.

Directors: John Huston, Kenneth Hughes, Val Guest, Robert Parrish, Joseph McGrath. *Additional sequences:* Val Guest. *Producers:* Charles K. Feldman and Jerry Bresler. *Screenplay:* Wolf Mankowitz, John Law, Michael Sayers. *Associate producer:* John Dark. *Editor:* Bill Lenny. *Director of photography:* Jack Hildyard. Panavision. Technicolor. *Additional photography:* John Wilcox, Nicolas Roeg. *Second unit directors:* Richard Talmadge, Anthony Squire. *Production designer:* Michael Stringer. *Art directors:* John Howell, Ivor Beddoes, Lionel Couch. *Costume designer:* Julie Harris. *Special effects:* Cliff Richardson, Roy Whybrow. *Titles and montage effects:* Richard Williams. *Music:* Burt Bacharach. *Lyrics:* Hal David. *Main title theme played by:* Herb Alpert and the Tijuana Brass. 'The Look of Love' *performed by:* Dusty Springfield. *Certificate:* A. *Running time:* 130 mins.

Cast: Peter Sellers (Evelyn Tremble – 'James Bond 007'), Ursula Andress (Vesper Lynd – 'James Bond 007'), David Niven (Sir James Bond), Orson Welles (Le Chiffre), Joanna Pettet (Mata Bond), Daliah Lavi (The Detainer – 'James Bond 007'), Woody Allen (Jimmy Bond/Dr Noah), Deborah Kerr (Agent Mimi, *aka* Lady Fiona), William Holden (Ransome), Charles Boyer (Le Grand), John Huston (McTarry – M), Kurt Kasznar (Smernov), George Raft (Himself), Jean-Paul Belmondo (French Legionnaire), Terence Cooper (Agent Cooper – 'James Bond 007'), Barbara Bouchet (Moneypenny), Jacqueline Bisset (Miss Goodthighs), Angela Scoular (Buttercup), Gabriella Licudi (Eliza), Tracey Crisp

---

* Roland Culver is actually listed on the credits as 'Foreign Secretary' but is referred to as 'Home Secretary' in the film itself.

** Blofeld is again uncredited, though his voice is clearly that of Joseph Wiseman (not, on this occasion, Eric Pohlmann as suggested by some sources).

(Heather), Elaine Taylor (Peg), Alexandra Bastedo (Meg), Anna Quayle (Frau Hoffer), Ronnie Corbett (Polo), Bernard Cribbins (Taxi driver), Derek Nimmo (Hadley), Geoffrey Bayldon (Q), John Wells (Q's assistant), John Bluthal (Casino doorman & MI5 man), Tracy Reed (FANG Leader), Duncan MaCrea (Inspector Mathis), Richard Wattis (British Army officer), Vladek Sheybal (Le Chiffre's representative), Graham Stark (Cashier), Chic Murray (Chic), Jonathan Rowth (John), Percy Herbert (1st Piper), Penny Riley (Control girl), Jeanne Roland (Captain of the Guard).*

You Only Live Twice

United Artists/Eon Productions. 1967.

Director: Lewis Gilbert. *Producers:* Harry Saltzman and Albert R. Broccoli. *Screenplay:* Roald Dahl. *Additional story material:* Harry Jack Bloom. *Production supervisor:* David Middlemas. *Second unit director and supervising editor:* Peter Hunt. *Director of photography:* Freddie Young. Panavision. Technicolor. *Aerial photography:* John Jordan. *Underwater photography:* Lamar Boren. *Production designer:* Ken Adam. *Art director:* Harry Pottle. *Wardrobe supervisor:* Elsa Fennell. *Action sequences:* Bob Simmons. *Special effects:* John Stears. *Main titles:* Maurice Binder. *Music:* John Barry. *Title song performed by:* Nancy Sinatra. *Lyrics:* Leslie Bricusse. *Certificate:* A. *Running time:* 116 mins.

Cast: Sean Connery (James Bond), Donald Pleasence (Ernst Stavro Blofeld), Akiko Wakabayashi (Aki), Mie Hama (Kissy Suzuki), Tetsuro Tamba (Tiger Tanaka), Teru Shimada (Osato), Karin Dor (Helga Brandt), Bernard Lee (M), Lois Maxwell (Miss Moneypenny), Desmond Llewelyn (Q), Charles Gray (Henderson), Tsai Chin (Chinese girl – Hong Kong), Burt Kwouk (SPECTRE #3), Michael Chow (SPECTRE #4), Ronald Rich (Hans), Jeanne Roland (Bond's masseuse), David Tiguri (Bedroom assassin), Alexander Knox (American president), Robert Hutton (President's aide), John Stone (Submarine captain), Richard Marner (Russian officer), Anthony Ainley, Patrick Jordan (Military policemen), Norman Jones, Paul Carson (Astronauts: 1st American spacecraft), Laurence Herder, Richard Graydon (Astronauts: Russian spacecraft), Bill Mitchell, George Roubeck (Astronauts: 2nd American spacecraft).

On Her Majesty's Secret Service

United Artists/Eon Productions. 1969.

Director: Peter Hunt. *Producers:* Albert R. Broccoli and Harry Saltzman. *Screenplay:*

---

* Peter O'Toole made an uncredited appearance as a Scottish piper.

Richard Maibaum. *Additional dialogue:* Simon Raven. *Associate producer:* Stanley Sopel. *Production supervisor:* David Middlemas. *Editor and second unit director:* John Glen. *Director of photography:* Michael Reed. Panavision. Technicolor. *Aerial photography:* John Jordan. *Ski photography:* Willy Bogner, Alex Barbey. *Stock car sequence director:* Anthony Squire. *Production designer:* Syd Cain. *Art director:* Peter Lamont. *Costume designer:* Marjory Cornelius. *Stunt arranger:* George Leech. *Special effects:* John Stears. *Main titles:* Maurice Binder. *Music:* John Barry. *Lyrics:* Hal David. 'We Have All the Time in the World' *performed by:* Louis Armstrong. 'Do You Know How Christmas Trees Are Grown?' *performed by:* Nina. *Certificate:* A. *Running time:* 140 mins.

Cast: George Lazenby (James Bond),* Diana Rigg (Tracy), Telly Savalas (Ernst Stavro Blofeld), Gabriele Ferzetti (Draco), Ilse Steppat (Irma Bunt), George Baker (Sir Hilary Bray), Lois Maxwell (Miss Moneypenny), Bernard Lee (M), Bernard Horsfall (Campbell), Desmond Llewelyn (Q), Yuri Borienko (Grunther), Virginia North (Olympe), Geoffrey Cheshire (Toussaint), Irvin Allen (Che Che), Terry Mountain (Raphael), James Bree (Gumbold), John Gay (Hammond), Brian Worth (Manuel), Norman McGlen (Janitor), Dudley Jones (Hall porter), John Crewdson (Draco's helicopter pilot), Josef Vasa (Piz Gloria receptionist), Les Crawford (Felsen), George Cooper (Braun), Reg Harding (Blofeld's driver), Richard Graydon (Draco's driver), Bill Morgan (Klett), Bessie Love (American guest), Steve Plytas (Greek tycoon), Robert Rietty (Chef de Jeu), Elliott Sullivan (American guest). *The Girls:* Angela Scoular (Ruby), Catherina von Schell (Nancy), Julie Ege (Scandinavian), Mona Chong (Chinese), Sylvana Henriques (Jamaican), Dani Sheridan (American), Joanna Lumley (English), Zara (Indian), Anoushka Hempel (Australian), Ingrit Back (German), Helena Ronee (Israeli), Jenny Hanley (Irish).

Diamonds Are Forever

United Artists/Eon Productions. 1971.

Director: Guy Hamilton. *Producers:* Albert R. Broccoli and Harry Saltzman. *Screenplay:* Richard Maibaum and Tom Mankiewicz. *Associate producer:* Stanley Sopel. *Production managers:* Milton Feldman, Claude Hudson. *Editors:* John W. Holmes, Bert Bates. *Director of photography:* Ted Moore. Panavision. Technicolor. *Production designer:* Ken Adam. *Art directors:* Bill Kenney, Jack Maxsted. *Wardrobe supervisors:* Elsa Fennell, Ted Tetrick. *Stunt arrangers:* Bob Simmons, Paul Baxley. *Special effects:* Whitey McMahon, Leslie Hillman. *Main titles:* Maurice Binder. *Music:* John Barry. *Title song performed by:* Shirley Bassey. *Lyrics:* Don Black. *Certificate:* A. *Running time:* 120 mins.

---

* Lazenby was dubbed by George Baker during his impersonation of Sir Hilary Bray.

Cast: Sean Connery (James Bond), Jill St John (Tiffany Case), Charles Gray (Ernst Stavro Blofeld), Lana Wood (Plenty O'Toole), Jimmy Dean (Willard Whyte), Bruce Cabot (Bert Saxby), Bruce Glover (Mr Wint), Putter Smith (Mr Kidd), Norman Burton (Felix Leiter), Joseph Furst (Dr Metz), Bernard Lee (M), Desmond Llewelyn (Q), Lois Maxwell (Miss Moneypenny), Laurence Naismith (Sir Donald Munger), Leonard Barr (Shady Tree), Margaret Lacey (Mrs Whistler), Joe Robinson (Peter Franks), David de Keyser (Doctor), David Bauer (Morton Slumber), Donna Garratt (Bambi), Trina Parks (Thumper), Burt Metcalf (Maxwell), Ed Bishop (Klaus Hergersheimer), Henry Rowland (Dentist), Marc Lawrence, Michael Valente (Gangsters), Shane Rimmer (Tom), Constantin de Goguel (Aide to Metz), Clifford Earle (US Immigration officer), Max Latimer (Blofeld's double), Frank Olegario (Man in fez), Denise Perrier (Marie).

Live and Let Die

United Artists/Eon Productions. 1973.

Director: Guy Hamilton. *Producers:* Harry Saltzman and Albert R. Broccoli. *Screenplay:* Tom Mankiewicz. *Production supervisor:* Claude Hudson. *Editors:* Bert Bates, Raymond Poulton, John Shirley. *Director of photography:* Ted Moore. Eastman Colour. *Supervising art director:* Syd Cain. *Costume designer:* Julie Harris. *Choreography:* Geoffrey Holder. *Stunt co-ordinators:* Bob Simmons, Ross Kananga, Jerry Comeaux, Bill Bennet, Eddie Smith, Joie Chitwood. *Special effects:* Derek Meddings. *Main titles:* Maurice Binder. *Music:* George Martin. *Title song by:* Paul and Linda McCartney. *Performed by:* Paul McCartney and Wings. *Certificate:* A. *Running time:* 121 mins.

Cast: Roger Moore (James Bond), Yaphet Kotto (Kananga/Mr Big), Jane Seymour (Solitaire), Clifton James (Sheriff Pepper), Julius W. Harris (Tee Hee), Geoffrey Holder (Baron Samedi), Gloria Hendry (Rosie), Bernard Lee (M), Lois Maxwell (Miss Moneypenny), Tommy Lane (Adam), Earl Jolly Brown (Whisper), Roy Stewart (Quarrel Jr), Lon Satton (Strutter), Arnold Williams (Cab driver), Ruth Kempf (Mrs Bell), Joie Chitwood (Charlie), Madeline Smith (Italian girl), Michael Ebbin (Dambala), Kubi Chaza (Sales girl), B. J. Arnau (Singer).

The Man With the Golden Gun

United Artists/Eon Productions. 1974.

Director: Guy Hamilton. *Producers:* Albert R. Broccoli and Harry Saltzman. *Screenplay:* Richard Maibaum and Tom Mankiewicz. *Associate producer:* Charles

Orme. *Production supervisor:* Claude Hudson. *Editors:* John Shirley, Raymond Poulton. *Directors of photography:* Ted Moore, Oswald Morris. Eastman Colour. *Production designer:* Peter Murton. *Art directors:* John Graysmark, Peter Lamont. *Wardrobe supervisor:* Elsa Fennell. *Special effects:* John Stears. *Miniatures:* Derek Meddings. *Stunt co-ordinator:* W. J. Milligan Jr. *Main titles:* Maurice Binder. *Music:* John Barry. *Title song performed by:* Lulu. *Lyrics:* Don Black. *Certificate:* A. *Running time:* 125 mins.

Cast: Roger Moore (James Bond), Christopher Lee (Scaramanga), Britt Ekland (Mary Goodnight), Maud Adams (Andrea Anders), Hervé Villechaize (Nick Nack), Clifton James (J. W. Pepper), Richard Loo (Hai Fat), Soon Taik Oh (Hip), Bernard Lee (M), Lois Maxwell (Miss Moneypenny), Desmond Llewelyn (Q), James Cossins (Colthorpe), Marne Maitland (Lazar), Carmen Sautoy (Saida), Marc Lawrence (Hitman), Chan Yiu Lim (Chula), Gerald James (Frazier), Michael Osborne (Naval lieutenant), Michael Fleming (Communications officer).

The Spy Who Loved Me

United Artists/Eon Productions. 1977.

Director: Lewis Gilbert. *Producer:* Albert R. Broccoli. *Screenplay:* Christopher Wood and Richard Maibaum. *Associate producer:* William P. Cartlidge. *Production manager:* David Middlemas. *Special assistant to the producer:* Michael G. Wilson. *Second unit directors:* Ernest Day, John Glen. *Editor:* John Glen. *Director of photography:* Claude Renoir. Panavision. Eastman Colour. *Ski photography:* Willy Bogner. *Underwater photography:* Lamar Boren. *Production designer:* Ken Adam. *Art director:* Peter Lamont. *Wardrobe supervisor:* Rosemary Burrows. *Action sequences:* Bob Simmons. *Ski jump performed by:* Rick Sylvester. *Special visual effects:* Derek Meddings. *Main titles:* Maurice Binder. *Music:* Marvin Hamlisch. 'Nobody Does It Better' *performed by:* Carly Simon. *Lyrics:* Carole Bayer Saiger. *Certificate:* A. *Running time:* 125 mins.

Cast: Roger Moore (James Bond), Barbara Bach (Anya Amasova), Curt Jurgens (Stromberg), Richard Kiel (Jaws), Caroline Munro (Naomi), Walter Gotell (General Gogol), Geoffrey Keen (Sir Frederick Gray),* Bernard Lee (M), George Baker (Captain Benson), Robert Brown (Admiral Hargreaves), Shane Rimmer (Commander Carter), Desmond Llewelyn (Q), Lois Maxwell (Miss Moneypenny), Edward de Souza (Sheik Hossein), Nadim Sawalha (Fekkesh),

---

* The character of the Minister of Defence, played by Keen from *The Spy Who Loved Me* until *The Living Daylights*, is referred to by name, as Sir Frederick Gray, in both *The Spy Who Loved Me* and *Moonraker*. Bond calls him 'Freddie' in *The Spy*, but reverts to a more formal 'Minister' thereafter. Sir Frederick is unique as the only Cabinet minister to have served in successive Labour *and* Conservative governments!

Vernon Dobtcheff (Max Kalba), Michael Billington (Sergei), Sue Vanner (Log cabin girl), Eva Rueber-Staier (Rublevich),* Milton Reid (Sandor), Sidney Tafler (*Liparus* Captain), Valerie Leon (Hotel receptionist), Marilyn Galsworthy (Stromberg's assistant), Cyril Shaps (Dr Bechmann), Milo Sperber (Professor Markovitz), Rafiq Anwar (Mujaba Club waiter), Albert Moses (Barman), Bryan Marshall (Captain Talbot), Felicity York, Dawn Rodriques, Anika Pavel, Jill Goodall and The Egyptian Folklore Group (Arab beauties).

Moonraker

United Artists/Eon Productions and Les Productions Artistes Associes. 1979.

Director: Lewis Gilbert. *Producer:* Albert R. Broccoli. *Screenplay:* Christopher Wood. *Executive producer:* Michael G. Wilson. *Associate producer:* William P. Cartlidge. *Production managers:* Jean-Pierre Spiri-Mercanton (France), Terence Churcher (GB). *Second unit directors:* Ernest Day, John Glen. *Editor:* John Glen. *Director of photography:* Jean Tournier. Panavision. Technicolor. *Production designer:* Ken Adam. *Art directors:* Max Douy, Charles Bishop. *Costume designer:* Jacques Fonteray. *Action sequences:* Bob Simmons. *Space consultant:* Eric Burgess. *Visual effects supervisor:* Derek Meddings. *Visual effects art director:* Peter Lamont. *Main titles:* Maurice Binder. *Music:* John Barry. *Title song performed by:* Shirley Bassey. *Lyrics:* Hal David. *Certificate:* A. *Running time:* 126 mins.

Cast: Roger Moore (James Bond), Lois Chiles (Holly Goodhead), Michael Lonsdale (Drax), Richard Kiel (Jaws), Corinne Clery (Corinne Dufour), Emily Bolton (Manuela), Toshiro Suga (Chang),** Geoffrey Keen (Sir Frederick Gray), Bernard Lee (M), Desmond Llewelyn (Q), Lois Maxwell (Miss Moneypenny), Michael Marshall (Colonel Scott), Walter Gotell (General Gogol), Irka Bochenko (Blonde beauty), Anne Lonnberg (Museum guide), Nicholas Arbez (Drax's boy), Blanche Ravelac (Dolly), Arthur Howard (Cavendish), Alfie Bass (Consumptive Italian), Lizzie Warville (Gogol's girl), Jean-Pierre Castaldi (Pilot, private jet), Leila Shenna (Hostess, private jet), Douglas Lambert (Mission Control director), Brian Keith (US Shuttle captain), George Birt (Boeing 747 captain), Kim Fortune (RAF officer), Claude Carliez (Gondolier), Chichinou Kaeppler, Christina Hui, Françoise Gayat, Nicaise Jean-Louis, Catherine Serre and Beatrice Libert (Drax's Girls).

---

* Former Miss World Eva Rueber-Staier had cameo roles in three Bond films as General Gogol's secretary, and on each occasion her character's name was spelled differently on the credits: as 'Rubelvitch' in *The Spy Who Loved Me*, 'Rublevich' in *For Your Eyes Only* and 'Rublevitch' in *Octopussy*. I have opted for 'Rublevich'.

** The character is credited as 'Chang', but is referred to as 'Char' in the film itself.

For Your Eyes Only

United Artists/Eon Productions. 1981.

Director: John Glen. *Producer:* Albert R. Broccoli. *Screenplay:* Richard Maibaum and Michael G. Wilson. *Executive producer:* Michael G. Wilson. *Associate producer:* Tom Pevsner. *Production supervisor:* Bob Simmonds. *Second unit director and photographer:* Arthur Wooster. *Editor:* John Grover. *Director of photography:* Alan Hume. Panavision. Technicolor. *Ski photography:* Willy Bogner. *Aerial photography:* James Devis. *Underwater photography:* Al Giddings. *Production designer:* Peter Lamont. *Art director:* John Fenner. *Costume designer:* Elizabeth Waller. *Action sequences:* Bob Simmons. *Driving stunts:* Remy Julienne. *Visual effects supervisor:* Derek Meddings. *Visual effects photography:* Paul Wilson. *Main titles:* Maurice Binder. *Music:* Bill Conti. *Title song performed by:* Sheena Easton. *Lyrics:* Michael Leeson. *Certificate:* A. *Running time:* 127 mins.

Cast: Roger Moore (James Bond), Carole Bouquet (Melina Havelock), Topol (Columbo), Lynn-Holly Johnson (Bibi), Julian Glover (Kristatos), Cassandra Harris (Lisl), Jill Bennett (Jacoba Brink), Michael Gothard (Locque), John Wyman (Kriegler), Jack Hedley (Sir Timothy Havelock), Lois Maxwell (Miss Moneypenny), Desmond Llewelyn (Q), Geoffrey Keen (Minister of Defence), Walter Gotell (General Gogol), James Villiers (Tanner),* John Moreno (Ferrara), Toby Robins (Iona Havelock), Graham Crowden (First Sea Lord), Noel Johnson (Vice-Admiral), Charles Dance (Claus), Paul Angelis (Karageorge), Jack Klaf (Apostis), Stag Theodore (Nikos), Stefan Kalipha (Gonzales), William Hoyland (McGregor), Eva Rueber-Staier (Rublevich), Fred Bryant (Vicar), Robbin Young (Girl in flower shop), Graham Hawks (Mantis Man), John Wells (Denis), Janet Brown (Prime Minister), Lalla Dean, Evelyn Drogue, Laoura Hadzivageli, Koko, Chai Lee, Kim Mills, Tula, Vanya, Viva, Lizze Warville and Alison Worth (Girls at poolside).

Octopussy

MGM-United Artists/Eon Productions. 1983.

Director: John Glen. *Producer:* Albert R. Broccoli. *Screenplay:* Richard Maibaum and Michael G. Wilson. *Story:* George MacDonald Fraser. *Executive producer:*

---

*Bill Tanner is the British Secret Service Chief of Staff in Fleming's novels. When Bernard Lee died shortly before filming his scenes for *For Your Eyes Only*, it was decided not to replace him in this film. Moneypenny tells Bond that M is 'on leave'. The script reveals that the lines written for M were simply assigned to Tanner. It also reveals that the scene later in the film where Bond meets Q in disguise as a Greek Orthodox priest was originally to have been for M.

Michael G. Wilson. *Associate producer:* Tom Pevsner. *Production supervisor:* Hugh Harlow. *Second unit director and photographer:* Arthur Wooster. *Supervising editor:* John Grover. *Director of photography:* Alan Hume. Panavision. Technicolor. *Production designer:* Peter Lamont. *Art director:* John Fenner. *Costume designer:* Emma Porteous. *Action sequences:* Bob Simmons. *Driving stunts:* Remy Julienne. *Special effects supervisor:* John Richardson. *Main titles:* Maurice Binder. *Music:* John Barry. 'All Time High' *performed by:* Rita Coolidge. *Lyrics:* Tim Rice. *Certificate:* PG. *Running time:* 131 mins.

Cast: Roger Moore (James Bond), Maud Adams (Octopussy),* Louis Jourdan (Kamal Khan), Kristina Wayborn (Magda), Steven Berkoff (General Orlov), Kabir Bedi (Gobinda), David Meyer (Twin One), Anthony Meyer (Twin Two), Vijay Amritraj (Vijay), Desmond Llewelyn (Q), Robert Brown (M),** Lois Maxwell (Miss Moneypenny), Michaela Clavell (Penelope Smallbone), Walter Gotell (General Gogol), Geoffrey Keen (Minister of Defence), Douglas Wilmer (Fanning), Albert Moses (Sadruddin), Andy Bradford (009), Bruce Boa (US General), Paul Hardwick (Soviet Chairman), Suzanne Jerome (Gwendoline), Cherry Gillespie (Midge), Peter Porteous (Lankin), Dermot Crowley (Kamp), Eva Rueber-Staier (Rublevich), Jeremy Bullock (Smithers), Tina Hudson (Bianca), William Derrick (Yo-yo thug), Stuart Saunders (Major Clive), Patrick Barr (British Ambassador), Ken Norris (Colonel Toro), Tony Arjuna (Mufti), Gertan Klauber (Bubi), Hugo Bower (Karl), Brian Coburn (South American VIP), Mary Stavin, Carolyn Seaward, Carole Ashby, Cheryl-Anne, Jani-Z, Julie Martin, Joni Flynn, Julie Barth, Kathy Davies, Helene Hunt, Gillian De Terville, Safira Afzal, Louise King, Tina Robinson, Alison Worth, Janine Andrews and Lynda Knight (The Octopussy Girls), Suzanne Dando (Gymnasts supervisor), Teresa Craddock, Kirsten Harrison, Christine Cullers, Lisa Jackman, Jane Aldridge, Christine Gibson, Tracy Llewellyn and Ruth Flynn (Gymnasts), Robert Germains (Ringmaster), Richard Graydon (Francisco the Fearless), The Hassani Troupe, The Flying Cherokees, Carol Richter, Josef Richter, Vera Fossett, Shirley Fossett and Barrie Winship (Circus Performers).

---

* Maud Adams, who had previously played Scaramanga's mistress in *The Man With the Golden Gun*, is the only actress to have had two major parts as a 'Bond girl'.

** Robert Brown, the new M, had previously played Admiral Hargreaves in *The Spy Who Loved Me*, though it seems likely that his M is meant to be the same character previously played by the late Bernard Lee. He played M for four films, until *Licence To Kill*. Brown had previously played Gurth to Roger Moore's Ivanhoe in the Anglo-American television series *Ivanhoe* (1957–58).

Never Say Never Again

Warner Bros./Taliafilm/Woodcote Productions. 1983.

Director: Irvin Kershner. *Producer:* Jack Schwartzman. *Screenplay:* Lorenzo Semple Jr. Based on an original story by Kevin McClory, Jack Whittingham and Ian Fleming. *Executive producer:* Kevin McClory. *Associate producer:* Michael Dryhurst. *Production supervisor:* Alex de Grunwald. *Second unit director:* Michael Moore. *Underwater sequences director:* Ricou Browning. *Supervising editor:* Robert Lawrence. *Director of photography:* Douglas Slocombe. Panavision. Technicolor. *Production designers:* Philip Harrison, Stephen Grimes. *Supervising art director:* Leslie Dilley. *Costume designer:* Charles Knode. *Stunt co-ordinator:* Vic Armstrong. *Supervisor of special visual effects:* David Dryer. *Music:* Michael Legrand. *Title song performed by:* Lani Hall. *Trumpet solo:* Herb Alpert. *Lyrics:* Alan and Marilyn Bergman. *Certificate:* PG. *Running time:* 134 mins.

Cast: Sean Connery (James Bond), Klaus Maria Brandauer (Largo), Max Von Sydow (Blofeld), Barbara Carrera (Fatima Blush), Kim Basinger (Domino), Bernie Casey (Felix Leiter), Alec McCowen (Q – Algernon), Edward Fox (M), Pamela Salem (Miss Moneypenny), Rowan Atkinson (Nigel Small-Fawcett), Valerie Leon (Lady in Bahamas), Milow Kirek (Kovacs), Pat Roach (Lippe), Anthony Sharp (Lord Ambrose), Prunella Gee (Patricia Fearing), Gavan O'Herlihy (Captain Jack Petachi), Ronald Pickup (Elliott), Robert Rietty and Guido Adorni (Italian ministers), Vincent Marzello (Culpepper), Christopher Reich (No. 5), Billy J. Mitchell (Captain Pedersen), Manning Redwood (General Miller), Saskia Cohen Tanugi (Nicole), Anthony Van Laast (Kurt), Sylvia Marriott (French Minister), Dan Meaden (Bouncer), Michael Medwin (Dr Wain), Lucy Hornak (Nurse), Derek Deadman (Porter), Joanna Dickens (Cook), Tony Alleff (Auctioneer), Paul Tucker (Steward), Brenda Kempner (Masseuse), Jill Meager (Receptionist at health spa), Roy Bowe (Ship's captain), John Stephen Hill (Communications officer), Wendy Leech (Girl hostage).

A View To A Kill

MGM-United Artists/Eon Productions. 1985.

Director: John Glen. *Producers:* Albert R. Broccoli and Michael G. Wilson. *Screenplay:* Richard Maibaum and Michael G. Wilson. *Associate producer:* Tom Pevsner. *Production supervisor:* Anthony Waye. *Second unit director and photographer:* Arthur Wooster. *Ski director:* Willy Bogner. *Editor:* Peter Davies. *Director of photography:* Alan Hume. Panavision. Technicolor. *Production designer:* Peter Lamont. *Art director:* John Fenner. *Costume designer:* Emma Porteous. *Action sequences:* Martin Grace. *Driving stunts:* Remy Julienne. *Special effects supervisor:*

John Richardson. *Main titles:* Maurice Binder. *Music:* John Barry. *Title song performed by:* Duran Duran. *Written by:* Duran Duran and John Barry. *Certificate:* PG. *Running time:* 131 mins.

Cast: Roger Moore (James Bond), Christopher Walken (Max Zorin), Tanya Roberts (Stacey Sutton), Grace Jones (May Day), Patrick Macnee (Sir Godfrey Tibbett), Patrick Bachau (Scarpine), David Yip (Chuck Lee), Fiona Fullerton (Pola Ivanova), Manning Redwood (Bob Conley), Alison Doody (Jenny Flex), Willoughby Gray (Dr Carl Mortner), Desmond Llewelyn (Q), Robert Brown (M), Lois Maxwell (Miss Moneypenny),* Walter Gotell (General Gogol), Geoffrey Keen (Minister of Defence), Jean Rougerie (Aubergine), Mary Stavin (Kimberley Jones), Daniel Benzali (Howe), Bogdan Kominowski (Klotkoff), Papillon Soo Soo (Pan Ho), Dominique Risbourg (Butterfly act compere), Carole Ashby (Whistling girl), Anthony Chin (Taiwanese tycoon), Lucien Jerome (Taxi driver), Joe Flood (US police captain), Gerard Buhr (Auctioneer), Dolph Lundgren (KGB man), Tony Sibbald (Mine foreman), Bill Ackridge (O'Rourke), Sian Adey-Jones, Samina Afzal, Celine Cawley, Nike Clark, Helen Clitherow, Maggie Defreitas, Gloria Douse, Caroline Hallett, Deborah Hanna, Josanne Haydon-Pearce, Ann Jackson, Terri Johns, Karen Loughlin, Angela Lyn, Patricia Martinez, Kim Ashfield Norton, Elke Ritschel, Lou-Anne Ronchi, Helen Smith, Jane Spencer, Paula Thomas, Mayako Torigai and Toni White (The Girls).

The Living Daylights

MGM-United Artists/Eon Productions. 1987.

Director: John Glen. *Producers:* Albert R. Broccoli and Michael G. Wilson. *Screenplay:* Richard Maibaum and Michael G. Wilson. *Associate producers:* Tom Pevsner and Barbara Broccoli. *Production supervisor:* Anthony Waye. *Second unit director and photographer:* Arthur Wooster. *Editors:* John Grover, Peter Davies. *Director of photography:* Alec Mills. Panavision. Technicolor. *Production designer:* Peter Lamont. *Art director:* Terry Ackland Snow. *Costume designer:* Emma Porteous. *Stunt supervisor:* Paul Weston. *Driving stunts:* Remy Julienne. *Aerial stunt arranger:* B. J. Worth. *Special visual effects:* John Richardson. *Main titles:* Maurice Binder. *Music:* John Barry. *Title song performed by:* a-ha. *Written by:* Pal Waaktaar and John Barry. 'Where Has Everybody Gone' and 'If There Was A Man'

---

* *A View to A Kill* marked Lois Maxwell's farewell apprearence as Miss Moneypenny, having played the role of M's secretary in fourteen consecutive films from *Dr No*. Hereafter a new actress has been cast as Moneypenny opposite each new James Bond. Maxwell claims she suggested to the producers that after stepping down as Moneypenny, she should herself play M, though the idea was turned down. A female M was of course introduced with Dame Judi Dench in *GoldenEye*.

performed by: The Pretenders. *Lyrics:* Chrissie Hynde. *Certificate:* PG. *Running time:* 131 mins.

Cast: Timothy Dalton (James Bond), Maryam d'Abo (Kara Milovy), Jeroen Krabbé (General Georgi Koskov), Joe Don Baker (Brad Whitaker), John Rhys-Davies (General Leonid Pushkin), Art Malik (Kamran Shah), Andreas Wisniewski (Necros), Thomas Wheatley (Saunders), Desmond Llewelyn (Q), Robert Brown (M), Geoffrey Keen (Minister of Defence), Caroline Bliss (Miss Moneypenny), Walter Gotell (General Anatol Gogol),* John Terry (Felix Leiter), Virginia Hey (Rubavitch),** John Bowe (Colonel Feyador), Julie T. Wallace (Rosika Miklos), Kell Tyler (Linda), Catherine Rabett (Liz), Dulice Liecier (Ava), Nadim Sawalha (Chief of Police, Tangier), Alan Talbot (KGB man), Carl Rigg (Imposter), Frederick Warder (004), Glyn Baker (002), Tony Cyrus (Chief of the Snow Leopard Brotherhood), Ken Sharrock (Russian jailer), Peter Porteous (Gas works supervisor), Derek Hoxby (Sergeant Stagg), Anthony Carrick (Male secretary, Blaydon), Bill Weston (Butler, Blaydon), Leslie French (Lavatory attendant), Michael Moor, Sumar Khan (Mujaheddin), Odette Benatar, Dianna Casale, Sharon Devlin, Femi Gardiner, Patricia Keefer, Ruddy Rodriguez, Mayte Sanchez, Cela Savannah, Karen Seeberg, Waris Walsh and Karen Williams (The Girls).

Licence To Kill

MGM-United Artists/Eon Productions. 1989.

Director: John Glen. *Producers:* Albert R. Broccoli and Michael G. Wilson. *Screenplay:* Michael G. Wilson and Richard Maibaum. *Associate producers:* Tom Pevsner and Barbara Broccoli. *Production supervisor:* Anthony Waye. *Second unit director and photographer:* Arthur Wooster. *Editor:* John Grover. *Director of photography:* Alec Mills. Panavision. Technicolor. *Production designer:* Peter Lamont. *Art director:* Michael Lamont. *Costume designer:* Jodie Tillen. *Stunt co-ordinator:* Paul Weston. *Driving stunts:* Remy Julienne. *Aerial stunt supervisor:* 'Corkey' Fornof. *Special visual effects:* John Richardson. *Main titles:* Maurice Binder. *Music:* Michael Kamen. *Title song performed by:* Gladys Knight. 'If You Asked Me To' *performed by:* Patti LaBelle. *Written by:* Diana Warren. *Certificate:* 15. *Running time:* 133 mins.

---

* This was the only occasion on which Gogol's first name was included in the credits: although billed here as 'Anatol', M had called him 'Alexis' in *The Spy Who Loved Me*.

** This character, Pushkin's mistress, is presumably not the same as Gogol's secretary Rublevich, despite the similarity in their names – unless successive heads of the KGB keep the same female companion.

Cast: Timothy Dalton (James Bond), Carey Lowell (Pam Bouvier), Robert Davi (Franz Sanchez), Talisa Soto (Lupe Lamora), Anthony Zerbe (Milton Krest), Frank McRae (Sharkey), Everett McGill (Killifer), Desmond Llewelyn (Q), Wayne Newton (Professor Joe Butcher), Pedro Armendariz Jr (President Hector Lopez), Don Stroud (Heller), David Hedison (Felix Leiter),* Pamela Barnes (Della Churchill), Robert Brown (M), Caroline Bliss (Miss Moneypenny), Benicio del Toro (Dario), Anthony Starke (Truman-Lodge), Grand L. Bush (Hawkins), Cary-Hiroyuki Tagawa (Kwang), Alejandro Bracho (Perez), Guy de Saint Cyr (Braun), Rafer Johnson (Mullens), Diana Lee-Hsu (Loti), Christopher Neame (Fallon), Claude Brook (Montelongo), Jeannine Bisignano (Stripper), Edna Bolkan (Waitress), Eddie Enderfield (Clive), Cynthia Fallo (Consuello), Teresa Blake (Ticket agent), Samuel Benjamin Lancaster (Della's uncle).

GoldenEye

MGM-United Artists/Eon Productions. 1995.

Director: Martin Campbell. *Producers:* Michael G. Wilson and Barbara Broccoli. *Screenplay:* Bruce Ferstein. *Story:* Jeffrey Caine and Michael France. *Executive producer:* Tom Pevsner. *Associate producer:* Anthony Waye. *Editor:* Terry Rawlings. *Director of photography:* Phil Meheux. Panavision. Technicolor. *Additional photography:* Arthur Wooster. *Production designer:* Peter Lamont. *Supervising art director:* Neil Lamont. *Costume designer:* Lindy Hemming. *Stunt co-ordinator:* Simon Crane. *Driving stunts:* Remy Julienne. *Parachute stunt co-ordinator:* B. J. Worth. *Special effects supervisor:* Chris Courbold. *Miniatures:* Derek Meddings. *Main titles:* Daniel Kleinman. *Music:* Eric Serra. *Title song performed by:* Tina Turner. *Written by:* Bono and The Edge. 'The Experience of Love' *written and performed by:* Eric Serra. *Certificate:* 12. *Running time:* 130 mins.

Cast: Pierce Brosnan (James Bond), Sean Bean (Alec Trevelyan), Izabella Scorupco (Natalya Simonova), Famke Janssen (Xenia Onatopp), Joe Don Baker (Jack Wade), Judi Dench (M), Robbie Coltrane (Valentin Zukovsky), Gottfried John (General Ourumov), Tcheky Karyo (Defence Minister Dimitri Mishkin), Alan Cumming (Boris Grishenko), Desmond Llewelyn (Q), Samantha Bond (Miss Moneypenny), Michael Kitchen (Tanner), Serena Gordon (Caroline), Billy J. Mitchell (Admiral Chuck Farrel), Minnie Driver (Irina), Michelle Arthur (Anna), Simon Kunz (Severnaya duty officer).

---

* Hedison is the only actor to have played Felix Leiter twice, having previously appeared in *Live and Let Die*.

Tomorrow Never Dies

MGM-United Artists/Eon Productions. 1997.

Director: Roger Spottiswoode. *Producers:* Michael G. Wilson and Barbara Broccoli. *Screenplay:* Bruce Ferstein. *Line producer:* Anthony Waye. *Second unit director:* Vic Armstrong. *Aerial director:* Marc Wolff. *Underwater director:* Pete Romano. *Editors:* Dominique Fortin, Michel Arcand. *Director of photography:* Robert Elswit. Pana-vision. Technicolor. *Production designer:* Allan Cameron. *Art directors:* Stephen Scott, Giles Masters, Tony Reading, Jonathan Lee, Ken Court. *Costume designer:* Lindy Hemming. *Stunt supervisor:* Dicky Beer. *HALO Jump co-ordinator:* B. J. Worth. *Special effects supervisor:* Chris Courbold. *Miniatures:* John Richardson. *Main titles:* Daniel Kleinman. *Music:* David Arnold. *Title song performed by:* Sheryl Crow. *Written by:* Sheryl Crow and Mitchell Froom. *End title song performed by:* k. d. lang. *Certificate:* 12. *Running time:* 119 mins.

Cast: Pierce Brosnan (James Bond), Jonathan Pryce (Elliot Carver), Michelle Yeoh (Wai Lin), Teri Hatcher (Paris Carver), Joe Don Baker (Jack Wade), Ricky Jay (Henry Gupta), Götz Otto (Stamper), Vincent Schiavelli (Dr Kaufman), Judi Dench (M), Desmond Llewelyn (Q), Samantha Bond (Miss Moneypenny), Colin Salmon (Robinson), Geoffrey Palmer (Admiral Roebuck), Julian Fellowes (Minister of Defence), Terence Rigby (General Bukharin), Cecilie Thomsen (Professor Inga Bergstrom), Nina Young (Tamara Steele), Daphne Deckers (Carver's PR girl), Colin Stinton (Dave Greenwalt), Michael Byrne (Admiral Kelly), Mark Spalding (Stealth Boat captain), Bruce Alexander (Captain of HMS *Chester*), Christopher Bowen (Captain of HMS *Devonshire*), Philip Kwok (General Chang).

Bibliography

The James Bond novels

This bibliography lists all the James Bond novels, by various authors, in chronological order. The publication details refer to the original editions; the Ian Fleming titles have subsequently been published in paperback editions by Pan, Triad and Coronet (the paperback division of Hodder and Stoughton). Novelisations of film screenplays are indicated by an asterisk (*).

By Ian Fleming:

Casino Royale (London: Jonathan Cape, 1953).
Live and Let Die (London: Jonathan Cape, 1954).
Moonraker (London: Jonathan Cape, 1955).
Diamonds Are Forever (London: Jonathan Cape, 1956).
From Russia, With Love (London: Jonathan Cape, 1957).
Dr No (London: Jonathan Cape, 1958).
Goldfinger (London: Jonathan Cape, 1959).
For Your Eyes Only (London: Jonathan Cape, 1960).
Thunderball (London: Jonathan Cape, 1961).
The Spy Who Loved Me (London: Jonathan Cape, 1962).
On Her Majesty's Secret Service (London: Jonathan Cape, 1963).
You Only Live Twice (London: Jonathan Cape, 1964).
The Man With the Golden Gun (London: Jonathan Cape, 1965).
Octopussy and the Living Daylights (London: Jonathan Cape, 1966).

(When originally published, the last volume comprised just two short stories, 'Octopussy' and 'The Living Daylights'. A third story, 'The Property of A Lady', was included in later editions, with the volume entitled just *Octopussy*. However, the most recent Coronet paperback edition contains all three stories but reverts to the volume title *Octopussy and the Living Daylights*.)

By Kingsley Amis (writing as Robert Markham):

Colonel Sun (London: Jonathan Cape, 1968).

By Christopher Wood:

James Bond, The Spy Who Loved Me (London: Triad/Panther, 1977).*
James Bond and Moonraker (London: Triad/Panther, 1979).*

By John Gardner:

Licence Renewed (London: Jonathan Cape/Hodder and Stoughton, 1981).
For Special Services (London: Jonathan Cape/Hodder and Stoughton, 1982).
Icebreaker (London: Jonathan Cape/Hodder and Stoughton, 1983).
Role of Honour (London: Jonathan Cape/Hodder and Stoughton, 1984).
Nobody Lives For Ever (London: Jonathan Cape/Hodder and Stoughton, 1986).
No Deals, Mr Bond (London: Jonathan Cape/Hodder and Stoughton, 1987).
Scorpius (London: Hodder and Stoughton, 1988).
Win, Lose or Die (London: Hodder and Stoughton, 1989).
Licence To Kill (London: Hodder and Stoughton/Coronet, 1989).*
Brokenclaw (London: Hodder and Stoughton, 1990).
The Man From Barbarossa (London: Hodder and Stoughton, 1991).
Death is Forever (London: Hodder and Stoughton, 1992).
Never Send Flowers (London: Hodder and Stoughton, 1993).
Sea Fire (London: Hodder and Stoughton, 1994).
GoldenEye (London: Hodder and Stoughton/Coronet, 1995).*
Cold (London: Hodder and Stoughton, 1996).

By Raymond Benson:

Zero Minus Ten (London: Hodder and Stoughton, 1997).
Tomorrow Never Dies (London: Hodder and Stoughton/Coronet, 1997).*
The Facts of Death (London: Hodder and Stoughton, 1998).

British Film Institute Unpublished Scripts

S6500: *Dr No. From the Novel by Ian Fleming.* Fourth Draft Screenplay, by Richard Maibaum and Wolf Mankowitz, 12 December 1961.
S6501: *Ian Fleming's From Russia With Love.* Final Draft Screenplay, by Richard Maibaum, 18 March 1963.
S6508: *Ian Fleming's Goldfinger.* Final Draft Screenplay, by Richard Maibaum and Paul Dehn, 26 February 1964.
S6502: *Diamonds Are Forever.* Final Draft Screenplay, by Tom Mankiewicz, no date.
S4498: *The Spy Who Loved Me.* Revised Final Shooting Script [by Christopher Wood], 23 August 1976.
S17894: *For Your Eyes Only.* Screen Story and Screenplay, by Richard Maibaum and Michael G. Wilson, 12 August 1980.
S18120: *Octopussy.* Screenplay by Richard Maibaum and Michael G. Wilson, based on a draft screenplay by George MacDonald Fraser, 10 June 1982.
S18050: *License To Kill* [sic]. Final Draft Screenplay, by Michael G. Wilson and Richard Maibaum, no date.

Newspapers and periodicals

My chapter notes indicate which newspapers and periodicals I have used for film reviews. Many of these are taken from the press clippings provided on the British Film Institute's microfiche collection, an invaluable source for researchers, though occasionally prone to inaccuracy. I have quoted from reviews and articles appearing in the following British newspapers and periodicals: *Daily Express, Daily Telegraph, Daily Worker, Evening News, Evening Standard, Financial Times, Guardian, Independent, New Statesman, News of the World, Observer, Punch, Scene, Spectator, Sunday Express, Sunday People, Sunday Times* and *The Times*. These represent a range of opinion from both the quality and the popular press and from across the political spectrum. For the United States I have quoted from the following newspapers and periodicals: *Esquire, New York Times, New Yorker, Playboy, Saturday Review, Time* and *Village Voice*. Reviews of the Bond films can be found in the following volumes of *The New York Times Film Reviews: 1959–1968, 1969–1970, 1971–1972, 1973–1974, 1977–1978, 1979–1980* (all published in New York by Times Books and Arno Press, 1970, 1971, 1973, 1975, 1979 and 1981 respectively), and *1981–1982, 1983–1984, 1985–1986, 1987–1988, 1989–1990, 1995–1996* (all published in New York by Times Books and Garland Publishing, 1984, 1986, 1988, 1990, 1992 and 1998 respectively). Some film-related articles are extracted from Gene Brown (ed.), *The New York Times Film Encyclopedia* (New York: Times Books, 1984).

Film journals and trade papers

Again sources can be traced through the chapter notes. For reviews I have drawn on *Films and Filming* as representative of the middle-brow film journalism in Britain for much of the period during which the Bond films have been made, and on the *Monthly Film Bulletin* and *Sight and Sound* as (until their merger and subsequent dumbing-down) the nearest thing to an intellectual film culture in Britain. Separate articles on the Bond films, as distinct from reviews, are listed under 'articles and chapters' below. For background on the British film industry I have used the trade papers *Kinematograph Weekly* and *Today's Cinema* until the end of the 1960s, and *Screen International* thereafter. *American Cinematographer* provided much useful technical information on the Bond films, while US trade papers *Hollywood Reporter, Motion Picture Herald* and *Variety* have been used for reviews and information about the reception of the films in the United States. Reviews of the Bond films from *Variety* can be found in the following volumes of *Variety's Film Reviews* (all published by R. R. Bowker, New York until *Vol. 18*, thereafter R. R. Bowker, New Providence, NJ): *Vol. 10: 1959–1963* (1983), *Vol. 11: 1964–1967* (1983), *Vol. 12: 1968–1970* (1983), *Vol. 13: 1971–1974* (1983), *Vol. 14: 1975–1977* (1983), *Vol. 15: 1978–1980* (1983), *Vol. 17: 1981–1982* (1983), *Vol. 18: 1983–1984* (1986), *Vol. 19: 1985–1986* (1988), *Vol. 20: 1987–1988* (1991), *Vol. 21: 1989–1990* (1991) and *Vol. 24: 1995–1996* (1997). (*Vol. 16* [1983] is the *Index of Titles, 1907–1980*.)

The review of the television *Casino Royale* from *Daily Variety* on p. 43 is taken from *Variety's Television Reviews, Vol. 1: 1946–1956* (New York: Garland Publishing, 1988). Statistics regarding the negative costs and box-office performance of the Bond films can be found in the following trade paper special issues: 'James Bond: 25 Years', *Variety*, 13 May 1987; 'James Bond's 25th Anniversary', *Hollywood Reporter*, 14 July 1987; and '35 Years of Unrivaled Success', *Screen International*, 5 December 1997.

Fan magazines

'Fanzines' represent a different type of source to film journals and trade papers, being celebratory, anecdotal and uncritical, but magazines such as *Cinefantastique*, *Starburst* and *Starlog* provide background information on the production of the films and sometimes feature interviews with actors and production personnel. In addition, the following James Bond fanzines are worthy of particular mention: *Bondage* (published by the now defunct James Bond 007 Fan Club of America), *007 Magazine* (published by the British-based James Bond 007 International Fan Club, PO Box 007, Addlestone, Surrey KT15 1DY), and *Goldeneye* (published by the Ian Fleming Foundation, PO Box 1850, Burbank, CA 91507, USA). The articles and correspondence in these publications provide a useful insight into the ways in which the James Bond fan culture engages with the films.

Biographies, autobiographies and diaries

Broccoli, Albert R., with Donald Zec, *When the Snow Melts: The Autobiography of Cubby Broccoli* (London: Boxtree, 1998).

Creighton, Christopher, *Op. JB: The Last Great Secret of the Second World War* (London: Simon and Schuster, 1996). (An example of the 'secret history' genre of fiction, the author's account of a secret mission entitled 'Operation James Bond' supposedly undertaken with Ian Fleming in April and May 1945.)

Davie, Michael (ed.), *The Diaries of Evelyn Waugh* (London: Weidenfeld and Nicolson, 1976).

Fiegel, Eddi, *John Barry, A Sixties Theme: From James Bond to Midnight Cowboy* (London: Constable, 1998).

Freedland, Michael, *Sean Connery: The Untouchable Hero* (London: Virgin, 1993).

Lycett, Andrew, *Ian Fleming* (London: Weidenfeld and Nicolson, 1995).

Moore, Roger, *Roger Moore as James Bond: Roger Moore's own account of filming Live and Let Die* (London: Pan, 1973).

Moseley, Roy, with Philip and Martin Masheter, *Roger Moore: A Biography* (London: New English Library, 1985).

Pearson, John, *The Life of Ian Fleming* (London: Jonathan Cape, 1966).

— *James Bond: The Authorised Biography of 007* (London: Sidgwick and Jackson, 1973). (An ingenious 'fictional biography' based on the premise that James Bond was a real person, and Fleming his biographer.)

Simmons, Bob, with Kenneth Passingham, *Nobody Does It Better: My 25 Years of Stunts with James Bond and Other Stars* (Poole, Dorset: Javelin Books, 1987).

Thatcher, Margaret, *The Downing Street Years* (London: HarperCollins, 1993).

Trevelyan, John, *What the Censor Saw* (London: Michael Joseph, 1973).

Young, Freddie, *Seventy Light Years: A Life in the Movies* (London: Faber and Faber, 1999).

Books and monographs

Aldgate, Anthony, *Censorship and the Permissive Society: British Cinema and Theatre 1955–1965* (Oxford: Clarendon Press, 1995).

Amis, Kingsley, *The James Bond Dossier* (London: Jonathan Cape, 1965; Pan Books, 1966).

Armes, Roy, *A Critical History of British Cinema* (London: Secker and Warburg, 1978).

Barnes, Alan, and Marcus Hearn, *Kiss Kiss Bang! Bang!: The Unofficial James Bond Film Companion* (London: B. T. Batsford, 1997).

Barr, Charles, *Ealing Studios*, rev. edn (London: Studio Vista, 1993).

Belton, John, *American Cinema/American Culture* (New York: McGraw-Hill, 1994).

Bennett, Tony, et al., *The Making of 'The Spy Who Loved Me': DE 353 Broadcasting Handbook 3* (Milton Keynes: Open University Press, 1977).

Bennett, Tony, and Janet Woollacott, *Bond and Beyond: The Political Career of a Popular Hero* (London: Macmillan, 1987).

Benson, Raymond, *The James Bond Bedside Companion* (London: Boxtree, 1988).

Bergan, Ronald, *The United Artists Story* (London: Octopus, 1986).

Booker, Christopher, *The Neophiliacs: A Study of the Revolution in English Life in the Fifties and Sixties* (London: Collins, 1969).

— *The Seventies: Portrait of a Decade* (London: Allen Lane, 1980).

Boyd, Ann S., *The Devil with James Bond!* (Richmond: John Knox Press, 1967; Westport: Greenwood Press, 1975).

Brosnan, John, *James Bond in the Cinema*, 2nd edn (London: Tantivy Press, 1981).

Cawelti, John G., *Adventure, Mystery, and Romance: Formula Stories as Art and Popular Culture* (Chicago: University of Chicago Press, 1976).

Del Buono, Oreste, and Umberto Eco (eds), *The Bond Affair*, trans. R. A. Downie (London: Macdonald, 1966).

Denning, Michael, *Cover Stories: Narrative and Ideology in the British Spy Thriller* (London: Routledge and Kegan Paul, 1987).

Dickinson, Margaret, and Sarah Street, *Cinema and State: The Film Industry and the British Government, 1927–84* (London: British Film Institute, 1985).

Drummond, Lee, *American Dreamtime: A Cultural Analysis of Popular Movies and their Implications for a Science of Humanity* (Lanham, Maryland: Littlefield Adams, 1996).

Durgnat, Raymond, *A Mirror for England: British Movies from Austerity to Affluence* (London: Faber and Faber, 1970).

Eagleton, Terry, *Literary Theory: An Introduction* (Oxford: Basil Blackwell, 1983).

Haining, Peter, *James Bond: A Celebration* (London: Planet Books, 1987).

Harmon, Jim, and Donald F. Glut, *The Great Movie Serials: Their Sound and Fury* (London: Woburn Press, 1973).

Hibbin, Sally, *The Official James Bond 007 Movie Book* (London: Hamlyn, 1987).

Hirschhorn, Clive, *The Columbia Story* (London: Pyramid, 1989).

Landy, Marcia, *British Genres: Cinema and Society, 1930–1960* (Princeton: Princeton University Press, 1991).

Lane, Andy, and Paul Simpson, *The Bond Files: The Unofficial Guide to the World's Greatest Secret Agent* (London: Virgin, 1998).

Lane, Sheldon (ed.), *For Bond Lovers Only* (London: Panther, 1965).

McFarlane, Brian (ed.), *An Autobiography of British Cinema* (London: Methuen, 1997).

McGilligan, Pat (ed.), *Backstory: Interviews with Screenwriters of Hollywood's Golden Age* (Berkeley: University of California Press, 1986).

McInnerney, Jay, Nick Foulkes, Neil Norman, Nick Sullivan, with Colin Woodhead, *Dressed To Kill: James Bond, the Suited Hero* (Paris: Flammarion, 1996).

Marwick, Arthur, *British Society Since 1945*, 3rd edn (London: Penguin, 1996).

— *The Sixties: Cultural Revolution in Britain, France, Italy, and the United States c.1958–1974* (Oxford: Oxford University Press, 1998).

Merry, Bruce, *Anatomy of the Spy Thriller* (Dublin: Gill and Macmillan, 1977).

Morgan, Kenneth O., *The People's Peace: British History 1945–1990* (Oxford: Oxford University Press, 1990).

Murphy, Robert, *Sixties British Cinema* (London: British Film Institute, 1992).

Naremore, James (ed.), *North by Northwest; Alfred Hitchcock, director* (New Brunswick: Rutgers University Press, 1993).

Palmer, Jerry, *Thrillers: Genesis and Structure of a Popular Genre* (London: Edward Arnold, 1978).

Pearce, Garth, *The Making of GoldenEye* (London: Boxtree, 1995).

— *The Making of Tomorrow Never Dies* (London: Boxtree, 1997).

Pearson, Roberta E., and William Uricchio (eds), *The Many Lives of the Batman: Critical Approaches to a Superhero and his Media* (London: British Film Institute, 1991).

Peary, Danny, *Cult Movies 3* (New York: Simon and Schuster, 1988).

Perry, George, *The Great British Picture Show* (London: Michael Joseph, 1974).

— *Movies from the Mansion: A History of Pinewood Studios* (London: Pavilion, 1986).

Petrie, Duncan, *The British Cinematographer* (London: British Film Institute, 1996).

Pfeiffer, Lee, and Philip Lisa, *The Incredible World of 007* (London: Boxtree, 1992).

Pfeiffer, Lee, and Dave Worrall, *The Essential Bond: The Authorized Guide to the World of 007* (London: Boxtree, 1998).

Polmar, Norman, and Thomas B. Allen, *The Spy Book: The Encyclopedia of Espionage* (London: Greenhill, 1997).

Ray, Robert B., *A Certain Tendency of the Hollywood Cinema, 1930–1980* (Princeton: Princeton University Press, 1985).

Richards, Jeffrey, *Films and British National Identity: From Dickens to Dad's Army* (Manchester: Manchester University Press, 1997).

Rissik, Andrew, *The James Bond Man: The Films of Sean Connery* (London: Elm Tree Books, 1983).

Roddick, Nick, and Martin Auty (eds), *British Cinema Now* (London: British Film Institute, 1985).

Rubin, Steven Jay, *The James Bond Films: A Behind the Scenes History* (London: Talisman Books, 1981).

Rufo, Patrick, *The James Bond Story* (Paris: WIN Productions, 1987).

Ryall, Tom, *Alfred Hitchcock and the British Cinema* (London: Croom Helm, 1986).

Rye, Graham, *The James Bond Girls* (London: Boxtree, 1989).

Snelling, O. F., *James Bond: A Report* (London: Panther, 1965).

Street, Sarah, *British National Cinema* (London: Routledge, 1997).

Sutherland, John A., *Fiction and the Fiction Industry* (London: Athlone Press, 1978).

Thompson, Kristin, and David Bordwell, *Film History: An Introduction* (New York: McGraw-Hill, 1994).

Thumim, Janet, *Celluloid Sisters: Women and Popular Cinema* (London: Macmillan, 1992).

Truffaut, François, with Helen G. Scott, *Hitchcock*, rev. edn (London: Paladin, 1986).

Turner, Adrian, *Goldfinger: Bloomsbury Movie Guide No. 2* (London: Bloomsbury, 1998).

Usborne, Richard, *Clubland Heroes: A Nostalgic Study of Some Recurrent Characters in the Romantic Fiction of Dornford Yates, John Buchan and Sapper*, rev. edn (London: Barrie and Jenkins, 1974).

Walker, Alexander, *Hollywood, England: The British Film Industry in the Sixties* (London: Michael Joseph, 1974; rev. edn London: Harrap, 1986).

— *National Heroes: British Cinema in the Seventies and Eighties* (London: Harrap, 1985).

Watson, Colin, *Snobbery With Violence: English Crime Stories and their Audience*, rev. edn (London: Methuen, 1987).

Williams, Raymond, *Keywords: A Vocabulary of Culture and Society*, rev. edn (London: Fontana, 1983).

Wood, Linda (ed.), *British Film Industry: BFI Information Guide No. 1* (London: British Film Institute, 1980).

Wood, Robin, *Hitchcock's Films*, rev. edn (London: Tantivy Press, 1977).

Worrall, Dave, *The Most Famous Car in the World: The Complete History of the James Bond Aston Martin DB5* (Christchurch: Solo Publishing, 1991).

Articles and chapters

Anez, Nicholas, 'James Bond', *Films in Review*, 18/9–10, September/October 1992, pp. 311–19; 'James Bond (Part 2)', 18/11–12, November/December 1992, pp. 383–8; 'James Bond (Part 3)', 19/1–2, January/February 1993, pp. 30–6.

Baron, Cynthia, '*Doctor No*: Bonding Britishness to Racial Sovereignty', *Spectator: The University of Southern California Journal of Film and Television Criticism*, 14/2, Spring 1994, pp. 68–81.

Bear, Andrew, 'Intellectuals and 007: High Comedy and Total Stimulation', *Dissent*, Winter 1966, pp. 23–7.

Bennett, Tony, 'Text and Social Process: the Case of James Bond', *Screen Education*, 41, Winter/Spring 1982, pp. 3–14.

— 'James Bond as Popular Hero', Unit 21 of Open University course U203 *Popular Culture*, in *Politics, Ideology and Popular Culture 2* (Milton Keynes: Open University Press, 1982).

— 'James Bond in the 1980s', *Marxism Today*, 27/6, June 1983, pp. 37–9.

Bergonzi, Bernard, 'The Case of Mr Fleming', *Twentieth Century*, March 1958, pp. 220–8.

Burgess, Eric, 'The Making of *Moonraker*', *New Scientist*, 21 June 1979, pp. 984–7.

Cannadine, David, 'James Bond and the Decline of England', *Encounter*, 53/3, November 1979, pp. 46–55.

Douglas, Andy, 'Bond Never Dies', *British Film and Television Facilities Journal*, 9, Winter 1998, pp. 17–27.

Fleming, Ian, 'How To Write A Thriller', *Books and Bookmen*, May 1963, pp. 14–19.

Gow, Gordon, 'Thrill A Minute: Adventure Movies of the '60s', *Films and Filming*, 13/4, January 1967, pp. 5–11.

Grant, Barry Keith, 'Introduction', Grant B. K. (ed.), *Film Genre Reader II* (Austin: University of Texas Press, 1995), pp. xv–xx.

Gross, Larry, 'Big and Loud', *Sight and Sound*, New Series, 5/8, August 1995, pp. 6–10.

Hoberman, J., 'When Dr No Met Dr Strangelove', *Sight and Sound*, New Series, 3/12, December 1993, pp. 16–21.

Houston, Penelope, '007', *Sight and Sound*, 34/1, Winter 1964–65, pp. 14–16.

'James Bond Special', *Film Review*, Special 21, 1997, pp. 18–59.

Johnson, Ian, '007 + 4', *Films and Filming*, 12/1, October 1965, pp. 5–8.

Kirkham, Pat, 'Dots and Sickles', *Sight and Sound*, New Series, 5/12, December 1995, pp. 10–12.

Lane, John Francis, 'Young Romantic', *Films and Filming*, 13/5, February 1967, pp. 58–60.

Marwick, Arthur, '*Room at the Top*, *Saturday Night and Sunday Morning*, and the "Cultural Revolution" in Britain', *Journal of Contemporary History*, 19/1, January 1984, pp. 127–52.

Moniot, Drew, 'James Bond and America in the Sixties: An Investigation of the Formula Film in Popular Culture', *Journal of the University Film Association*, 28/3, Summer 1976, pp. 25–33.

Mulvey, Laura, 'Visual Pleasure and Narrative Cinema', *Screen*, 16/3, August 1975, pp. 6–18.

Petley, Julian, 'The Lost Continent', in Charles Barr (ed.), *All Our Yesterdays: 90 Years of British Cinema* (London: British Film Institute, 1986), pp. 98–119.

Petley, Julian, and Alan Burton, 'Introduction', *Journal of Popular British Cinema*, 1, 'Genre and British Cinema', 1998, pp. 2–5.

Price, James, 'Our Man in the Torture Chamber', *London Magazine*, July 1962, pp. 67–70.

Richler, Mordecai, 'Ian Fleming: A Voice for Little England', *Nova*, January 1970, pp. 2–12.

Rissik, Andrew, 'Indiana Jones and the 007 Myth', *Films and Filming*, 362, November 1984, p. 13.

Schatz, Thomas, 'The New Hollywood', in Jim Collins, Hilary Radner and Ava Preacher Collins, *Film Theory Goes to the Movies* (London: Routledge, 1993), pp. 8–36.

Thumim, Janet, 'The "Popular", Cash and Culture in the Postwar British Cinema Industry', *Screen*, 32/3, Autumn 1991, pp. 245–71.

Wills, Ron, 'Sadism for the Family', *Cinema* (Berkeley), 1/5, August/September 1963, pp. 32–3.

Woollacott, Janet, 'The James Bond Films: Conditions of Production', in James Curran and Vincent Porter (eds), *British Cinema History* (London: Weidenfeld and Nicolson, 1983), pp. 208–25.

Index

Note: References to 'Bond films' and the character 'James Bond' appear too frequently in the text to be worthwhile indexing individually. Page numbers in italics indicate an illustration. An *(n)* indicates that the reference is to a footnote on the page cited. Page numbers in bold type indicate the filmography entry for the film concerned.